Core Criminal Law

Core Criminal Law

Learning Through Multiple-Choice Questions

Kathy Swedlow

Carolina Academic Press

Durham, North Carolina

ISBN 978-1-5310-1898-6
e-ISBN 978-1-5310-1899-3
LCCN 2020948327

Carolina Academic Press
700 Kent Street
Durham, North Carolina 27701
Telephone (919) 489-7486
Fax (919) 493-5668
www.cap-press.com

Printed in the United States of America

Contents

Preface

There are many excellent hornbooks on the market to help students with their classroom studies. These materials provide comprehensive coverage, but not in the format that students need to master the subject for the bar exam. At the same time, study aids and bar preparation materials are ill-suited for formative use, as they sample topics instead of presenting a comprehensive review, and sample subtopics students have not yet studied.

This book was written to fill that gap: it provides bar-style multiple-choice questions that can be used formatively, when students are enrolled in a law school Criminal Law class.

The first half of the book is divided into three parts—General Principles, Crimes, and Defenses—and each part has multiple chapters. Each chapter begins with questions addressing basic concepts and definitions, and then presents the variations students can expect to encounter when studying that particular topic, including any crime-specific defenses. The focus is primarily on the common law,[1] but each chapter ends with a few statutory examples, so students can get a sense of how the law has changed over time. Statutory homicide, which is a significant part of any Criminal Law class, has its own chapter. Collectively, the questions in this book track the topics covered in most law school Criminal Law classes.

The questions in this book follow the format used by the National Conference of Bar Examiners on the Multistate Bar Exam. Since these questions were written to present and test one concept at a time, students will find it useful to use this book first and then move on to questions provided by bar review companies and/or released by the bar examiners.

The second half of the book consists of answers for each question. The answers are concise and rule-based, with the intention that students will refer to their casebooks for more detailed information.

In writing this book, I've had the support and advice from some terrific friends: Erika Breitfeld generously answered my questions; Terry Cavanaugh cheered me on; and Marilena David-Martin, Linda Kisabeth, Tonya Krause-Phelan, Stacie Toal, Marinda van Dalen, and Heather Waara provided wonderful friendship. My far-flung siblings and their families also buoyed me through many Sunday-afternoon pandemic Zoom calls; I cannot wait to see them all again in person.

Most importantly, I thank Erik Altmann and Max and Min for being such great stay-at-home companions, and for everything else.

1. Readers should assume the common law applies unless a question directs otherwise.

Core Criminal Law

Part I

General Principles

Introductory Concepts

1. A man was in a car accident that caused the death of a pedestrian. The pedestrian's estate sued the man and he was found liable. The jury's verdict required the man to pay the pedestrian's estate $1 million.

Has the man been punished for killing the pedestrian?

A. Yes; the man has to pay $1 million to the pedestrian's estate.

B. Yes; the man will likely go bankrupt as a result of the jury's verdict.

C. No; the man will be able to forgive the debt in bankruptcy and move on.

D. No; the man was not convicted of any crime as a result of the accident.

2. A county commission was considering a proposal to fund a specialty court for drug users in its jurisdiction. Under the proposal, defendants convicted of certain drug crimes could have their jail sentences suspended if they agreed to accept routine drug testing and treatment. The author of the proposal noted that drug courts in other jurisdictions had drastically reduced the recidivism rate for first-time drug offenders.

For what purpose has the proposal been designed?

A. To incapacitate drug offenders.

B. To rehabilitate drug offenders.

C. To show retribution to drug offenders.

D. To deter would-be drug offenders.

3. A prosecutor was assigned the task of deciding whether and how to charge a young father who had left his baby daughter unattended in his truck. The baby died.

The prosecutor believed the baby's death was completely accidental and that the young father showed genuine remorse. Despite this, the prosecutor believed it was important to charge the father with some form of homicide so that other parents would learn to be more careful with their children.

What theory of punishment is motivating the prosecutor's charging decision?

A. General deterrence, because the prosecutor wants the public to learn from the father's case.

B. Specific deterrence, because the prosecutor wants the public to learn from the father's case.

C. Bounded deterrence, because the prosecutor wants the public to learn from the father's case.

D. Universal deterrence, because the prosecutor wants the public to learn from the father's case.

4. A state trial judge proposed that her jurisdiction devote resources to a mental health treatment court, where some first-time offenders would be given treatment and counseling in lieu of jail or prison time. If a participant successfully completed his treatment and counseling, the criminal conviction would be erased from his record. As part of the proposal, the judge estimated that the state would save a significant amount of money if it was not required to incarcerate these offenders.

On what theory of punishment is the judge's proposal based?

A. Utilitarianism.

B. Retributivism.

C. Empiricism.

D. Rationalism.

5. A state legislature commissioned an in-depth study of the costs of maintaining the state's death penalty. The study showed that the financial cost of imposing and carrying out capital sentences far exceeds the financial cost of life-without-parole sentences. After the report was released, a legislator moved to abolish the state's death penalty, arguing that it was not worth the cost to maintain. The legislator also proposed that the money saved be put into the state public school budget. Several legislators opposed the motion, arguing that capital sentencing should always be an option for heinous crimes, no matter what the financial cost.

How should the legislators opposing the motion be described?

A. They are victim advocates because they seek the best solutions for victims of crime.

B. They are safety advocates because they seek to keep society safe, no matter what the cost.

C. They are utilitarians because they believe that capital sentencing is best for society.

D. They are retributivists because they emphasize punishment over other considerations.

6. A state legislator proposed that the state amend its penal code to make possession of any amount of any illegal drug a felony. Under the existing provisions in the state's penal code, felonies are punishable by one year to life in prison. After the proposal was put to a vote, it was overwhelmingly rejected by legislators from both parties, even those who bragged about being "tough on crime."

Why would the "tough on crime" legislators vote against this proposed amendment?

A. Because some of those legislators probably feared being imprisoned under the new law.

B. Because retributivists sometimes agree with utilitarians about excessive punishments.

C. Because being "tough on crime" is a position on crimes against the person, not drug crimes.

D. Because prosecutors already have exclusive authority to decide how to charge drug crimes.

7. A first-term law student was reviewing her notes from her first Criminal Law class. At one place in her notes, the student had written the words, "Sources of the Criminal Law," but had written nothing below that.

What should the student add to her notes to make them complete?

A. "The common law."

B. "The common law and statutory law."

C. "The Model Penal Code."

D. "The common law, the Model Penal Code, and statutory law."

8. A state's penal code includes the following language in its introductory provisions:

> Common law crimes abolished: No conduct constitutes a crime unless it is a crime under this title or another statute of this state.

How should this provision be interpreted?

A. The jurisdiction has rejected the common law in its entirety in favor of the Model Penal Code.

B. The jurisdiction may rely on common law concepts, but all crimes are codified in the penal code.

C. This jurisdiction is essentially lawless, having eliminated the common law and all of its crimes.

D. This provision cannot be enforced, as it is unconstitutional to reject the common law.

9. A state legislator proposed that her state rewrite portions of its penal code and adopt the Model Penal Code's definitions of murder and manslaughter. But the legislator also proposed keeping other provisions intact. The legislator's opponent objected to this and claimed that the state would have to adopt the Model Penal Code in its entirety, or not at all.

Is the opponent correct?

A. No; many states have incorporated individual provisions of the Model Penal Code into their penal codes.

B. No; the Model Penal Code is intended to be a guide and no part of it can be adopted by any jurisdiction.

C. Yes; the Model Penal Code was intended to be a unified code and its provisions cannot be separately adopted.

D. Yes; provisions of the Model Penal Code cannot be separately adopted without undercutting the entire code.

10. A man took his dog to the veterinarian after the dog began acting strangely. After conducting an exam, the veterinarian began to suspect that the dog had been sexually assaulted by a human. The veterinarian reported his suspicions to the state police. After an investigation, the local prosecutor charged the man with sexually assaulting the dog.

The man hired an attorney, who discovered that the state's penal code does not address sexual assault of an animal, although it prohibits other forms of animal abuse. The attorney filed a motion to dismiss the charges.

How should the judge rule on the motion?

A. The judge should grant the motion because the man's conviction would violate the *Ex Post Facto* Clause of the Constitution.

B. The judge should grant the motion because the principle of legality prohibits prosecution for a crime that does not exist.

C. The judge should deny the motion because the man should have known that bestiality is morally repugnant and wrong.

D. The judge should deny the motion because the drafters of the penal code mistakenly omitted bestiality from its text.

11. A state legislator proposed an addition to the penal code that would make robocalling a felony:

> It is unlawful for any person to use a telephone for the purpose of offering any goods or services for sale, or for conveying information regarding any goods or services for the purpose of soliciting the sale or purchase of the goods or services when the use involves an automated system for the selection and dialing of telephone numbers and the playing of recorded messages when a message is completed to the called number.

Can the state criminalize robocalling?

A. No; the state may only criminalize conduct that was known to exist at the time of the common law.

B. No; the state may not criminalize legitimate business practices, even if robocalls are very annoying.

C. Yes; the state may criminalize robocalling, assuming the proposed law does not violate the Constitution.

D. Yes; a state may criminalize robocalling but the resulting crime cannot be categorized as a felony.

12. A woman pleaded guilty to sexually assaulting her nephew 20 years prior, when he was just a toddler. At the time the woman committed this offense, the maximum punishment for this crime was 15 years in prison. Three years after committing the offense, the legislature increased the penalty to a maximum of life in prison.

At the woman's sentencing, the judge imposed a 50-year sentence, but declined to impose a life sentence. The woman filed paperwork for an appeal.

Should the woman's sentence be vacated on appeal?

A. No; the woman molested her nephew, and so she deserved the sentence she received.

B. No; the judge was permitted to sentence the woman using the more recent statute.

C. Yes; the sentence violates the *Ex Post Facto* Clause and should be no more than 15 years.

D. Yes; the judge was required to sentence the woman to a maximum of life in prison.

13. Police discovered that a crematory owner had failed to cremate hundreds of bodies and found bodies strewn all over his property. In this jurisdiction, it is a crime to desecrate a grave or a cemetery, but there is no law prohibiting the abandonment of a corpse.

After a newspaper reported on this gap in the law, and to help the prosecutor secure a conviction in this case, a state legislator drafted a bill criminalizing a crematory owner's failure to cremate the remains of any corpse if the crematory owner had agreed to do so. The bill also included penalties for leaving corpses unattended on a crematory owner's property.

Will the bill survive constitutional scrutiny?

A. No; the bill is a prohibited Bill of Attainder because it was written to retrospectively punish this individual crematory owner.

B. No; the bill is unconstitutional because it seeks to regulate interstate commerce, a right that belongs to the federal government.

C. Yes; there is an obvious gap in the state's penal code, and the bill will address the omission for this case and any that arise in the future.

D. Yes; without this bill, the prosecution will be limited in the charges it can file, and the crematory owner's crimes require proper charges.

14. A young man was trimming a tree in his front yard one day when he accidentally dropped the saw on his foot. The young man began to swear. A woman was walking nearby, pushing her sleeping baby in a stroller. The woman reported the incident to the police, who later arrested the man. He was charged with the following crime:

> Any person who shall use any indecent, immoral, obscene, vulgar or insulting language in the presence or hearing of any woman or child shall be guilty of a misdemeanor.

How should the young man fight this charge?

A. The young man should argue that the baby was sleeping and so was not harmed in any way.

B. The young man should argue that the statute restricts his First Amendment freedom of speech.

C. The young man should argue that the statute unconstitutionally fails to refer to male victims.

D. The young man should argue that his swearing was involuntary, and so cannot be criminalized.

15. An inspector boarded a fishing boat and found the captain had caught undersized fish in violation of several fishing regulations. The inspector told the captain to bring the undersized fish to port. The captain instead threw all the undersized fish back into the ocean.

The captain was later charged with interfering with a fishing violation inspection. The relevant statute states:

> Any person who knowingly alters, destroys, mutilates, conceals, covers up, falsifies, or makes a false entry in any record, document, or tangible object with the intent to impede, obstruct, or influence an investigation, is guilty of a felony.

The captain's attorney filed a motion to dismiss the charge, arguing that the fish did not meet the statutory definition of a "tangible object."

How should the judge rule on the motion?

A. The motion should be granted because the statute only addresses paperwork, not fish.

B. The motion should be granted because fish are living beings and are not objects.

C. The motion should be granted because the inspector failed to properly secure the fish.

D. The motion should be granted because the rule of lenity supports the captain's argument.

16. A law school teaching assistant was preparing to give his first review for some first-term criminal law students. In the first class, the professor had provided students with a general definition of a common law crime, but the teaching assistant forgot to write it down. The teaching assistant drafted several definitions on his own and then emailed the professor to ask which one he should use.

Which definition should the professor select?

A. A crime is formed exclusively from a guilty mind (a *mens rea*) and a guilty act (an *actus reus*).

B. A crime consists of a *mens rea* and a concurrent *actus reus*, which together cause a social harm.

C. A crime consists solely of the subjective (the *mens rea*) and the objective (the *actus reus*).

D. A crime consists of a *mens rea* and a concurrent *actus reus*, combined with some identified harm.

17. A woman broke into her neighbor's house one morning, intending to steal some jewelry. The neighbor was home, though, and stopped the woman before she took anything. The woman was charged with burglary: the breaking and entering of the dwelling house at night with the intent to commit a felony therein.

At her bench trial, the woman admitted to breaking and entering with the intent to steal the jewelry, but argued that she was not guilty of burglary. The prosecutor responded that since she had established the woman's *mens rea* and her concurrent *actus reus*, the woman must be convicted.

Who is correct?

A. The woman is correct because burglary also requires that the prosecutor prove an attendant circumstance, which is not present here.

B. The woman is correct because the neighbor stopped her before she took any jewelry, and so she is not guilty of the charged crime.

C. The prosecutor is correct because the woman only had to intend to steal the jewelry from inside the house and not actually steal it.

D. The prosecutor is correct because she proved the woman's *mens rea* and her concurrent *actus reus*, which is all that is required.

18. A woman confronted her sister over the handling of their father's estate. The woman believed that the sister, the estate executor, had stolen from the estate. The sister denied the woman's claims and added that their father hated the woman and often said that he wished she had never been born. The woman became very upset, pulled a gun from her purse, and shot and killed her sister.

What caused the sister's death?

A. The sister caused her own death when she stole from the estate; the woman only asked about what was rightfully hers.

B. The sister caused her own death when she insulted the woman; no one should be subject to such mean and nasty comments.

C. The woman caused her sister's death because the sister would not have died but for the woman shooting her with a gun.

D. The two women are equally responsible for the death because each played a role in the events leading to the sister's death.

19. Two men were involved in a drug deal and the first man shot the second man in the neck, paralyzing him. A year later, the second man died. The autopsy report showed that the second man had pneumonia at the time of his death and was using powerful narcotics. The report indicated that the pneumonia was linked to the second man's paralysis and that he took narcotics to deal with chronic pain associated with the shooting.

The prosecutor charged the first man with murder. Before the trial, the first man's attorney filed a motion to dismiss the charges, arguing that the first man did not cause the second man's death—pneumonia and narcotics did.

How should the judge rule on the motion?

A. The motion should be granted because the first man had no way of knowing his actions would lead to this result.

B. The motion should be granted because the second man died due to intervening causes and not the first man's acts.

C. The motion should be denied because the first man's actions were the proximate cause of the second man's death.

D. The motion should be denied because the first man's actions were the direct cause of the second man's death.

20. A woman detested her neighbor's kids because they were loud and sometimes drew with chalk on her driveway. The woman sometimes thought about harming or killing the kids, but did not act on these thoughts because she did not want to go to prison.

One day, as the woman backed her car out of her driveway, she ran over one of the neighbor's kids, killing her. The child had been crouched on the woman's driveway, drawing with chalk. Although the woman hit the child by accident, she was secretly happy that the child had died. The woman was later charged with the intentional murder of the child.

How should the woman defend herself at trial?

A. The woman should explain how the kids drew with chalk on her driveway and how that irritated her.

B. The woman should explain that the neighbor should have done a better job controlling her kids.

C. The woman should explain that there was no concurrence between her *mens rea* and *actus reus*.

D. The woman should explain that she is remorseful and does not want to go to prison.

21. A man was arrested after a bar fight. He had no criminal history and this was his first arrest. He retained a lawyer, who later told the man that he had been charged with misdemeanor battery.

What type of sentence can the man expect, if he is convicted?

A. The man may face any sentence short of the death penalty, as that punishment is reserved for homicides.

B. The man may face a fine and/or a sentence of up to one year in jail, but he will likely not go to prison.

C. The man will likely serve a year in prison unless the judge gives him probation instead.

D. The man will only be fined because this is his first arrest and he has no other criminal history.

22. A man was charged with common law murder for the killing of his stepfather.

What type of crime has the man been charged with?

A. A *malum prohibitum* crime because murder is a prohibited wrong.

B. A *mare liberum* crime because convicted murderers go to prison.

C. A *malum in se* crime because murder is morally wrong.

D. A *jus commune* crime because murder is a common law crime.

23. A college sophomore pleaded guilty to violating the following statute and had to pay a $500 fine:

> A person shall not knowingly cause litter or any object to fall or to be thrown into the path of or to hit a vehicle traveling upon a highway.

What type of crime has the college sophomore committed?

A. A *malum prohibitum* offense, because littering is prohibited.

B. A misdemeanor, because the college sophomore did not go to jail.

C. A misdemeanor, because the college sophomore paid a large fine.

D. A *malum in se* offense, because it is morally wrong to litter.

24. A police officer saw a man walking down the street, singing loudly. The officer arrested him for public drunkenness, which is defined as:

> A person who shall be and appear in an intoxicated condition in any public place or within the curtilage of any private residence not his own other than by invitation of the owner or lawful occupant, which condition is made manifest by boisterousness, by indecent condition or act, or by vulgar, profane, loud, or unbecoming language, is guilty of a misdemeanor.

The man was convicted; he appealed, challenging the statute as a "victimless" crime.

How should the prosecutor respond?

A. The prosecutor should concede error as the man's hangover was enough punishment for his public drunkenness.

B. The prosecutor should concede error as no one is harmed when a drunk person sings loudly in public, as the man did here.

C. The prosecutor should explain that the innocent people who had to listen to the man's loud singing were harmed.

D. The prosecutor should explain that an element of harm is not necessarily required in a criminal statute.

25. A man was arrested and charged under state law with the murder of his father. Two days later, the county prosecutor received a call from a federal prosecutor, who explained that he was going to take over the case. When the county prosecutor asked why, the federal prosecutor explained that while the homicide victim had no federal ties and the killing did not occur on federal land, his office had better resources and could probably do a better job with the prosecution.

Can the federal prosecutor assume jurisdiction over this case?

A. Yes; with better funding, his office will be more likely to secure a conviction.

B. Yes; the federal prosecutor's office has a right of first refusal in homicide cases.

C. No; the county prosecutor should not rely on federal funds for a state case.

D. No; the federal prosecutor's office lacks jurisdiction over non-federal cases.

26. A man from one state was visiting a friend who lived in another state. Several days into the visit, the two argued and the friend shot and killed the man. Police investigation revealed that the friend's gun had been purchased years before in a third state.

Which state has jurisdiction to prosecute the homicide?

A. The friend's home state, because the homicide was committed there.

B. The man's home state, so it can vindicate the rights of its former resident.

C. The third state, because the friend purchased the murder weapon there.

D. The state that files charges first will have jurisdiction to prosecute.

27. While living in a state on the east coast, two men conspired to kill a third man who lived in a midwestern state. The two men purchased a gun for the crime in their east coast state, and then one of the men drove to the midwestern state and, using the gun, killed the third man.

Does a prosecutor in the east coast state have jurisdiction to prosecute the two men for any crimes?

A. The prosecutor may only prosecute the two men for conspiracy to commit murder, as that was the only crime that occurred in her state.

B. The prosecutor cannot prosecute the two men for any crimes, as the target of the conspiracy (murder) was committed in another state.

C. The prosecutor may prosecute the two men for the conspiracy and the murder, even though the murder was not committed in her state.

D. The prosecutor cannot prosecute the two men for any crimes, as the more serious crime (murder) was committed in the midwestern state.

28. A man robbed a bank and was prosecuted in state court for robbery. After he was convicted, the man was charged under federal law for the same bank robbery. The man's attorney filed a motion to dismiss the federal charges, arguing that the state courts had exclusive jurisdiction over substantive crimes.

How should the judge rule on the motion?

A. The motion should be granted because the attorney has presented a legally correct jurisdictional argument.

B. The motion should be granted because the federal prosecution violates the protection against double jeopardy.

C. The motion should be denied because it is premature; jurisdiction is an element to be established at trial.

D. The motion should be denied because the state and federal courts have concurrent jurisdiction.

29. In her closing argument in a murder trial, a prosecutor told the jury:

> As the judge told you, I have the burden of proving this crime beyond a reasonable doubt. No one saw the crime but the victim and her killer, so I cannot give you any real evidence that the defendant committed the crime. But ask yourselves: if the defendant did not kill the victim, then who did? He had a motive. He disliked the victim. And now she is dead. I urge you to find the defendant guilty because no one else could have committed this crime.

The jury returned a guilty verdict. The defense appealed and argued that the prosecutor's argument established that his conviction should be vacated.

How should the appellate court rule?

A. The defendant should not receive a new trial because the prosecutor was being honest with the jury about the case.

B. The defendant should not receive a new trial because the prosecutor's failure to prove her case is harmless error.

C. The defendant should receive a new trial because the prosecutor's argument demonstrates that he is innocent.

D. The defendant should receive a new trial because the prosecutor's argument shows she did not meet the burden of proof.

30. A man was on trial for murder and wanted to argue to the jury that he acted in self-defense. The man asked his attorney how the defense would work, and the attorney explained that under state law, they—the defense—would have the burden to present some evidence showing that the man killed by necessity. The man expressed surprise and told the attorney that he thought the state had the burden of proof.

How should the attorney respond?

A. The attorney should not try to explain complex legal concepts to an uneducated layperson.

B. The attorney should explain that the state's burden of proof works differently in self-defense cases.

C. The attorney should explain how the burden of proof is different from the burden of production.

D. The attorney should tell the man that the law is unconstitutional and should offer to challenge it.

31. At a murder trial, the prosecutor argued in closing:

> You heard the witnesses and what they said. One of them testified that he saw a man with red hair commit the killing. Guess what? The defendant has red hair! Now, that alone may not be enough for a conviction, but that's where the other witnesses come in. One of them testified that the defendant had a grudge against the deceased and another one testified that the defendant wasn't at work on the afternoon of the killing. Put all this testimony together and what do you have? A man with a motive to kill, with the opportunity to kill, and who coincidentally had the same hair color as the killer. And since the defendant hasn't given you anything to disprove this, you are required by law to accept all of this testimony as true.

Is the prosecutor's argument correct?

A. Yes; a defendant can be convicted based solely on circumstantial evidence.

B. Yes; the prosecutor's argument helpfully summarized the witness testimony.

C. No; the prosecutor's argument shifted the burden of proof to the defendant.

D. No; the prosecutor's argument shifted the burden of production to the defendant.

32. At the close of testimony in a murder case, the judge gave the jury its instructions. As to reasonable doubt, the judge explained:

> Reasonable doubt is difficult to define and that's why I like to think of it in terms of percentages. It's probably more than 50%. And it's less than 100%. It's probably something in between those two figures, although, of course, the higher the percentage the guiltier the defendant is.

The defense attorney objected to the judge's definition.

What is the basis of the objection?

A. Due process forbids the quantification of the reasonable doubt standard.

B. The judge's instruction will confuse jurors who don't understand math.

C. The judge's instruction diluted the prosecutor's required burden of proof.

D. The judge's instruction shifted the burden of proof to the defense.

33. A man and his friend agreed to rob a bank together. The robbery itself was committed by the friend, while the man stayed in his car outside the bank, ready to drive quickly away. During the robbery, the friend became agitated and shot and killed the bank manager.

Later, after the man and his friend were arrested and charged, the man learned that he had been charged with the bank manager's death. The man asked his lawyer to explain how he could be charged for his friend's crime.

How should the lawyer respond?

A. A person can be charged for his own direct acts as well as the acts of others if the person acts as an accomplice or a co-conspirator.

B. A person can only be charged for his own direct acts and not for the acts of others, and so the judge will dismiss the homicide charge.

C. A person can only be charged for the acts of others if he had advance notice of those acts, so the judge will dismiss the homicide charge.

D. A person can only be charged for crimes that he committed himself or helped with, so the judge will dismiss the homicide charge.

34. A state law makes it a crime to sell alcohol to minors and requires bartenders to check IDs and refuse service to would-be underage drinkers. Violators of the law are fined $100. The bartender at a neighborhood bar often ignored this law and routinely served underage drinkers. The bar owner suspected the bartender ignored the law, as he knew the bar's profits spiked whenever the local high school won a sporting event.

The police set up a sting and sent a 20-year-old police cadet into the bar to buy a drink. After the bartender served her without checking ID, the bartender was arrested and charged with violating this law. The prosecutor now wants to charge the bar owner with the same crime.

Can the bar owner be properly charged with this crime?

A. No, because criminal charges can only be based on direct liability and not vicarious liability.

B. No, because the bar owner did not know for certain that the bartender ignored the law.

C. Yes, because the criminal law permits limited charging based on vicarious liability.

D. Yes, because the bar owner was getting rich from the bartender's violation of the law.

35. A man owned a landscaping business and relied on a manager to handle all the day-to-day business. The manager routinely hired young teens to perform gardening tasks, did not require them to obtain work permits, and frequently made them work long hours—all in violation of the state child labor law. A violation under this law is a felony and carries a 20-year sentence.

One of the teens complained to his mother, who contacted the police. The prosecutor charged the business owner with violating state law and he now faces prison time. His attorney has filed a motion to dismiss the charge.

What argument should the attorney offer in support of the motion?

A. Criminal charges against a defendant can only be based on direct liability and never on vicarious liability.

B. The criminal law only permits prosecution for a misdemeanor under vicarious liability, never a felony.

C. The business owner can be prosecuted using vicarious liability, but the punishment must be limited.

D. The business owner did not commit any *actus reus* associated with this crime and so the charges should be dismissed.

Mens Rea

36. A man shot his neighbor and killed him.

How should the man be punished?

A. The man should receive the death penalty because it is morally wrong to take another life.

B. The man should receive a life sentence and should never be given the possibility of parole.

C. The man's punishment cannot be determined on these facts alone; more information is needed.

D. The man should receive a term of years sentence so that he can maintain hope for his future.

37. The parents of a young woman reviewed their will with her; under the will, the young woman would inherit all of their money. Because the parents had saved their money and invested wisely, the young woman would never need to work and could live a life of leisure.

Two weeks later, the parents were murdered in their home. The coroner's report indicated that the parents had been shot "execution-style" with single bullet wounds to the head. The young woman could not produce an alibi for the evening in question. Then, when the investigating officer learned about the parents' will, he urged the prosecutor to charge the young woman in the crime.

How should the prosecutor respond to the police?

A. The young woman had a motive to kill her parents but that does not also mean that she had the *mens rea* for the crime.

B. All children inherit money from their parents and so the young woman's motive is no different from anyone else's.

C. The young woman had a motive to kill her parents, which demonstrates that she also had the *mens rea* for the crime.

D. The young woman did not have a motive to kill her parents because estate taxes would have reduced her inheritance.

38. A high school senior was charged with burglarizing his coach's house. At the senior's bench trial, the defense attorney urged the judge to acquit him, arguing:

> As you know, my client did not testify. And he doesn't have to. Instead, the prosecutor has to prove every element of the crime. But she hasn't. And she can't. How can the prosecutor prove what my client was thinking that night? Unless my client testifies to that point, the prosecutor cannot meet her burden.

Is the defense attorney correct?

A. No, because the senior's *mens rea* can be established through the use of inductive and deductive reasoning.

B. No, because the senior's *mens rea* can be established by making reasonable inferences from the facts.

C. Yes, because no one can know what was in the senior's heart and mind unless he testifies to those facts.

D. Yes, because the senior's constitutional right to silence takes precedence over the need to prove *mens rea*.

39. A man was arrested while hiding in the backyard of an enemy's house. The man was wearing dark clothing and had a semi-full five-gallon can of gasoline with him. He also had glass bottles, some old rags, and several boxes of matches in his backpack.

The man was charged with attempted arson. The man's attorney filed a motion to dismiss, arguing that the prosecutor could not prove that he specifically intended to commit arson.

How should the judge respond to the motion?

A. The prosecutor does not need to prove specific intent because arson is a general intent crime.

B. The man's *mens rea* can be reasonably inferred from the circumstances when he was arrested.

C. All reasonable fact-finders will agree that the man specifically intended to commit arson.

D. Under the Fifth Amendment, the prosecutor can force the man to testify as to his *mens rea*.

40. A man was on trial for intentionally killing his wife by shooting her. The man claimed that his gun had accidentally discharged and that he had not intended to kill his wife.

In his instructions to the jury, the judge explained that "the law presumes that the people intend the consequences of their actions," and the jury convicted the man. On appeal, the man argued that the judge's instruction violated his due process rights.

How should the appellate court rule?

A. The judge's instruction relieved the prosecution of its burden of proof by allowing the jury to presume the man's intent to kill from his use of a gun.

B. The judge's instruction relieved the prosecution of its burden of proof by allowing the jury to presume the man's *actus reus* from his use of a gun.

C. The judge's instruction only stated the obvious: that the jurors could presume the man's intent to kill because he used a gun to shoot and kill his wife.

D. The judge's instruction relieved the prosecution of its burden of proof, but because the wife died, the error was harmless beyond a reasonable doubt.

41. A woman decided to see what would happen if she added gasoline to a pile of leaves her neighbor was carefully burning in his yard. The woman threw a bottle of gasoline over the fence between their properties and onto the leaf pile. The bottle exploded and the flames leapt out of control, quickly engulfing a shed on the neighbor's property, razing it.

At the woman's subsequent trial for arson, she tearfully testified that she never intended to destroy the shed.

What is the legal relevance of the woman's testimony?

A. The woman's testimony has no legal relevance because arson does not require proof of any *mens rea.*

B. The woman's testimony has no legal relevance because arson does not require specific intent to destroy.

C. The woman's testimony is relevant because it demonstrates that the neighbor was at fault and not her.

D. The woman's testimony is relevant because it shows she lacked the *mens rea* for an arson conviction.

42. In his second week of law school, a student was asked in class to give examples of general intent crimes.

How should the student properly respond?

A. Burglary, arson, and all malice crimes.

B. Assault, battery, and rape.

C. Common law murder, arson, and the inchoate crimes.

D. Rape, battery, and arson.

43. At a criminal trial, the prosecutor offered testimony showing that one night at about 10:00 P.M., a woman hurled a rock through a window of a dwelling house and then crawled through the opening. The prosecutor then rested his case.

Can the woman be properly convicted of burglary?

A. No; the woman cannot be convicted until she testifies in her own defense.

B. No; the prosecutor has not established the woman's *mens rea* for the crime.

C. Yes; the *mens rea* for the burglary can be inferred by the woman's acts.

D. Yes; the woman broke and entered the dwelling house of another at night.

44. A law professor was writing an essay exam and drafted a fact pattern where a woman was charged with conspiracy to commit rape. The professor wanted students to write a short answer explaining whether that crime was a specific or general intent crime.

What answer should receive full credit?

A. Conspiracy to commit rape is a specific intent crime because conspiracy has dual intents: intent to agree and intent that the rape be committed.

B. Conspiracy to commit rape is a specific intent crime because when two crimes are combined, each crime's distinct *mens rea* must be separately proven.

C. Conspiracy to commit rape is a general intent crime because conspiracy is always a general intent crime, no matter the target of the conspiracy.

D. Conspiracy to commit rape is a general intent crime because rape is always a general intent crime, no matter if it also involves a conspiracy.

45. An attorney was walking to her car after work when she saw something sparkle on the ground. The attorney knelt down to the ground and picked up the sparkler: a large diamond ring. Sincerely believing the ring had been abandoned, the attorney kept it.

The ring actually belonged to a college student who had accidentally dropped it earlier in the day. The college student reported the loss to the police, who were able to identify the attorney using surveillance video from a nearby building.

Can the attorney be properly charged with larceny of the ring?

A. Yes; as a licensed attorney, she should be held to a higher standard of conduct than non-attorneys.

B. Yes; the attorney should have known that people don't abandon diamond rings on public sidewalks.

C. No; the attorney sincerely thought the ring was abandoned, so she lacked the *mens rea* for larceny.

D. No; the attorney was under no obligation to report her discovery of the diamond ring to the police.

46. A man and a woman went on a dinner date. At the end of the evening, they went to the man's apartment for a drink. After mutually kissing for a few minutes, the man began to undress the woman. She told the man "no," but he believed she was being coy and wanted him to continue—so he did. The woman again said "no," but the man had sexual intercourse with her anyway, continuing to believe she was being coy. Later, the woman reported what happened to the police.

The man was charged with rape. The man told his attorney that he sincerely believed that the woman had consented and was being coy when she told him "no." The man asked whether this information would be helpful in his defense.

How should the attorney respond?

A. The attorney should tell the man that since he sincerely believed the woman consented, he lacked the *mens rea* for rape.

B. The attorney should tell the man that since he reasonably believed the woman consented, he lacked the *mens rea* for rape.

C. The attorney should advise the man that his beliefs regarding the woman's consent have absolutely no relevance at all.

D. The attorney should advise the man that his beliefs regarding the woman's consent must be both sincere and reasonable.

47. A man was inside his neighbor's house, stealing jewelry. Because it was dark and he could not see, the man lit matches to guide him as he went through the house, dropping the burned-out matches to the ground. One of the matches fell onto a carpet and the house caught fire.

Later, the man was charged with theft and arson. The judge instructed the jury that it could reasonably infer that the man intentionally burned the house if it found that he had burglarized the house with the intent to steal the jewelry.

Was the judge's instruction correct?

A. No, because the intent to commit one crime generally cannot be grafted onto the act of committing another crime.

B. No, because the man only lit the matches to help him see and to aid him in committing larceny of the jewelry.

C. Yes, because when a person acts intentionally in one respect, he acts intentionally in all other respects.

D. Yes, because the dropping of burned matches on the carpet shows a reckless disregard for a high risk of burning.

48. A woman decided to kill her ex-husband and waited outside his office to shoot him. After the woman waited for about an hour, the ex-husband walked out of the building. The woman aimed her gun and fired it, but instead she accidentally killed a teenager who had been walking closely behind the ex-husband.

Can the woman be properly charged for the intentional murder of the teenager?

A. No; the woman should instead be charged with depraved heart murder because she showed a reckless disregard for the teenager's life.

B. No; the woman only intended to kill her ex-husband and, absent proof that she also intended to kill the teenager, the charge should be dropped.

C. Yes; the woman intended to kill her ex-husband and did not, but her intent to kill can be ascribed to the eventual killing of the teenager.

D. Yes; the woman intended to kill her ex-husband and if she is not prosecuted for this crime now, she will likely try to kill him again in the future.

49. A woman robbed a bank. During the robbery, the woman became agitated because she believed the teller was moving too slowly, and so the woman fired a warning shot from her gun at the wall. The bullet ricocheted off a desk and hit and killed a baby, who was being held by a bank customer.

The woman was later charged with felony murder of the baby, based on the underlying felony of bank robbery. The woman filed a motion to dismiss, arguing that the prosecution could only show that she had the intent to commit the robbery.

How should the judge rule on the woman's motion?

A. The motion should be denied because the felony murder rule holds a defendant strictly responsible for all crimes that occur during the felony.

B. The motion should be denied because the felony murder rule allows a finding of constructive malice when death occurs during the felony.

C. The motion should be granted because the woman only intended to rob the bank and the baby's death was just an unfortunate accident.

D. The motion should be granted because the woman fired the shot at the wall and so there is no proof that she intentionally killed the baby.

50. A man was charged with burglary: the breaking and entering of the dwelling house of another with the intent to commit a felony inside. The man moved to dismiss the charge, claiming that his intent to break and enter into the house could not be "transferred" to show an intent to commit a felony inside the house.

How should the judge rule on the man's motion?

A. The motion should be granted because the intent to break and enter into the house cannot be used to show the intent to commit a felony once inside.

B. The motion should be granted because a crime is only permitted to have one *mens rea* associated with it, and this crime has two different *mens reas.*

C. The motion should be denied because the intent to commit a felony is an additional element of the crime and not an impermissible transfer of intent.

D. The motion should be denied because the intent to break and enter into the house can be used to show the intent to commit a felony once inside.

51. A woman received a $50 ticket for failing to wear her seat belt.

What type of offense has the woman most likely committed?

A. The woman has most likely committed a strict liability offense, i.e., one that does not require proof of *mens rea.*

B. The woman has most likely committed a misdemeanor, and the officer gave her a break with the $50 ticket.

C. The nature of the woman's offense cannot be determined until after she exercises her right to a jury trial.

D. The nature of the woman's offense cannot be determined until she is formally arraigned on the charges.

52. A law student received a ticket for violating her state's jaywalking law. The relevant statute states:

> A pedestrian shall not cross an intersection diagonally unless authorized by official traffic-control devices.

What type of offense this is?

A. A *malum prohibitum* offense, because it prohibits a pedestrian's conduct.

B. A strict liability offense, because the statute does not include a *mens rea*.

C. A criminal infraction, because the law student was only issued a ticket.

D. A misdemeanor, because a person cannot go to prison for jaywalking.

53. A woman received a ticket for speeding after an officer stopped her for driving 65 MPH in a 50-MPH zone. In this jurisdiction, speeding is statutorily defined as:

> Except when a special hazard exists that requires a lower rate of speed, no person shall drive any motorized vehicle in excess of the posted speed limit.

During the traffic stop, the officer told the woman that a posted traffic sign limited her speed to 50 MPH. The woman explained that she believed had misread the sign and thought it said 65 MPH.

How should the officer respond?

A. The officer should explain that the woman's mistake of fact about the limit on the posted sign negates her *mens rea* for the crime.

B. The officer should explain that the woman's mistake of fact about the limit on the posted sign is irrelevant for a strict liability crime.

C. The officer should explain to the woman that he is not authorized to dismiss a ticket once it has been issued, but the judge can.

D. The officer should explain to the woman that her mistake of fact is a defense that can only be evaluated by a judge or jury.

54. A 19-year-old college student and his 15-year-old girlfriend were in love. But when the girlfriend's mother found out that the two were having sex, she contacted the police and reported the college student. He was later charged with statutory rape. In meeting with his defense attorney, the college student said that he only ever intended to have consensual sex with his girlfriend, and asked the attorney to explain that to the judge.

How should the attorney respond?

A. Statutory rape is a strict liability crime as to age, and so it does not matter if the sex was consensual.

B. Statutory rape is a strict liability crime, and so it does not matter if the sex was consensual.

C. Rape is a general intent crime and so the college student's *mens rea* is very relevant to his guilt.

D. The college student's claims will only negate one element of the charged crime, but not the others.

55. A statute requires individuals to register any fully automatic weapons with a central registry and makes it a crime to "possess a weapon that should be registered" under the statute. The penalties for a violation of this statute include a fine of up to $5,000 and up to 10 years in prison.

A woman was in possession of an unregistered machine gun and was charged with violating the statute. The woman claimed that she did not know that she was required to register the weapon; her attorney argued to the judge that the woman's *mens rea* was critical to the question of her guilt.

How should the judge respond?

A. The woman's *mens rea* is irrelevant in this situation because she has been charged with a strict liability offense.

B. The statute is unconstitutional because it interferes with the woman's rights under the Second Amendment.

C. The statute is unconstitutional because it permits incarceration without proof of the woman's *mens rea*.

D. Even though the statute appears to be strict liability, its penalties require that the prosecutor prove a *mens rea*.

Acts and Omissions

56. An employee was frustrated with her supervisor because she thought he treated her unfairly, and she fantasized about different ways that she could kill him. One evening after drinking a glass of wine, the employee told her roommate that she had experienced these thoughts. Alarmed, the roommate called the police and reported the employee for attempted murder.

How should the police respond to the roommate's concerns?

A. The police should warn the supervisor that he is in imminent danger from one of his employees.

B. The police should go to the employee's apartment and arrest her for the attempted murder of her supervisor.

C. The police should tell the roommate to calm down because everyone fantasizes about killing their supervisor.

D. The police should explain to the roommate that the employee has not committed any crime.

57. A woman and her husband went out drinking one evening and the woman had a lot to drink. Later, as they slept in their shared bed, the woman was restless and kept on tossing and turning. At one point, the woman rolled over, violently throwing her arm across her husband's body and hitting his face with the back of her hand. The woman's wedding ring hit her husband's nose, breaking it.

Can the woman be charged with battery of her husband?

A. No, because the woman's physical actions against her husband were neither conscious nor voluntary.

B. No, because the woman was still intoxicated when she battered her husband and broke his nose.

C. Yes, because the woman used unlawful force against her husband, which resulted in harm to him.

D. Yes, because the woman used unlawful force in an attempt to cause fear or apprehension to her husband.

58. A man lived on a block with several families with young children. One day while driving home from work, a little girl darted out in front of the man's car and he hit her. The man felt the thud against his bumper, got out of the car, and realized he hit the little girl. When the man saw what had happened, he was happy because he did not like kids and thought they should stay indoors. The little girl later died from her injuries.

Can the man be properly charged with intentionally killing the little girl?

A. No, because the little girl darted out in front of the man's car, and so he is not at fault.

B. No, because there was no concurrence between the man's *mens rea* and his *actus reus*.

C. Yes, because the man clearly hates children and he should be punished for what he did.

D. Yes because the man caused the little girl's death and was happy about doing what he did.

59. A student was walking to his parked car when he heard yelling nearby. The student looked over and saw a man pointing a gun at a woman. The woman saw the student and pleaded with him to call the police. The student did not respond, but just watched. After several more minutes of yelling back and forth between the man and the woman, the man shot and killed her.

Can the student be charged with murder?

A. No, because the student's failure to act in this situation does not constitute the *actus reus* for murder.

B. No, because one person cannot be held responsible for the criminal actions of another person.

C. Yes, because the student could have called the police for help and had ample time to do so.

D. Yes, because the woman pleaded with the student to call the police and he failed to do so.

60. A husband was visiting his wife in her hospital room; she was waking up from surgery to fix a broken leg, but was very groggy. During the visit, a nurse came into the room and explained that she was going to give the wife an injection of particular pain medicine. The husband knew that his wife was allergic to this particular medicine, but he said nothing. Seconds after receiving the injection, the wife's face began to swell and she started to cough and choke. The nurse tried to save the wife, but she died.

Does the husband bear any criminal responsibility for his wife's death?

A. Yes, because it would have been very easy for the husband to stop the nurse, but he instead did nothing.

B. Yes, because the husband's failure to act in this situation can constitute the *actus reus* for a crime.

C. Yes, because the marriage vows include a promise to take care of each other, in sickness and in health.

D. Yes, because the husband knew that his wife had a drug allergy, so he had the *mens rea* for criminal homicide.

61. An adult son was worried about his elderly mother, who lived alone in another state. The son contracted with an elder care agency to bring his mother one meal a day. The contract specified that an agency employee would have in-person contact with the mother at each visit and that the employee would immediately report any concerns about the mother's condition to an agency supervisor.

For the first two weeks, the arrangement worked perfectly. But after that, the mother stopped answering her doorbell and so the agency employee left the meal on the doorstep. The employee left six daily meals before he told his supervisor about the issue. The supervisor asked the police to conduct a welfare check on the mother; the police found her on the floor of her kitchen, barely alive and suffering from pneumonia. She was taken to the hospital, where she later died.

Does the agency and its employees have any criminal responsibility for the mother's death?

A. Yes; the agency and its employees had a duty to care for the mother and the failure to properly do so can constitute the *actus reus* for a crime.

B. Yes; the agency and its employees had a moral duty to alert the son that the mother had not answered the doorbell for six days in a row.

C. No; the mother was elderly and in need of care and the son should have helped her directly instead of outsourcing this work to strangers.

D. No; the mother's failure to answer the doorbell and alert the agency employee that she had pneumonia was the direct cause of her death.

62. A kindergarten teacher suspected that a girl in her class was being physically abused at home. The girl sometimes came to school with odd bumps and bruises on her body; when the teacher asked where they came from, the girl would not respond. The teacher also noticed that the girl seemed afraid of her mother and had once seen the mother slap the girl.

Midway through the school year, the girl's mother was arrested and charged with child abuse. The principal asked the teacher if she had witnessed any signs of abuse and the teacher related what she had seen. The principal then asked the teacher why she hadn't said anything earlier, explaining that state law required teachers to report suspected physical abuse of their students.

Does the teacher bear any criminal responsibility in this situation?

A. No, because the teacher asked the girl about the cause of her injuries and the girl would not respond to her.

B. No, because the teacher only suspected that the girl was being abused by her mother, but was not certain.

C. Yes, because the teacher could have prevented the girl's abuse by reporting the mother, but failed to do so.

D. Yes, because state law imposed a duty on the teacher to report the suspected abuse, and she failed to do so.

63. A woman was driving home on a rainy evening when she saw a jogger lying on the side of the road. The woman pulled her car over and went to the jogger, who was bleeding and unconscious. The woman dragged the jogger off the road and retrieved her phone to call an ambulance for him. But right then, the woman's daughter called to remind her that she had promised to take her to the mall. The woman rushed back to her car and drove home. Twenty minutes later, another car came by; the driver did not see the jogger and hit and killed him.

Can the woman be charged in the jogger's death?

A. Yes, because the woman assumed a duty to help the jogger when she pulled over and began to give him help.

B. Yes, because the woman only had to call an ambulance, and her failure to do so contributed to the jogger's death.

C. No, because the woman dragged the jogger to safety and so the other driver was completely to blame for his death.

D. No, because the woman did not know the jogger and so had no duty to help him beyond the help she already gave.

64. A man decided to landscape his front yard. Using an excavator, the man began to dig a series of deep holes into which he planned to plant mature trees. As the man was digging, a girl rode by on her bike. The girl was intrigued by what the man was doing so she stopped and asked if she could watch; the man agreed. But the girl stood too close to the excavator and as the man dug, the ground shifted and the girl fell into the hole. The man didn't know what to do so he took a lunch break. Unfortunately, the girl broke her neck in the fall and died.

Can the man be charged in the girl's death?

A. No; this issue should be resolved under the attractive nuisance doctrine.

B. No; the girl was solely at fault because she stood too close to the excavator.

C. Yes; the man dug the hole into which the girl fell and so owed her a duty.

D. Yes; the man should have refused the girl's request to watch him digging.

65. A physician suspected that one of his elderly patients was being abused, but did not know who was responsible. The patient suffered from mild dementia and the physician had seen strange bruises on her arms and legs. The patient lived with her husband, who was her sole caretaker.

In this jurisdiction, the physician is considered to be a mandated reporter; the relevant statute states:

> If any mandated reporter has reason to believe that an eligible adult, who because of a disability or other condition or impairment is unable to seek assistance for himself or herself, has, within the previous 12 months, been subjected to abuse, neglect, or financial exploitation, the mandated reporter shall, within 24 hours after developing such belief, report this suspicion to an agency designated to receive such reports under this Act.

After reviewing the statute, the doctor determined that his elderly patient met the definition of an "eligible adult."

What are the physician's responsibilities under this statute?

A. The physician should first determine the source of the patient's bruises, before reporting to the agency.

B. The physician should ask the patient about the bruises, and then consider reporting to the agency.

C. The physician should ask the husband about the bruises, then consider reporting to the agency.

D. The physician should immediately report his suspicions to the agency, as required by the statute.

Parties to a Crime

66. A woman got into an argument with a co-worker about the right way to add paper to the office copier. After listening to the argument for several minutes, a supervisor walked up and handed the woman a pistol. The supervisor told the woman that she was correct and suggested that she shoot the co-worker because he was wrong. The woman shot and killed the co-worker.

Can the supervisor be charged in the co-worker's death?

A. Yes, because the supervisor's pistol was used to shoot the co-worker and so she is criminally responsible for his death.

B. Yes, because the supervisor intended that the woman kill the co-worker and assisted in the crime by providing the pistol.

C. No, because the supervisor did not shoot the co-worker and so cannot be held criminally responsible for his death.

D. No, because the supervisor had no way of knowing the woman would follow her suggestion and kill the co-worker.

67. A woman asked a friend if he would help her buy and sell drugs. The friend replied that he did not want to be involved in drug dealing, but that he would loan her money so she could start her drug dealing business.

The woman used the friend's loaned money to start her business. Several months later, she paid him back with interest. Shortly after that, the woman was arrested and charged with drug dealing.

Can the friend also be charged with this crime?

A. No; the friend had no tangible connection to the commission of the crime.

B. No; the friend's involvement ended when the woman repaid his loan.

C. Yes; the friend's loan was a tangible connection to the commission of the crime.

D. Yes; the friend can be charged even though he personally did not deal drugs.

68. A woman was heartbroken after her boyfriend broke up with her. The woman asked her neighbor to borrow one of his handguns and told the neighbor that she wanted to use the handgun to kill the boyfriend. The neighbor readily agreed and told the woman she was doing the right thing.

The next day, the woman shot and killed the boyfriend using the neighbor's handgun. The woman was charged with first degree murder.

How should the neighbor be charged?

A. The neighbor should be charged with the crime of accessory before the fact.

B. The neighbor should be charged with the crime of accessory before the fact to murder.

C. The neighbor should be charged with the crime of murder.

D. The neighbor should be charged as an accessory before the fact to murder.

69. A law student was studying for her final exam in Criminal Law. The law student asked her roommate—who had gotten an "A" in the class the year before—to help her create a proper list of the "parties to a crime."

If the roommate wants the law student to get a good grade, too, what list should she provide?

A. Principal to the Crime, Accessory Before the Fact, and Accessory After the Fact.

B. Principal in the First Degree, Principal in the Second Degree, Accessory Before the Fact, and Accessory After the Fact.

C. Principal to the Crime, Principal Before the Crime, Principal During the Crime, and Accessory After the Fact.

D. Principal, Aider and Abettor Before the Crime, and Accessory After the Fact.

70. A woman shot and killed her boyfriend after she caught him cheating on her. When police interrogated the woman, she refused to answer questions about whether she received help from anyone else in committing the crime. After additional investigation, the police concluded that the woman acted alone. Now, the prosecutor wants to charge the woman as a principal in the first degree to murder.

Is this charge appropriate?

A. Yes; as police have concluded that the woman acted alone when she committed the crime, she should be charged as a principal in the first degree.

B. Yes; as the woman acted alone when she committed the crime, she should be charged as a principal in the first degree.

C. No; as the woman acted alone when she committed the crime, she should not be charged as a principal in the first degree.

D. No; because the woman would not verify if she acted alone, she should be charged as a principal in the first degree, in case police later find her helper.

71. Two brothers created a plan to rob a bank. According to the plan, the younger brother would drive the car and serve as a lookout, and the older brother would perform the actual robbery.

On the appointed day, the brothers executed their plan. They were arrested by police after the robbery, about a mile away from the bank.

How should the brothers be charged?

A. Both brothers are principals in the first degree because they both participated in the commission of the crime.

B. The older brother is the principal in the first degree and the younger brother is the principal in the second degree.

C. The younger brother is the principal in the first degree and the older brother is the principal in the second degree.

D. The brothers are co-conspirators because they both participated in the commission of the crime.

72. A mother told her two adult sons that they would either need to start paying rent or move out of her house. The older son pointed out that he and his brother were unemployed and asked his mother how she thought they would be able to find money. The mother pulled a handgun out of a dresser drawer and suggested that they use it to rob the local bank.

Two days later, the sons did exactly as their mother suggested. The older son drove the car and served as a lookout, and the younger son robbed the bank.

Can the mother be convicted of bank robbery?

A. Yes; she is an accessory before the fact because she provided the handgun and suggested the robbery but was not present when the crime was committed.

B. Yes; she is a principal in the second degree because she was constructively present at the crime as the sons used her handgun to rob the bank.

C. No; she has no criminal liability because she only provided the handgun and suggested the robbery, but the sons actually committed the crime.

D. No; because she provided the handgun and suggested the robbery she is a principal in the first degree and there is no need to use accomplice liability.

73. A college student called his father and explained that on a recent date, he and a classmate had engaged in "rough sex." The student told his father that the classmate had gone to the police and accused him of raping her, that he had been charged with rape, and that a warrant had been issued for his arrest. The father directed the student to meet him at the airport.

When the student arrived, the father was waiting with his passport, a packed suitcase, and several thousand dollars in cash. The father told the student that there was a one-way international plane ticket for him at the ticket counter.

Can the father be charged with a crime?

A. No; because the father's actions were completely legal, he cannot be charged with a crime.

B. No; without forensic evidence to prove the classmate's story, the father cannot be charged with a crime.

C. Yes, the father can be charged as an accessory after the fact to the student's rape of his classmate.

D. Yes, the father can be charged with failing to report a crime and aiding a fugitive from justice.

74. A man coveted his girlfriend's new sportscar, but as his license was suspended, she would not let him drive it. The man convinced the girlfriend's best friend to give him a copy of the spare car key, but falsely told her that his license had been restored and the girlfriend was okay with him driving the car.

The best friend delivered the car key to the boyfriend and he accidentally drove the car into a guardrail, totaling it. The prosecutor now wants to charge both the boyfriend and the best friend with automobile theft.

How should the boyfriend and the best friend be charged?

A. The boyfriend should be charged with automobile theft but the best friend should not be charged because she did not know she had been lied to.

B. The boyfriend should be charged as a principal in the first degree, and the best friend should be charged as an accessory before the fact.

C. The boyfriend should be charged as a principal in the first degree, and the best friend should be charged as a principal in the second degree.

D. Neither the boyfriend nor the best friend should be charged as this is a private situation and the prosecutor really should not get involved.

75. A prosecutor charged a woman as the principal to a crime and charged her husband as her accessory before the fact. The woman was very sick with cancer, though, and to allow her to recover before the trial, the prosecutor decided to hold the husband's trial first. The husband's attorney objected but the prosecutor told the judge that the woman might die if she had to stand trial while undergoing cancer treatment.

How should the judge rule on the objection?

A. The trials must be held together because the defendants are married to one another.

B. The trials must be held together because the defendants are charged as parties to the same crime.

C. The husband's trial may be held first because the woman's poor health gave the prosecutor no other option.

D. The husband's trial may only be held after the woman is first tried and convicted.

76. A prosecutor charged a woman with her mother's murder and charged the woman's older sister as an accessory before the fact to the murder. After a lengthy trial, the jury acquitted the woman of the crime. The older sister's attorney filed a motion to dismiss the charge against her client and the prosecutor objected.

How should the judge rule on the motion?

A. The motion should be granted; the woman's acquittal demonstrated that the jury disbelieved that a crime even occurred.

B. The motion should be granted; the older sister cannot be convicted on the basis of derivative liability if the woman has been acquitted.

C. The motion should be denied; the judge must hear testimony about the older sister's role in the crime before reaching a decision.

D. The motion should be denied; the woman was acquitted for her conduct, but the older sister must still answer for what she did to her mother.

77. A woman was charged as an accomplice in the murder of her ex-husband. At the woman's trial, the prosecutor presented a recording of the woman telling an undercover officer that she was glad her ex-husband had been killed because he had been abusive to her. In his closing argument, the prosecutor argued that the recording established that the woman had the specific intent that her husband be killed. The woman's attorney filed a motion for a directed verdict.

How should the judge rule on the woman's motion?

A. The motion should be granted because the prosecutor has not established that the woman had the *mens rea* to be an accomplice.

B. The motion should be granted because the prosecutor must prove the woman's *actus reus*, and he has only proven her *mens rea*.

C. The motion should be denied because the prosecutor has established that the woman had the *mens rea* to be an accomplice.

D. The motion should be denied because the woman probably wished her abusive ex-husband dead at many points in the marriage.

78. A man was in an unhappy marriage and so decided to kill his husband. The man explained his plan to a neighbor and asked to borrow her handgun. The neighbor was horrified but lent the man her handgun because she was afraid that he might kill her too if she declined. As soon as the man left the neighbor's house, she reported him to the police. But before the police could arrive to investigate the neighbor's claim, the man used the handgun to kill his husband.

Can the neighbor be properly charged as an accessory before the fact to murder?

A. Yes; she intentionally lent the man her handgun knowing that he intended to use it to kill his husband.

B. Yes; she intentionally lent the man her handgun without first trying to talk him out of killing his husband.

C. No; she intentionally lent the man her handgun but did not know he would act so quickly to kill his husband.

D. No; she intentionally lent the man her handgun but had no intent that he kill his husband.

79. A woman was charged as an accessory before the fact to arson. At her trial, the woman testified at length that she had no idea that the principal was going to commit the arson. When instructing the jury, the judge stated:

> The second thing that has to be proven is that the defendant intended that the principal commit a crime. It need not be proven that the defendant intended for the principal to commit any particular crime. All the prosecutor must prove is that the defendant intended that the principal commit a crime.

The defense objected to the judge's instruction.

What is the basis for the objection?

A. The instruction misstates the required *mens rea* for the woman to be convicted as an accomplice.

B. The instruction refers to the woman as "the defendant," which is impersonal and dehumanizing.

C. The instruction is unconstitutionally vague because it fails to address the charged crime of arson.

D. The instruction fails to address the woman's trial testimony about what she knew about the arson.

80. Despite many trips to rehab, a man remained addicted to narcotics. Because of his addiction, the man could not keep a job and so he moved in with his sister. The sister gave the man extra cash when she could, knowing that he would likely spend the money on drugs but hoping he would not. One day, while buying drugs with the money his sister had given him, the man was arrested and charged with possession of narcotics.

Can the sister be properly charged as an accessory to the man's crime?

A. No, because the sister did not intend for the man to buy drugs with the money she gave him.

B. No, because the sister was not present when the man bought drugs with the money she gave him.

C. Yes, because the sister knew the man would buy drugs with the money she gave him.

D. Yes, because the sister assisted in the man's possession of drugs when she gave him money.

81. A woman was laid off from her job and went into a bar to have a drink. After one drink, the woman wanted another and the bartender obliged. After downing several more drinks, the woman got in her car and began to drive home. On the way, she drove erratically, crashed the car, and killed a pedestrian.

The prosecutor charged the woman with involuntary manslaughter and the bartender as an accessory before the fact to manslaughter. The bartender's attorney filed a motion to dismiss. The judge dismissed the charges.

What sentence should appear in the judge's dismissal order?

A. "The bartender provided the woman with alcohol to get drunk but the woman killed the pedestrian through her own free will."

B. "The bartender provided the woman with alcohol to get drunk but did not know with certainty that she would get in an accident."

C. "While the bartender provided the woman with alcohol to get drunk, he could not intend to commit manslaughter."

D. "The woman made the voluntary choice to drink and drive and the bartender should not be held liable for the woman's bad choices."

82. A man asked his friend if he could borrow her car to drive across town and sell some drugs. The friend agreed and gave the man her car keys. During the drug sale, the man was arrested. The prosecutor later filed drug charges against the man and also charged the friend as his accomplice.

Prior to trial, the friend filed a motion to quash the charges, arguing that the prosecutor could not establish that she committed the necessary *actus reus* to be considered an accessory.

How should the judge rule on the motion?

A. The motion should be denied as the woman's act provided the man with assistance to commit the crime.

B. The motion should be denied as the woman's act was an indispensable element in the man's plan to sell drugs.

C. The motion should be granted as the woman had no real control over where the man would take her car.

D. The motion should be granted as the woman was only helping the man with his transportation needs.

83. A young woman was considering selling drugs to help pay her college tuition bill. She had some uncertainty, though, and so she called her father to ask for his advice. The father told the young woman that he believed that she could be successful at anything she wanted to do in her life.

Buoyed by her father's helpful words, the young woman set up her first drug sale. She was arrested leaving the sale.

Can the father be properly charged as an accessory before the fact to the drug sale?

A. No, because the father only did what any loving and supportive parent would do for his child.

B. No, because the father's assistance was not tangible, and so he cannot be considered an accomplice.

C. Yes, because the father provided an act of assistance to the young woman's sale of the drugs.

D. Yes, because but for the father's helpful words, the young woman would not have sold the drugs.

84. Late one afternoon, two teenage boys finished swim practice at their high school. The swim coach told the boys that he needed to finish some work in his office and instructed the boys to leave the school directly. Instead, the first boy ran down the hall and smashed the windows of several classroom doors. The second boy stood in the hallway and watched.

The first boy was later charged with vandalism. The prosecutor also wants to charge the second boy, arguing that he acted as a lookout to warn the first boy if the swim coach came by.

Is the prosecutor correct?

A. Yes, because the first boy acted as he did because he knew the second boy was acting as his lookout.

B. Yes, because even though the second boy never had to warn the first boy, he could have if he needed to.

C. No, because the second boy never had to issue a warning to the first boy, he cannot be charged with a crime.

D. No, because the second boy's mere presence in the hallway is insufficient to convert him into a principal.

85. A man asked his friend to come along with him as he robbed a bank. The man told the friend that all she had to do was sit in the car and text him if the police arrived. The man also told the friend that, without her help, he was too frightened to rob the bank himself. The friend agreed to help the man as he had asked.

The next day, the man and the friend drove to the bank. The man went inside to rob the bank and the friend sat in the passenger seat. As the police did not arrive, the friend did not have to text the man.

Can the friend be properly charged as an accomplice to the bank robbery?

A. No, because the police never arrived and the friend never had to send a text, she cannot be charged as a principal or accessory.

B. No, because the friend's mere presence in the parking lot of the bank is not enough to convert her into a principal or accessory.

C. Yes, because the friend's agreement to text the man if the police arrived emboldened the man to commit the bank robbery.

D. Yes, because the friend intended that the man rob the bank and stayed in the car while the robbery occurred.

86. A man was sitting in the corner of a bar, drinking a glass of wine and texting with a friend, when a woman walked into the bar. The woman was wearing a mask and had a gun in her hand. The woman pointed the gun at the bartender and demanded money from the cash register. Terrified, the bartender complied. A few minutes later, the woman ran out of the bar, cash in hand. The man watched these events as he sipped his wine.

The prosecutor charged the man as an accessory to the robbery, based on his failure to call or text the police while the robbery was in progress. The defense filed a motion to dismiss the charge.

How should the judge rule on the defense motion?

A. The motion should be granted because the man's failure to act in this situation cannot form the basis for accomplice liability.

B. The motion should be granted because the man's mere presence during the robbery did not make him a principal or accessory.

C. The motion should be denied because the jury should decide whether the man's failure to act was helpful to the woman.

D. The motion should be denied because the man's failure to act in this situation constituted an act of assistance to the woman.

87. A sixth-grade student told her gymnastics coach that her father often beat her. The student also showed the coach some bruises on her back and explained that her father had kicked her repeatedly for not setting the dinner table properly. The coach told the student that she sympathized, but was powerless to do anything to help.

Two weeks later, the father beat the student to death, and the prosecutor charged him with murder. When a police officer interviewed the coach, she related what the student had told her. The officer told the coach that she was required by state law to report to suspected abuse, without exception, she replied that she had not known that.

Can the prosecutor properly charge the coach as an accessory to the murder?

A. Yes, because the coach had a duty to report the abuse of the student and failed to fulfill that duty.

B. Yes, even though the student never told the coach that her father's abuse might end in a homicide.

C. No, because the student was too young to provide the coach with a credible report about her father's abuse.

D. No, because the coach did not know she had a duty to report and so lacked the *mens rea* to be an accessory.

88. An unemployed man needed rent money; the man asked his roommate for help, but the roommate had no cash to spare. The roommate offered the man his handgun, though, and suggested he use it to rob a gas station.

Later that day, the man robbed the gas station. In the course of the robbery, the man lost his temper and used the roommate's handgun to kill the clerk. The man was arrested and charged with armed robbery and intentional murder; the prosecutor also wants to charge the roommate as an accessory before the fact to both crimes.

Can the prosecutor properly charge the roommate with these crimes?

A. No; the roommate only knew about the armed robbery and so he should not be held criminally responsible for the murder.

B. No; the roommate had no way of knowing that the man would lose his temper and use the gun to shoot and kill the clerk.

C. Yes; as an accessory before the fact to armed robbery, the roommate is responsible for the natural and probable consequences of that crime.

D. Yes; as an accessory before the fact to armed robbery, the roommate knew that someone would probably die in the commission of that crime.

89. Two high school football players collaborated on a plan to steal the playbook from the coach of a rival football team. The quarterback drove to the house and acted as a lookout and the placekicker broke into the house and stole the playbook. While inside the house, the placekicker spray-painted his team's name on the walls of the dining room.

The football players were arrested and charged as principals in the first degree (the placekicker) and second degree (the quarterback) to home invasion, theft, and vandalism. The quarterback's attorney moved to dismiss the vandalism charge.

How should the prosecutor respond?

A. The prosecutor should argue that because teenagers often do stupid things, it was foreseeable that the placekicker would spray paint the team's name on the dining room wall.

B. The prosecutor should argue that because teenagers often do stupid things, it was probable that the placekicker would spray paint the team's name on the dining room wall.

C. The prosecutor should argue that although vandalism isn't usually a natural and probable consequence of home invasion and theft, it was here because the crime involved rival teams.

D. The prosecutor should acknowledge that vandalism is not a natural and probable consequence of either home invasion or theft, and he should also dismiss the charge.

90. A man was convicted as an accessory before the fact to first degree murder. The prosecutor asked the judge for a sentence of 50 years in prison—the same sentence that the principal in the first degree received when he was convicted of first degree murder. Defense counsel objected, arguing that her client deserved a drastically reduced sentence as he did not perform the killing, but only provided the murder weapon and encouragement for the crime.

Can the man receive the same sentence as the principal in the first degree?

A. Yes; the sentences can be the same because the man was convicted of first degree murder based on derivative liability.

B. Yes; the sentences can be the same because people who provide murder weapons and encourage crimes must be punished.

C. No; the sentences cannot be the same because the person who pulled the trigger should always receive a harsher sentence.

D. No; the sentences cannot be the same because prison sentences should be individually crafted for each unique defendant.

91. One night, a woman was reading in bed when her best friend knocked on her back door and begged for help. The best friend explained that she had gotten into a fight with her boyfriend and stabbed him with a knife. The woman gave the best friend some clean clothes and agreed to wash the best friend's blood-soaked clothes. The woman gave the best friend all the cash from her wallet, and the best friend got into her car and drove away.

The police came to the woman's house the next day and, after executing a search warrant, found the best friend's washed clothes. Both women were later arrested; the best friend pled guilty to attempted murder and the woman pled guilty to being an accessory after the fact to attempted murder.

How should the woman be sentenced?

A. The woman's sentence should be the same as the best friend's sentence because covering up a stabbing is as bad as stabbing someone.

B. The woman's sentence should be the same as the best friend's sentence because she impeded a police investigation by washing the clothes.

C. The woman's sentence should be less than the best friend's sentence because she only learned about the stabbing after it happened.

D. The woman's sentence should be greater than the best friend's sentence because she failed to call the police and report the stabbing.

92. A man and a woman agreed to rob a bank together. They drove to a bank together and while the woman went inside the bank and committed the robbery, the man stayed in the car. When the woman finished, she got into the car, and the man quickly drove away.

What is the man's relationship to the woman?

A. The man is either the woman's co-conspirator or her accomplice.

B. The man is the woman's accomplice but not her co-conspirator.

C. The man is the woman's co-conspirator but not her accomplice.

D. The man is the woman's co-conspirator and also her accomplice.

93. A woman went into a store to rob it. As a customer in the back of the store watched, the woman pulled out a gun and pointed it at the cashier. As the customer watched, she noticed that the store owner had parked his car at the rear of the store and was walking toward the back door, to enter the store. The customer slipped out of the back door and began chatting with the store owner. In the meantime, the woman completed the robbery and drove away.

What is the customer's relationship to the woman?

A. The customer is the woman's co-conspirator because, by her actions, she agreed to help her rob the store.

B. The customer is a principal in the second degree because she intended that a robbery be committed and helped with its commission.

C. The customer has no relationship with the woman because there is no indication that the two knew each other.

D. The customer has no relationship with the woman because the woman did not know the customer assisted with the robbery.

94. A woman and her brother agreed to steal money from their elderly parents. Before they could act on their plan, though, the woman was arrested for drug possession and locked up in the county jail. Over the next few weeks, the brother continued with the plan and stole thousands of dollars from the parents' checking account. The parents eventually realized what was happening and called the police; the brother was later arrested.

What is the woman's relationship to her brother?

A. The woman is her brother's accomplice, but just to the drug crime.

B. The woman is her brother's accomplice but not his co-conspirator.

C. The woman is her brother's co-conspirator but not his accomplice.

D. The woman is her brother's co-conspirator and his accomplice.

95. A state legislature is considering adding the following provision to its penal code:

> Every person involved in the commission of an offense, whether he directly commits the act constituting the offense or procures, counsels, aids, or abets in its commission, may be prosecuted and on conviction shall be punished as if he had directly committed that offense.

What does this provision do?

A. It combines the principal in the first and second degrees into one category for the purposes of prosecution and punishment.

B. It combines all common law parties to a crime into one category for the purposes of prosecution and punishment.

C. It eradicates the distinction between principals and accessories before the fact for the purposes of prosecution and punishment.

D. It eradicates the distinction between accessories before and after the fact for the purposes of prosecution and punishment.

Model Penal Code

96. A woman was charged with murdering her husband. Prior to trial, the defense filed a motion claiming the woman should be convicted of manslaughter because she acted under "the influence of an extreme emotional disturbance for which there was a reasonable explanation or excuse."

A law student was assigned to review the motion and was told that the homicide provisions in the state's penal code were derived from the Model Penal Code.

The student told her supervisor that the Model Penal Code's manslaughter provision referred to an "extreme mental or emotional disturbance"—not merely an "extreme emotional disturbance." The student asked the supervisor whether the state's penal code had a typo.

How should the supervisor respond?

A. The supervisor should applaud the student for discovering a gap in the state's penal code and should contact her legislator to make the correction.

B. The supervisor should explain that the state adopted only part of the provision from the Model Penal Code and was not required to adopt it verbatim.

C. The supervisor should tell the student that her job description does not involve second-guessing the work of experienced criminal practitioners.

D. The supervisor should advise the student not to worry because if there was a typo in the state's penal code, someone would have already noticed it.

97. A law professor was writing an article about the Model Penal Code. She wanted to begin the article by summarizing the Code's approach to mental states.

What sentence should be included in the text?

A. "The Model Penal Code adopts common law *mens rea* terminology, but uses extensive commentary to define each term."

B. "The Model Penal Code recognizes four new mental states in addition to adopting common law *mens rea* terminology."

C. "The Model Penal Code rejects inquiry into a defendant's *mens rea* and instead focuses exclusively on the defendant's *actus reus*."

D. "The Model Penal includes only four mental states in its crime definitions: purposely, knowingly, recklessly, and negligently."

98. A law professor asked a student in her class to identify a common law corollary to the Model Penal Code's definition of "purposely." Under the Code:

> A person acts purposely with respect to a material element of an offense when:
>
> > (i) if the element involves the nature of his conduct or a result thereof, it is his conscious object to engage in conduct of that nature or to cause such a result; and
> >
> > (ii) if the element involves the attendant circumstances, he is aware of the existence of such circumstances or he believes or hopes that they exist.

How should the student respond?

A. When a common law crime requires a *mens rea* of "intentionally," that is the same as the Code's definition of "purposely."

B. When a common law crime requires a *mens rea* of "premeditatedly," that is the same as the Code's definition of "purposely."

C. When a common law crime requires a *mens rea* of "deliberately," that is the same as the Code's definition of "purposely."

D. There is no common law corollary to the Code's definition of "purposely;" the point of the Code was to reject common law concepts.

99. A man approached a woman from behind, pushed his cellphone into her back and demanded she give up her wallet. The woman was terrified and did as she was told. The man was charged with robbery using the Model Penal Code's definition of that crime:

> A person is guilty of robbery if, in the course of committing a theft, he:
>
> > (a) inflicts serious bodily injury upon another; or
> >
> > (b) threatens another with or purposely puts him in fear of immediate serious bodily injury; or
> >
> > (c) commits or threatens immediately to commit any felony of the first or second degree.

The man claims that the prosecutor cannot prove the elements of this offense.

How should the judge respond?

A. The man cannot be charged with robbery because he only used a cellphone to threaten the woman, and a cellphone cannot cause any sort of physical injury to anyone.

B. The man cannot be charged with robbery because any claim that the woman might have feared immediate serious bodily injury from the cellphone is unreasonable.

C. The man acted purposely when he pushed his cellphone into the woman's back, because it was his conscious object to put her in fear of immediate serious bodily injury.

D. The man acted purposely when he pushed his cellphone into the woman's back, because it was his conscious object to threaten her with immediate serious bodily injury.

100. A man and his husband got into a fight about money; the man shot his husband in the chest and killed him. When he was interviewed later by the police, the man explained that he was a long-time gun owner and appreciated the lethal damage that could be caused by a gunshot. The man also explained that he loved his husband and had not wanted him to die. Instead, the man said that he wanted his husband to reflect on his spending habits and save more of his income. In this jurisdiction:

> A person acts knowingly with respect to a material element of an offense when:
>
> > (i) if the element involves the nature of his conduct or the attendant circumstances, he is aware that his conduct is of that nature or that such circumstances exist; and
> >
> > (ii) if the element involves a result of his conduct, he is aware that it is practically certain that his conduct will cause such a result.

Did the man knowingly cause the death of his husband?

A. Yes, because the man was aware that it was practically certain the gunshot would kill the husband.

B. Yes, because the man's experience with guns shows that he lied to the police about his intentions.

C. No, because the man's statement to the police indicates that he did not intend for his husband to die.

D. No, because the man only appreciated that guns can kill, but did not know for certain his husband would die.

101. A woman invited a friend to dinner. During the meal, the two got into a fight; the friend wanted to leave but the woman took the friend's car keys and said he would have to stay until the fight was resolved. The woman knew the friend had diabetes and had to get home to take his medication. The woman was charged with felonious restraint in a jurisdiction that follows the Model Penal Code:

> A person commits a felony of the third degree if he knowingly:
>
> > (a) restrains another unlawfully in circumstances exposing him to risk of serious bodily injury; or
> >
> > (b) holds another in a condition of involuntary servitude.

Can the woman be properly convicted of this crime?

A. No, because she did not knowingly expose the friend to a risk of serious bodily injury.

B. No, because she did not know how sick her friend might become without his medication.

C. Yes, because she kept her friend from his medication, creating a risk of serious bodily injury.

D. Yes, because she knowingly restrained her friend and exposed him to a risk of serious bodily injury.

102. One sunny afternoon, a police officer gave a woman a ticket for reckless driving after he caught her driving 6 MPH above the posted limit. Reckless driving is defined as "the reckless operation of an automobile, so as to create a significant danger to others." The penal code uses the Model Penal Code definition of recklessly:

> A person acts recklessly with respect to a material element of an offense when he consciously disregards a substantial and unjustifiable risk that the material element exists or will result from his conduct. The risk must be of such a nature and degree that, considering the nature and purpose of the actor's conduct and the circumstances known to him, its disregard involves a gross deviation from the standard of conduct that a law-abiding person would observe in the actor's situation.

Should the officer have issued this ticket?

A. No, because the woman failed to be aware of the risk to others and did not consciously disregard the risk.

B. Yes, because the woman's speeding posed a substantial and unjustifiable risk of danger to others.

C. No, because the woman's speeding did not pose a substantial and unjustifiable risk of danger to others.

D. Yes, because the woman consciously disregarded a substantial and unjustifiable risk of danger to others.

103. A nurse put an advertisement online, offering to perform breast and buttock implants at a reduced price. A woman contacted the nurse and arranged surgery for the following week, to be performed in the nurse's dining room. During the surgery, the woman had a heart attack and died. The autopsy revealed that she had a heart abnormality that would have been survivable, had the heart attack occurred in a hospital.

The nurse was charged with reckless murder. The penal code uses the Model Penal Code definition of recklessly:

> A person acts recklessly with respect to a material element of an offense when he consciously disregards a substantial and unjustifiable risk that the material element exists or will result from his conduct. The risk must be of such a nature and degree that, considering the nature and purpose of the actor's conduct and the circumstances known to him, its disregard involves a gross deviation from the standard of conduct that a law-abiding person would observe in the actor's situation.

In a motion to dismiss the charges, the nurse conceded that the home surgery was quite risky. But she argued that she was not aware of the specific risk that the woman might have a heart attack because she had no training in cardiology.

How should the judge rule on the motion?

A. The motion should be granted because the nurse could not consciously disregard something she did not know.

B. The motion should be granted because the nurse should lose her nursing license and not be convicted of a crime.

C. The motion should be denied because the nurse should not be allowed to evade responsibility for the woman's death.

D. The motion should be denied because the nurse conceded that she knew of the risks of death from the home surgery.

104. On a criminal law exam, a law professor asked her students to explain the difference between Model Penal Code recklessness and negligence. The exam provided the following definitions:

> A person acts *recklessly* with respect to a material element of an offense when he consciously disregards a substantial and unjustifiable risk that the material element exists or will result from his conduct. The risk must be of such a nature and degree that, considering the nature and purpose of the actor's conduct and the circumstances known to him, its disregard involves a gross deviation from the standard of conduct that a law-abiding person would observe in the actor's situation.
>
> A person acts *negligently* with respect to a material element of an offense when he should be aware of a substantial and unjustifiable risk that the material element exists or will result from his conduct. The risk must be of such a nature and degree that the actor's failure to perceive it, considering the nature and purpose of his conduct and the circumstances known to him, involves a gross deviation from the standard of care that a reasonable person would observe in the actor's situation.

How should the students respond?

A. The degree of risk is different, and a reckless defendant shows a conscious disregard for the risk while a negligent defendant fails to be aware of the risk.

B. The degree of risk is identical, but a reckless defendant shows a conscious disregard for the risk while a negligent defendant fails to be aware of the risk.

C. The conduct for crimes involving recklessness is much riskier, and so the defendant faces greater liability because he consciously disregards the risk.

D. The conduct for crimes involving negligence involves ordinary risk, and so the defendant faces reduced liability because he fails to be aware of the risk.

105. A teenage boy and his brother broke into a gun safe belonging to their mother. The teenage boy jokingly pointed the gun at his brother, not realizing that it was loaded; his finger slipped on the trigger and the gun discharged. The bullet grazed the brother's arm.

The teenage boy was charged with simple assault in a jurisdiction that follows the Model Penal Code. The statute states:

> (1) Simple Assault. A person is guilty of assault if he:
>
> > (a) attempts to cause or purposely, knowingly or recklessly causes bodily injury to another; or
> >
> > (b) negligently causes bodily injury to another with a deadly weapon; or
> >
> > (c) attempts by physical menace to put another in fear of imminent serious bodily injury.

Can the teenage boy be convicted of this crime?

A. Yes, because the teenage boy caused bodily injury to his brother and failed to be aware of the risk of harm associated with using the gun.

B. Yes, because the teenage boy caused bodily injury to his brother, consciously disregarding the risk of harm associated with using the gun.

C. No, because labeling the shooting of a person with a gun as "simple assault" ignores the inherent danger associated with such an act.

D. No, because the teenage boy did not know the gun was loaded and his finger slipped on the trigger; this was just an unfortunate accident.

106. A lawyer was reviewing her state's penal code in preparation for an upcoming oral argument. The lawyer anticipated being asked to list the ways murder can be committed under the penal code and she wanted to have the right answer. This jurisdiction has adopted a definition of murder from the Model Penal Code:

> A criminal homicide constitutes murder when:
>
> (a) it is committed purposely or knowingly; or
>
> (b) it is committed recklessly under circumstances manifesting extreme indifference to the value of human life. Such recklessness and indifference are presumed if the actor is engaged in or is an accomplice in the commission of, or an attempt to commit, or flight after committing or attempting to commit robbery, rape or deviate sexual intercourse by force or threat of force, arson, burglary, kidnapping or felonious escape.

What answer should the lawyer be prepared to give?

A. In this jurisdiction, murder can be committed purposefully or knowingly.

B. In this jurisdiction, murder can be committed purposefully, knowingly, or recklessly.

C. In this jurisdiction, murder can be committed purposefully, knowingly, or recklessly under circumstances manifesting an extreme indifference to the value of human life.

D. In this jurisdiction, murder can be committed purposefully, knowingly, or by committing a killing in conjunction with one of the felonies enumerated in the statute.

107. A man killed a teller while robbing a bank. He was charged with reckless murder in a jurisdiction that follows the Model Penal Code. The relevant provision states:

> A criminal homicide constitutes murder when it is committed recklessly under circumstances manifesting extreme indifference to the value of human life. Such recklessness and indifference are presumed if the actor is engaged or is an accomplice in the commission of, or an attempt to commit, or flight after committing or attempting to commit robbery, rape or deviate sexual intercourse by force or threat of force, arson, burglary, kidnapping or felonious escape.

In its deliberations, the jurors agreed that the man committed a robbery, but that the killing was purely accidental.

Should the jury return a guilty verdict?

A. Yes, because the jurors agreed that he committed felony murder: he killed the bank teller while committing an enumerated felony.

B. Yes, because by committing robbery, the man demonstrated that he had an extreme indifference to the value of human life.

C. No, because the man did not act recklessly although his actions did manifest an extreme indifference to the value of human life.

D. No, because the jurors agreed that the man did not act under circumstances manifesting extreme indifference to the value of human life.

108. Under the Model Penal Code, manslaughter can be committed in one of two ways. First, the homicide can be committed recklessly. Second:

> [A] homicide which would otherwise be murder is committed under the influence of extreme mental or emotional disturbance for which there is reasonable explanation or excuse. The reasonableness of such explanation or excuse shall be determined from the viewpoint of a person in the actor's situation under the circumstances as he believes them to be.

How does this second provision compare to common law voluntary manslaughter?

A. It is identical: the defendant has to act suddenly in response to a particular type of provocation; he must not have time to cool off; and his conduct will be judged according to an objective, reasonable man standard.

B. It is nearly identical: the defendant has to act suddenly in response to a particular type of provocation and his conduct will be judged according to an objective, reasonable man standard.

C. It bears no resemblance to, and has nothing in common with, common law voluntary manslaughter; the two crimes are conceptually separate and should not be compared to one another.

D. It is similar to but distinct from common law voluntary manslaughter: the defendant does not need to be provoked by a person or event; there is no cooling-off requirement; and his conduct will be judged with some subjectivity.

109. A man was convicted of murder in a state that has adopted the Model Penal Code in its entirety. Before the man's sentencing, the judge confessed to her law clerk that she was unsure how to sentence the man, given that the state's penal code did not separate murder into degrees. The judge asked the law clerk how the Model Penal Code resolved this situation.

How should the law clerk respond?

A. The law clerk should explain that the judge has identified one of the gaping holes in the Model Penal Code.

B. The law clerk should explain that the Model Penal Code only defined crimes, but did not address sentencing.

C. The law clerk should explain that the Model Penal Code classified crimes into degrees for sentencing purposes.

D. The law clerk should explain that due to the age of the Model Penal Code, it should not be used as an authority.

110. A state currently follows the common law. But the legislature is considering adopting the definition of negligent homicide from the Model Penal Code, which states that "criminal homicide constitutes negligent homicide when it is committed negligently." According to the Code:

> A person acts negligently with respect to a material element of an offense when he should be aware of a substantial and unjustifiable risk that the material element exists or will result from his conduct. The risk must be of such a nature and degree that the actor's failure to perceive it, considering the nature and purpose of his conduct and the circumstances known to him, involves a gross deviation from the standard of care that a reasonable person would observe in the actor's situation.

A state legislator opposes the proposed adoption because he believes it will allow defendants who commit involuntary manslaughter—as that crime is defined at common law—to evade responsibility.

Is the state legislator correct?

A. No; the Model Penal Code's definition of negligent homicide is the same as the common law definition of involuntary manslaughter.

B. No; the Model Penal Code treats common law involuntary manslaughter as a form of murder, so the legislator need not worry.

C. Yes; the Model Penal Code's definition of negligent homicide replaces common law involuntary manslaughter with a more restrictive definition.

D. Yes; the drafters of the Model Penal Code failed to account for involuntary manslaughter when they produced their Code.

Part II

Specific Crimes

Homicide (Common Law)

111. A hunter shot and killed a buck two days before the start of deer season. The hunter was arrested and charged with homicide. The very next day, the hunter's attorney filed a motion to quash the charges, conceding that the hunter broke the law by hunting early but arguing that the homicide charge should be dismissed anyway.

How should the judge rule on the motion?

A. The motion should be denied because a jury should decide whether the hunter is guilty or not of the charged crime.

B. The motion should be denied because it was filed right after the arrest and additional investigation is required.

C. The motion should be granted because hunting before the start of deer season is only a technical violation of the law.

D. The motion should be granted because when the hunter shot and killed the buck, he did not commit a homicide.

112. After a woman was convicted of murder, a jury sentenced her to death. The woman appealed her conviction and sentence, but was unsuccessful. The woman was later executed.

How should the woman's execution be described?

A. The woman's execution was a homicide.

B. The woman's execution was a culpable homicide.

C. The woman's execution was a criminal homicide.

D. The woman's execution was excusable euthanasia.

113. A woman believed her husband had been unfaithful to her. The woman confronted her husband with her suspicions and demanded an explanation. The husband denied cheating and told the woman that she was delusional. Outraged by her husband's statement, the woman pulled a handgun out of her purse and shot him dead.

How should the woman be charged under the common law?

A. With second degree murder, because the husband provoked the woman when he called her delusional.

B. With murder, because the woman killed her husband with malice aforethought and without justification or excuse.

C. With manslaughter, because the woman did not exhibit malice aforethought when she killed her husband.

D. With second degree manslaughter, because the husband provoked the woman when he called her delusional.

114. A law clerk was preparing a memo for her judge, to be used in an upcoming murder trial. The law clerk needed to provide the legal definition of common law murder in her memo, and so she looked on the internet for help. She found four possible definitions.

Which of the following definitions is correct?

A. Murder is a killing with *malum in se*, express or implied.

B. Murder is a killing accompanied by the intent to harm the victim.

C. Murder is a killing with *malum prohibitum*.

D. Murder is a killing with malice aforethought, express or implied.

115. A woman was at a grocery store after work. The woman was tired from a long day and was in a sour mood. In the fruit section of the store, the woman reached for a bunch of ripe bananas but a man grabbed them first. The woman pulled a gun from her purse and shot the man in the chest, killing him. According to bystanders, the entire interaction between the man and the woman took only a few seconds.

Can the woman be convicted of common law murder?

A. No, because the woman had insufficient time to develop malice aforethought.

B. No, because it is impossible to determine the woman's *mens rea* toward the man.

C. Yes, because the woman had sufficient time to develop malice aforethought.

D. Yes, because the woman did not give the man a chance to return the bananas.

116. A law student was studying for her final exam in her first term Criminal Law class. The student was creating flashcards to use while studying. On the front of one card, the student wrote "forms of malice aforethought."

What should the student write on the back of the notecard?

A. Malice aforethought can be express or implied, or unilateral or bilateral.

B. Malice aforethought includes intent to kill, intent to cause harm to another, corrupt heart, and intent to commit a felony that results in death.

C. Malice aforethought can be express or implied, or intentional or negligent.

D. Malice aforethought includes intent to kill, intent to cause great bodily harm, depraved heart, and intent to commit a felony that results in death.

117. A young man shot and killed his roommate. There were no witnesses to the crime but the prosecution established at trial that the young man shot his roommate once in the head. The young man declined to testify in his own defense.

Can a jury properly convict the young man of common law murder?

A. No, because the jury lacks sufficient information by which to determine the young man's *mens rea* at the time of the shooting.

B. No, because a murder conviction requires testimony from either an eyewitness to the crime or from the defendant himself.

C. Yes, because the fact-finder can presume the young man's *mens rea* from the weapon he used and the location of the gunshot.

D. Yes, because the fact-finder can infer the young man's *mens rea* from the weapon he used and the location of the gunshot.

118. A retired man begged his wife to retire and spend more time with him, but she did not want to. Furious, the retired man put rat poison into a lunch he prepared for his wife. The retired man knew the poison was highly toxic and would likely cause his wife's death, but he hoped it would instead leave her too sick to work and she would retire. But because the poison was so toxic, the woman died shortly after eating her lunch.

The retired man was charged with the intentional murder of his wife. His attorney plans to argue that he did not intend to kill her, but only intended for her to become sick and then retire.

Can the retired man be properly convicted of intentional murder?

A. No, because the retired man did not have an intent to kill his wife.

B. No, because the retired man intended only that his wife become sick.

C. Yes, because it was foreseeable that the rat poison would kill the wife.

D. Yes, because the retired man's claims are completely implausible.

119. A college sophomore was driving down the street when she spotted her girlfriend and another woman, smiling and chatting at an outdoor café. The sophomore became enraged with jealousy; she turned the steering wheel, put her foot on the accelerator, and drove the car into the table where the girlfriend and the other woman were sitting. Both the girlfriend and the other woman died in the crash.

At the sophomore's subsequent trial on intentional murder charges, the prosecutor asked the judge to instruct the jurors that they could infer the sophomore's intent to kill from her use of a deadly weapon, i.e., the car. The defense objected, claiming that cars are not deadly weapons.

How should the judge rule on the objection?

A. For the defense, because cars are designed and manufactured to transport people, and not to kill people.

B. For the defense, because cars are designed with many safety features designed to save lives and not end lives.

C. For the prosecution, because the sophomore intentionally used her car in a way that was likely to cause death.

D. For the prosecution, because any device that causes death is a deadly weapon, regardless of its design or manufacture.

120. A college student was in the common area of her dormitory, looking out the window. The student's friend saw her and walked toward her. The friend stopped about 15 feet away, tossed a hockey puck at the student and yelled out "think fast!" The student turned around but before she could raise her hands to catch the puck, it hit her in the middle of the forehead. The student slumped over and later died from the blow to the head.

At the friend's subsequent trial on intentional murder charges, the prosecutor asked the judge to instruct the jurors that they could infer the friend's intent to kill from his use of a deadly weapon. The defense objected, claiming that hockey pucks are not deadly weapons.

How should the judge rule?

A. For the defense, because hockey pucks are designed and manufactured for hockey matches, and not to kill people.

B. For the defense, because this hockey puck was not designed, manufactured, or intentionally used to cause death.

C. For the prosecution, because the hockey puck was used to cause death, even though it was not designed or manufactured for that purpose.

D. For the prosecution, because any device that causes death is a deadly weapon, regardless of its design or manufacture.

121. A teenage boy got into a fight with his friend because he thought the friend had stolen his new video game, but the friend denied doing so. The two pushed and shoved one another, and then the teenage boy grabbed a nearby lamp and used it to smack his friend across the face. The friend was stunned and stopped moving for a few seconds. He then confessed that he had indeed stolen the video game and apologized. The two agreed to forget the incident and remain friends.

Later that night, the friend died in his sleep. An autopsy showed that his death was caused by the blow to the head from the lamp.

Can the teenage boy be convicted of common law murder?

A. Yes, because the teenage boy intended great bodily harm to his friend, which caused the friend's death.

B. Yes, because the teenage boy is old enough to be held responsible for the consequences of his actions.

C. No, because the teenage boy had no intent to kill his friend, which is required for common law murder.

D. No, because the teenage boy is not fully mature and teenagers should not be convicted of adult crimes.

122. A man thought his roommate was a slob; despite the roommate's promises to improve, she continued to leave her belongings around the house. One evening and to make a point to the roommate, the man grabbed her dirty laundry from a pile in the hallway and tossed it onto the couch in the living room. He moved the roommate's crusty dishes from the kitchen sink to the coffee table in the living room. And he took the roommate's mildewed towels from the floor of the bathroom and put them on the floor of the living room.

Twenty minutes later, the roommate came home. When she opened the front door and saw the mess, she thought the house had been burglarized. Fearful that the burglar might still be in the house, the roommate had a heart attack and died of fright. The man was later arrested and charged with common law murder. The defense anticipates filing a motion to dismiss the charges.

What should the defense argue in its motion?

A. The man might be a terrible roommate but he is not a murderer.

B. The man did not intend significant enough harm to the roommate.

C. The prosecutor cannot prove the man's acts caused the roommate's death.

D. The roommate brought this on herself by being such a slob.

123. Two men wanted to park their cars in the same parking space. After yelling at one another from their separate cars for several minutes, the men got out of their cars and began fighting. In the fight, the first man punched the second man in the jaw. The second man stumbled and then fell to the ground and died. A later autopsy revealed that he had a vein abnormality in his brain, and the first man's punch had caused it to hemorrhage.

At the first man's subsequent murder trial, he argued that he should be acquitted because he had no way of knowing that the second man had the vein abnormality in his brain.

How should the judge respond?

A. The first man is correct because the vein abnormality was an equal, contributing factor in the second man's death.

B. The first man is correct because the second man likely knew he had the vein abnormality, but fought anyway.

C. The first man is incorrect because lack of knowledge of a victim's physical frailty is not a defense to a criminal charge.

D. The first man is incorrect because his punch was an equal, contributing factor to the second man's death.

124. Two high school seniors decided to skip school. After driving around aimlessly for several hours, the seniors went to a local park and collected some large rocks. The seniors then drove to a bridge above a highway and threw the rocks over the railing. One of the rocks hit the pavement in front of an SUV. The driver swerved out of the way; the SUV rolled over several times and the driver was ejected from the SUV. The driver died at the scene. The subsequent police investigation revealed that the driver did not have a valid license and was not wearing a seat belt.

Can the seniors be properly charged with murder?

A. No, because the seniors had no intent to kill or intent to cause great bodily harm to the driver.

B. No, because the driver was unlicensed and was contributorily negligent for not wearing a seat belt.

C. Yes, because the seniors engaged in a dangerous act that ultimately led to the driver's death.

D. Yes, because the seniors acted with reckless indifference and their act caused the driver's death.

125. Running late to work, a man was driving on the highway. Anxious about the time, he drove 10 MPH above the posted speed limit. Seemingly out of nowhere, a deer jumped onto the highway and in front of the man's car. The man swerved his car to avoid the deer, but hit a car in the next lane, killing its driver.

Can the man be properly convicted of common law depraved heart murder?

A. No; the deer was contributorily negligent for the accident, and so the man should not be convicted of depraved heart murder.

B. No; while the man took a risk when he exceeded the speed limit, it was not significant enough for a depraved heart conviction.

C. Yes; the man took a significant risk in exceeding the speed limit, was aware of the risk he took, and someone died as a result.

D. Yes; the man's failure to obey the posted speed limit shows a depraved indifference to the value of other drivers' lives.

126. A college senior invited his friends over to his house for a party on New Year's Eve. A few minutes before midnight, the senior told his guests to go outside to watch the fireworks show he had arranged for them. As one of the guests left the house, he grabbed a jacket from a coatrack near the door, believing it to be his own. The jacket actually belonged to the senior.

Once outside, the guest put his hands in a pocket of the jacket and found a loaded revolver. As the clock struck midnight, the guest pulled out the revolver and fired a shot into the house, believing that no one was inside. But the senior was still inside the house and was struck and killed by the bullet.

Can the guest be properly convicted of common law depraved heart murder?

A. No; the senior was contributorily negligent by leaving his revolver in the jacket, and so the guest should not be convicted.

B. No; while the guest took a risk when he fired the revolver in the house, the risk was negated by his belief that no one was inside.

C. Yes; the guest took a significant risk by firing the revolver into the house, even though he believed that no one was inside.

D. Yes; the guest's failure to obey basic weapons safety rules shows a depraved indifference to the value of the lives of others.

127. One summer day, a man drove to the grocery store to pick up some food for dinner. The man's daughter was strapped into her car seat in the back seat, sleeping. Once at the store, the man parked the car and cracked the front windows a few inches. Although the man had read several news stories about small children dying in parked cars, he did not want to wake his daughter.

The man went into the store. When he returned 45 minutes later, his daughter was dead.

How should father's *mens rea* be described?

A. The father acted negligently, as he breached his duty to protect his daughter when he left her alone in the car.

B. The father acted with criminal negligence as he failed to be aware of the risk that his daughter might die in the car.

C. The father intentionally killed his daughter, as he knew that there was a significant risk that she might die if left in the car.

D. The father acted with extreme recklessness because he was aware of and ignored a significant risk to his daughter's life.

128. A woman needed rent money and so she decided to rob a bank. The woman planned to show a gun to the bank teller to scare him into giving her money. But the woman was a pacifist and had absolutely no intention of using the gun to hurt anyone. The robbery did not go as planned; when the woman showed the teller the gun, it accidentally discharged, killing a bank customer.

Can the woman be charged with murder?

A. Yes, because the woman killed the bank customer while committing a robbery.

B. Yes, because the woman intended great bodily harm to the bank customer.

C. No, because the gun discharged accidentally and so the woman is not to blame.

D. No; the woman had no intent to kill or cause great bodily harm to the teller.

129. A brother asked his sister for a big favor: to serve as his driver for a bank robbery he was planning. The sister agreed. On the appointed day, the sister drove the brother to the bank and waited in the parking lot while he robbed the bank. As the brother was running from the bank after the robbery, he tripped and fell, fatally breaking his neck. The sister was arrested and charged with felony murder, a crime carrying a mandatory 50-year prison sentence. By contrast, in this jurisdiction, the penalty for armed robbery is 5–15 years in prison.

The defense filed a motion to dismiss, arguing that it would be unfair to convict the sister of murder because the brother died because of his own clumsiness.

Should the judge grant or deny the motion?

A. Grant; the sister is only responsible for reasonably foreseeable deaths that occurred during the commission of the robbery.

B. Grant; the sister is only responsible for the deaths of non-felons, and cannot be responsible for the death of another felon.

C. Deny; the sister is responsible for any deaths that occurred during the commission of the robbery.

D. Deny; the sister makes a good point in her motion, but it is one that should be submitted to the jury for it to decide.

130. A law student was discussing common law felony murder with her roommate, who was a lawyer. The law student explained that she thought it was unfair to convict a person of murder based only on his *mens rea* for the underlying crime, and wondered why the common law allowed such convictions.

How should the roommate respond?

A. Common law scholars were deeply concerned about unfairness under the felony murder rule, and many called for the rule to be abolished.

B. Common law scholars knew that the felony murder rule could be unfair, but they were more focused on drafting a model penal code.

C. Common law scholars did not think that felony murder convictions were unfair because the punishment for all felonies at that time was death.

D. Common law scholars did not think that felony murder convictions were unfair because fairness is a modern concept that did not exist then.

131. A man went into a convenience store and robbed it. The man then drove away in his car. A few minutes later, police spotted the man driving on the highway and began to chase him. During the chase, the man's car sideswiped a minivan, causing it to spin off the road. The driver of the minivan was thrown from the vehicle and died.

The man was later captured and charged with robbery and felony murder. The man's lawyer filed a motion to dismiss the murder charge.

How should the judge rule on the motion?

A. The motion should be denied because the death occurred during the *res gestae* of the robbery.

B. The motion should be denied because the death occurred during the *corpus delicti* of the robbery.

C. The motion should be granted because the death did not occur during the robbery, but after it.

D. The motion should be granted because the accident would not have happened if the police weren't chasing the man.

132. A law professor was writing a book about homicide and wanted one chapter to consist of an overview about the different forms of common law manslaughter.

What topics should the professor address in the chapter?

A. Voluntary manslaughter, involuntary manslaughter, and *amicus curiae* manslaughter.

B. First degree manslaughter, second degree manslaughter, and misdemeanor manslaughter.

C. Voluntary manslaughter, involuntary manslaughter, and misdemeanor manslaughter.

D. Voluntary manslaughter, involuntary manslaughter, and strict liability manslaughter.

133. A teaching assistant was conducting a review session for a first-term criminal law class. One of the students asked the teaching assistant for help distinguishing murder from manslaughter. The teaching assistant replied that the primary distinction between murder and manslaughter is the presence of malice aforethought, or its absence.

Is the teaching assistant correct?

A. Yes; murder requires proof of malice aforethought but manslaughter does not include malice in its definition.

B. Yes; although the teaching assistant should have added that this distinction has been eliminated by modern law.

C. No; there are many ways to distinguish the two crimes and malice aforethought is just one of them.

D. No; manslaughter can be committed with malice aforethought, such as when a defendant exhibits an intent to kill.

134. A woman came home from her office unexpectedly one afternoon to retrieve some work papers she had left by her bed. The woman walked into the bedroom and found her husband naked in the bed with another woman. The woman was shocked and without thinking, reached into her purse, pulled out her gun, and shot and killed her husband. After the woman was arrested, police confirmed that the woman did not have a license for the gun, which is a felony in this jurisdiction.

How should the prosecutor charge the woman?

A. The woman intentionally killed her husband, so she can only be charged with one form of homicide: intent to kill murder.

B. The woman intentionally killed her husband, but because of the attendant circumstances, she may be charged with involuntary manslaughter.

C. The woman intentionally killed while committing a felony, so she can only be charged with felony murder or intent to kill murder.

D. The woman intentionally killed her husband, but because of the attendant circumstances, she may be charged with voluntary manslaughter.

135. A woman was charged with murder for shooting and killing her husband after he had slapped her face. Despite the prosecutor's arguments, the jury convicted the woman of voluntary manslaughter. The evening after the verdict, the presiding judge was having dinner with her teenage daughter and was telling her about the trial. The teenage daughter asked her mother to explain the legal rationale for why the jury might not have returned a murder conviction.

How should the judge respond?

A. By recognizing that some types of provocation can cause a heat of passion and lead to an intentional killing, the verdict was a concession to human frailty.

B. The judge should not discuss a gruesome murder with her daughter, and should probably change the subject and discuss something more pleasant.

C. The jury's voluntary manslaughter verdict was an act of nullification and an example of jurors ignoring their oaths and their obligation to follow the law.

D. The verdict showed recognition that the woman was not in her right mind at the time of the crime and that she deserves a reduced punishment as a result.

136. A man came home from work and found his wife having sex with her colleague from work. The man did not love his wife and was planning on divorcing her. Still, the man was annoyed that she had cheated on him, and so he shot and killed her.

The prosecutor later charged the man with intentional murder. At the man's bench trial, the man's lawyer argued that the only proper verdict was voluntary manslaughter.

How should the judge respond?

A. The judge should convict the man as charged because annoyance does not equate to a heat of passion.

B. The judge should convict the man as charged because the man was planning to divorce his wife anyway.

C. The judge should convict the man of manslaughter because he was probably angrier than he claimed to be.

D. The judge should convict the man of manslaughter because he discovered his wife in an act of adultery.

137. A man left his office to get a sandwich for lunch. While walking to the deli, the man was surprised to see his wife standing on a nearby street corner. Then, a second man walked up to the wife and the two hugged. The man had long suspected that his wife was having an affair and became very upset when he saw this. He pulled out his concealed pistol and shot and killed his wife and the second man.

The man was charged with intentional murder and wants to argue that the charges should be reduced to voluntary manslaughter.

Will the argument be successful?

A. Yes, because the man saw his wife engage in adultery.

B. Yes, because the man was very upset by his wife's actions.

C. No, because the man did not take steps to verify what he saw.

D. No, because the man only saw his wife hug another man.

138. A man suspected his wife was having an affair with their neighbor. He had no direct proof of an affair, but noticed that his wife and the neighbor had exchanged phone numbers at the annual holiday party. One night while cooking dinner, the man told his wife about his suspicions. She denied the affair and called him a "crazy, jealous lunatic." The man snapped, grabbed a butcher knife, and stabbed his wife in the chest. She died instantly. The man was later arrested and charged with intentional murder.

At the man's trial, the defense attorney argued that the man should instead be convicted of voluntary manslaughter.

How should the prosecutor respond?

A. The man should be convicted of murder because his wife denied having an affair with the neighbor.

B. The man should be convicted of murder because his wife's name-calling was not legally adequate provocation.

C. The man should be convicted of murder because he had no direct proof of an affair with the neighbor.

D. The man should be convicted of murder because he was not provoked by his wife's name-calling.

139. A young man who had been bullied for most of his life decided to take boxing lessons, with the hope that they would help his self-esteem. After the first class, the young man was about to leave the gym when his boxing coach walked by and started to shadowbox directly in front of him. Terrified, the young man pulled out a gun and shot the boxing coach in the chest, killing him.

The young man was later convicted of intentional murder. On appeal, the defense argued that the judge should have instructed the jury on voluntary manslaughter as the young man's history as a victim of bullying made him unusually fearful of aggression from other people.

How should the appeals court rule?

A. The trial court erred because a reasonable person in the young man's position would have been provoked by the coach's shadowboxing.

B. The trial court erred because the young man's actions showed that he was provoked by the coach's shadowboxing.

C. The trial court did not err because a reasonable person would not have been provoked by the coach's shadowboxing.

D. The trial court did not err because the young man obviously failed to realize that the coach was just joking around.

140. A driver was trying to leave a parking ramp and was having trouble using her credit card at the automated payment machine. The man in the car directly behind the woman honked his horn and yelled at her to hurry up. The woman continued to try to use the machine, but without success. After waiting several minutes, the man got out of his car and walked to the woman's car, waving his arms and yelling. The woman was terrified and pulled out her pistol; she aimed it at the man and fired. The gunshot did not hit the man, but instead hit and killed a parking ramp worker who was walking over to help.

At the woman's trial for intentional murder, her defense attorney argued that she should instead be convicted of voluntary manslaughter.

Is the defense attorney correct?

A. No, because the woman was safe in her car and did not need to shoot anyone.

B. No, because the woman was not provoked by the parking ramp worker.

C. Yes, because the woman acted in a heat of passion from adequate provocation.

D. Yes, because it would be unfair to convict the woman of murder on these facts.

141. After speaking to a man about his loan application, a loan officer denied the application. The man became very angry and had to be escorted from the bank by a security officer. Once on the street, the man tried to push his way back inside, but the security officer stopped him. The man kept pushing, and so the security officer punched the man in the face. The man pulled out a gun and shot and killed the security officer.

The man's defense attorney has argued to the prosecutor that voluntary manslaughter is the only proper charge that can be filed under these circumstances.

Is the defense attorney correct?

A. Yes; the man killed the security officer intentionally, in a heat of passion, and due to adequate provocation.

B. Yes; although the man pushed the security officer, she escalated the violence by punching him in the face.

C. No; because banks are federally regulated, intentional killings on or near bank property must be treated as murder.

D. No; although the security officer's punch was adequate provocation, it did not cause the man to suffer from a heat of passion.

142. A woman was standing in line in a coffee shop. A man came up behind her and put his hand on her shoulder. The woman told the man to remove his hand. The man laughed and grabbed the woman's breasts. Outraged, the woman left the coffee shop and sat in her parked car. After a few minutes of deep breathing, she felt calmer. She pulled her handgun from the glove compartment, walked back into the coffee shop, and shot and killed the man.

The prosecutor assigned to this case has argued to her supervisor that the woman should be charged with voluntary manslaughter and not murder.

How should the supervisor respond?

A. The woman should not be charged with voluntary manslaughter because she acted deliberately when she killed the man.

B. The woman should not be charged with voluntary manslaughter because she had time to cool off after the man provoked her.

C. The woman should be charged with voluntary manslaughter because the man's conduct was aggressive, offensive, and outrageous.

D. The woman should be charged with voluntary manslaughter because she intentionally killed the man after he provoked her.

143. A woman came home from work and found her wife in bed with their neighbor. The woman became outraged and ran out of the house. To try to calm down, the woman walked around the block. But the walking did not help, so the woman went inside the house, grabbed a gun from her gun safe, and shot and killed her wife.

Before the start of the woman's trial, her attorney filed a motion to have the charges reduced from murder to manslaughter.

How should the judge rule on the motion?

A. The motion should be denied because the woman had ample time to cool off as demonstrated by the time it took her to walk around the block.

B. The motion should be denied because the woman's decision to walk around the block shows that she was aware that she had a short temper.

C. The motion should be granted because the woman killed while suffering from a heat of passion, which was caused by adequate provocation.

D. The motion should be granted because the woman killed her wife, and marital killings are better treated as manslaughter, not murder.

144. A woman developed a plan to kill her husband with poison and use the profits from his life insurance policy to travel the world. The day before the plan was to be deployed, the woman came home from work and found her husband in bed with her best friend. Despite the woman's plan, she was filled with jealousy. The woman grabbed a gun and shot her husband in the head, killing him.

Can the woman be properly convicted of voluntary manslaughter?

A. Yes, because she killed her husband intentionally, with a heat of passion, and due to adequate provocation.

B. Yes, because she intentionally killed her husband after she caught him engaged in an act of adultery.

C. No, because the husband committed adultery, and so he got just what he deserved when she killed him.

D. No, because the woman had a preexisting intent to kill her husband, despite jealousy at finding him cheating.

145. One evening after work, a man was driving through a residential area in heavy rain. As the man approached a turn in the road, he slowed down briefly, causing his car to hydroplane on the wet road and crash into a car driving in the opposite direction. The driver of the other car was killed in the accident, and the man was charged with involuntary manslaughter. By reviewing the "black box" from the man's car, police learned that at the moment of impact, the man was driving 20 MPH over the posted speed limit.

Can the man be properly convicted of involuntary manslaughter?

A. Yes; the man failed to be aware of a substantial and unjustifiable risk of death to others, but should have been aware of that risk.

B. Yes; the man killed another driver in a traffic accident and these deaths are traditionally treated as manslaughter and not murder.

C. No; the man was only exceeding the speed limit slightly, and it would be wrong to punish the man for something most of us do every day.

D. No; the only reason the man's car hydroplaned is that he slowed down at the turn, and so he should have continued speeding.

146. A young man was the father of an eight-month-old baby. One day, the baby became sick with a fever. The young man gave the baby some aspirin and stayed home from work to be with her. The fever did not break. After 48 hours and at the urging of his aunt, the young man took the baby to the hospital. By the time they arrived, the baby was in acute distress and she died a few hours later.

An autopsy showed that if the baby had received medical treatment within 24 hours of starting her fever, she would have lived. When asked by police why he did not take the baby to the hospital earlier, the young man explained that he didn't think she was that sick.

Is the young man guilty of involuntary manslaughter?

A. Yes; the young man owed a duty to his baby, breached the duty that he owed to her, and the baby died as a result.

B. Yes; the young man's failure to seek timely medical care for his baby was a gross deviation from the ordinary standard of care.

C. No; the young man's failure to seek timely medical care for his baby may have been negligent, but it was not criminally negligent.

D. No; the young man's failure to seek timely medical care for his baby was due to his ignorance of her medical condition.

147. One winter afternoon, a mother was out running errands in her car, and the mother's newborn baby was in a car seat in the back. The mother parked her car in the parking lot of a grocery store to do some quick shopping and left the baby in the car to sleep. When the mother came back 20 minutes later, the baby had died of hypothermia.

The prosecutor charged the mother with involuntary manslaughter. At trial, defense counsel asked the judge to instruct the jury that the mother's conduct should be assessed according to the "ordinary, sleep-deprived, new parent" standard.

How should the judge respond?

A. The judge should instruct the jury as requested because the proposed standard describes the reasonable person.

B. The judge should instruct the jury as requested because the proposed standard describes the new mother exactly.

C. The judge should not instruct the jury as requested because the proposed standard is not fully objective.

D. The judge should not instruct the jury as requested because there is no evidence that the mother was sleep deprived.

148. A young boy found the key to his father's locked gun safe and removed a handgun. The boy showed the handgun to his teenage brother, who jokingly pointed it at the boy and pulled the trigger. The teenager assumed the handgun was unloaded because his father had told him that he never stored loaded weapons in the safe. But the handgun was loaded, and the boy died.

The teenager's parents hired an attorney, and the attorney contacted the prosecutor to find out if the teenager would be charged with a crime. The prosecutor said that she was considering filing a depraved heart murder charge against him.

How should the defense attorney respond?

A. Involuntary manslaughter is a more appropriate charge because the teenager reasonably believed that the handgun was unloaded.

B. The father should be charged instead of the teenager because the father failed to properly hide the key to the gun safe.

C. If the teenager is convicted of murder, his reasonable belief that the handgun was unloaded should be considered at sentencing.

D. Involuntary manslaughter is a more appropriate charge because the teenager was too young to know about weapon safety.

149. A woman was driving in a residential area when she hit and killed a child who had been playing in the street. The woman later confessed to police that, just before hitting the child, she had picked up her phone to check the time. This jurisdiction is "hands-free," and holding a phone in any way while driving is a misdemeanor.

Can the woman be properly charged with manslaughter?

A. Yes; the woman failed to be aware of a substantial and unjustifiable risk of death and should have been aware.

B. Yes; the woman caused the child's death while committing the misdemeanor of holding a phone while driving.

C. No; death during the commission of a misdemeanor cannot form the basis of any type of homicide charge.

D. No; the child's death was an unfortunate accident, and criminal charges should not be filed in this situation.

150. A high school student met six of her friends in the school parking lot. They all piled into the student's car: the student sat in the driver's seat, two friends sat together in the front passenger seat, and the remaining friends shared the back seat. The student knew that the seatbelts in the back seat did not work.

The student pulled out of the parking lot and drove down the street, rocking the steering wheel back and forth to the beat of the music on the car radio. But the student lost control of the car, causing it to flip over and eject the friends in the back seat, killing them. A review of the "black box" from the student's car showed that she was driving 25 MPH over the speed limit at the time of the crash.

In this jurisdiction, misdemeanor reckless endangerment occurs when a person "recklessly engages in conduct not amounting to drive-by shooting but that creates a substantial risk of death or serious physical injury to another person." The penal code defines recklessness as "knowing of and disregarding a substantial risk that a wrongful act may occur," where the "disregard of such substantial risk is a gross deviation from conduct that a reasonable person would exercise in the same situation." The jurisdiction also follows the common law of homicide.

How should the prosecutor charge the student?

A. With no crime, because the student was not involved in a drive-by shooting, and she only lost control of the car by accident.

B. With involuntary manslaughter, because the student acted with gross criminal negligence and as a result, killed her friends.

C. With involuntary manslaughter, because the student failed to be aware of the substantial risks she took, but should have been.

D. With misdemeanor manslaughter, because the student was aware of the substantial risks she took, but disregarded them.

Homicide (Modern and Statutory)

151. A state has relied exclusively on the common law in its criminal prosecutions. But members of the legislature are considering drafting a penal code to review and codify all crimes. One legislator has proposed separating common law murder into degrees, based on severity.

What is a valid reason for the legislator's proposal?

A. If murder is separated into degrees, lawyers and judges will not have the onerous task of remembering all the different forms of malice aforethought.

B. If murder is separated into degrees, the jurisdiction will show its commitment to a progressive criminal justice model that reflects modern norms and values.

C. If murder is separated into degrees, the jurisdiction can punish offenders more precisely, varying punishments based on the degree of murder committed.

D. If murder is separated into degrees, people who commit crimes will be given the security of knowing how they will be charged and convicted.

152. A woman killed her wife intentionally, but without premeditation or deliberation. In this jurisdiction, the penal code includes the following definition of murder:

> *First degree*: Killings committed by poison or lying in wait, or any other type of willful, premeditated, and deliberate killing.
>
> *Second degree*: All other forms of murder.

Can the woman be properly charged with either degree of murder?

A. She can be charged with first degree murder because she killed intentionally, and "willful" and "intentional" mean the same thing.

B. She can be charged with second degree murder because intentional killings are subsumed into the "all other forms of murder" category.

C. She can be charged with either first or second degree murder depending on the egregiousness of the circumstances surrounding the homicide.

D. She cannot be charged with murder because intentional killings committed without premeditation or deliberation are not addressed by this statute.

153. A man was furious because his property taxes had been increased. Carrying his gun, the man went to the next meeting of his city council. In the middle of the meeting, the man shot and killed the mayor. This jurisdiction's penal code includes the following definitions:

> First degree murder: the killing of any on-duty police or corrections officer, or the killing of any person elected to state office, while in the course of official duties.
>
> Second degree murder: any form of willful, premeditated, and deliberate killing.
>
> Third degree murder: any killing that occurs during the commission of a burglary, arson, robbery, sexual assault, or kidnapping.
>
> Fourth degree murder: all other forms of murder.

How can the man be charged?

A. The man can be charged with first degree murder because he killed an elected official while she was in the course of her official duties.

B. The man can be charged with second or fourth degree murder because he killed intentionally, and maybe with premeditation and deliberation.

C. The man cannot be charged under this statute because it only provides for killing of an official elected to state office, but not a local office.

D. The man can only be charged with fourth degree murder, because intentional killings are subsumed into the "all other forms of murder" category.

154. A woman learned that her boss had given her a bad performance review, but that it had not yet been finalized. The woman decided to kill her boss before he placed the review in her personnel file. That evening, the woman waited in the parking lot after work hours; when her boss came out to his car, she shot and killed him with a bow and arrow.

In this jurisdiction, first degree murder includes those "committed by poison, lying in wait, or any other type of willful, premeditated, and deliberate killing."

Can the woman be properly convicted of first degree murder?

A. Yes, because killing was willful, premeditated, and deliberate.

B. Yes, because the woman acted willfully, albeit with an antiquated weapon.

C. No, because the statute requires the killing be committed by poison.

D. No, because the antiquated means of killing falls outside the statute.

155. A man detested his long-time neighbor. Over the years, the man had seriously considered killing his neighbor and had even gone so far as to develop a plan to shoot the neighbor while she was out gardening. But the man never acted on his plan.

One evening, the neighbor was mowing her front lawn as the man was driving down the street. The man's foot accidentally slipped on the accelerator, causing the car to speed up and hit and kill the neighbor.

In this jurisdiction, first degree murder includes all "willful, premeditated, and deliberate" killings, and case law ascribes independent meaning to each adjective.

What is the best way to describe the killing?

A. The killing was willful, but not premeditated or deliberate.

B. The killing was willful, premeditated, and deliberate.

C. The killing was willful and premeditated, but not deliberate.

D. The killing was not willful, but was arguably premeditated and deliberate.

156. A woman discovered that her husband had gone to a casino and gambled most of their life savings. The woman confronted her husband, hoping that he would admit his mistake. But he denied the claims. Furious, the woman picked up a knife from the kitchen counter asked her husband if he wanted to reconsider his answer. He said no, so the woman stabbed him in the chest, killing him.

The woman was charged with first degree murder which, in this jurisdiction, includes all "willful, premeditated, and deliberate" killings. The defense has filed a motion to dismiss, arguing that the woman acted very quickly and premeditation and deliberation require at least a few minutes to develop.

How should the judge rule on the motion?

A. The judge should grant the motion because it does take a few minutes to premeditate and deliberate.

B. The judge should grant the motion because the woman had time to premeditate but not time to deliberate.

C. The judge should deny the motion because there is no set time period required for premeditation and deliberation.

D. The judge should deny the motion because the woman's ready access to the knife shows her premeditation and deliberation.

157. A state appellate court is reviewing a first degree murder conviction, imposed under the following statute:

> All murders committed by means of poison or lying in wait, or any other type of willful, premeditated, and deliberate killing shall be considered first degree murder. To prove the killing was premeditated and deliberate, it is not necessary to prove that the defendant maturely and meaningfully reflected upon the gravity of his or her act. First degree murder is punishable by life imprisonment without the possibility of parole.
>
> All murders committed intentionally shall be considered second degree murder. Second degree murder is punishable by any term of imprisonment, up to 25 years.

In his appellate brief, the defendant admitted that he acted intentionally, but argued that he did not premediate or deliberate. In response, the prosecution argued that because first degree murder does not require proof of mature and meaningful reflection, it only requires proof of an intentional killing.

How should the appellate court interpret the statute?

A. The plain language of the statute indicates that there is no difference between first and second degree murders.

B. The statutory reference to mature and meaningful reflection requires some level of thought beyond the intent to kill.

C. The state and federal separation of powers doctrine prohibits the appellate court from ruling on this issue.

D. It is unfair to sentence a defendant to a non-parolable life sentence without proof that he also premeditated and deliberated.

158. A man went out to drink with his friends. After several drinks, the friends suggested the man take a cab home but he refused. The man got into his car and began driving home. As he turned onto a main road, the man decided to see how fast the car would drive. After speeding up over a one-mile stretch of roadway, the man lost control of the car and crashed into a second car. The impact killed the three people inside the second car.

Police later recovered the "black box" from the man's car, which showed that he was driving 136 MPH when he hit the second car. The man has now been charged with third degree murder under the following statute:

> First degree murder includes any form of willful, premeditated, and deliberate killing.
>
> Second degree murder includes any killing committed during the commission of burglary, arson, robbery, rape, or kidnapping.
>
> Third degree murder includes all other forms of murder.

Can the man be properly convicted of third degree murder?

A. No, because the man was intoxicated and so he was not aware of the high risk he created in his driving.

B. No, because third degree murder does not specifically include vehicular homicide.

C. Yes, because the extreme rate of speed shows that the man acted intentionally, and not recklessly.

D. Yes, because the man showed an extreme indifference to a very high risk of death in his driving.

159. A man killed his friend during a game of "Russian Roulette." The local prosecutor has described the crime as "extremely reckless," and wants to charge the man using the following statute:

> First degree murder includes any form of willful, premeditated, and deliberate killing.
>
> Second degree murder includes all other forms of murder.

How should the man be charged?

A. He should be charged with second degree murder, because extremely reckless killings are subsumed into the "all other forms of murder" category.

B. He should be charged first degree murder, because "Russian Roulette" is an inherently risky game that often leads to a player's death.

C. He should be charged with either first or second degree murder, depending on the egregiousness of the circumstances surrounding the homicide.

D. He cannot be charged with murder at all because extremely reckless killings are not addressed by this statute.

160. A computer hacker developed a program to steal bank account information stored in computers. The hacker deployed the program by sending legitimate-looking emails offering a discount on car insurance. If the recipient clicked on the offer, the program would install itself on the recipient's computer and relay bank account information back to the hacker.

One of the people who clicked on the discount offer was a wealthy man, and the hacker quickly wiped out his accounts. When the wealthy man found out he had been hacked, he had a heart attack and died. The hacker was charged with felony murder based on the predicate felony of Unlawful Access to the Computer System of Another. The jurisdiction's murder statute, which was drafted in 1965, defines second degree murder as "a killing committed during the commission of any felony." The defense has moved to dismiss.

How should the judge rule on the motion?

A. The motion should be granted because it would be ridiculous to convict the hacker for murder under these circumstances.

B. The motion should be granted because computer crimes could not have been anticipated when the murder statute was drafted.

C. The motion should be denied because the hacker committed a felony and the wealthy man died as a result.

D. The motion should be denied because the hacker's motion presents a question of fact and should be decided by the jury.

161. A woman set fire to her neighbor's potting shed in retaliation for the neighbor cutting down a tree that shaded the woman's yard. Because the woman only wanted to teach the neighbor a lesson, she picked a rainy day to set the fire, assuming the rain would quickly extinguish the fire. But the fire quickly burned out of control and spread to the roof of the woman's house and burned it to the ground, killing her elderly mother who was inside.

The woman was charged with felony murder based on the arson of the neighbor's potting shed. Prior to trial, the defense moved to dismiss the charge, arguing that the woman tried to commit a "safe arson" and had no desire to kill her own mother.

How should the judge rule on the motion?

A. The motion should be granted because the house fire really was a freak accident that the woman could not have anticipated.

B. The motion should be granted because the woman took every precaution to burn the potting shed as safely as possible.

C. The motion should be denied because the woman's motion presents a question of fact that should be decided by the jury.

D. The motion should be denied because arson is an inherently dangerous crime, even if no harm to life was intended.

162. A man came home from work one evening and found his husband in bed with their neighbor. The man was furious and immediately shot and killed his husband. The man was convicted of felony murder based on the predicate felony of assault with a deadly weapon.

What should the defense argue on appeal?

A. The felony murder conviction should be vacated because the assault with a deadly weapon merged into the homicide.

B. The felony murder conviction should be vacated because the man was justified in using force because of the husband's adultery.

C. The felony murder conviction should be vacated because the man acted with a heat of passion based on adequate provocation.

D. The felony murder conviction should be vacated because the man should have only been charged with voluntary manslaughter.

163. A father was angry with his teenage son because the son ignored his curfew. One evening when the son came home late, the father confronted him. The two argued and the father pushed the son against a wall, putting his forearm against the son's throat. The son began to choke, but the father pressed harder. The son died.

The father was prosecuted for felony murder based on the predicate felony of battery. On appeal and as a matter of first impression, the father argued that the battery merged with the homicide, rendering the resulting felony murder conviction unfair.

How should the prosecutor respond?

A. There was no unfairness because the father could have been alternatively convicted of intentional murder.

B. The prosecutor should concede error, because the battery merged with the homicide, and so the conviction is unfair.

C. There is no unfairness because the father could have been alternatively convicted of intent to cause great bodily harm murder.

D. There is no unfairness because the father could have been alternatively convicted of two other forms of murder.

164. A state's penal code includes the following definitions of murder:

> *First degree*: A person is guilty of first degree murder when he kills willfully and with premeditation and deliberation, or when he kills during the commission of any burglary, arson, robbery, sexual assault, or kidnapping.
>
> *Second degree*: A person is guilty of second degree murder when he kills during the commission of any felony, including any assaultive felony not specifically enumerated in the first degree statute.
>
> *Third degree*: A person is guilty of third degree murder when he commits any other form of murder.

A woman was charged with second degree murder based on the predicate crime of felonious assault, which is defined as "knowingly causing serious harm to another person with a deadly weapon."

The woman filed a motion to dismiss and argued that the assault should merge with the homicide and so she should be convicted of third degree murder instead. The prosecutor argued that the charge was proper.

How should the judge respond?

A. While assault might ordinarily merge with the homicide, this statute permits a felony murder conviction based on the predicate felony of felonious assault.

B. While assault is not usually a predicate felony for felony murder, this is an issue that would be better resolved in an appeal to a higher court.

C. As assault is an attempted battery; the only crime it merges with is battery and so assault cannot merge with any form of homicide.

D. As felonious assault is not specifically listed in either the first or second degree murder provisions, it cannot be used for a second degree murder conviction.

165. As a practical joke, two teenagers decided to break into their track coach's house and steal his television. The two went to the coach's house together, riding in the first teenager's car. At the house, the first teenager stayed in the car and the second teenager tried to get into the house through a side window. But the coach was at home and, not realizing who was trying to get in through the window, shot and killed the second teenager. The first teenager was arrested and charged with felony murder.

Can the first teenager be properly convicted of felony murder?

A. Yes, because the first teenager should have anticipated that the coach might use deadly force to defend his home.

B. Yes, because as a co-felon, he is responsible for deaths that occurred during the commission of the felony.

C. No, because he did not have a malicious *mens rea*: the intent to kill, intent to cause great bodily harm, or a depraved heart.

D. No, because he can only be convicted for the death of a non-felon, and cannot be responsible for the death of another felon.

166. A husband and wife robbed a bank. During the robbery, one of the bank customers reached into her bag, pulled out a handgun, and fired at the wife. The shot missed and killed the bank security officer instead. The husband and wife were arrested and charged with bank robbery and felony murder.

Prior to trial, the defense moved to dismiss the felony murder charges, arguing that the husband and wife were not responsible for the acts of the bank customer. This jurisdiction follows the majority rule for killings by non-felons.

How should the judge rule on the motion?

A. The judge should grant the motion because the husband and wife could not reasonably foresee that the bank customer would kill the security officer.

B. The judge should grant the motion because the bank customer was not acting as an agent of the husband or wife when she killed the security officer.

C. The judge should deny the motion because by robbing the bank, the husband and wife were the proximate cause of the security officer's death.

D. The judge should deny the motion because she lacks adequate information to decide it, and the question should be given to the jury to decide.

167. A woman robbed a liquor store. A police officer walking nearby noticed the robbery and entered the liquor store. He pulled his weapon and fired at the woman, but accidentally killed the clerk of the liquor store instead. The woman was charged with robbery and felony murder.

The woman's attorney filed a motion to dismiss the felony murder charges. This jurisdiction follows the minority rule for killings by non-felons.

How should the judge rule on the motion?

A. The judge should deny the motion because the proper time for the woman's claim is on appeal, after she is convicted.

B. The judge should deny the motion because the woman was the proximate cause of the store clerk's death.

C. The judge should grant the motion because the woman should not be held responsible for the officer's bad aim.

D. The judge should grant the motion because the officer was not acting as the woman's agent when he killed the store clerk.

168. A brother convinced his sister to help with the burglary of his neighbor's house. The brother told the sister that since the neighbor was in the hospital, no one would be at home and so no one would be hurt. The brother explained that he would be armed, but promised to abandon the plan if there was a threat to anyone's safety. The sister reluctantly agreed to help.

While the brother was burglarizing his neighbor's home, the sister waited outside in her car. But the neighbor was at home and confronted the brother; during the confrontation, the brother shot and killed the neighbor. The sister has now been charged with felony murder. The relevant statute states:

> It is an affirmative defense to prosecution under this section that the defendant:
>
> (1) Did not commit the homicidal act or in any way solicit, command, induce, procure or aid the commission thereof;
>
> (2) Was not armed with a dangerous weapon, or other weapon which under circumstances indicated a readiness to inflict serious bodily injury;
>
> (3) Reasonably believed that no other participant was armed with such a weapon; and
>
> (4) Reasonably believed that no other participant intended to engage in conduct likely to result in death or serious bodily injury.

Does the sister have a defense under this statute?

A. Yes, because she took every possible precaution to ensure that no one would be hurt.

B. Yes, because although she knew the brother was armed, he promised he would not use the weapon.

C. No, because she agreed to help commit the burglary, she is responsible for any resulting deaths.

D. No, because she knew that the brother was carrying a weapon, although he promised he would not use it.

169. A man robbed his local bank. During the robbery, the man forced the bank customers into the bank manager's office. One of the customers tripped and fell and cracked his head open on the marble floor. The customer later died from the injury to his head.

In this jurisdiction, second degree murder is defined as follows:

> Second degree murder includes any killing that occurs during the commission of any burglary, arson, robbery, sexual assault, or kidnapping, and which is committed with actual malice.

Can the man be properly convicted of second degree murder?

A. No; the bank customer only tripped and fell because she was clumsy and the man had nothing to do with her death.

B. No; the man did not exhibit an intent to kill, intent to cause great bodily harm, or a depraved heart when he robbed the bank.

C. Yes; the man's act of forcing the bank customers into the office was malicious and caused the customer's death.

D. Yes; the man committed one of the statutory predicate felonies and so is responsible for any resulting deaths.

170. A woman who was addicted to opiates robbed a pharmacy. At first, the pharmacist refused to give the woman any money or drugs, but then the woman threatened to kill him if he didn't comply with her demand. While the woman held the gun to the pharmacist's head, he packed money and drugs into a paper bag. But the woman's finger slipped on the trigger and the gun discharged, killing the pharmacist.

In this jurisdiction, murder includes "any killing that occurs during the commission of any burglary, arson, robbery, sexual assault, or kidnapping, and which is committed with actual malice."

Can the woman be properly convicted of murder?

A. Yes; the woman showed intent to kill, a form of malice, when she threatened to kill the pharmacist and put the gun to his head.

B. Yes; the woman committed one of the statutory predicate felonies, a robbery, and so is responsible for any resulting deaths.

C. No; the woman's finger slipped and so the act that caused the act pharmacist's death was accidental and not intentional.

D. No; the woman's opiate addition mitigates her crime and she should be sent to drug rehabilitation and not prison.

171. A state's penal code has three degrees of murder, and second degree murder consists of felony murder only.

A state senator wants to introduce legislation to abolish second degree murder and to collapse the statute to two degrees only. The senator's staff must now write a press release to accompany the legislation.

What should the press release say?

A. The proposed legislation will save tax dollars because it will stop all prosecutions against defendants who kill while committing felonies that are dangerous to human life.

B. The proposed legislation will still allow prosecutions for killings committed during certain felonies, but these cases will now be prosecuted as manslaughter instead of murder.

C. The proposed legislation will save tax dollars by preventing most prosecutions against defendants who kill while committing felonies that are dangerous to human life.

D. The proposed legislation will still allow most murder prosecutions to proceed, but will eliminate those where defendants play a minimal or nonexistent role in the victim's death.

172. A woman saw that a political group was holding a rally. The woman walked up to listen to the speaker, who was well known for his extreme views and hateful rhetoric. The woman was outraged by his words and the cheering of the crowd. She reached into her pocket, pulled out a gun, and shot and killed the speaker.

After her arrest, the woman was charged with murder. At her trial, the defense argued that she should be convicted of voluntary manslaughter instead. According to the defense, modern law no longer restricts provocation to limited, narrow categories, and so the speaker's comments could be considered legally adequate provocation.

How should the prosecutor respond?

A. While modern law may recognize new forms of provocation, the woman was provoked by the crowd and not by the speaker.

B. While modern law may recognize new forms of provocation, the speaker was speaking to the crowd and not to the woman directly.

C. While modern law may recognize new forms of provocation, the speaker was acting lawfully when the woman shot him.

D. While modern law may recognize new forms of provocation, the woman could have just walked away and returned to her group.

173. A car was stopped at a red light. A bicyclist rode his bike along the passenger's side of the car, also stopping at the light. The driver rolled down the passenger window and told the bicyclist to move away from his car. The bicyclist did not move. The driver then got out of the car and, with a tire iron in his raised hand, jogged over to the bicyclist while yelling racial slurs at him. The bicyclist pulled out a knife and stabbed the driver three times, killing him.

At the bicyclist's murder trial, the defense asked the jury to be instructed on voluntary manslaughter. The prosecutor objected.

If the judge grants the motion, what fact will be critical to her ruling?

A. The driver's use of racial slurs.

B. The driver's brandishing of a tire iron.

C. That the driver began the altercation.

D. That the driver had time to cool off.

174. A woman was driving home one evening after work. A block from her house, the woman saw her daughter playing in the street just as a speeding car came down the street. The car ran into the girl, knocking her to the ground. The mother stopped her car, ran to her daughter, and then ran over to the driver of the other car and began to slap him as he sat in his car. A neighbor who witnessed the entire scene rushed over and tried to pull the mother off of the driver. The mother pulled a handgun out of her pocket and shot and killed the neighbor.

The mother was charged with murder. The defense attorney requested that the jury be instructed on voluntary manslaughter, based on the following statute:

> A person who kills an individual without lawful justification commits voluntary manslaughter if at the time of the killing he is acting under a sudden and intense passion resulting from serious provocation by:
>
> (1) the individual killed; or
>
> (2) another whom the actor endeavors to kill, but he negligently or accidentally causes the death of the individual killed.

Should the judge instruct the jury on voluntary manslaughter?

A. Yes, because the statute permits such an instruction when a defendant negligently or accidentally kills an innocent third party.

B. Yes, because the mother was trying to kill the driver of the other car and negligently killed the neighbor instead.

C. No, because the mother did not act negligently or accidentally, but instead recklessly killed the neighbor.

D. No, because the mother was not trying to kill the driver of the other car when the neighbor intervened.

175. A woman suffered from mental illness and struggled with visual delusions. One day, the woman was at the grocery store when she saw a man coming toward her with a baseball bat in his hand. Afraid that he was about to attack her, the woman grabbed a gun from her purse and killed him. Eyewitnesses told police that the man did not have a baseball bat in his hand, but was instead holding a bunch of bananas.

At the woman's bench trial for intentional murder, the defense moved for a voluntary manslaughter conviction, claiming that the "modern, reasonable person" now also includes the "reasonable delusional and mentally ill person."

How should the judge rule on the motion?

A. The motion should be denied because even a modern reasonable person standard does not include the subjective features the woman requests.

B. The motion should be denied because the woman should pursue an insanity acquittal and not a conviction for voluntary manslaughter.

C. The motion should be granted because, relative to when the common law developed, we now better understand the impact of mental illness.

D. The motion should be granted because the woman is mentally ill and it would be manifestly unfair to convict her of murder on these facts.

Rape

176. A student on the law review was writing a note about recent changes to her home state's sexual assault statute. The student intended to begin the article discussing the common law crime of rape and then review all the statutory developments over the past several decades before addressing the most recent statutory scheme.

What definition should the student use in the discussion of common law rape?

A. Rape is the carnal knowledge of another, by force and without consent.

B. Rape is the carnal knowledge of a woman, by force and without consent.

C. Rape is the forceful and carnal knowledge of another, without consent.

D. Rape is the forceful and carnal knowledge of a child, without consent.

177. The manager and the head chef of a restaurant were working late one night after the other workers had left. The head chef suggested having a quick drink before going home, and the manager agreed. The two men instead had several drinks and got drunk. Out of the blue, the manager began to kiss the head chef, but the head chef resisted and tried to push the manager away. The manager wrestled the head chef to the ground, pulled off his clothes, and had anal sex with him.

The head chef later went to the hospital; his medical examination that showed physical trauma consistent with forced anal sex. After review, the prosecutor charged the manager with rape. In response, the manager's attorney filed a motion to quash the charge.

How should the judge rule on the motion?

A. The motion should be denied because the jury should decide how the head chef's drinking affected his credibility.

B. The motion should be denied because the medical examination results support the head chef's claim that he was raped.

C. The motion should be granted because the head chef was drunk when he was assaulted, so he will not be a credible witness.

D. The motion should be granted because the manager's actions toward the head chef do not constitute common law rape.

178. Two college juniors were assigned to live together as part of a "semester abroad" program. The women had not met before, and so they arranged to have drinks before their trip began. The two got very drunk and so they decided to stay at a mutual friend's house instead of driving home. One of the women quickly fell asleep; the other woman took a sex toy from her purse and used it to penetrate the sleeping woman's vagina. The sleeping woman woke up as this was happening and called the police.

The prosecutor now wants to charge the other woman with rape of the sleeping woman.

Should the prosecutor file this charge?

A. No, because rape requires a sexual act performed by a man, and the act here was performed by a woman.

B. No, because the sleeping woman was drunk and may have a cloudy memory of what actually happened.

C. Yes, because the other woman raped the sleeping woman when she used a sex toy to penetrate her.

D. Yes, because the sleeping woman woke up during the act and so she can testify as to what happened.

179. A married couple had a turbulent relationship and the husband had been arrested several times for beating up his wife. The wife was very scared of the husband and each time the police tried to investigate him, the wife would refuse to cooperate.

One day the husband and wife got into a horrible fight that left the wife with a dislocated shoulder and a broken cheekbone. Still, the husband demanded that the wife have sex with him. She refused, but the husband forced her to the floor and had sexual intercourse with her anyway. Later, after the husband fell asleep, the wife went to the police and reported what had happened. The wife also promised that this time, she would cooperate with the police in their investigation.

Can the husband be properly charged for raping his wife?

A. No, because in spite of the wife's promise, the police cannot guarantee that she will cooperate with the prosecution.

B. No, because a husband cannot be prosecuted for raping his wife, no matter if the other elements of the crime are met.

C. Yes, because the husband engaged in the carnal knowledge of a woman, by force and without her consent.

D. Yes, because the wife's injuries are sufficient to rebut the presumption that a man cannot be convicted of raping his wife.

180. A woman and a man went out to dinner on a first date. At the end of the evening, the man drove the woman home. The man parked his car in the woman's driveway and asked her if he could come inside her house, but the woman said no. The man then tried to kiss the woman; she became very afraid and did not respond in any way. Assuming the woman's lack of response was a signal for him to continue, the man climbed on top of the woman and had sexual intercourse with her.

Did the man's actions meet the *actus reus* for rape?

A. Yes, because the man had sexual intercourse with the woman and she was too afraid to fight back against him.

B. Yes, because the woman did not give consent to the sexual intercourse, and the man should have realized that.

C. No, because the sexual intercourse was accomplished without force and with the woman's apparent consent.

D. No, because the woman only said the man he couldn't come in the house, but did not say no to the sexual intercourse.

181. A woman was walking home from the store one afternoon when a man came up behind her and pulled her into an alley. The woman kicked and screamed but the man overpowered her. After punching the woman several times, the man forced her to perform oral sex on him. The man then punched the woman one more time and ran from the alley. A jogger found the woman lying in the alley, crying and dazed from being punched so many times. The police later arrested the man and the prosecutor has charged him with rape.

Can the man be properly convicted of this crime?

A. No, because the woman never told the man that she did not consent to giving him oral sex.

B. No, because the man did not force the woman to perform non-consensual sexual intercourse.

C. Yes, because the man forced the woman to perform oral sex that she did not consent to.

D. Yes, because the man overpowered the woman by pulling her into the alley and punching her.

182. A woman was riding in an elevator alone when a man got on the elevator. When the doors closed, the man turned to the woman and began to fondle her breasts. The woman pushed the man away but he continued. When the elevator doors opened, the woman ran out and went straight to the police. She explained that the man was "like an octopus," and the officer confirmed that there had been several complaints identical to the woman's over the past two weeks.

Can the man be properly convicted of rape?

A. Yes, because he groped the woman by force and without her consent.

B. Yes, because he groped many women by force and without their consent.

C. No, because his actions, while disturbing, do not constitute rape.

D. No, because the woman has no forensic evidence to support her claim.

183. A man broke into a woman's house one night while she was sleeping. The man crept into the woman's bedroom and quietly climbed into her bed. The man then began to have sexual intercourse with her. As the man penetrated her, the woman woke up and started to scream. The woman's screaming woke her dog, who ran into the bedroom and bit the man on the leg. The man pushed the dog away and ran out of the house.

The woman called the police and reported that the sexual intercourse had lasted "about five seconds" before the man ran away. The man was later arrested and the prosecutor charged him with rape.

Can the man be properly convicted of this crime?

A. Yes, because the man engaged in carnal knowledge of a woman, by force and without consent.

B. Yes, because the man entered the woman's house and her bed without her consent.

C. No, because the sexual intercourse was brief and rape requires intercourse to be completed.

D. No, because the man did not use force to engage in sexual intercourse with the woman.

184. A woman reported to the police that she had been on a date the night before and that her date had raped her. The investigating officer asked the woman if she had any bruises or other marks on her body that she could show a nurse, and the woman said that she did not. But, the woman explained, the man had sexual intercourse with her without first obtaining her consent.

Will the prosecutor be able to establish that the woman was raped?

A. No, because the woman gave her consent when she agreed to go on the date.

B. No, because according to the woman's explanation, the man did not use force.

C. Yes, because according to the woman's explanation, she did not consent to sex.

D. Yes, because the woman reported the rape within 24 hours of its occurrence.

185. A man and a woman met at a party, had several drinks, and went back to the woman's apartment. The man began to kiss the woman but she pushed him away and said "no." The man tried a second time, and the woman pushed back again. The man tried a third time but the woman neither said nor did anything in response. The two had sexual intercourse and the man left the woman's apartment.

A week later, the woman reported to the police that she had been raped. An officer then interviewed the man, who explained that the woman had been "very, very still" during intercourse, but he believed it had been consensual. The officer told the woman that after speaking to the man, rape charges would not be filed. She asked for an explanation.

How should the officer respond?

A. The prosecutor will be unable to prove the woman did not give consent to the sexual act because the man thought she consented.

B. The prosecutor will be unable to prove the intercourse occurred because the woman did not go to the hospital immediately.

C. The prosecutor will be unable to prove the woman did not give consent to the sexual act because she said "no" just once.

D. The prosecutor will be unable to prove the force element because the woman failed to adequately resist the man's advances.

186. A college student was on a first date with an older man she met at her gym. After having a few drinks at a local bar, the man drove the college student to his apartment and invited her inside. The college student did not want to go into the man's apartment, but she was worried that he would think she was immature if she said no. Inside the apartment, the man kissed the college student, took off her clothes, and had sex with her. The college student stayed silent throughout the encounter because, as she later told the police, she was terrified that the man might hurt her if she tried to leave. The prosecutor charged the man with rape.

Will the man be convicted?

A. Yes, because the college student's fear overcame her ability to resist.

B. Yes, because the man did not have the college student's consent to have sex.

C. No, because the college student did not resist so there is no proof of force.

D. No, because the man and the college student were on a consensual date.

187. A woman was sunbathing on her back deck when a stranger walked into her yard with a gun in his hand. Pointing the gun at the woman, the stranger directed the woman into her house and into a bedroom. Once inside the bedroom, the stranger had sexual intercourse with her; during the intercourse, the stranger kept the gun in his hand. When the stranger finished, he left the house.

Later, in an interview with the police, the woman explained that she had not resisted because she was afraid the stranger would shoot her if she did. The prosecutor is debating whether to charge the stranger with rape but is concerned that she will not be able to prove that the stranger forced the woman to have sexual intercourse.

Does the prosecutor have a legitimate concern?

A. No, because the stranger's use of the gun was a serious threat against the woman's life, so she did not have to resist.

B. No, because force can be demonstrated by the stranger making the woman participate in non-consensual sexual intercourse.

C. Yes, because the stranger did not use any force beyond what was necessary to accomplish the sexual act.

D. Yes, because the stranger did not specifically threaten the woman while he was having sexual intercourse with her.

188. A man and a woman went out for a first date. The date went well, so the woman invited the man to her apartment for a drink. Once inside the apartment, the two began to kiss. The man began to fondle the woman's breasts; the woman did not pull away or move the man's hands away. The man kept going and moved the woman onto the couch, where he had sexual intercourse with her. The woman did not speak or respond in any way during the intercourse. Later that night, the woman went to the police station and reported that the man had raped her.

After a review of the police file, the prosecutor filed a rape charge against the man.

What defense argument should the prosecutor anticipate at the upcoming trial?

A. The defense will argue that the woman consented because she invited the man into her apartment.

B. The defense will argue that this case involves regret and not rape and so the charges should be quashed.

C. The defense will argue that rape involves sex between acquaintances and so the charges should be quashed.

D. The defense will argue that the prosecutor cannot show that the woman did not consent to the intercourse.

189. A young woman was dating a young man who had a twin brother; the young woman did not know he was a twin. The brothers looked identical, except one had blue eyes and the other had brown eyes. One evening, the twins decided to play a joke on the young woman.

The brown-eyed twin went to the young woman's apartment and pretended to be his brother. The young woman asked him why his eye color was different than before; he lied and said he was wearing colored contact lenses. The young woman accepted this explanation and later had sexual intercourse with him.

The following week, the young woman discovered that she had been deceived. She went to the police and reported that the brown-eyed twin had raped her.

How should the police respond?

A. The sexual intercourse was not rape because the young woman consented to it.

B. The brown-eyed twin cannot be charged because the young woman waited too long to file a report.

C. The brown-eyed twin cannot be charged because the twins were just playing a joke on her.

D. The sexual intercourse was not rape because the young woman was dating the blue-eyed twin.

190. During cancer surgery, a woman suffered a serious stroke. The woman never regained consciousness and so, with the consent of her family, she was transferred to a 24-hour care facility.

Three months after entering the facility, a night nurse had sexual intercourse with the woman while he was on his dinner break. The night nurse did not realize that a hidden camera in the woman's room captured the event. When the night nurse's supervisor saw the camera footage, she called the police. A subsequent medical exam showed that the woman has not suffered any physical injuries from the intercourse.

Can the night nurse be properly charged with rape?

A. Yes, because the night nurse failed to secure the woman's consent before he had intercourse with her.

B. Yes, because the night nurse had intercourse with a woman incapable of giving consent.

C. No, because the woman's family implicitly consented to this act when they placed her in the care facility.

D. No, because there was no evidence that the night nurse used force to accomplish the sexual act.

191. A 19-year-old college sophomore had sex with his 15-year-old high school girlfriend. When the girl's mother found out about this, she confronted the girl, who tearfully explained that she was in love and had been a willing participant in the sex. The mother was unmoved and called the police. She also forced the girl to have a physical exam, but no evidence was collected because too much time had passed.

After an investigation, the police recommended that the prosecutor file a rape charge against the sophomore. When the sophomore's father learned about the possible charges, he asked an attorney whether his son could really be charged with rape for having consensual sex with his girlfriend.

How should the attorney respond?

A. The attorney should explain that rape charges will not be filed because the girlfriend is too young to be a reliable witness.

B. The attorney should explain that rape charges will not be filed because the sophomore has not yet reached the age of full majority.

C. The attorney should explain that if the girlfriend is below the jurisdiction's age of consent, her willing participation is irrelevant.

D. The attorney should explain that because juries won't convict without forensic evidence, the sophomore will not be convicted of rape.

192. A man went to his local bar after work. While waiting for his beer, the man began to talk with a young woman standing nearby. She explained that it was her 21st birthday, and she was waiting for her friends to join her for a celebration. A few minutes later, the young woman's friends came into the bar and wished her a happy birthday.

As the evening progressed, the man joined the young woman and her friends, and the group stayed at the bar until closing time. The man drove the young woman home and they had sex in her bedroom. Two days later, the man was charged with rape. When the police arrested him, they told the man that the young woman was really 14 years old. The man was shocked and told the police that he thought she was 21 years old.

In light of his belief about the young woman's age, can the man be properly convicted?

A. The man can be properly convicted because he was charged with a strict liability crime.

B. The man can be properly convicted because his beliefs about the girl's age are irrelevant.

C. The man should be acquitted because he reasonably thought the girl was 21 years old.

D. The man should be acquitted because he sincerely thought the girl was 21 years old.

193. A woman called the police to report that a colleague from work had confronted her in the parking garage and kissed her without consent. The woman told police that her colleague had also grabbed her breasts and buttocks.

In this jurisdiction, the penal code includes "non-consensual sexual contact" within its "sexual assault" statute. The penal code classifies "non-consensual sexual contact" as "the intentional touching of the victim's or actor's intimate parts or the intentional touching of the clothing covering the immediate area of the victim's or actor's intimate parts, if that intentional touching can reasonably be construed as being for the purpose of sexual arousal or gratification."

The colleague was charged under this statute and retained an attorney to defend him. At their first meeting, the colleague asked the attorney for his opinion as to whether he would be convicted.

How should the attorney respond?

A. The colleague will not be convicted because there is no proof that he had sexual intercourse with the woman or used force against her.

B. The colleague will not be convicted because there is no proof that he was sexually aroused or gratified when he grabbed the woman.

C. The colleague will likely be convicted because the woman's story establishes the elements of nonconsensual sexual contact.

D. The colleague will likely be convicted because he did not have the woman's consent when he kissed her in the parking garage.

194. A married couple decided to divorce. Because money was tight, the two continued to live in the same house, although they kept separate bedrooms and schedules. One night, the husband crawled into the wife's bed and had sexual intercourse with her. During intercourse, the husband held the wife's arms down as she struggled to get away from him.

The prosecutor charged the husband with first degree sexual assault which, in this jurisdiction, is defined as "nonconsensual sexual intercourse with another person by forcible compulsion." "Forcible compulsion" is defined as "the use of physical, intellectual, moral, emotional or psychological force, either express or implied, to accomplish the prohibited act."

Can the husband be properly convicted of this crime?

A. No, because a husband cannot be prosecuted for raping his wife, no matter if the other elements of the crime are met.

B. No, because the wife did not suffer any injuries and so there is no proof that the husband used any force against her.

C. Yes, because the husband engaged in the carnal knowledge of a woman, by force and without her consent.

D. Yes, because the husband had nonconsensual sexual intercourse with his wife, by means of forcible compulsion.

195. A young man was walking to his parked car one evening when a second man appeared from behind a building. The second man put a knife to the young man's throat and pushed him to the ground. The second man had anal sex with the young man; during the encounter, the young man did not protest because he was terrified.

Later, the young man went to the police and reported the attack. The second man was arrested and has now been charged with "first degree sexual assault." In this jurisdiction, this crime includes "nonconsensual sexual penetration," where sexual penetration is defined as:

> sexual intercourse in its ordinary meaning, cunnilingus, fellatio, anal intercourse, or any intrusion, however slight, of any part of the actor's or victim's body or any object manipulated by the actor into the genital or anal openings of the victim's body which can be reasonably construed as being for non-medical, non-health, or non-law enforcement purposes. Sexual penetration shall not require emission of semen.

At the close of the prosecution's case, the second man's attorney filed a motion to dismiss, arguing that a man cannot be convicted of raping another man.

How should the judge rule on the motion?

A. The judge should deny the motion because the second man wielded a knife and so the young man was too scared to fight back.

B. The judge should deny the motion because the statutory definition of nonconsensual sexual penetration is gender-neutral.

C. The judge should grant the motion because common law rape requires a female victim, and the victim here was a man.

D. The judge should grant the motion because the young man never indicated that he did not consent to the sexual act.

Assault and Battery

196. A woman was at a block party with her wife when she learned from a neighbor that her wife had been unfaithful. Upon hearing the news, the woman hurled a can of soda at her wife, barely missing the wife's face. The woman later told a friend that she did not want to hit her wife, but instead wanted to show her that she could do so if she wanted to.

What crime has the woman committed?

A. Battery.

B. Assault.

C. Mayhem.

D. Attempted mayhem.

197. A new law firm associate was assigned to work with the firm's senior partner. On her first day, the associate reported to the partner's office; he met her at the door with a baseball bat in his hand. During the meeting, the partner twirled the bat around over his head, slapped the bat into the palm of his free hand, and banged the bat onto the floor to emphasize his words as he spoke. Later, after the associate reported the partner's behavior, he explained that he had no intention of using the bat to hit the associate, but merely wanted her to be scared of him.

Can the partner be properly charged with assault?

A. No, because the partner had no intent to use the bat to hit the associate.

B. No, because the partner never tried to hit the associate with the bat.

C. Yes, because the partner tried but failed to hit the associate with the bat.

D. Yes, because the partner used the bat to make the associate afraid.

198. A father was walking his daughter to elementary school. As they approached the school, a crossing guard instructed them to stop at the corner and to wait for her signal to cross the street. The father told the crossing guard that she was an idiot for making them wait because there were no cars driving on the street. The crossing guard was frightened by the father's words and reported him to the police.

Can the father be properly charged with assault?

A. No; the father may have insulted the crossing guard when he called her an idiot, but he did not use fighting words.

B. No; the father's insult was not enough to reasonably create fear or apprehension in the mind of the crossing guard.

C. Yes; the father's insult was enough to reasonably create fear or apprehension in the mind of the crossing guard.

D. Yes; the father reasonably insulted the crossing guard when he called her an idiot because he used fighting words.

199. A man received a bill from his credit card company, stating that his payment was overdue. The man looked at his checking account and could see that his payment had been received on time, and so he called the credit card company. The clerk told the man that his payment was past due and that the issue would be reported to a collection agency; the man protested and tried to explain that he had paid on time. The man became so frustrated that he told the clerk: "I am going to hunt you down and make you pay for destroying my credit rating!" The clerk was aghast and reported the threat to his supervisor. The supervisor called the police and asked whether the man could be charged with assault.

How should the police respond to the supervisor's question?

A. The man cannot be charged with assault because he was legitimately upset about the damage to his credit rating.

B. The man cannot be charged with assault because he has proof that he paid on time and that he was billed in error.

C. The man cannot be charged with assault because he had no present ability to follow through with his threat.

D. The man cannot be charged with assault because his threat was vague and he did not threaten bodily harm to the clerk.

200. A man attended a baseball game and was seated next to a group of rival fans. The rival fans booed the man's team, which annoyed him. The man told the rival fans to shut up and one of them threw a beer bottle directly at him. The man ducked, though, and the bottle instead hit an empty seat and shattered.

Can the rival fan who threw the bottle be properly charged with assault?

A. Yes, because the rival fan attempted to batter the man, but did not succeed.

B. Yes, because the rival fan tried to scare the man by throwing the bottle at him.

C. No, because the rival fan did not actually hit the man with the beer bottle.

D. No, because the rival fan was only trying to scare the man and not hit him.

201. A man cut down a cherry tree that he believed was on the edge of his property; in reality, the tree was on the edge of a neighbor's property. When the neighbor saw what had happened to the tree, he held up a rake in his hands and shouted: "if you ever do that again, I'll smack you with this rake!" At the time, the neighbor was standing 60 feet away from the man. The man also had his back to the neighbor at the time and did not hear the neighbor's words because he was deaf.

Can the neighbor be properly charged with assault?

A. No, because the neighbor only intended to threaten the man and did not intend to hit him.

B. No, because the man did not hear the neighbor and so did not experience fear or apprehension.

C. Yes, because the neighbor threatened the man and so should be punished for acting dangerously.

D. Yes, because when the neighbor threatened the man, he intended to commit a battery against him.

202. A woman was visiting her elderly and comatose mother in the hospital. The woman had just learned her mother had disinherited her, and the woman was furious. The woman raised her hand to strike her mother, but a nurse standing nearby saw what was about to happen and grabbed the woman's arm. The woman was later charged with assault of her mother.

Can the woman be properly convicted of this crime?

A. No, because the mother was in a coma and did not see the woman's acts.

B. No, because the nurse stopped the assault before it actually happened.

C. Yes, because being disinherited did not warrant the woman's response.

D. Yes, because the woman attempted to batter her mother, but failed.

203. A man was sitting by himself at a bar, drinking a beer. A woman walked up to him and asked if she could buy him a drink, but the man declined. The woman told the bartender to give the man another beer, and the man told the woman that he did not want another beer and did not want to talk with her. Angered by the man's comments, the woman slapped him across the face. The man's cheek turned bright red from the slap, but he did not suffer any other injury.

What crime has the woman committed?

A. Battery, because the woman used unlawful force when she slapped the man and caused him injury.

B. Assault, because when the woman slapped the man, she intended for him to suffer fear and apprehension.

C. Attempted battery, because the man did not suffer any real injury from the slap, just a reddened face.

D. Assault and battery, because the woman raised her hand for the slap (assault) and then followed through (battery).

204. A woman was drinking a glass of wine at a bar when a man offered to buy her a drink. The woman declined, but the man persisted. After saying no to the man several times, the woman became frustrated and asked him to leave her alone. The man sat down at the bar next to the woman so she threw her glass of wine at him. The breaking glass cut the man's face next to his eye, but he did not need stitches.

Can the woman be properly charged with battery?

A. No, because the woman had to act as she did because the man was being a jerk.

B. No, because the man's injuries were *de minimis* and he did not need stitches.

C. Yes, because the woman could have just moved to a different seat at the bar.

D. Yes, because the man was injured by the woman's intentional use of force.

205. A plastic surgeon performed breast augmentation surgery on a patient who had requested breast reduction surgery instead. The patient reported the issue to the state medical board. In a final report detailing its investigation into the matter, the medical board found that the surgeon had not reviewed his pre-surgery notes before operating and had ignored several comments from a surgical nurse that he was performing the wrong surgery. The final report also noted that this was the third time this surgeon had performed the wrong surgery in the past five years.

Can the surgeon be properly charged with battery of the patient?

A. Yes, because the surgeon had made the same mistake twice in past.

B. Yes, because the patient was injured by the surgeon's criminal negligence.

C. No, because the surgeon committed medical malpractice and not a crime.

D. No, because the hospital is responsible for maintaining the surgeon on staff.

206. A woman was driving her car down a residential street, exceeding the speed limit by 8 MPH. A pedestrian stepped out in front of the car but the woman could not stop in time and hit him. Because of the impact, the pedestrian broke his arm.

The prosecutor charged the woman with battery; her attorney filed a motion to dismiss.

How should the judge rule on the motion?

A. The motion should be granted because the pedestrian stepped in the car's way and caused the accident.

B. The motion should be granted because the pedestrian was contributorily negligent for the accident.

C. The motion should be denied because the woman failed to meet her duty to brake in time to stop the accident.

D. The motion should be denied because the pedestrian's injury was due to the woman's unlawful act.

207. A woman was sitting in a bar having a glass of wine with her best friend. A work colleague entered the bar and, seeing the woman, walked up to her table. The work colleague touched the woman's hand and remarked how nice it was to run into her outside of work. The woman was deeply offended and withdrew her hand. The next day, the woman went to the prosecutor's office and demanded the work colleague be charged with battery.

How should the prosecutor respond?

A. The prosecutor should explain that sexual harassment is a civil issue, and so she should retain an attorney to sue the colleague.

B. The prosecutor should explain that a reasonable person would not have been offended by the colleague's actions at the bar.

C. The prosecutor should explain that the woman should go to the police, who will investigate and then give him a report.

D. The prosecutor should explain that the colleague was only being friendly, and the woman is being too sensitive.

208. A high school student was on his school's hockey team. In the first game of the year, the student cross-checked another player with his hockey stick. The blow broke the other player's cheekbone and left him with a concussion. Still, the referee did not call a penalty. After reviewing tape of the game, the local prosecutor charged the student with battery.

Can the student be properly convicted of this crime?

A. Yes, because the student intentionally used force to harm the other player, beyond what is ordinarily accepted in hockey.

B. Yes, because cross-checking is prohibited in hockey, and the student used his hockey stick to cross-check the other player.

C. No, because by agreeing to play a dangerous sport like hockey, the other player consented to this use of force.

D. No, because the referee did not call a penalty, the student's actions cannot be deemed objectively unreasonable.

209. Late one evening, a woman walked into a grocery store to do her weekly shopping. The greeter at the front of the store told the woman that the store would be closing in 10 minutes and suggested that she either shop very quickly or come back another day. The woman spit on the ground and went back to her car.

In this jurisdiction, the relevant portion of the penal code states:

> A person is guilty of simple assault if he attempts to cause or intentionally, knowingly or recklessly causes bodily injury to another, or if he attempts by physical menace to put another in fear of bodily injury.

The prosecutor wants to charge the woman with simple assault. Can she properly do so?

A. No, because the common law did not recognize the crime of "simple assault," only the crime of assault.

B. No, because the statute unconstitutionally describes both assault and battery, instead of one or the other.

C. No, because the woman did not intentionally cause bodily injury to the greeter when she spit on the ground.

D. No, because the woman did not attempt by physical menace to put the greeter in fear of bodily injury.

210. A teenager asked to borrow her father's sports car, but he refused. Undaunted, the teenager snuck the spare key from her father's desk and took the sports car out for a ride. When the father found out, he went to the driveway to wait for the teenager to come home. As the teenager pulled into the driveway an hour later, she saw her father. Figuring that she could avoid an argument with her father if he was hospitalized with a few broken bones, the teenager put her foot on the accelerator and drove the sports car into her father.

The prosecutor now wants to charge the teenager under the following statute:

> A person who assaults and batters another person with the intent to do great bodily harm less than the crime of murder is guilty of a felony punishable by imprisonment of not more than 10 years or a fine of not more than $5,000, or both.

Can the teenager be properly convicted under this statute?

A. No, because the extent of the father's injuries is unclear.

B. No, because the teenager did not intend to murder her father.

C. Yes, because the teenager intended great bodily harm to her father.

D. Yes, because the teenager intended to murder her father.

Burglary

211. A man was jealous of his brother because the brother lived in a large home filled with expensive furnishings. The home included a library filled with rare books. One night while the brother and his family were asleep, the man armed himself with a gun, broke into the brother's house and took some books from the library.

If the man is guilty of common law burglary, how is his crime best described?

A. As a crime against the person, because the man created a danger to human life when he armed himself with a gun.

B. As a crime against possession, because the man interfered with the brother's possession of real and personal property.

C. As a crime against habitation, because the man interfered with the brother's right to live peacefully in his own home.

D. As a crime against the people, because the burglary diminished society, even though it was committed against one person.

212. A man knew that his neighbor kept his expensive watch collection at his home. The man also knew that the neighbor kept a spare key on his back porch under a flower pot. One night when the neighbor was out of town on a business trip, the man took the spare key from under the flower pot; as he did so, he tipped over the flower pot and broke it. Using the key, the man let himself into the neighbor's house and took the watches.

Did the man's actions constitute a breaking?

A. No, because the man did not break anything valuable.

B. No, because the man used a key to enter the house.

C. Yes, because the man tipped the flower pot and broke it.

D. Yes, because the man created an entry into the house.

213. One evening, a woman knocked on her neighbor's door. When the neighbor answered, the woman explained that she was collecting donations for needy children and asked if the neighbor would like to donate. This was a lie; the woman really wanted to steal a diamond bracelet she had seen the neighbor wearing the day before.

The neighbor agreed to help and opened the door so the woman could come inside. While the woman stood in the entryway, the neighbor went to get some money. In the meantime, the woman saw the bracelet on a table and quickly put it in her pocket. The neighbor returned a few minutes later and gave the woman $5 for the needy children.

Can the woman be convicted of common law burglary?

A. No, because common law burglary requires a breaking, and the woman did not break anything.

B. No, because common law burglary requires a breaking and the neighbor opened the door.

C. Yes, because a breaking occurred when the woman lied to gain entry to the neighbor's house.

D. Yes, because all the other requirements of common law burglary are met, except for breaking.

214. A woman contracted with a builder to remodel her kitchen. The woman provided the builder with a house key and the two agreed that he would only use it while the woman was at work, from 9:00 A.M. to 5:00 P.M., on weekdays.

One evening while the woman was out of town, the builder realized that he had left his cellphone inside the woman's house. The builder used the key to open the locked door, went inside, and recovered his cellphone.

Did the builder's actions constitute a breaking?

A. Yes, because the builder used the key to create a breach or an opening in the house.

B. Yes, because the builder did not have the woman's consent to use the key as he did.

C. No, because the builder wanted his own property and had no intent to commit a theft.

D. No, because the woman and the builder only had a verbal agreement about the key.

215. One sweltering summer evening, a man opened several windows in his house to get some fresh air. He also opened his front door, leaving the screen door closed but unlocked. Later, the man went to bed, forgetting to close the front door.

While the man was sleeping, a neighbor's teenage son opened the screen door and came inside the man's house. The teenage son found the man's wallet on the kitchen counter and stole it.

Did the teenage son commit a breaking?

A. No, because the man left his front door open, inviting the teenage son and other strangers to enter his home.

B. No, because the common law only recognized entry through solid doors, not screened doors, as a breaking.

C. Yes, because the teenage son created a breach by opening the screen door, even though the door was unlocked.

D. Yes, because the teenage son failed to secure the man's consent to open the door and enter his home.

216. A woman was jealous of her friend because the friend had a large diamond ring.

One evening when the friend was out of town, the woman drove to the friend's house with her seven-year-old daughter in the car. The woman pulled into the friend's driveway and grabbed a spare house key from under a flowerpot by the front door. The woman used the house key to open the door and then instructed her daughter to go inside the house and get the ring from the friend's bedside table. When the daughter asked why, the woman said that the friend had asked her to keep the ring for safekeeping while she was away. The daughter did as she was told.

Can the woman be convicted of burglary?

A. Yes, because the woman lied to her daughter about the friend's instructions.

B. Yes, because the woman used her daughter to break and enter into the house.

C. No, because the woman did not herself break or enter into the friend's house.

D. No, because the woman did not steal the ring; instead, the daughter did.

217. One evening, a teenager snuck over to a friend's house and used a golf club to break a window in the back of the house. Neither the friend nor her parents heard the sound of the breaking glass or noticed the broken window.

Late the following evening, the teenager came back to the friend's house and crept in through the broken window. Once inside, the teenager stole some of her friend's jewelry.

Is the teenager guilty of burglary?

A. No, because there was more than a 24-hour gap between the breaking and the entering.

B. No, because as a minor the teenager cannot be charged with adult crimes like burglary.

C. Yes, because there was a causal relationship between the acts of breaking and entering.

D. Yes, because the teenager is old enough to be charged with adult crimes like burglary.

218. A man was charged with the burglary of a summer home and the theft of an expensive painting. The prosecutor argued that the man, who was very thin, had entered the house by lowering himself down the chimney. The man was later arrested when he tried to sell the painting to an undercover officer. In a pretrial motion to dismiss, the man's lawyer argued that if the prosecutor was correct and the man had come in through the chimney, no breaking occurred.

How should the judge rule on the motion?

A. The judge should deny the motion because even though the chimney had an opening, it was not an invitation to enter.

B. The judge should deny the motion because requiring homeowners to cap chimneys would jeopardize public safety.

C. The judge should grant the motion because the man's attempted sale of the painting demonstrates that he stole it.

D. The judge should grant the motion because a chimney's opening is considered by law as an invitation to enter the house.

219. A teenager learned that his friend's father kept his tools in a locked shed behind the house. Late one night, the teenager crept into the friend's backyard. Using a tire iron, he broke the padlock on a shed next to the house, went inside, and lifted the toolbox off the shelf. But the toolbox was very heavy and the teenager could not carry it very far. After just a few steps, he dropped it on his foot and screamed in pain. The screaming woke the friend's family, who called the police.

Can the teenager be convicted of burglary?

A. No, because the shed is not part of the dwelling house.

B. No, because he did not actually steal the toolbox.

C. Yes, because he took the toolbox from the shelf.

D. Yes, because the shed is part of the dwelling house.

220. A wealthy woman owned a house in the small town where she was raised; she stayed at the house several weeks every year. The rest of the time, the woman traveled around the world or stayed at one of her many vacation properties.

One night, a man broke into the woman's house and stole some valuable jewelry from the safe in the bedroom. The woman was not at home at the time and had not been to the house in the past six months. But when the woman returned to the house several weeks later, she discovered the theft and immediately reported it to the police.

Did the man commit a burglary?

A. No; the woman had been away from the house for six months and so the house lost its character as a dwelling house.

B. No; the woman discovered the theft weeks after it occurred, and so the prosecutor will be unable to get a conviction.

C. Yes; the house is still a dwelling house even though the woman was on an extended vacation at the time of the theft.

D. Yes; once a structure is considered a dwelling house, it will remain a dwelling house until the structure is demolished.

221. One day, the manager of a restaurant fired one of the cooks for stealing food. The cook was furious and decided to get even. That evening after the restaurant closed, the cook hurled a large rock through the front window and then hoisted himself through the opening and into the restaurant. The cook grabbed several thousand dollars from the restaurant safe and threw food all over the floor. The cook then doused the restaurant with gasoline and set the building on fire.

Has the cook committed common law burglary?

A. Yes, because the cook broke and entered the restaurant at night and committed an atrocious crime inside.

B. Yes, because the cook broke and entered the restaurant at night and had the intent to commit a crime inside.

C. No, because the cook's last act was to set fire to the restaurant, and so he should instead be charged with arson.

D. No, because the cook's acts, although atrocious, do not meet the elements of common law burglary.

222. A retired baker told his friends that he would bake cookies and small cakes for them, charging them only to cover his costs. Word soon spread, and the baker began to receive requests for much more elaborate cakes. Because the baker did not want to return to full-time work, he decided to accept just a few cake requests a month and no more. Still, the baker only charged enough to cover his costs.

After learning that the baker kept a valuable coin collection in his house, a local man broke into the house one evening. Once inside, the man found the coin collection stored in the oven. He quickly grabbed it and ran from the house.

Did the man commit a burglary?

A. Yes, because the baker lived in the house (in addition to baking there) it is still considered a dwelling house.

B. Yes, because the baker did not profit financially from his business, his home is considered a dwelling house.

C. No, because the baker's use of his house as a business means that it cannot also be considered a dwelling house.

D. No, because the baker collected money from his customers, no matter how little, his house was a really a commercial kitchen.

223. A woman owed a lot of money on her credit cards and needed money. After announcing to friends that she was going to the beach for a week, the woman checked into a local motel. Several nights later and wearing dark clothing, the woman snuck back to her house. She broke several windows with a rock and entered, grabbed her jewelry from her bedroom, and went back to the motel. The woman stayed there for two more days and then went back home.

When she returned, the woman pretended to be surprised by the apparent break-in. She called the police and the insurance company and reported the missing jewelry. Unfortunately for the woman, both the police and the insurance company quickly realized that she was the culprit.

If the woman is later charged with burglary, how should she defend herself?

A. The woman should argue that no breaking occurred because she had a property interest in the house.

B. The woman should argue that no entry occurred because she had a property interest in the house.

C. The woman should argue that no burglary occurred because one cannot burglarize one's own home.

D. The woman should argue that she lacked the *mens rea* to commit any sort of crime inside the house.

224. To avoid the heat, a runner trained in the early morning hours. The runner was also a burglar, and used his early morning runs to check out potential targets for his crimes.

One morning as he ran through a posh neighborhood, the runner opened the unlocked back door of a fancy house and went inside. The runner saw a wallet sitting on a table next to the door, grabbed it, and then ran away from the house. Unfortunately for the runner, the homeowner had a camera at the back door which recorded the entry and theft. The recording showed that the runner opened the door and entered the home exactly 11 minutes after sunrise, but that it was still dark outside.

Did the runner commit a burglary?

A. No, because the owner invited entry by leaving the door unlocked.

B. No, because the breaking and entry were committed after sunrise.

C. Yes, because the breaking and entry were committed after sunrise.

D. Yes, because the recording indicated that it was still dark outside.

225. A man and woman lived together for many years, co-owning their home. After they broke up, the man signed the house over to the woman and moved away. One evening when the woman was out on a date, the man returned to the house to retrieve some belongings he had left in the attic. Because the woman owed the man some money, he decided also to take the woman's valuable coin collection.

As the man broke and entered into the house, a neighbor saw him because a streetlamp was shining brightly on the woman's house. The neighbor called the police and the man was soon arrested.

Is the man guilty of burglarizing the woman's house?

A. Yes, and the light from the streetlamp does not affect the man's guilt in any way.

B. Yes, because man had the intent to steal some of the woman's property, in addition to taking his own.

C. No, because there was enough light by which to see the man break and enter into the house.

D. No, because the man had a valid claim of right over his property that he wanted from the attic.

226. One night, a man went out to celebrate his promotion at work. After drinking for many hours, the man was too drunk to drive home, and the bartender confiscated his keys. The man began to walk home but then remembered that his friend lived close to the bar and so he walked to the friend's house. Once at the house, the man used a rock to break open a window in the back of the house; he crawled through the window and immediately passed out on the floor.

Can the man be convicted of common law burglary?

A. Yes; the man broke and entered the dwelling house of another at night, and these actions constitute a felony.

B. Yes; the man broke and entered the dwelling house of another at night and intended to commit a felony inside.

C. No; although the other elements of burglary are present, the man had no intent to commit a felony in the house.

D. No; although the other elements of burglary are present, the man was too drunk to form any *mens rea*.

227. One fall, a novice camper went on a weeklong camping trip in the woods. On the third night, the temperature dropped unexpectedly, and the camper began to suffer from hypothermia. The camper began hiking back to her car and soon came across a small cabin. The door was locked, and no one was inside.

The camper found a key on a hook next to the woodpile and used it to open the door to the cabin. Once inside, she started a fire. While the camper was sitting in front of the fire, she saw a wallet on the mantelpiece with some cash sticking out. After she had fully warmed up, the camper poured ash over the fire to put it out, took the cash from the wallet, and continued her hike—carefully locking the door behind her as she left the cabin.

Did the camper commit common law burglary?

A. No, because the camper left the cabin as she found it.

B. No, because the camper lacked the *mens rea* for burglary.

C. Yes, even though the camper left the cabin as she found it.

D. Yes, even though the camper lacked the *mens rea* for burglary.

228. An incumbent was running for local office; the challenger lived in the same neighborhood, two blocks away. As the election drew near, the incumbent became concerned that some of her long-time supporters were donating to the challenger's campaign. To find out for sure, the incumbent broke into the challenger's house one night while he was out at a campaign rally. While in the house, the incumbent went through the challenger's records and discovered her hunch was wrong: the challenger had not received any donations from her supporters.

Has the incumbent committed common law burglary?

A. No, because the incumbent had no intent to commit a felony when she broke and entered the challenger's house.

B. No, because the incumbent only intended to learn information and was not going to take anything with her.

C. Yes, because the incumbent intended to commit a campaign finance violation inside the challenger's house.

D. Yes, because the incumbent intended to interfere with an election by going through the challenger's records.

229. A woman learned that her neighbor had a wine cellar, stocked with rare and expensive wines. One night, while the neighbor was away on vacation, the woman decided to go into the neighbor's house and take a few bottles of wine.

The woman used a brick to smash a window in the back of the house and then crawled in through the broken window. But the woman did not realize that by smashing the window, she had tripped the silent alarm. Within just a few minutes, and before the woman even got to the wine cellar, the police arrived and arrested her.

Should the woman be charged with common law burglary?

A. Yes, because the woman had the intent to steal wine from her neighbor.

B. Yes, because the woman would have stolen the wine if she wasn't arrested.

C. No, because the police arrived before the woman could steal the wine.

D. No, because the woman did not commit a felony inside the neighbor's house.

230. A woman walked into a clothing store to look for new clothes. After browsing for a while, the woman found a sweater that she loved. But the sweater was expensive and so the woman snuck it into her purse, planning to steal it. The store owner saw this, confronted the woman, and asked her to return the sweater and then leave the store. The woman denied doing anything wrong and refused to leave. The store owner called the police, who arrested the woman.

The woman has now been charged with burglary, which, in this jurisdiction, is defined as: "entering and remaining unlawfully in a building with the intent to commit a crime."

What should the woman argue in her defense?

A. Because she did not actually or constructively break, the woman cannot be guilty of burglary.

B. Because the clothing store is not a dwelling house, the woman cannot be guilty of burglary.

C. Because she did not go into the clothing store at night, the woman cannot be guilty of burglary.

D. Because she had no criminal intent when she entered, the woman cannot be guilty of burglary.

Arson

231. A new law professor was creating teaching materials for her very first class. The law professor looked through her law school notes for a definition of common law arson and found four different definitions.

Which definition should the law professor put in her teaching materials?

A. Arson is the intentional burning of a dwelling house.

B. Arson is the malicious burning of a dwelling house.

C. Arson is the burning of a dwelling house of another.

D. Arson is the malicious burning of a dwelling house of another.

232. A woman burned down her neighbor's house and was charged with arson.

How should the woman's crime be classified?

A. As a crime against society, because the arson diminishes us all even though only the neighbor's house was burned.

B. As a crime against the person, because the woman created a danger to human life when she burned the neighbor's house.

C. As a crime against possession, because the woman interfered with the neighbor's possession of real and personal property.

D. As a crime against habitation, because the woman interfered with the neighbor's right to live peacefully in his own home.

233. A woman was angry with her sister. One night while the sister was away, the woman used her key to enter the sister's house. The woman doused the living room with gasoline, tossed a lit match onto the couch, and ran from the house. The fire caught quickly and the house burned to the ground. The woman was arrested and charged with arson.

Can the woman be convicted of this crime?

A. No, because she acted intentionally, but without malice.

B. No, because the sister had given her a key to the house.

C. Yes, because she maliciously burned her sister's house.

D. Yes, because she burned the dwelling house of another.

234. One fall day, a woman raked leaves into a pile in the bottom of her backyard and set the pile on fire. The woman did not have the necessary permit to burn the leaves but assumed that the fire would be safe because her yard was large and the leaf pile was relatively isolated. As she started the fire, a neighbor came out from his house to watch; the woman reassured him that she would closely monitor the fire. But sparks from the fire flew onto a nearby tree; the tree began to burn. Soon, sparks flew from tree to tree and onto the neighbor's roof. The neighbor's house burned to the ground.

Can the woman be properly charged with arson?

A. No, because she did not show a reckless disregard for a high risk that the neighbor's house would burn.

B. No, because the sparks flying from the trees to the roof were an intervening cause for the fire.

C. Yes, because she burned leaves in her yard without first obtaining the necessary permit.

D. Yes, because she plainly did not closely monitor the fire as she told the neighbor she would.

235. A high school junior was bored and looking for something fun to do. The junior hooked up the backyard sprinkler system at his mother's house to the gas line. The junior then turned on the gas and threw a match in the air. Instead of water, the sprinkler released tall flames, which quickly consumed the mother's house and the house next door. The junior was charged with arson.

Prior to trial, the junior's attorney filed a motion to dismiss, arguing that the fire was "a huge mistake, borne out of restlessness and juvenile idiocy, but not ill will."

How should the judge rule on the motion?

A. The motion should be granted because the junior could not know that his acts would cause the houses to burn.

B. The motion should be granted because arson charges should be reserved for criminals and not bored teenagers.

C. The motion should be denied because the junior showed a reckless disregard for a high risk of burning.

D. The motion should be denied because the attorney is wrong and the juvenile's acts demonstrated ill will.

236. A man tried to set fire to his friend's house by stuffing a gasoline-soaked rag under the front door and then lighting the edge of the rag. Because no oxygen could get to the rag, though, the fire never started and the rag only emitted smoke. The friend was at home and smelled the smoke; he found the rag and poured water on it.

Can the man be properly charged with arson?

A. No, because there was no burning of the dwelling house of another.

B. No, because the friend put out the fire before it caused any damage.

C. Yes, because he tried to intentionally burn his friend's dwelling house.

D. Yes, because he created a grave risk to human life when he lit the rag.

237. A young man built a homemade bomb from some materials he bought at a local hardware store. The young man planned to drive the bomb out to the desert to detonate it, but it exploded one day when he was at work. The bomb destroyed the young man's house and blew off part of the roof of the house next door.

The prosecutor charged the young man with arson; the young man's attorney plans to file a motion to dismiss.

What argument should the attorney include in the motion?

A. The young man did not have the *mens rea* for arson and so cannot be held criminally liable for the explosion.

B. While the young man may have been reckless, the explosion did not result in a burning of the house next door.

C. The only damage to the house next door was to the roof, which is not significant enough for an arson charge.

D. The young man's plan to detonate the bomb in the desert shows that he did not intentionally detonate the bomb.

238. A woman learned that her best friend had gossiped about her. To retaliate, the woman filled a bottle with gasoline, added a wick and lit it, and then threw the flaming bottle through a window of the best friend's house. The best friend was at home and quickly doused the burning bottle with water. Part of the wooden floor in the house was charred, and a much larger area of the floor was warped by water damage.

Can the woman be properly charged with arson?

A. Yes, because part of the floor in the best friend's house was charred by the fire from the flaming bottle.

B. Yes, because the woman intentionally created a high risk of burning of the best friend's house.

C. No, because most of the damage to the floor occurred due to the best friend's use of water.

D. No, because the woman's actions only resulted in relatively minor damage to the best friend's house.

239. A man was burning leaves in his backyard on a windy day, and the fire spread from the leaf pile to a tree branch. The fire then jumped to the house next door: the neighbor had a window open and a blowing curtain caught the flame. The neighbor saw this happen, pulled the curtain from the curtain rod, and stamped out the flames.

The neighbor called the police and demanded the man be charged with arson.

How should the police respond to the neighbor's request?

A. The prosecutor files charges, not the police, and so the neighbor should contact the prosecutor for help.

B. The man did not commit arson as neither the neighbor's dwelling house nor its permanent fixtures were burned.

C. The man did not intentionally set fire to the neighbor's curtain and so he cannot be arrested for arson.

D. The man did not commit arson as the fire only accidentally spread from the leaves to the tree to the curtain.

240. A contractor was hired to build a large house. In the middle of construction, the contractor's wife filed for divorce. In need of cash to pay a divorce attorney, the contractor set fire to a bulldozer at the build site, with the plan to use the insurance proceeds to pay the attorney. The fire destroyed the bulldozer and the half-built house.

Can the contractor be properly charged with arson of the house?

A. Yes, because he intentionally set fire to the bulldozer, which then caused the house to burn.

B. Yes, because he intentionally set fire to the bulldozer in order to commit insurance fraud.

C. No, because he intentionally set fire to his own property and not the dwelling house of another.

D. No, because the half-built house should not be considered the dwelling house of another.

241. A man instructed his teenage sons to rake the back lawn and then burn the leaves when they were done. The sons did as they were told. But the sons were checking their email on phones as the leaves burned and did not notice that the fire had spread to a small shed on a neighbor's property. Once the sons saw the shed was burning, they put the fire out.

Can the sons be properly charged with arson?

A. Yes, because they were on their phones and not watching the fire.

B. Yes, because they maliciously burned the dwelling house of another.

C. No, because only the shed burned and not the neighbor's house.

D. No, because the father should have better supervised the sons' work.

242. A woman was facing foreclosure on her house. Believing she had no other choice, the woman decided to set it on fire and collect the insurance proceeds. One evening, the woman put a lit cigarette in a trash can in her bathroom and then quickly drove across town to her favorite restaurant for dinner. The woman made sure to chat with the bartender and the waiters at the restaurant, hoping that if she ever needed an alibi, they would remember her.

Back at the house, the lit cigarette caught fire and the woman's house burned to the ground. Later, after an investigation by the fire marshal, the prosecutor charged the woman with arson.

Can the woman be properly convicted of arson?

A. Yes, because the woman intentionally burned a dwelling house at night.

B. Yes, because the woman intentionally burned a house for insurance money.

C. No, because the woman had an alibi for the time when the house was burning.

D. No, because the woman did not burn the dwelling house of another.

243. A landlord owned several rental houses. One house had been rented to the same woman for a decade. When the landlord was offered the opportunity to invest in a large high-rise building with dozens of apartments, he readily agreed. The landlord set fire to the house the woman was renting, intending to use the insurance proceeds to invest in the high-rise project. The house burned to the ground and the landlord was later charged with arson.

Prior to trial, the landlord's attorney filed a motion to dismiss, arguing that since the landlord owned the house, he could not be convicted of arson.

How should the prosecutor respond?

A. The woman's long-term rental of the house means that the landlord effectively burned her house to the ground.

B. Dismissing the charge would reward the landlord for committing insurance fraud and set a bad precedent.

C. The landlord burned the house intentionally and so he plainly acted with a *mens rea* of maliciousness.

D. The landlord's intentional burning of the house demonstrated a reckless disregard for the life of the woman.

244. As a joke and while visiting a friend at her house, a man put a roll of toilet paper in the sink and lit it on fire. The friend turned on the faucet and put out the fire, but the flames scorched a small spot on the wall beside the sink.

The prosecutor charged the man with second degree arson, a 20-year felony:

> Any person who intentionally burns, destroys or causes damage by fire or explosive to a dwelling of another, regardless of whether it is occupied, unoccupied, or vacant at the time of the fire or explosion, or its contents, is guilty of second degree arson.

The statute also defines "damage" as including "charring, melting, singeing, scorching, or burning." The man's attorney filed a motion to dismiss.

How should the judge rule on the motion?

A. The motion should be denied because the man's intentional act caused "damage" to the friend's dwelling house, as defined by the statute.

B. The motion should be denied because the damage could have been worse if the friend had not acted so quickly to turn on the faucet.

C. The motion should be granted because the man only burned the toilet paper as a joke and should not face 20 years in prison for that.

D. The motion should be granted because the man burned the toilet paper as a joke and so did not act intentionally, as required by the statute.

245. A woman was annoyed with her husband because he spent a lot of time riding his fancy bicycle instead of spending time with her. One night while her husband slept, the woman set fire to the bicycle, which was worth $5,000.

The prosecutor now wants to charge the woman with fifth degree arson, which includes the "wilful or malicious burning of any personal property having a value of $1,000 or more, but less than $20,000."

Can this charge be sustained?

A. No, because the bicycle was marital property and so was not the property "of another."

B. No, because arson is a crime against habitation and the woman burned a bicycle.

C. Yes, because the woman intentionally burned personal property worth $1,000–$20,000.

D. Yes, because the woman intentionally burned the personal property of another, at night.

Theft

246. A hungry man walked into a grocery store and shoplifted a frozen dinner. A store security officer witnessed this. The officer followed the man to the parking lot and arrested him.

What crime has the hungry man committed?

A. No crime, because the grocery store is a business entity and so the frozen dinner cannot be considered the personal property "of another."

B. No crime, because the store security officer is not a sworn peace officer and so did not have the authority to arrest the hungry man for shoplifting.

C. Embezzlement, because the man had lawful possession of the frozen dinner while in the store, and converted it for his own use when he left.

D. Larceny, because the man took the personal property of another without consent and then carried it away, and had no intent to return it.

247. A girl set up a lemonade stand on the driveway of her house. The girl put a tip jar on the lemonade stand. A man walked up the lemonade stand, reached into the jar and pulled the tip money out, and then walked away.

What type of crime has the man committed?

A. A crime against nature, because it is unnatural and wrong for a grown man to steal from a child.

B. A crime against possession, because the man interfered with the girl's right to possess her tip money.

C. A crime against the person, because the man stole the tip money from the girl's immediate presence.

D. A crime against habitation, since the girl was near her house when the man took the tip money.

248. A lawyer accepted a job at a law firm, which supplied her with an office and a desktop computer with a monitor and keyboard. When the lawyer started her job, the password was set to "12345," and the firm's system administrator told the lawyer to change the password to "678910." The lawyer did as she was instructed.

What possessory interest does the lawyer have in the desktop computer?

A. The lawyer has custody of the computer because she has relatively little control over it.

B. The lawyer has possession of the computer because she was permitted to change the password.

C. The lawyer has title to the computer because her employer gave it to her to use in her job.

D. The lawyer has no possessory right to the computer at all, as the computer belongs to the law firm.

249. A doctor worked at a university hospital. As part of the doctor's employment contract, the university provided her with a new laptop computer every other year. The contract specified that the doctor was required to surrender her old laptop before the university would replace it with a new one. The contract also permitted the doctor to use the laptop for personal use and to bring it with her during personal travel.

What possessory interest does the doctor have in the laptop computer?

A. The doctor has custody of the laptop because her use of the laptop is controlled by the employment contract.

B. The doctor has possession of the laptop because the university places few limits on how she is allowed to use it.

C. The doctor has title to the laptop because the employment contract did not restrict its use to work-related matters.

D. The lawyer has no possessory right to the laptop because, according to the contract, it belongs to the university.

250. A law professor went to the law school's bookstore and selected a textbook for a course she planned to teach the following term. The bookstore clerk charged the cost of the book to the professor's professional development fund, which was furnished by the university and used to pay for textbooks, conferences, and related expenditures. The professor then spent several weeks reading the textbook, writing notes in the margins as she went along. She also brought the textbook to her home several times and took it with her for a spring vacation at the beach.

What possessory interest does the professor have in the textbook?

A. The professor has custody of the textbook because she did not pay for it with her own money.

B. The professor has no possessory right to the textbook because the university ultimately paid for it.

C. The professor has title to the textbook because the university does not want a used textbook.

D. The professor has possession of the textbook because she has few restrictions on its use.

251. A woman wearing an expensive bracelet was walking down the street. The clasp on the bracelet was broken and the bracelet fell from the woman's wrist. Two men were walking behind the woman and saw this. The first man quickly picked the bracelet up from the ground and put it in his pocket. The second man, who also wanted the bracelet but did not act quickly enough, accused the first man of larceny of the bracelet.

What can the first man plausibly say in his defense?

A. The woman abandoned the bracelet when she allowed it to drop to the ground, so he did not take it by trespass.

B. The woman did not have possession of the bracelet when it was on the ground, so he did not take it by trespass.

C. The prosecutor cannot prove the *mens rea* for larceny because she does not know what the first man intended.

D. The second man is trying to deflect attention from himself by accusing the first man of larceny of the woman's bracelet.

252. A clerk in a clothing shop was helping a customer. The clerk suggested that the customer try on a sweater and handed it to him so he could go into the dressing room. Instead, the customer walked out of the store, taking the sweater with him.

The prosecutor charged the customer with larceny. The customer's attorney filed a motion to dismiss, arguing that the clerk surrendered her lawful possession of the sweater when she handed it to the customer.

How should the judge rule on the motion?

A. The motion should be denied because the clerk retained constructive possession of the sweater when she handed it to the customer.

B. The motion should be denied because the customer stole the sweater when he walked out of the store without paying for it first.

C. The motion should be granted because the clerk voluntarily handed the sweater to the customer, giving him legal possession.

D. The motion should be granted because the customer interfered with the shop owner's possessory right to the sweater and not the clerk's.

253. A bicycle store had a large inventory, including bicycles, clothing, and other equipment. The store was owned by an attorney and was managed by the attorney's brother. The two met monthly to discuss the store's finances; otherwise, the attorney focused on his law practice and had little to do with the store's daily operations.

What possessory interest does the lawyer have in the store's inventory?

A. The lawyer has no possessory interest in the store's inventory, because he has little to do with the store's daily operations.

B. The lawyer is the title holder of the store's inventory, even though he has little to do with the store's daily operations.

C. The lawyer has constructive possession over the store's inventory, because he has little to do with the store's daily operations.

D. The lawyer does not have any interest in the store's inventory, as it is unethical for him to own a business while practicing law.

254. A woman was walking in a residential neighborhood when she passed by a house with a parked car in the driveway. As the woman walked by the car, she noticed a wallet sitting on the dashboard. The woman looked in both directions and, seeing no one watching, opened the car door and took the wallet. She then walked quickly down the street and away from the car.

Has the woman committed larceny?

A. Yes, because the woman took unlawful possession of the wallet, with the intent to permanently deprive the owner of it.

B. Yes, because the woman trespassed on the driveway and dispossessed the wallet owner of the wallet without his consent.

C. No, because the woman did not take the wallet directly "from another," she cannot be convicted of larceny of the wallet.

D. No, because without knowing whether there was any cash in the wallet, the woman cannot be convicted of larceny.

255. A college student needed money to pay her tuition. The only real thing of value she owned was her car, which was insured. The student gave her keys to a friend and asked him to take the car so she could report it stolen and collect the insurance money. The friend agreed and asked if the student if she wanted the car back. The student told him that he could keep the car.

The next day, the friend took the car and parked it in his garage. But the student changed her mind about her plan and reported that her car really had been stolen. The police arrested the friend and the prosecutor charged him with larceny.

How should the friend defend himself against this charge at trial?

A. The friend should explain that he only intended to help the student, and not to permanently deprive her of the car.

B. The friend should ask the prosecutor for a deal to testify against the student for attempted insurance fraud.

C. The friend should explain that he did not take the car by trespass because the student gave him the keys.

D. The friend should explain that the student was the mastermind of the plan, and he just was just trying to help.

256. A man was charged with larceny. At his trial, the prosecution presented evidence that established that the man had gone into a jewelry store and asked to see several expensive rings. As the clerk was showing the man the rings, he concealed one under his hand as it rested on the jewelry counter. A security guard witnessed this and forced the man to turn his hand over, revealing the ring.

At the close of the prosecution's case, the man's attorney filed a motion to dismiss, arguing that the prosecution had not established that he carried away the ring.

How should the judge rule on the motion?

A. The motion should be granted because the man did not carry away the ring, but instead merely concealed it.

B. The motion should be granted because the clerk should not have shown so many rings at the same time.

C. The motion should be denied because the judge should not usurp the jury's role by deciding this legal issue.

D. The motion should be denied because even a small movement toward trespassory taking will suffice.

257. A woman went into a store intending to shoplift some jewelry. The woman asked the clerk if she could see a pair of earrings in a jewelry case, claiming falsely that she wanted to buy her mother a gift. As the clerk put the earrings on the counter, one accidentally fell onto the floor. The woman picked up the earring and placed it back on the counter.

While the clerk inspected the earring to see if it had been damaged in the fall, the woman grabbed a bracelet from an open display and put it in her purse. The woman was later arrested and charged with larceny of the earrings and the bracelet.

Can the woman be properly convicted of larceny of the earrings?

A. No, because the woman did not carry the earrings away from the store.

B. No, because the woman did not carry the earrings away as part of a taking.

C. Yes, because the woman lied about why she wanted to see the earrings.

D. Yes, because the woman exploited the clerk's clumsiness to steal the bracelet.

258. A man invited several friends out for drinks to help him celebrate making the last payment on his mortgage. At the bar, the man showed his friends the paper deed the loan officer had handed him earlier that afternoon. But the man had too much to drink that night and did not notice when one of his friends took the paper deed from him. The next day, when the man realized what had happened, he asked the local prosecutor to charge the friend with larceny.

How should the prosecutor respond?

A. The prosecutor should explain to the man that the low value of the paper deed is not worth filing criminal charges.

B. The prosecutor should tell the man that the deed would not have been stolen if he hadn't had so much to drink.

C. The prosecutor should suggest to the man that anyone who would steal from him is not really a good friend.

D. The prosecutor should advise the man that the paper deed is not personal property so no larceny occurred.

259. A student wanted to attend the homecoming football game but did not have enough money to pay the $30 admission fee. The student broke the lock on a side door to the football arena, snuck into the bleachers, and watched the game. Unfortunately for the student, a video camera recorded her entry through the door, and she was later arrested and charged with larceny.

How should the student defend herself at trial?

A. The student should explain that she did not take any personal property.

B. The student should explain that she did not trespass on school property.

C. The student should challenge the authenticity of the video recording.

D. The student should challenge the chain of custody of the video recording.

260. A woman was late paying her mortgage and came up with a plan to get some money from her insurance company. The woman went to her neighborhood bar for a few beers. Having been seen by several people at the bar, the woman snuck out of the bar and walked back to her house, leaving her car in the bar's parking lot. She broke into a back window of her house, grabbed her best jewelry, and then went back to the bar. After another beer, the woman went home.

Back at her house, the woman called the police and reported that she had been burglarized. The investigating officer quickly saw through the woman's alibi and recommended to the prosecutor that the woman be charged with larceny of the jewelry.

How should the prosecutor respond?

A. The prosecutor should charge the woman with larceny because she took the jewelry during a burglary.

B. The prosecutor should charge the woman with attempted larceny because she never completed the crime.

C. The prosecutor should not charge the woman with larceny because she did not take the jewelry from another.

D. The prosecutor should not charge the woman with larceny because she never reported the break-in to her insurer.

261. A teenager wanted to borrow his mother's car for a date on a school night, but he was only allowed to use the car for weekend dates. The teenager snuck the keys from his mother's purse anyway and left the house in the car. While the teenager was driving to pick up his date, a police officer pulled him over and told him that his mother had reported him for theft of her car.

Later, after he was charged with larceny, the teenager's attorney filed a motion to quash the charge.

What argument should the attorney make in support of the motion?

A. The teenager did not commit larceny because he had not yet picked up his date when he was arrested.

B. The teenager did not commit larceny because a child cannot be convicted of stealing from his parent.

C. The teenager did not commit larceny because his mother called the police, so she knew he had the car.

D. The teenager did not commit larceny because he had no intent to permanently deprive his mother of her car.

262. A man was at his local library when he saw a new laptop sitting unattended in a reading carrel. After checking to make sure that no one was watching, the man packed up the laptop, wrapped it in his jacket, and went home.

The owner of the laptop used tracking software to locate it at the man's house and called the police with the information. The police then went to the man's house and arrested him for larceny. After he was charged, the man hired an attorney for his trial. During their first consultation, the man explained that he never intended to keep the laptop, but instead just wanted to borrow it for a few hours.

How should the attorney advise the man?

A. The attorney should tell the man that his claim, if believed, will negate an element of the charged crime.

B. The attorney should tell the man that he would not have been charged with larceny if he had a credible defense.

C. The attorney should tell the man that his claim, even if believed, will have no effect on the jury's verdict.

D. The attorney should tell the man that because he did not take the laptop from its owner, he will be acquitted.

263. A man was jealous of his older brother because the brother was very successful and flaunted his wealth. One evening after a family dinner at the brother's house, the man snuck into his brother's dressing room and took one of his expensive watches from his watch display case. The man then put the watch in the trash.

Later, the brother's maid discovered the watch in the trash. The brother called the police and reported the man, and the prosecutor charged the man with larceny. Before trial, the man's attorney filed a motion to dismiss.

How should the judge rule on the motion?

A. The motion should be denied because the man took the brother's watch without permission, with the intent to permanently deprive him of it.

B. The motion should be denied because the man's jealousy provides proof that he intended to permanently deprive the brother of the watch.

C. The motion should be granted because the watch stayed in the brother's house at all times and was quickly recovered in the trash.

D. The motion should be granted because although the man took the watch without permission, he did not destroy it or use it for himself.

264. A teenager went to a grocery store to pick up some things for his mother. The mother was very strict, and the teenager knew he would be in trouble if he purchased anything that was not on his mother's list.

The teenager paid for his mother's groceries with her credit card, but also shoplifted a new video game for himself. As the teenager was walking away from the cash register, a store security officer stopped him and asked him to hand over the video game.

What crime has the teenager committed?

A. The teenager did not commit any crime because he was stopped as he left the cash register and never left the store.

B. The teenager committed larceny, but he should be allowed to keep the video game because his mother is very strict.

C. The teenager committed larceny of the groceries and the video game because he took both in the same transaction.

D. The teenager committed larceny of the video game because he took it by trespass and did not intend to return it.

265. A woman was having dinner with a friend in a busy pub. After the meal, the woman excused herself to use the restroom. Inside the restroom, the woman saw a small purse sitting on the sink. Inside the purse was a wallet with credit cards, photo ID, and several hundred dollars. The woman called out, but she was the only person in the restroom and so no one answered. The woman tucked the purse into her handbag and left the restaurant. The next day, a second woman reported the missing purse to the restaurant.

Has the woman committed larceny?

A. Yes, because the purse was not abandoned but was instead constructively possessed by its owner.

B. Yes, because the woman had a legal obligation to report her discovery to the pub manager, but did not.

C. No, because the woman called out in the restroom and no one answered, so she had a right to keep the purse.

D. No, because the woman had no legal obligation to report her discovery or seek out the owner of the purse.

266. A student attending a high school football game did not have a sweater or coat and was cold. The student spotted an old, threadbare sweatshirt on the grass under the bleachers; she hopped off the bleachers and grabbed the sweatshirt. The student later wore the sweatshirt home.

When the student wore the sweatshirt to school two days later, a classmate recognized it as one he had lost at the game. The classmate complained to the school resource officer, who then asked the student to meet with him in his office.

What information should the resource officer seek from the student?

A. The resource officer should ask the student whether she had ever seen the classmate wearing the sweatshirt.

B. The resource officer should ask the student whether she thought anyone owned the sweatshirt when she found it.

C. The resource officer should ask the student whether she has a history of stealing other people's clothing.

D. The resource officer should ask the student whether she can provide the names of anyone to corroborate her story.

267. A wealthy woman planned a visit to her vacation home and put her assistant in charge of logistics for the trip. But the woman packed her own jewelry, placing it in a large case that she handed to the assistant to carry. On the flight to the vacation home, the assistant grew bored and opened up the jewelry case. He selected a diamond brooch and put it in his pocket, with the plan to give it to his mother.

Two weeks later, the woman realized that the brooch was missing. She complained to the police and the assistant was arrested and charged with larceny of the brooch.

How should the assistant try to defend himself?

A. The assistant should explain that the woman put him in charge of all the logistics for the trip, and so he did not take the brooch by trespass.

B. The assistant should explain that the woman gave him lawful possession over the case and its contents, so he did not take the brooch by trespass.

C. The assistant should explain that his job is difficult and demanding and so he considered the brooch to be fair compensation for his hard work.

D. The assistant should explain that the woman's delayed realization that the brooch was missing shows reasonable doubt about his guilt.

268. A museum wanted to move a priceless collection of historic dresses into storage. Museum workers put the dresses into linen bags to protect them from light and dirt. A mover was hired to move the bagged dresses.

Curious about the linen bags in the back of his truck, the mover opened one to see its contents. Recognizing a designer name, he pulled out a dress to give to his girlfriend and then zipped the bag closed again.

The mover was arrested and charged with larceny of the dress. The mover's attorney filed a motion to dismiss.

Following modern law, how should the judge rule on the motion?

A. The motion should be denied because the mover was given lawful possession over the linen bags but only custody over their contents.

B. The motion should be denied because it was the responsibility of the mover to check the contents of the bags and to see what he was moving.

C. The motion should be granted because the mover was given lawful title over the bags and their contents, so he did not take by trespass.

D. The motion should be granted because the mover was being a good boyfriend and his record should not be marred by a criminal conviction.

269. A woman rented a car for the weekend and signed a rental agreement promising to return the car the following Monday morning. At the time of the rental, the woman had plans to drive across the country and never return the car, but she realized that the rental agency would never rent to her if she was truthful about her intentions.

What possessory interest does the woman have in the rental car?

A. The woman took the car by trespass because she had a duty to disclose her real plans when she signed the rental agreement.

B. The woman took the car by trespass because she only obtained possession of the car by lying about her true intentions.

C. The woman has lawful possession of the car and will continue to do so until she fails to return the car on Monday morning.

D. The woman has lawful possession of the car because she had a valid, binding rental agreement with the car rental agency.

270. A woman asked her friend if she could borrow her diamond earrings. The woman told her friend that she wanted to wear the earrings to a garden party, but she really planned to wear them to a rock concert. Figuring that the precious earrings would be safe at a garden party, the friend agreed.

After putting on the earrings and admiring how nice they looked on her, the woman changed her mind and decided that she would keep the earrings for herself.

Will the prosecutor face any obstacles if she prosecutes the woman for larceny?

A. Yes; the prosecutor cannot show that the woman really wanted to wear the earrings to the rock concert.

B. Yes; the woman only formed the *mens rea* for larceny after she gained unlawful possession of the earrings.

C. No; the woman committed larceny by trick when she lied to her friend to gain unlawful possession of the earrings.

D. No; the friend knew the woman wanted to wear the earrings to an event, and the type of event does not matter.

271. A man asked a friend if he could borrow the friend's truck. In making the request, the man lied and told the friend that he wanted to use the truck to go on a date. In reality, the man was going to use the truck to haul firewood. The friend lent the man his truck. After using the truck to haul several cords of wood, the man decided that he wanted to keep the truck for himself.

What crime has the man committed?

A. The man has not committed any crime because truck owners realize their trucks will sometimes be borrowed for hauling.

B. The man has not committed any crime because it is only relevant that the friend agreed to loan the truck, not why.

C. Larceny by trick, because the man was not truthful and lied about his reason for wanting to borrow the truck.

D. Larceny by continuous trespass, because the man formed the intent to steal the truck after he lied to obtain possession.

272. The owner of a coffee shop placed a large jar on the counter next to the cash register. He put a sign on the jar with a photo of a cute toddler; the sign read:

> This little boy is very sick and has been in and out of hospitals many times during his short life. His parents need your help. Your donations will help this family through their terrible crisis.

Several customers felt sorry for the boy and put money in the jar. But the owner had invented the story and taken the photo from the internet. The owner kept the donations for himself.

Has the owner committed a crime?

A. The owner is not guilty of any crimes; the customers should have been aware of the risk that the owner made up the story.

B. The owner is guilty of larceny by trick because he tricked his customers into giving him possession of their money.

C. The owner is guilty of larceny by false pretenses because he tricked his customers into giving him title to their money.

D. The owner is guilty of larceny by continuous trespass because he only formed the intent to steal after the donations were made.

273. A high school senior asked her father if she could borrow the father's car for the evening. The senior explained that she was going to go to the movies with her friends. But the senior lied; instead, she planned to drive to the beach and start a new life with her history teacher—who she had secretly been dating.

Based on the senior's story about going to the movies, the father gave her a set of car keys. The senior then got in the car and drove away.

What crime has the senior committed?

A. Larceny by false pretenses, because she took title to her father's car and had no intent to return the car to him.

B. Larceny by trick, because she took unlawful possession of her father's car and had no intent to return the car to him.

C. Attempted larceny by false pretenses because the senior's crime will not be complete until she arrives at the beach.

D. The senior has not committed any theft crime; instead, her history teacher should be charged with statutory rape.

274. A woman posted flyers around her neighborhood, asking for donations. The flyers had a photo of a family and explained that both parents had both been laid off, but that they each had gotten new jobs and would begin working again in three weeks. The flyer stated that all donations would be used for the family's rent during the layoff period. The flyer included the woman's name and address and explained that she would arrange for all donations to be given to the family's landlord.

Several of the woman's neighbors donated money. But the woman made up the story about the family and kept the donated money for herself.

Has the woman committed any crimes?

A. The woman has not committed any crimes but she is a terrible person and ought to be driven out of the neighborhood.

B. The woman has committed larceny by trick because she tricked her neighbors into giving her possession of their money.

C. The woman has committed larceny by false pretenses because she tricked her neighbors into giving her title to their money.

D. The woman has committed larceny because knew at the time she posted the signs that she would keep the money for herself.

275. A woman managed a clothing store for its absentee owner; the woman made all the buying choices, paid the bills from the store account, and oversaw the staff. One afternoon, the woman took an outfit from the store without paying for it. She reasoned that she worked hard and deserved something new to wear.

Has the woman committed common law larceny?

A. No; the woman had lawful possession over the outfit and so did not unlawfully dispossess anyone when she took the outfit.

B. No; as the trusted store manager, the woman probably had the right to take from the store's inventory for her personal use.

C. Yes; the woman took an outfit without permission or payment, which is the same as if a customer had shoplifted from the store.

D. Yes; the woman only had custody over the outfit and so she unlawfully dispossessed the owner when she took the outfit.

276. The chief financial officer of a large corporation wanted to buy a new vacation home, but the bank turned him down for a loan. The officer began skimming money from one of the corporate accounts and saving the money in a special account for the house down payment. The officer's assistant noticed the discrepancy and asked him about it, but he lied to her and explained that the CEO of the company had authorized him to take the money from the corporate accounts.

What crime has the chief financial officer committed?

A. Larceny by trick, because the officer lied about his authority over the account.

B. Larceny by false pretenses, because the officer lied about what the CEO said.

C. Embezzlement, because the officer had lawful possession over the account.

D. Larceny, because the officer took personal property that did not belong to him.

277. The treasurer for a neighborhood association was having trouble paying her bills, but also anticipated that she would receive a large tax refund in a few months. To get by until she received the refund, the treasurer took money from the association's account. Once the treasurer received the refund, she paid back the money she had borrowed, with interest. Six months after that, a routine audit showed the unusual account activity. The neighborhood association president confronted the treasurer and accused her of embezzlement.

Did the treasurer embezzle from the neighborhood association?

A. No, because the treasurer paid the money back, with interest.

B. No, because the treasurer had lawful authority over the account.

C. Yes, because the treasurer converted the association's money for her own use.

D. Yes, because the treasurer did not first ask the president's permission.

278. A woman was visiting a friend at his house when she saw a watch sitting on the kitchen counter; the watch was similar to one the woman had recently misplaced. The woman was upset to realize that her friend might have stolen a watch from her and so she quickly put it in her pocket and left his house. Later, the friend realized the watch was missing and reported the woman to the police as the possible suspect in the theft.

When the police came to speak to the woman about the watch, she explained that she thought the watch was hers and that her friend had taken it from her. But the woman was mistaken, as the watch actually belonged to the friend's wife.

If the woman is later charged with larceny, does she have a defense?

A. No, because the watch was similar but not identical to the woman's watch, she was wrong to believe it was hers.

B. No, because the woman should have asked the friend if he stole the watch from her instead of jumping to conclusions.

C. Yes, because the woman reasonably thought the watch was hers, she lacked the *mens rea* for a larceny charge.

D. Yes, because the woman honestly thought the watch was hers, she lacked the *mens rea* for a larceny charge.

279. A woman needed money for a house down payment. Instead of applying for a mortgage, the woman decided to take a more direct approach. The woman drove to her bank and, pointing a gun at the teller, directed him to hand over $20,000. The teller was terrified and refused. The woman hit the teller across the face with the pistol, and he then did as she directed.

What crime has the woman committed?

A. Robbery, because she committed a larceny by force and by taking the money directly from the teller.

B. Bank robbery, because she stole from a bank by force and by taking money directly from the teller.

C. Larceny by force, because she committed larceny and used force when she hit the teller with the gun.

D. Taking title by force, because she took unlawful title to the bank's money and used force to do so.

280. A man was waiting in line at a farmer's market vegetable stand and was frustrated because the check-out clerk was moving so slowly. The man walked to the front of the line and told the clerk that he could not wait any longer and so he was just going to leave without paying for his vegetables. The man added that if the clerk called the police, he would slash the tires of her car. Afraid to confront the man because of the threat, the clerk allowed the man to walk away with several bags of vegetables.

Can the man be properly convicted of robbery?

A. No, because the man did not take anything of real value, only vegetables.

B. No, because the man only threatened future, conditional harm to property.

C. No, because the man took the vegetables from the stand, and not the clerk.

D. No, because the man was being rude, but that does not mean he is a criminal.

281. A young man was riding home on a city bus after work and fell asleep. The woman sitting across the aisle noticed that the young man was sleeping, and that he had an expensive laptop sitting on the seat next to him. The woman quietly changed her seat and then gently took the young man's laptop from the seat. The woman got off at the next stop. When the young man woke up a few minutes later, he realized that his laptop was gone.

Can the woman be properly charged with robbery?

A. No, because the young woman did not use any force to take the laptop from the young man's seat.

B. No, because the young man did not take adequate steps to protect his laptop while he slept.

C. Yes, because the woman forcefully interfered with the young man's personal bodily integrity.

D. Yes, because the woman took the laptop by force and directly from the young man's presence.

282. Two men came up with a plan to steal from a wealthy neighbor. One day while the neighbor was out jogging in the park, the first man came up to the neighbor and put a gun to her back. He told her to hold still or he would shoot her. While this was happening, the second man broke into the neighbor's house and stole all her jewelry.

Have the two men committed a robbery?

A. Yes, because the first man used force when he threatened the neighbor with a gun, while the second man simultaneously stole her jewelry.

B. Yes, because even though the jewelry was not taken from the neighbor's immediate presence, it was taken from an area she controlled.

C. No, because the men cannot be prosecuted for the same crime if they were not physically in the same place when that crime was committed.

D. No, because even though the first man used force against the neighbor, the jewelry was not taken from an area within her actual control.

283. A woman realized that her favorite bracelet was missing, and she suspected that her former roommate—who had borrowed the bracelet many times in past—had taken it when she moved out. The woman went to the former roommate's new house and rang the doorbell. When the former roommate answered, the woman saw that she was wearing a bracelet that looked just like hers; the woman demanded it back. The former roommate insisted that the bracelet was hers. The woman smacked the former roommate across the face, yanked the bracelet from her wrist, and drove back home.

The former roommate went to the police and filed a complaint. After the prosecutor was satisfied that the woman did not own the bracelet in question, he charged her with robbery.

Does the woman have a defense?

A. Yes, because the woman honestly thought the bracelet was hers, she lacked the *mens rea* for a robbery charge.

B. Yes, because the woman did not use any sort of weapon to take the bracelet back from the former roommate.

C. No, because even though the woman honestly thought the bracelet was hers, her use of force negates any defense.

D. No, because even though the woman reasonably thought the bracelet was hers, her use of force negates any defense.

284. A man coveted his neighbor's motorcycle. One night while the neighbor was sleeping, the man snuck over to his driveway and wheeled the motorcycle into his garage.

This jurisdiction's penal code includes the following definition of theft:

> A person commits theft if he willfully or knowingly obtains or exerts unauthorized control over property, and if the person:
>
> (1) intends to deprive the owner of the property;
>
> (2) willfully or knowingly uses, conceals, or abandons the property in a manner that deprives the owner of the property; or
>
> (3) uses, conceals, or abandons the property knowing the use, concealment, or abandonment probably will deprive the owner of the property.

Has the man committed theft, according to this statute?

A. No, because the man wheeled the motorcycle from the neighbor's driveway and did not carry it away, as required for larceny.

B. No, because the prosecutor cannot prove that the man intended to deprive the neighbor of the motorcycle, only that he coveted it.

C. Yes, because the man took the neighbor's motorcycle by trespass and carried it away, with the intent to permanently deprive him of it.

D. Yes, because the man intentionally took unauthorized control over the motorcycle and hid it so the neighbor could not use it.

285. A state's penal code divides theft into different categories, based on the value of the property stolen. Under the penal code, theft of property valued between $750 and $1,500 is an aggravated misdemeanor, and theft of property over $1,500 is a felony.

A man purchased a new laptop for $1,700 and, two days later, his friend stole it. The friend was charged with felony theft, but filed a motion to quash the charges or, in the alternative, reduce the charge to a misdemeanor. According to the friend, he would not be able to resell the laptop for more than $1,000.

Should the friend's motion prevail?

A. Yes; if the laptop is worth less than $1,000, the friend should not be charged with felony theft.

B. Yes; the laptop's value should be evaluated based on its current value and not its purchase price.

C. No; because the laptop was brand-new, its value should be based on the purchase price.

D. No; the laptop probably had some emotional value to the man, as well as monetary value.

Solicitation

286. A law student joined a study group and was tasked with outlining the inchoate offenses for the group's criminal law outline.

What definition should the student provide for the crime of solicitation?

A. Solicitation occurs when a person asks, commands, incites, counsels, induces, urges, or encourages another person to commit a crime.

B. Solicitation occurs when a person asks, commands, incites, counsels, induces, urges, or encourages another person to commit a crime, with the intent that the crime be committed.

C. Solicitation occurs when a person asks, commands, incites, counsels, induces, urges, or encourages another person to join her in the commission of a crime.

D. Solicitation occurs when a person asks, commands, incites, counsels, induces, urges, or encourages another person to assist in the commission of a crime.

287. A woman went out for drinks with her friend. During the discussion, the woman confided that she had recently discovered her boyfriend had cheated on her. The woman was very upset and asked her friend what she thought she should do. The friend jokingly replied, "I would kill him if I were you."

Is the friend guilty of solicitation to commit murder?

A. Yes, because the friend counseled the woman to commit a crime, i.e., to murder her boyfriend.

B. Yes, because the woman was upset and vulnerable and probably could not tell the friend was joking.

C. No, because the friend was joking, she did not intend that the woman murder her boyfriend.

D. No, because the friend did not suggest anything the woman had probably not already considered.

288. A man was talking with his husband about how he was having a tough time at work because his supervisor was so demanding. The conversation continued:

> *The man*: I should really do something about this awful situation at work.
>
> *The husband*: Why don't you slash her tires?
>
> *The man*: You really think that's a good idea?
>
> *The husband*: Sure, then she'll know how you really feel.

At what point in this conversation did a solicitation occur?

A. When the man stated that he should really do something about the awful situation at work.

B. When the husband replied that the man should slash the tires on the supervisor's car.

C. When the man asked the husband whether he really thought slashing the tires was a good idea.

D. When the husband replied that by slashing the tires, the supervisor would know how the man really felt.

289. A wealthy woman had grown sick of her husband, and so she decided to kill him. The wealthy woman told her gardener about the plan and asked if she could borrow his handgun. The wealthy woman told the gardener she would fire him if he said no, and so the gardener complied with the wealthy woman's request. Two days later, the police learned of the wealthy woman's plan and arrested her.

Can the prosecutor properly charge the wealthy woman with solicitation to commit murder?

A. No, because the wealthy woman asked the gardener for his gun so she could commit the crime herself.

B. No, because when the gardener provided the gun, the solicitation merged into a completed conspiracy.

C. Yes, because the wealthy woman asked the gardener to commit a crime, i.e., to provide a murder weapon.

D. Yes, because the wealthy woman took advantage of the gardener's employment status to access to the gun.

290. A prisoner wrote a letter to her brother, offering to pay him to kill her ex-husband, who had testified against her at trial. She placed the letter in the prison mail but it was intercepted by prison authorities. The prosecutor charged the prisoner with solicitation to commit murder. In this jurisdiction:

> Every person who, with the intent that the crime be committed, solicits another to commit murder shall be punished by imprisonment in the state prison for no more than nine years. A solicitation must be communicated.

Can the prisoner be convicted of this crime?

A. Yes, because otherwise, the prisoner will be rewarded for her bad conduct and the prison authorities will be punished for their diligence.

B. Yes, because when the prisoner offered to pay her brother to kill the ex-husband, she solicited another to commit murder, as required by the statute.

C. No, because the sister's request to her brother only marked the beginning of the negotiations, and no other details were discussed.

D. No; because the letter was never received by its intended recipient, the prisoner can instead be convicted of attempted solicitation.

291. A professor coveted her dean's vintage sports car and wanted it for her own. After stealing the car keys from the dean's office, the professor handed them to one of her students and falsely explained that that she just bought the car from the dean. The professor asked the student if he would take the car from the parking lot and drive it to her house.

Has the professor solicited the student to commit a crime?

A. Yes; the professor has asked the student to steal valuable property that does not belong to him.

B. Yes; the professor has asked the student to commit a crime, which makes the student complicit.

C. No; the professor has only asked the student to move the car, and so no crime has been committed.

D. No; the professor is using the student to commit a crime for her, and so she has not solicited a crime.

292. A man broke up with his boyfriend after he learned that the boyfriend had cheated on him. The man was devastated and asked his co-worker if she would beat up the boyfriend. The woman agreed. The woman later had a change of heart and reported the conversation to the police, who arrested the man.

How should the prosecutor properly charge the man?

A. The man should be charged with solicitation to commit battery because he asked the woman to commit a crime (battery).

B. The man should be charged with conspiracy to commit battery because he and the woman agreed to commit a crime (battery).

C. The man should not be charged with any crime because the woman went to the police and the battery was not committed.

D. The man should be charged with both solicitation and conspiracy because the merger rule does not apply to conspiracy.

293. A woman was angry with her neighbor and so offered her brother $1,000 to kill her. The brother said nothing in response, but the next day he shot and killed the neighbor. Two weeks after that, the woman was arrested. The prosecutor is now contemplating whether to charge the woman with solicitation to commit murder.

Can the woman be properly charged with this crime?

A. No, because the solicitation merged into the completed crime of murder.

B. No, because it is unclear if the brother acted because of the woman's request.

C. Yes, because the woman offered her brother money to commit a murder.

D. Yes, because it is clear that the brother acted because of the woman's request.

294. A woman had cared for her elderly father for many years, and it had become a tremendous financial, emotional, and financial burden. One day when the woman was feeling particularly frustrated, she posted an anonymous advertisement on a website, trying to recruit a hit man to kill her father. The woman quickly regretted the post and retracted it a few hours later. But the police saw the post and arrested her. The woman was charged with solicitation to commit murder.

In a jurisdiction that follows the common law, can the woman claim a defense of abandonment?

A. Yes, because the woman voluntarily and completely renounced her criminal purpose, and her father is not in any danger.

B. Yes, because the woman was under a lot of stress when she posted the advertisement and was not thinking clearly.

C. No, because the crime of solicitation was complete as soon as the woman posted the advertisement online.

D. No, because online postings never really disappear and so one can never abandon a virtual solicitation.

295. A teenage girl bet her friends $50 that she could persuade one of their teachers to have sex with her. One week, the girl tried to flirt with the teacher on a class trip, but the teacher did not respond in kind. The next week, the girl asked the teacher for a ride home, explaining that her car had broken down. The teacher reluctantly agreed. Once at the house, the girl invited the teacher inside and told him that since her parents were out of town, they could have sex and no one would ever find out.

Can the girl be properly charged with solicitation to commit statutory rape?

A. No; the girl is protected by the statutory rape law and so cannot be convicted of solicitation to commit statutory rape.

B. No; the girl only suggested to the teacher that they have sex, and did not invite, ask, induce, or encourage him to have sex.

C. Yes; despite the fact that the girl is protected by the statutory rape law, she needs to be taught that her actions are wrong.

D. Yes; the girl invited and encouraged her adult teacher to commit a crime, i.e., to commit the crime of statutory rape.

Attempt

296. A lawyer volunteered to serve on a state bar committee, which was tasked with writing model jury instructions for criminal cases. The committee chair asked the lawyer to draft a proposed definition for the crime of attempt.

What definition should the lawyer propose?

A. An attempt occurs when a defendant, with the intent to commit a specific crime, takes a substantial step beyond mere preparation and commits that crime.

B. An attempt occurs when a defendant, with the intent to commit a specific crime, is fully prepared to commit that crime.

C. An attempt occurs when a defendant, with the intent to commit a specific crime, takes a substantial step beyond mere preparation and toward committing that crime.

D. An attempt occurs when a defendant, with the intent to commit a specific crime, completes the preparation to commit that crime.

297. A middle-aged man detested his elderly mother. After thinking of all the terrible things she had done to him over the years, the man resolved to get even. Knowing that his mother was housebound, the man decided to set fire to her house—hoping that she would die either from the fire or from smoke inhalation. The man mentioned his decision to his girlfriend, who quickly reported him to the police.

Can the man be properly prosecuted for the attempted murder of his mother?

A. Yes, because the man developed a specific plan to kill his mother and the only missing step was putting the plan in action.

B. Yes, because unless the man is prosecuted, he will carry out his plan and kill his defenseless and elderly mother.

C. No, because although the man developed a specific plan to kill his mother, he still might change his mind and abandon his plan.

D. No, because although the man has developed a specific plan to kill his mother, he has not committed any sort of *actus reus*.

298. A college student disliked her roommate and decided to kill her. The college student methodically researched different types of lethal poisons and identified one that could be placed in the roommate's food and would be undetectable during an autopsy. One night when she thought the roommate wasn't looking, the college student sprinkled poison on the roommate's pizza; the college student then went out to a movie. But the roommate saw what the college student did and did not eat the pizza.

What crime has the college student committed?

A. Criminal attempt.

B. Attempted murder.

C. Attempt.

D. No crime, because the roommate did not eat the pizza.

299. A man had a gambling problem. The man developed a plan to rob a bank and use the proceeds from the crime to pay his debts. The man robbed the bank and then returned home. Three hours later, police arrested him.

How should the man be charged?

A. With robbery, because the man robbed the bank.

B. With attempted robbery, because the man was arrested before he could pay his debts, which was part of the larger plan.

C. The man should not be charged at all, because he was arrested before he paid his debts, which was part of the larger plan.

D. With attempted robbery and robbery, because the man planned to rob the bank and then robbed the bank.

300. A man broke up with his boyfriend. The boyfriend responded by hammering nails into the tires on the man's car. The next morning as the man was driving to work, two of the tires blew out and he lost control of the car. The car smashed into a concrete barrier and the man was badly injured.

Can the boyfriend be properly convicted of attempted murder?

A. No, because when the boyfriend intentionally hammered nails into the tires, he could not reasonably foresee that they would blow out.

B. No, because the boyfriend did not intend to kill the man, although he did act intentionally when he hammered nails into the tires.

C. Yes, because the boyfriend intentionally hammered nails into the tires, which constituted a substantial step beyond mere preparation.

D. Yes, because when the boyfriend intentionally hammered nails into the tires, he should have reasonably foreseen that they would blow out.

301. A woman walked into a bank, gun in hand. An off-duty police officer inside the bank noticed the woman and immediately stopped her. After her arrest, police discovered that the woman was wearing a wig, prosthetic nose, and a significant amount of make-up. When these items were removed, the woman looked much different. The woman was charged with attempted robbery and refused to give a statement to the police.

Prior to trial, the woman moved to dismiss the charges, claiming that since she would not give a statement the prosecutor could not prove that she had the *mens rea* for attempted robbery.

How should the prosecutor respond?

A. The woman's *mens rea* can be established by the fact that she wore a wig and make-up into the bank, a federally regulated facility.

B. The woman's *mens rea* can be established by the fact that she brought a gun into the bank, a federally regulated facility.

C. The woman's *mens rea* can be established by the gun in her hand and that she disguised her appearance inside the bank.

D. The woman's *mens rea* can be established by the fact that she wore a prosthetic nose without any legitimate reason to do so.

302. A woman set fire to a house that she thought was empty, wanting to watch the flames blaze in the night sky. The woman did not realize that a man was sleeping inside. A neighbor saw and reported the fire, and emergency workers were able to rescue the man and put out the fire. The woman has now been charged with attempted felony murder.

In a jurisdiction following the majority approach to this crime, can the woman be properly convicted as charged?

A. No, because the woman had no intent to kill and attempt crimes require an intent to commit the target crime.

B. No, because the woman did not know the man was in the house and so did not have malice, the *mens rea* for murder.

C. Yes, because when she intentionally set fire to the house, the woman took a substantial step toward killing the man.

D. Yes, because when she intentionally set fire to the house, the woman showed reckless indifference toward the man's life.

303. A man bought a new handgun and decided to have some fun by shooting out the windows of an abandoned house near where he lived. After firing several shots, the man heard a howling sound coming from inside the house. The man ran into the house and found a young woman, shot in the arm. The young woman was homeless and had been staying in the house. The man rushed the young woman to the hospital, where she was treated and released.

The prosecutor has charged the man with attempted depraved heart murder.

Can he be properly convicted of this crime?

A. Yes, because the man's act of shooting into the house is a classic example of depraved heart murder.

B. Yes, because the man's acts showed a deliberate indifference to the value of human life, a form of malice.

C. No, because attempt crimes require specific intent, and one cannot specifically intend an accident.

D. No, because attempt crimes require specific intent, and the man did not know anyone was in the house.

304. A woman learned that her boyfriend had cheated on her. Furious, the woman decided to get even with him by burning down his house. The woman filled a glass bottle with gasoline and fashioned a wick from a piece of cloth.

What crime has the woman committed?

A. Attempted arson, because the woman completed all necessary steps in preparation to commit arson.

B. Attempted arson, because the woman completed most of the necessary steps in preparation to commit arson.

C. No crime, because the woman did not set fire to the boyfriend's house and so did not commit arson.

D. No crime, because the woman has not taken a substantial step beyond preparing to commit arson.

305. A man planned to burglarize the home of a local jeweler. The man followed the jeweler home after work one day and saw that at 8:00 P.M., she left her house and drove to the gym. The next night around 7:45 P.M. the man drove to the jeweler's house and parked his car one block away.

What the man did not realize is that while he had been watching the jeweler, the police had been watching him. As soon as the man parked his car, the police arrested him. The man has now been charged with attempted burglary of the jeweler's house.

Can the man be properly convicted of this crime?

A. Yes, because the man was only 15 minutes away from committing the burglary when he was arrested by the police.

B. Yes, because the man was only one block away from the jeweler's house when he was arrested by the police.

C. No, because the man was still preparing to burglarize the jeweler's house when he was arrested by the police.

D. No, because the man had not taken a substantial step beyond preparing to burglarize the jeweler's house.

306. A woman learned that her co-worker had accused her of embezzling from the company where they both worked. The next day, the woman left work a little early and went to the company parking lot. The woman crouched behind a bush near the co-worker's parked car; in her hand, the woman held a sock filled with rocks.

As the co-worker was walking to her car, she noticed the woman crouched in the bushes. The co-worker called the police and the woman was arrested. The woman was later charged with attempted battery.

Can the woman be properly convicted of this crime?

A. Yes, because by crouching in the bushes with a weapon in her hand, the woman crossed the line from preparation to perpetration.

B. Yes, because the woman had a solid motive to want to harm the co-worker, which can be used to establish her guilt.

C. No, because the woman was caught before she had an opportunity to hit the co-worker and so did not take a step beyond preparation.

D. No, because the woman could have changed her mind and was stopped before she could exhibit her full *mens rea*.

307. A woman thought her neighbor was gossiping about her and stealing her mail. The woman made a little cloth doll that resembled the neighbor and stuck pins in it, sincerely believing that this would cause the neighbor's death. The neighbor was completely unaffected by the woman's actions.

When the police learned about the doll and the pins, they arrested the woman. The prosecutor charged the woman with attempted murder.

How should the woman defend herself against this charge?

A. The woman should claim she is not responsible by reason of insanity.

B. The woman should claim that the charged crime is impossible.

C. The woman should point out that the neighbor suffered no harm.

D. The woman should claim that she suffers from a diminished capacity.

308. A man advertised online for a "young girl" who would be willing to accompany him on a trip overseas. He received a response from someone who said that she liked older men, wanted to get away from school and her parents, and that she was 14 years old—but looked like she was 21. The man emailed back, suggesting a meeting at the local mall. The man also attached several photos of his genitalia to his message.

As the man arrived at the mall for the meeting, he was arrested. He later learned that he had emailed with a middle-aged male state police trooper and that the 14-year-old girl did not exist. The prosecutor charged the man with attempted distribution of pornographic material to a minor. Prior to trial, the defense filed a motion to dismiss, arguing that the crime was impossible to commit because no minor was involved. This jurisdiction follows a modern approach to impossibility defenses.

How should the judge rule?

A. The charges should be dismissed; because there was no minor, there could be no attempt to distribute anything to that minor.

B. The charges should be dismissed; the police arrested the man as he arrived at the mall and as he was still preparing to commit the crime.

C. The motion should be denied; the man has demonstrated that he is dangerous and to allow him this defense would ignore that fact.

D. The motion should be denied; by sending the photos, the man took a substantial step toward commission of the crime.

309. A woman walked into a bank, gun in hand, with the intent of robbing it. The woman walked up to the teller, gave her a note that demanded money, and displayed the gun. The teller began to shake and cry; she explained that this was her first day at work and she would be fired if she had to turn over the bank's money. The woman felt sorry for the teller, holstered her gun, and left the bank.

The woman was later arrested and charged with attempted bank robbery. The woman wants to defend herself by claiming that she abandoned her criminal purpose.

Should the woman's defense be allowed?

A. Yes; the fact-finder should be made aware of the woman's change of heart and permitted to give effect to that change of heart when rendering a verdict.

B. Yes; despite the woman's demand for money, her decision to end the robbery shows that her *mens rea* voluntarily changed, from criminal to noncriminal.

C. No; the woman only abandoned the bank robbery because she felt sorry for the teller and not because she realized that it is wrong to rob banks.

D. No; the woman had the *mens rea* for robbery and by demanding money and showing her gun, took a substantial step toward commission of the crime.

310. A man was devoted to his elderly father, who had dementia and lived in a nursing home. The man decided to put an end to his father's suffering.

At the man's next visit to the nursing home, he picked up a pillow and held it several inches above his father's face. But after a minute, the man put down the pillow. He later told his wife, "as I was holding that pillow, I realized what I was doing was wrong." But there was a hidden safety camera in the father's room, and the nursing home staff reported the man to the police. He was charged with attempted murder.

If this jurisdiction recognizes the abandonment defense, should the man be acquitted?

A. Yes; the man's statement to his wife demonstrates that he voluntarily and completely renounced his criminal intent to kill his father.

B. Yes; the man's intention to end his father's suffering was a noble one, and since the man didn't kill his father, no crime was actually committed.

C. No; the man had the intent to kill his father and by holding the pillow above his head, he took a substantial step toward commission of the crime.

D. No; no one has the right to take another person's life, no matter how much they love that other person or how much the other person is suffering.

Conspiracy

311. After realizing that they did not have enough money for their summer vacation, two men agreed to rob a bank. In preparation for the robbery, the two men bought weapons and face masks.

What crime has been committed?

A. Criminal attempt.

B. Attempted bank robbery.

C. Conspiracy to commit bank robbery.

D. No crime has yet been committed.

312. Two sorority sisters accepted a bet that they could not raise $10,000 for charity in a month. Halfway through the month, the sisters realized that they might lose the bet, so they decided to boost their fundraising by taking money from the sorority's grocery fund.

Have the sorority sisters committed a crime?

A. Yes; the sorority sisters agreed to raise money for charity by committing theft.

B. Yes; the sorority sisters deceived their sorority by taking from the grocery fund.

C. No; the sorority sisters are raising money for charity, which is not a crime.

D. No; the sorority sisters likely contributed to the fund and so can take from it.

313. A woman and her sister co-owned a house that they rented for extra income. After living in the house for a month, a renter demanded several repairs and threatened to withhold her rent unless the repairs were made. Annoyed, the woman and her sister decided to kill the renter. One afternoon when the renter was at work, the woman went to the house and blocked the exhaust vent for the furnace. Later that night, the renter came home and turned on the heat. The renter died in her sleep of carbon monoxide poisoning.

How should the prosecutor properly charge the woman?

A. Conspiracy to commit murder, attempted murder, and murder.

B. Conspiracy to commit murder and murder.

C. First degree premeditated and intentional murder.

D. Conspiracy to commit murder and attempted murder.

314. A woman and her wife were short on money and could not pay their mortgage. The women decided to rob their local bank and use the proceeds to pay off their debt. The women got into their car to drive directly to the bank, but police immediately arrested them as they were about to pull out of their driveway.

If the women never left their driveway, why should they be charged with conspiracy and punished?

A. To help the jurisdiction maintain accurate crime statistics.

B. To send a message that it is wrong to rob banks.

C. To let the women know that their actions are wrong.

D. Because group criminality is dangerous.

315. Two college gymnasts were angry with a teammate whose poor performance had cost the team the state championship. The two gymnasts decided to teach the teammate a lesson by putting poison in her protein shake. The two gymnasts went to the store and purchased rat poison to put in the teammate's shake.

What crime have the gymnasts committed?

A. No crime, because the gymnasts have not yet crossed the line between preparation and perpetration.

B. Conspiracy to commit battery, because they agreed to commit a battery and have the intent to commit a battery.

C. Attempted battery, because they agreed to commit a battery and took a substantial step by buying the poison.

D. Conspiracy to commit battery, because the purchase of the rat poison shows the agreement to commit a crime.

316. A brother called his sister to ask if she would help him rob a drug dealer. The brother told the sister that all he needed was a ride to and from the drug dealer's house, and she would not need to come inside or participate in the robbery. The sister agreed but had no real intention of helping her brother. Instead, as soon as the sister got off the phone with her brother, she called the police and reported him.

What crime has the sister committed?

A. No crime, because the sister lacked the *mens rea* for conspiracy.

B. No crime, because the sister lacked the *mens rea* for robbery.

C. Conspiracy to commit robbery, because the target crime was not completed.

D. Conspiracy to commit robbery, because the sister agreed to commit a crime.

317. An undercover officer infiltrated a drug ring and earned the trust of its members. One day, a drug ring member suggested to the undercover officer that they kill the ringleader and assume leadership of the drug ring. The undercover officer agreed. The two men met that night and drove to the ringleader's house for the hit. But because the undercover officer had alerted his supervisor to the plan, police pulled them over a mile from the ringleader's house. The police arrested the drug ring member and the prosecutor later charged him with conspiracy to commit murder.

Prior to trial, the defense filed a motion to quash the charge, arguing that there was no real agreement because the undercover officer never intended to kill the ringleader. This jurisdiction takes a modern approach to conspiracy law.

How should the judge rule on the motion?

A. The motion should be denied; the undercover officer pretending to agree is all that is required for a bilateral agreement under modern law.

B. The motion should be denied; the drug ring member thought he was entering into an agreement to kill the ringleader, which is sufficient.

C. The motion should be granted; modern conspiracy laws require a bilateral agreement and the undercover officer only pretended to agree.

D. The motion should be granted; the drug ring member was entrapped when the undercover officer pretended to agree to kill the ringleader.

318. Two men, driving on a highway, pulled over for gas. The men went into the gas station store together. Seeing that there was only one clerk in the store, the first man looked at the second man and smiled and then nodded at the clerk; the second man smiled back. The first man pulled out a gun and asked the clerk for the money in the cash register. The clerk pulled out her gun and shot and killed the first man.

The second man has now been charged with conspiracy to commit robbery and murder. His attorney has filed a motion to dismiss the conspiracy charge, arguing that the prosecutor cannot prove an agreement to commit a crime.

How should the judge rule on the motion?

A. The motion should be granted because an agreement cannot be established without the first man's testimony.

B. The motion should be granted because there was no agreement of any kind between the two men.

C. The motion should be denied because an agreement can be inferred from the attendant circumstances.

D. The motion should be denied because to do otherwise would violate the doctrine of *mortui non morden*.

319. Two co-workers met for some wine and gossip. One co-worker confessed she disliked their mutual supervisor and suggested that they kill her. The supervisor had recently placed the other co-worker on probation due to his poor performance and so he readily agreed that they should kill the supervisor.

What crime have the co-workers committed?

A. No crime, because the co-workers had not taken any acts in furtherance of their shared goal to kill the supervisor.

B. No crime, because the co-workers have no plan for how to kill the supervisor and have only agreed on the goal to kill her.

C. Conspiracy to commit murder, because the co-workers agreed to commit a crime, i.e., to kill their supervisor.

D. Conspiracy to commit attempted murder, because the co-workers agreed to try to commit a crime, i.e., to kill their supervisor.

320. A man and a woman were drinking beer one afternoon when the woman told the man that she had always disliked his wife. The man laughed and explained that he was about to ask his wife for a divorce because he did not like her either. The woman suggested that they kill the wife instead and then split the proceeds from her life insurance. The man agreed.

In a modern jurisdiction, what crime have the man and woman committed?

A. No crime, because neither the man nor the woman has taken any action in furtherance of the agreement to commit murder.

B. No crime, because the man and the woman were drinking beer and clearly not serious about their agreement to kill the wife.

C. Conspiracy to commit murder, because the man and the woman agreed to commit a crime, i.e., to kill the wife.

D. The woman has not committed any crime, but the man has committed adultery and conspiracy to commit adultery.

321. A woman decided to have her ex-husband killed, and hired a hit man to shoot him as he ran in an upcoming marathon. At the hit man's suggestion, the woman called her ex-husband and casually asked him if he was still planning on running in the marathon. The ex-husband explained that due to a hamstring injury, he wouldn't be able to compete in the marathon.

In a modern jurisdiction, what crime has been committed?

A. No crime; the woman's call to her ex-husband was legal, and so cannot constitute an overt act committed in furtherance of the conspiracy.

B. No crime; the woman's call to her ex-husband was preparatory, and so cannot constitute an overt act committed in furtherance of the conspiracy.

C. Conspiracy to commit murder, because the woman's call to her ex-husband was an overt act committed in furtherance of the conspiracy.

D. The woman has committed conspiracy to commit murder because she made the phone call, but the hit man has not committed any crime.

322. A man and his sister hatched a plan to steal money from unsuspecting older people by using personal information collected from phishing emails. The police learned of the plan and arrested the man, but the police could not locate the sister. While the man was in jail awaiting trial, the sister continued to send phishing emails and steal money. The police were able to establish that man and his sister stole $2 million before the man's arrest, and the sister stole another $2 million on her own, after his arrest.

The man has been charged with conspiracy, theft of $4 million, and various computer crimes. In a pretrial motion, the man argued that he should not be responsible for any crimes committed after his arrest.

How should the prosecutor respond?

A. The man is responsible for the conspiracy and all reasonably foreseeable crimes committed in furtherance of the conspiracy.

B. The man is responsible for the conspiracy and any crimes he personally committed in furtherance of the conspiracy.

C. The man is responsible for the conspiracy and all crimes committed by his co-conspirators, regardless of their foreseeability.

D. The man is responsible for the conspiracy and for all reasonably foreseeable crimes committed until his arrest.

323. A woman agreed to drive her neighbor to a liquor store so he could rob it, and to be a lookout during the robbery. During the robbery, the neighbor sexually assaulted one store customer and shot and killed another. The woman and the neighbor were arrested the following day.

The woman was charged with conspiracy to commit robbery, robbery, sexual assault, and murder. The defense has filed a motion to dismiss the sexual assault and murder charges, arguing that the woman only agreed to help with the robbery and so is only responsible for crimes related to that charge.

How should the judge rule on the motion?

A. The judge should dismiss the sexual assault charge because it was not reasonably foreseeable that the man would commit that crime.

B. The judge should dismiss the sexual assault and murder charges because the woman only conspired to commit the robbery of the liquor store.

C. The judge should deny the motion because as a co-conspirator, the woman is responsible for all crimes committed with the target crime.

D. The judge should deny the motion because as a co-conspirator, the woman is responsible for all crimes committed by her fellow conspirators.

324. A college student bought marijuana from a woman who lived in his apartment building. The marijuana sold by the woman came from a local farmer. One day, police arrested the college student for drunk driving and found some marijuana during a search of his car; the college student gave police the name of the woman. The police next arrested the woman, and she gave police the name of the farmer. When the farmer was arrested, police seized a large amount of dried marijuana from his farm.

The prosecutor has charged the college student, the woman, and the farmer with a single drug conspiracy. The college student's attorney has filed a motion to dismiss, arguing that while he knew the woman got her marijuana from an unidentified grower, he had no idea the farmer had such a large amount of marijuana at his farm. The college student also argued that he should only be charged, if at all, in a conspiracy with the woman because he never met the farmer or didn't even know his name.

How should the judge rule on the motion?

A. The judge should instruct the prosecutor that she can only charge a conspiracy between the college student and the woman.

B. The judge should wait for the evidence at trial to see if the college student is telling the truth about not knowing the farmer.

C. The judge should deny the motion because the facts demonstrate a three-person conspiracy to buy and sell marijuana.

D. The judge should grant the motion because the college student cannot conspire with someone he does not know.

325. An insurance agent offered to provide medical insurance billing to a local physician in return for a percentage of his reimbursements. The physician agreed. In the first year working with the insurance agent, the physician doubled his income. At a dinner party held at the agent's urging, the physician introduced the agent to three of his colleagues. The colleagues agreed to hire the agent on the same terms, and she quickly doubled their incomes, too.

The police later arrested the insurance agent and all four physicians, and the prosecutor charged them with a single conspiracy to commit insurance fraud. The physicians' defense attorneys filed motions to dismiss, arguing that none of the physicians were aware that the insurance agent was committing acts of fraud with the others. As such, the defense attorneys argued that the case involved a series of two-person conspiracies.

How should the prosecutor respond?

A. This was a single conspiracy because the agent was acting as a central hub, each physician had an identical, parallel arrangement with her, and the physicians knew one another.

B. This was a single conspiracy because the agent was acting as a central hub, she had an ongoing relationship with each physician, and each physician shared the broader criminal objective.

C. This was a single conspiracy because the agent was acting as a central hub, and each physician had an identical, parallel arrangement with the agent.

D. This was a single conspiracy because the agent was acting as a central hub, and each physician had to know the agent was committing some sort of fraud.

326. A man who lived in California sold tens of thousands of marijuana pipes over the internet; most of the sales were on the West Coast, but the man sold one pipe to a customer in Pennsylvania. The man was charged in a Pennsylvania court with taking part in a large conspiracy with dozens of other internet drug paraphernalia merchants.

The man called his long-time criminal lawyer in California and complained about the unfairness of having to defend himself in the Pennsylvania court—far away from his home and in a state where he had only sold one pipe. The man asked the lawyer whether a motion to dismiss raising these concerns would succeed.

How should the lawyer respond?

A. The motion will be successful because charging the man in Pennsylvania violates his rights under the Due Process Clauses of the United States Constitution.

B. The motion will be successful because the doctrine of *forum non conveniens* allows a person charged with a crime to demand his trial occur in a court closer to his home.

C. The motion will be unsuccessful because the proper venue for a conspiracy trial includes any jurisdiction where an act in furtherance of the conspiracy was committed.

D. The motion will be unsuccessful because the man participated in the global economy and now must pay the price—defending himself far from home—for his actions.

327. Three high school football players were suspended from playing in an upcoming game. Angry, they decided to break into the school and vandalize the principal's office. Later that night, the three met in the school parking lot as planned. But one of the players had second thoughts and told the others that he thought it would be wrong to continue. He begged them to reconsider, but they went ahead anyway.

Later, all three were arrested and charged with conspiracy to commit burglary and vandalism, as well as burglary and vandalism. At trial, the non-participating player claimed that he withdrew from the conspiracy. The judge accepted this defense.

What should the final ruling be?

A. The nonparticipating player should be acquitted of all charges and exonerated.

B. The nonparticipating player should be convicted of conspiracy only, because he communicated his withdrawal to his co-conspirators.

C. The nonparticipating player should be convicted of all charges, but will have a strong argument for leniency at sentencing.

D. The nonparticipating player should be convicted of all charges because he has no independent proof that he withdrew from the conspiracy.

328. A married woman had an affair with her unmarried co-worker. When the woman's husband discovered the affair, he called the police. The local prosecutor then charged the woman and the unmarried co-worker with conspiracy to commit adultery and adultery—a felony in this jurisdiction.

How should woman's attorney defend her at trial?

A. The defense attorney should plan to ask the judge to overturn the verdict if necessary, if the jury convicts the woman after hearing the evidence at trial.

B. The defense attorney should reach out to the legislature, to see if she can get the adultery statute rescinded before the woman's trial begins.

C. The defense attorney should concede that the woman committed both crimes, but should argue that the antiquated charges call for leniency in sentencing.

D. The defense attorney should argue that since adultery already requires a plurality, the woman cannot be convicted of conspiracy to commit adultery.

329. A high school teacher and a high school sophomore had sex one night after a school football game. The sophomore told his parents what happened, and the parents called the police. During the police investigation, the teacher told the police that the sophomore had seduced her, and that having sex had been the sophomore's idea.

Based on the teacher's statement, the prosecutor charged the sophomore with conspiracy to criminal sexual conduct with a minor.

How should the sophomore defend himself at trial?

A. The sophomore should argue that as a juvenile, his brain has not fully matured and so he cannot form the necessary *mens rea* for conspiracy.

B. The sophomore should argue that he since he is expressly protected by statutory rape laws, he cannot be convicted of conspiring to break those laws.

C. The sophomore should challenge the teacher's claim that the sex was his idea, and should focus on how the teacher took advantage of him.

D. The sophomore should argue that in the absence of DNA or other forensic evidence, the prosecutor cannot prove that a sexual act occurred.

330. After a bitter divorce, a woman asked her friend for help in murdering her ex-husband. The friend agreed. The women purchased handguns and then went to the ex-husband's house one evening with the intention of shooting him through a window. But the women did not realize that the ex-husband had moved from the house the week before and the house was empty. Before the women fired any shots, though, they were arrested by the police. The prosecutor charged the women with conspiracy to commit murder. In defense, the women argued that the crime was impossible because the ex-husband no longer lived in the house.

Should the court accept the women's defense?

A. No; the ex-husband may have moved from the house but the women were still acting as a dangerous group.

B. No; although the women did not kill the ex-husband as they intended, they might still kill him later.

C. Yes; the women were caught by the police before they were able to fire shots into the empty house.

D. Yes; the house was empty and so it would have been impossible for the women to kill anyone inside.

Part III

Defenses

Classification of Defenses

331. A burglar broke into a house one night and tried to sexually assault the homeowner while she slept. The homeowner shot and killed the burglar before the assault could be completed. After an investigation, the police recommended to the prosecutor that no charges be filed against the homeowner because she acted in self-defense.

What is the meaning of the police recommendation?

A. The police have concluded that the homeowner's actions should be excused.

B. The police have concluded that the homeowner's actions were justified.

C. The police have concluded that the burglar probably deserved what he got.

D. The police have concluded that the homeowner did not kill intentionally.

332. One evening, a woman and her wife were driving home from dinner when the wife passed out. The woman tried to resuscitate her wife but she remained unconscious. The woman shoved her wife from the driver's seat and then quickly drove the wife to a nearby hospital.

After police learned that the woman's license had been suspended the year before due to drunk driving, she was charged with driving without a valid license and violating the terms of her probation. The woman wants to defend herself by claiming necessity.

What type of defense does the woman propose?

A. A justification, because the woman is claiming that she made the right choice under the circumstances.

B. An excuse, because the woman is claiming that she is not morally culpable for driving without a license.

C. The woman is claiming both that she was justified and should be excused, and that she should be acquitted.

D. The woman is claiming that due to the unusual circumstances, the prosecutor cannot meet her burden of proof.

333. A woman walked into a shopping mall, pulled out a gun, and shot and killed two shoppers. The woman was charged with two counts of murder. At trial, the woman claimed insanity and presented an expert who testified that because of the woman's significant mental health problems, she sincerely believed that killing the shoppers was the right thing to do. The prosecution offered its own expert, who testified that the woman was not mentally ill at all and was malingering. The jury found the woman not guilty by reason of insanity.

What is the meaning of the jury's verdict?

A. The jury ignored the testimony offered by the prosecution expert.

B. The jury agreed with the woman that she was right to kill the shoppers.

C. The jury believed that the woman is not morally responsible for her actions.

D. The jury felt the defense expert was better than the prosecution expert.

334. A man learned that his wife was going to leave him for someone else. Despondent, the man went to a local bar and got very drunk. As he was finishing his last beer, the man's wife walked into the bar with her new lover. The man pulled out his gun and shot and killed both of them.

The man was charged with first degree murder in a jurisdiction that recognizes voluntary intoxication as a partial defense to homicide. The man wants to pursue this defense.

What type of defense does the man propose?

A. A justification, because the man claims that he was right to kill his wife and her lover.

B. An excuse, because the man claims that he lacks the moral culpability for first degree murder.

C. The man is not claiming justification or excuse, but that his wife and her lover deserved to die.

D. Neither, because the man is instead claiming that he lacked the *mens rea* for first degree murder.

335. A police officer was charged with accepting a bribe in violation of the following statute:

> A peace officer who receives from a defendant or from any other person any money or other valuable thing for omitting or delaying to arrest any defendant is guilty of a misdemeanor.

The officer was also charged with conspiracy to violate the statute. Prior to trial, the defense filed a motion to dismiss, arguing that the conspiracy charge violated Wharton's Rule.

How should the defense argument be categorized?

A. As a justification, because the officer's actions were permitted under the circumstances.

B. As an excuse, because the officer's actions were understandable under the circumstances.

C. As both a justification and an excuse, Wharton's Rule meets the criteria for both types of defense.

D. As neither a justification nor an excuse, but as a reason to dismiss the conspiracy charge.

Mistake

336. A college student was charged with receiving stolen property, which is defined as "receiving, retaining, or disposing of the property of another, knowing that it was stolen or probably stolen, and with the intent to permanently deprive the owner of the property."

The college student agreed that he "received" the property at issue, but wants to testify that he had no idea it was stolen.

What type of defense does the college student seek to assert?

A. Mistake of fact, because he claims he was not told the property was stolen when he received it.

B. Mistake of fact, because he claims he did not know the property was stolen when he received it.

C. Mistake of law, because he claims that he did not know it was wrong to take the property of another.

D. Mistake of law, because he claims he did not know he received stolen property belonging to another.

337. A man was charged with the rape of a woman he had met on a blind date. At the man's trial, he offered testimony showing that he honestly and reasonably believed the woman consented to having sex with him—the same standard set forth in the judge's instructions to the jury. The prosecutor did not contest the man's testimony and the jury found him to be a credible witness.

What verdict should the jury return?

A. Guilty of a lesser included offense, because otherwise the man would receive a windfall to which he is not entitled.

B. Guilty of a lesser included offense, because the man should not evade responsibility based on a technicality.

C. Not guilty, because if the man lacked the *mens rea* for the charged crime, he cannot be convicted of that crime.

D. Not guilty, because if the man did not commit the *actus reus* of the charged crime, he cannot be convicted of that crime.

338. A woman purchased a large property that included a dilapidated house and, in proximity, an old barn. The woman hired a contractor to raze the house and then build a new structure in its place. The contractor set up a burn of the house with the local fire department so that its members could get some hands-on training.

On the appointed day, the contractor started the fire. But the contractor also misunderstood the woman's directions, and so he set fire to both the house and the barn. The contractor was charged with arson of the barn. One of the proposed trial exhibits was an email from the woman to the contractor that stated: "I can't wait for you to get started. I don't like the view of that old barn!"

Will the contractor be able to assert a mistake of fact defense?

A. No; the email did not instruct the contractor to burn the barn, and he obviously misread the woman's words.

B. No; mistake of fact is not a defense to arson, as it is a *malum in se* crime that involves a threat to human life.

C. Yes; the email shows why the contractor honestly but mistakenly believed that he was told to burn the barn.

D. Yes; the email shows why the contractor honestly and reasonably believed that he was told to burn the barn.

339. An attorney thought she had arranged for her electricity bill to be automatically deducted from her checking account. But the attorney was also the executor for her father's estate and, when setting up the autopay arrangement, she accidentally used the estate checking account number instead of her own checking account number.

Several months later, the bank noticed the issue and reported the attorney to the police. The attorney was charged with embezzling from the estate.

Will the attorney be able to assert a mistake of fact defense?

A. No; as an officer of the court, the attorney should be held to a higher standard, and she cannot assert this defense.

B. No; mistake of fact is not a defense to specific intent crimes, and is only a defense to general intent crimes.

C. Yes; the attorney honestly but mistakenly believed that she provided the bank with the correct account information.

D. Yes; the attorney honestly and reasonably believed that she provided the bank with the correct account information.

340. A young man was set up on a date with a young woman by his roommate. During the date, the two split a bottle of wine; in their conversation, the young woman stated that she was a graduate student at a local university and that she had returned to school after several years traveling the world.

At the end of the evening, the two went to the young man's apartment, where they had sex. Afterward, she left, explaining that she had to go home and feed her dog. The next morning, the roommate told the young man that he had played a joke on him and that he had been set up with a 15-year-old high school student. The young woman's parents later learned about the date and the young man was charged with statutory rape.

Will the young man be able to assert a mistake of fact defense?

A. No, because the young man should not have relied on his roommate and should have asked for ID.

B. No, because mistake of fact is not a defense to statutory rape, no matter how reasonable the mistake.

C. Yes, because the young man honestly and reasonably believed the young woman was an adult.

D. Yes, because the young man had an objective, good faith belief that the young woman was an adult.

341. A woman was charged with stealing a tennis racquet from another woman's bag at the gym. In her defense, the woman claimed that she honestly believed the racquet was hers, as she thought it looked identical to one that had been taken from her locker the previous week. The woman showed the police a photo of her tennis racquet, which was dark blue. The racquet the woman was charged with taking was dark green.

Does the woman have a plausible defense?

A. Yes, because the woman honestly believed the racquet was hers, she lacks the *mens rea* for larceny.

B. Yes, because the woman reasonably believed the racquet was hers, she lacks the *mens rea* for larceny.

C. No, because the woman knew that her tennis racquet was dark blue, and the one she stole was dark green.

D. No, because claim of right is only a defense if the stolen property is identical to the defendant's property.

342. A woman was given a ticket for jaywalking after she crossed the street when the pedestrian signal was red. The jaywalking statute states: "A pedestrian shall obey the instructions of any official traffic control device specifically applicable to the pedestrian unless otherwise directed by a police officer."

When the officer was writing the ticket, the woman explained that she thought the signal was green when she crossed, and not red.

Does the woman have a plausible mistake of fact defense?

A. Yes, because the woman made an honest and reasonable mistake of fact, which negates her criminal *mens rea*.

B. Yes, because the woman made an honest mistake of fact, which negates her criminal *mens rea* for the crime.

C. No, because the woman received a ticket for a strict liability offense, and so her mistake of fact is irrelevant.

D. No, because the woman's claim about confusing a red light with a green light is patently unbelievable.

343. A married woman had an affair with one of her co-workers. When the woman's husband found out, he contacted the local police and reported her for the crime of adultery. In this jurisdiction, adultery is a felony.

The woman was charged and in her first meeting with her defense attorney, she asked whether it would be useful to tell the jury that she knew it was wrong to cheat on her husband, but she did not realize that adultery was a crime.

How should the attorney respond?

A. The attorney should tell the woman that her suggestion is a good one, and that it might help her get an acquittal.

B. The attorney should tell the woman that ignorance of the law can be an excuse, but only for *mala prohibita* crimes.

C. The attorney should tell the woman that ignorance of the law can be an excuse, but only for *mala in se* crimes.

D. The attorney should tell the woman that ignorance of the law is not an excuse, because she is presumed to know the law.

344. A law student asked her professor for the rationale of the mistake of law doctrine. The law student explained that attending law school had taught her that the law was very complex and that there were many more statutes that governed her behavior than she ever realized. The law student also said that she could not understand why the criminal law would impose a knowledge-of-law requirement on a person if she was honestly unaware that a certain law existed.

How should the professor respond?

A. The mistake of law doctrine is a remnant of the common law and is rarely followed by modern jurisdictions.

B. The mistake of law doctrine fosters society's adherence to the law by refusing to reward ignorance of the law.

C. The mistake of law doctrine keeps blameworthy defendants from being acquitted based on technicalities.

D. The mistake of law doctrine is an artifact of the common law from a time when there was limited access to books.

345. A woman was out for a long walk with her dog when it began to rain heavily. The woman tied the dog's leash to a utility pole and went inside a coffee shop for shelter, leaving the dog outside in the storm.

A police officer saw the dog in the rain and gave the woman a ticket for violating a new law making it a crime for a person to "tie, tether, or restrain an animal, either a pet or livestock, in a manner he knows is inhumane or is detrimental to its welfare." The statute had been enacted the day before and was posted to the state's website, but the woman was not aware of the new law.

Will the woman be able to assert a mistake of law defense?

A. Yes; there is a 72-hour grace period after a law's enactment before it can be enforced.

B. Yes; the woman can claim mistake of law until the statute appears in print in the penal code.

C. No; as a dog owner, the woman cannot claim ignorance of a law addressing dog ownership.

D. No; while the law was new, it was published and so the woman is presumed to know it.

346. A woman wanted to raze an unoccupied house located on her rural property, but could not afford to hire a contractor to do the work. The woman wrote to the local district attorney to ask whether it would be a crime to burn the house. The district attorney wrote back, providing his legal opinion that the woman's proposed actions would not violate the law. The woman burned the house to the ground.

Two weeks later, the state attorney general's office filed criminal charges against the woman for violating a statute that makes it a crime to "intentionally burn any dwelling, regardless of whether it is occupied or not."

Does the woman have a viable mistake of law defense?

A. Yes; the woman did all she could to adhere to the law and so she should not be punished with a conviction.

B. Yes; the woman can rely on the district attorney's advice in support of her mistake of law defense.

C. No; the woman obviously received bad advice from the district attorney and cannot rely on it in her defense.

D. No; the attorney general outranks the district attorney and so she cannot rely on the district attorney's advice.

347. A woman was appointed as the executor of her father's estate; the woman was the only heir to the estate. As executor, the woman had access to an estate account that has a large balance. The woman had retained an attorney to help her administer the estate, and she asked him whether she could pay her personal mortgage from the estate account. The attorney told her that it would be legal to do so.

The attorney's advice was incorrect, and after the woman paid her mortgage from the estate account, the bank reported her to the police. Later, the prosecutor charged the woman with embezzlement from the estate.

Can the woman assert mistake of law in her defense?

A. Yes, the woman can rely on the retained attorney's advice in support of her mistake of law defense.

B. Yes, because estate administration is so complex, the woman can be excused for not knowing the law.

C. No, the woman cannot rely on the retained attorney's advice in support of her mistake of law defense.

D. No, but the woman should explain that as the only heir to the estate, the money was hers to take anyway.

348. A young man was charged with violating a statute that makes it a crime to "willfully fail to file a state tax return." Under state law, "willfully" has been interpreted to require proof that the defendant "voluntarily and intentionally violated a known legal duty."

At his trial, the young man testified that he did not file his taxes because he thought his employer took money from his paycheck and paid the taxes for him. In support, the young man pointed to the difference between his gross and net pay, and that some of the difference was due to funds withheld by the state. Later, during deliberations, the jury agreed that the young man was a credible witness and that they thought he was being truthful.

What verdict should the jury return?

A. Guilty, because ignorance of the law is not an excuse as the young man is presumed to know the law.

B. Guilty, because the young man should have known that his employer would not pay his taxes for him.

C. Not guilty, because the young man honestly and reasonably did not know he needed to file a tax return.

D. Not guilty, because the young man's mistake of law negates the specific intent required by the statute.

349. A woman had married as a teenager, right after she graduated from high school. The marriage ended in divorce. Twenty years later, the woman married her second husband. However, the woman did not realize that her divorce had not been properly registered, as required by state law. As a result, the woman was still legally married to her first husband when she married her second husband.

In this jurisdiction, bigamy is defined as being married to more than one person at a time. The local prosecutor has now charged the woman under this statute.

Will the woman's mistake of law defense be successful?

A. Yes, because the woman did not know that she was still married to her first husband.

B. Yes, because the woman's mistake of law was not a mistake involving the criminal law.

C. No, because ignorance of the law is not an excuse, and the woman is presumed to know the law.

D. No, because the woman is claiming ignorance of civil law and not ignorance of the criminal law.

350. A man was given a ticket for jaywalking. The jaywalking statute states: "No pedestrian shall cross a roadway intersection diagonally unless authorized by official traffic control devices."

The man went to court to contest the ticket. When his case was called, the man told the judge that he knew he was not supposed to cross the street against the signal or cross in the middle of the street, but that he had never heard of a prohibition on crossing an intersection diagonally.

How should the judge respond?

A. The judge should explain that ignorance of the law is a limited defense and does not apply to strict liability crimes.

B. The judge should dismiss the ticket because the statute represents an example of governmental overreaching.

C. The judge should use her discretion to give the man a warning, but should make him promise to never jaywalk again.

D. The judge should dismiss the ticket because the man was not aware of the statute or that he was violating it.

Self-Defense and Defense of Others

351. A woman was sitting on her couch watching television when her ex-husband broke in through the back door and attacked her. The woman grabbed the gun she kept tucked in a couch cushion and shot and killed him. The prosecutor charged the woman with failing to properly secure a firearm and intentional murder.

Does the woman have a possible defense?

A. No; no one should ever use deadly force against another.

B. No; the firearms violation negates any self-defense claim.

C. Yes; deadly force can always be used against an attacker.

D. Yes; the woman can claim that she acted in self-defense.

352. A police officer arrested a woman at a protest. As the officer began the arrest, he held the woman's arms firmly behind her. The woman pulled free and slapped the officer across the face. Later, after the arrest, the woman was charged with battery of a police officer. At her upcoming trial, the woman plans to concede that the officer did not use excessive force, but wants to claim that she had the right to use proportional force to the force used against her.

Will the woman's proposed defense be successful?

A. No, because the police officer is protected by qualified immunity.

B. No, because the police officer used lawful force in making the arrest.

C. No, because one can never lawfully use force against a police officer.

D. No, because the police officer is protected by governmental immunity.

353. A man was walking to his car in a parking lot when a woman approached and accused him of stealing her lunch from the refrigerator in the office kitchen. The man denied the claim and tried to explain that he did not work with the woman and that she must have confused him with someone else. The woman insisted she had the right person. Enraged, she raised her hand to strike the man across the face.

May the man strike the woman in self-defense?

A. No; a man should never hit a woman for any reason.

B. No; self-defense is only a defense to homicide, and not battery.

C. Yes; the man is justified in using force under these circumstances.

D. Yes; the woman is mentally ill and needs to be subdued.

354. A man was sitting on a park bench eating his lunch. A stranger walked up to the man and asked him for a cigarette, but the man said he did not have one. The stranger asked for some money; the man declined and told the stranger to "go to hell." The stranger then pulled a gun out of his pocket, pointed it at the man, and demanded his wallet. In response, the man pulled out his own gun and shot and killed the stranger.

The prosecutor charged the man with murder and argued to the jury that the man could not claim self-defense because of what he said to the stranger.

Is the prosecutor correct?

A. Yes; the man's rudeness bars him from claiming that he killed in self-defense.

B. Yes; the man cannot claim self-defense because he was the initial aggressor.

C. No; the man's actions have no bearing whatsoever on his claim of self-defense.

D. No; the man may have been rude but the stranger was the initial aggressor.

355. Two men got into a fistfight at a neighborhood barbeque. According to witnesses, the fight began when the first man confronted the second man about his unkempt yard and then punched him in the face.

Several other men broke up the fight. The first man then walked away from the barbeque and smoked a cigarette. Five minutes later, the second man ran up to him and pointed a gun at him, calling him names. The first man pulled his own gun and shot and killed the second man.

Does the first man have a viable self-defense claim?

A. Yes; the first man started the fight but then retreated, and so the second man should be considered the initial aggressor.

B. Yes; the second man threatened to kill him over a fight about an unkept yard.

C. No; the first man started the fight with the second man and so the first man should be considered the initial aggressor.

D. No; once the initial aggressor starts a fight, he will retain that status going forward and cannot claim self-defense.

356. A college senior and his roommate got into a disagreement about who would do the dishes. The senior thought that since the roommate had dirtied most of the dishes, he should wash them. The roommate disagreed and claimed that since he did the dishes more often, the senior was responsible. After several minutes of yelling at one another, the senior picked up a plate and threw it against the wall close to where the roommate was standing. The roommate pulled out his gun and shot and killed the senior. The prosecutor charged the roommate with intentional murder.

Will the roommate be able to claim that he killed in self-defense?

A. Yes; the senior was the initial aggressor because he threw the plate at roommate.

B. Yes; the roommate was left with no choice but to kill the senior after he threw the plate.

C. No; the senior started the fight but the roommate escalated the violence by pulling a gun.

D. No; the roommate had to respond or else the senior would have the upper hand.

357. A woman got into an argument with her co-worker after the co-worker accused the woman of stealing the stapler from his desk. The two yelled back and forth until a supervisor broke up the fight. The co-worker then told the woman: "I will kill you if you ever do anything like that again!" Frightened for her life, the woman shot and killed the co-worker. The prosecutor later charged the woman with the intentional killing of the co-worker.

Does the woman have a viable self-defense claim?

A. No; although the co-worker threatened to kill the woman, the threat was not imminent.

B. No; although the co-worker threatened to kill the woman, the threat was conditional.

C. Yes; the co-worker threatened to kill the woman and the woman believed that he would.

D. Yes; the co-worker escalated an argument about a stapler by threatening the woman's life.

358. A woman was in her car in a parking lot. As she drove past a man on foot, he began to yell and gesture. The woman stopped the car and asked the man what was wrong. The man told her that she had driven too close to him and called her a "crazy driver." He put his hand in his pocket, and the woman believed he might be reaching for a gun. The woman then pulled out her own gun and shot and killed the man.

The woman was charged with the man's death. She asked her attorney whether she would be able to claim self-defense, pointing out that the police later found a gun in the man's pocket.

How should the attorney respond?

A. The attorney should explain that a self-defense claim will not be successful because the woman started the incident by driving too close to the man.

B. The attorney should explain that a self-defense claim will not be successful because the woman could have easily left the situation, but did not do so.

C. The attorney should explain that a self-defense claim will be successful because the police investigation showed the man did have a gun.

D. The attorney should explain that a self-defense claim will be successful because the man started the incident yelling and insulting the woman's driving.

359. A college professor was cooking dinner when she heard the sound of her front door opening; the professor lived alone so she had no idea who could have come into her house. She then heard someone walking down the hallway toward the kitchen. The professor knew that she could leave the house through the back door—which was located in the kitchen—but she instead pulled her gun from her purse. As the intruder walked into the kitchen, the woman saw that he was holding a gun in his hand. She shot and killed him.

Does the professor have a viable self-defense claim?

A. Yes; the professor had no duty to retreat from her own home, although she could have.

B. Yes; the professor shot and killed an intruder who invaded the sanctity of her home.

C. No; the professor could have easily avoided the intruder by leaving through the back door.

D. No; the professor knew that she could leave through the back door but chose to stay inside.

360. While two women were browsing clothing racks at a mall they converged on the same skirt, with each woman wanting the skirt for herself. The first woman tried to pull the skirt out of the second woman's hands. In response, the second woman picked up a loose hanger and used it to smack the first woman across the face. The first woman responded in kind. The store manager arrived and broke up the fight; the first woman had some bruises, but the second woman had a cut on her face that required a few stitches.

The prosecutor charged the first woman with aggravated assault and she wants to claim self-defense. The prosecutor has filed a motion to preclude the defense, arguing that the first woman's response was disproportionate.

How should the judge rule on the motion?

A. The motion should be granted because it is silly to use force in a fight about a skirt.

B. The motion should be granted because the injuries establish disproportionate force.

C. The motion should be denied because the first woman was the initial aggressor.

D. The motion should be denied because each woman used a hanger against the other.

361. A college senior was at a party when he overheard a freshman making fun of him. The senior confronted the freshman and told him to apologize. The freshman refused, and instead punched the senior. The senior responded by pulling out a knife and stabbing the freshman in the stomach several times. The freshman survived, but required extensive abdominal surgery because of the stab wounds.

The prosecutor charged the senior with attempted murder and the senior wants to argue that he acted in self-defense.

Will the senior's defense be successful?

A. No, because self-defense is only a defense to completed crimes, and not to attempt crimes.

B. No, because the senior's use of force was not proportional to the force used against him.

C. No, because the senior completely overreacted to the freshman's refusal to apologize to him.

D. No, because the senior would only be entitled to use a weapon if one had been used against him.

362. A woman was sleeping in her house one night when she woke up, realizing that a burglar had entered her house and was trying to get into her bed. Terrified, the woman pulled a gun from between the mattress and the box spring and used it to shoot and kill the burglar.

The prosecutor charged the woman with murder. In anticipation of the woman claiming self-defense, the prosecutor plans to argue that the woman used deadly force prematurely, because it was not clear that deadly force was required at the time of the shooting.

Is the prosecutor's argument legally sound?

A. Yes; at the time of the shooting, the woman did not know why the burglar was in her bedroom or what he wanted from her.

B. Yes; at the time of the shooting, the woman had only a subjective belief that the burglar was going to sexually assault her.

C. No; at the time of the shooting, the woman had a reasonable belief that the burglar was going to sexually assault her.

D. No; when a burglar enters a home, the law presumes that he intends death or serious bodily injury to those inside.

363. A man was waiting in line at a concession stand when a woman pushed ahead of him. The man told the woman to move to the end of the line but she refused, explaining that her movie was about to start and did not have time to wait. The man again told the woman to move, and she replied, "you can try to make me move, but you're going to regret it." As she spoke, the woman began to reach into her bag. The man believed the woman was reaching for a concealed weapon so he pulled his gun out first and shot the woman. The bullet grazed her arm.

After police established that the woman was reaching for her wallet and not a gun, the prosecutor charged the man with aggravated battery.

Does it matter that the woman did not have a gun in her bag?

A. Yes; the man's belief that the woman was reaching for a gun is only reasonable if it is also correct.

B. Yes; the man's belief that the woman was reaching for a gun is only sincere if it is also correct.

C. No; all that matters is that the man sincerely believed that the woman was reaching for a gun.

D. No; the man's belief that the woman was reaching for a gun has to be reasonable, not correct.

364. A woman shot and killed her husband after he tried to kill her during a divorce mediation session. The prosecutor charged the woman with murder and a trial was conducted. In its deliberations, the jury agreed the prosecutor had established the elements of intentional murder, but also that the woman had demonstrated that she acted in self-defense.

What will be the result of the trial?

A. The woman will be acquitted of murder.

B. The woman will be exonerated of murder.

C. The woman will be found guilty of a lesser offense.

D. The jury's findings will be used at sentencing.

365. A man killed his brother at a family gathering. The police investigation showed that the man killed his brother with an axe because he honestly but unreasonably believed that his brother was about to shoot him.

The man was charged with intentional murder, and he claimed self-defense. Like the police, the jury found that the man honestly but unreasonably believed that he had to use deadly force to protect himself.

What is the appropriate verdict under these circumstances?

A. The man should be found guilty of murder because there is no defense to killing someone with an axe.

B. The man should be found guilty of murder because he is unable to show he acted in self-defense.

C. The man should be found guilty of voluntary manslaughter because he acted in imperfect self-defense.

D. The man should be found guilty of unintentional murder because he acted in imperfect self-defense.

366. A man was sitting in his parked car on a residential street, waiting for a friend to meet him. The man saw a teenage girl walking down the street toward him; the girl had a gun in her hand and was pointing it at him. Fearful that the girl might shoot him, the man drew his weapon and killed the girl.

What type of self-defense statute will best serve the man in this situation?

A. One that has eliminated the duty to retreat.

B. One that adheres to the common law of self-defense.

C. One that does not measure the proportionality of force.

D. One that adopts the common law castle doctrine.

367. A lawyer was appointed to serve on a committee charged with reviewing the state's criminal jury instructions. The state had recently adopted a new self-defense statute, which included the following language:

> A person may use physical force upon another person when and to the extent he or she reasonably believes such to be necessary to defend himself, herself or a third person from what he or she reasonably believes to be the use or imminent use of unlawful physical force by such other person.

At a committee meeting, the chair argued that this provision required that the defendant act according to the objective, reasonable person standard. The chair then asked the lawyer if she agreed.

How should the lawyer respond?

A. The lawyer should agree with the committee chair if she wants to remain a member of the committee.

B. The lawyer should explain that the standard appears to include both subjective and objective components.

C. The lawyer should explain that when a statute uses the word "reasonably," the standard is wholly objective.

D. The lawyer should explain that when a statute refers to the defendant's belief, the standard is wholly subjective.

368. A man and woman were married for 30 years. During most of that time, the man routinely beat the woman, and she was hospitalized on several occasions. At other times, the man prevented the woman from going to the hospital, leaving her broken bones to heal without medical treatment. The man persistently berated and insulted the woman, telling her she was stupid and fat and that no one would ever love her. The woman was very isolated, as the man forbade her from having friends or seeing her family. The man also repeatedly told the woman that if she ever left him or told anyone about their home life, he would kill her.

One night while the man was sleeping, the woman set fire to their bed, killing him. The woman was charged with the man's murder.

Does the woman have a viable self-defense claim?

A. Yes, if the woman can offer testimony to show the abuse she endured from the man and how it affected her ability to perceive the situation.

B. Yes, if the woman can substantiate the abuse she suffered through neutral, third-party witnesses who can present the facts objectively.

C. No, because the woman was isolated from friends and family, she will not be able to corroborate her claims of abuse by the man.

D. No, because the force was unnecessary, disproportionate, and the woman should not have reasonably feared for her life at the time.

369. After enduring years of physical, mental, and emotional abuse, a husband killed his wife during an argument. The argument began when the wife discovered that the husband had not folded her laundry as she liked, and soon the wife was slapping and kicking the husband as he lay on the bedroom floor in the fetal position. But the husband reached for the gun the wife kept under the bed and used it to kill her.

The husband was charged with murder and his attorney plans on claiming self-defense. The attorney wants to offer expert testimony about the effects of the abuse on the husband.

What would be the relevance of this testimony?

A. It would show why the husband believed it was necessary to use deadly force against his wife.

B. It would show the wife was a horrible person and why the husband had to kill her.

C. It would have no relevance because the husband is trying to use a defense reserved for women.

D. It would have no relevance because the husband is trying to blame the victim for his problems.

370. A woman was at a family picnic when her teenage niece pushed ahead of her in the food line. The woman told the niece to go to the back of the line but the niece refused. The niece also told the woman that her father—the woman's brother—hated her, and then raised her soda cup to pour it over the woman's head. The woman reached out and blocked the teenager's arm, causing the soda in the cup to spill on the teenager. The niece's father called the police; the woman was later charged with simple battery.

Can the woman offer a self-defense claim?

A. No, because self-defense is only a defense to homicide charges and not a defense to lesser crimes.

B. No, because the worst thing that could have happened was that the niece spilled soda on the woman.

C. Yes, because the woman had a reasonable fear that the niece was about to use unlawful force against her.

D. Yes, because the woman felt threatened by the niece's use of force and by her use of fighting words.

371. A man was at a farmer's market when he got into a fistfight with a second man. According to witnesses, the second man was very aggressive and walked up to the first man and started the fight. The witnesses all agreed that the first man could probably just have walked away and that if he had, no blows would have been thrown. After considering the witness statements, the prosecutor charged the first man with battery.

Does the first man have a self-defense claim?

A. No, because he had the ability to retreat and did not try to retreat.

B. No, because he had a duty to retreat and did not try to retreat.

C. Yes, because he had no duty to retreat and so did not have to try to.

D. Yes, because the witnesses agreed that the second man was at fault.

372. A man was visiting his sister and her teenage son. On the second night of the visit, the teenage son came home after his curfew. The man's sister became angry and began to hit him with a wooden spoon. The man tackled his sister to the ground and pulled the wooden spoon from her hand.

The sister asked the man to leave and reported him to the police. He was charged with battery and wants to explain to the jury that he did not intend to hurt his sister, but only wanted to protect her teenage son.

Does the man's defense have any chance of success?

A. Yes; the man has a sympathetic story and it will help mitigate his sentence.

B. Yes; in some circumstances, a person can use force to defend a third party.

C. No; a person has no right to intervene in a parent's discipline of their child.

D. No; the teenage son did not ask for help so the man had no right to intervene.

373. While a college senior was at a public pool he noticed a couple standing nearby, fighting. The senior overheard the man insult the woman and watched as she started to cry. The man then told the woman to stop crying and raised his fist to her. The senior quickly ran up to the man, grabbed his arm, and twisted it behind his back.

The senior was later charged with battery and wants to offer a claim of defense of others.

Will the senior's defense be successful?

A. No, because the senior would only have a right to use force if he had a preexisting, close relationship with the woman.

B. No, because the senior did not know either the man or the woman and so he had no right to eavesdrop on their conversation.

C. Yes, because the force used was necessary and proportionate, and a reasonable person would have believed it was required here.

D. Yes, because the man was about to strike the woman and due to the senior's quick thinking, she was saved from the attack.

374. A lawyer walked into the break room in her office and saw a paralegal pointing a gun at a legal assistant. The lawyer immediately pulled out her own gun and shot and killed the paralegal. The lawyer was charged with murder.

Police later reviewed video footage of the encounter and learned that the legal assistant had started the fight with the paralegal and had drawn her weapon first. In the seconds before the lawyer walked into the break room, the paralegal had responded by kicking the legal assistant's gun from her hand and then drawing her own weapon.

Does the lawyer have a viable claim of self-defense?

A. Yes, because without the lawyer's intervention, the paralegal would have killed the legal assistant and maybe others.

B. Yes, because the force used was necessary and proportionate, and a reasonable person would have believed it was required.

C. No, because a party can only use non-deadly force in defense of third parties, not deadly force.

D. No; because the legal assistant did not have a right to use deadly force, the lawyer could not use deadly force to defend her.

375. A woman shot and killed a man she believed was raping an elderly neighbor. The police officer assigned to investigate the homicide reported that the woman had misunderstood the situation and that the man and the neighbor were having consensual sex. But the officer also reported that the neighbor was screaming "no, no, no," throughout the encounter, so he understood the woman's mistake.

The woman was charged with murder and wants to offer a self-defense claim. The relevant statute states:

> A person is justified in using force or deadly force against another to protect a third person if:
>
> (1) under the circumstances as the actor reasonably believes them to be, the actor would be justified in using force or deadly force to protect himself against the unlawful force or unlawful deadly force he reasonably believes to be threatening the third person he seeks to protect; and
>
> (2) the actor reasonably believes that his intervention is immediately necessary to protect the third person.

Will the woman's defense be successful?

A. No; because the neighbor was not in any peril, the woman had no right to intervene with force (deadly or otherwise) to defend her.

B. No; the woman mistakenly believed the neighbor was being raped and that intervention was immediately necessary to protect her.

C. Yes; the woman reasonably believed the neighbor was being raped and that intervention was immediately necessary to protect her.

D. Yes; under the doctrine of *defensionem aliorum*, the woman could use deadly force to protect her neighbor, even though she was wrong.

Defense of Property and Habitation

376. A gymnast was getting dressed in the locker room of her gym. She laid her diamond necklace on a counter and was sitting on a nearby bench, putting on her shoes. A woman walked into the locker room and seeing the necklace—but not the gymnast—quickly scooped it into her hand. The gymnast stood up, grabbed the woman's arm, and pried the necklace out of her hand.

The woman later asked her friend, a law student, whether she should report this event to the police. The woman's arm and hand were badly bruised in the exchange, and she thought the police should be alerted.

How should the friend respond?

A. The friend should encourage the woman to go to the police and report the gymnast for her violent and disproportionate conduct.

B. The friend should tell the woman that the gymnast had the right to use nondeadly force to protect her property.

C. The friend should tell the woman that he is not yet licensed to practice law and so cannot provide legal advice.

D. The friend should tell the woman that if she continues to steal, she will face the same consequences, or worse.

377. A man's briefcase was stolen from his car. The briefcase had been a college graduation gift and held great sentimental value to the man. A week after the theft, the man saw a woman on the street holding the briefcase. The man walked up to the woman and punched her, which caused her to drop the briefcase to the ground. He then picked up the briefcase and walked away.

The man was charged with battery. At his trial, he asserted that he had the right to use nondeadly force to defend his property.

Is the man correct?

A. Yes; the man would have been permitted to use force to stop the theft, so he could use the same force a week later.

B. Yes; a person may always use nondeadly force to defend his own property, but he cannot resort to deadly force.

C. No; the man would have been permitted to use force earlier to stop the theft, but could not use force a week later.

D. No; the man was not permitted to use force in this instance because the briefcase only had sentimental value.

378. A woman managed a small jewelry boutique. A man walked into the boutique one day and tried to steal several pieces of jewelry. The woman confronted the man and told him to return the jewelry, but he laughed at her. The woman punched the man in the head; stunned, he dropped the jewelry.

The man later reported the woman to the police and she was charged with battery. The woman planned to claim at trial that she was authorized in using force to protect property. But the prosecutor objected, claiming that the defense is reserved for titleholders and not those in mere possession of someone else's property.

How should the judge respond?

A. The judge should tell the lawyers to reserve their arguments for trial, so that the jury can decide the issue.

B. The judge should explain that the woman cannot raise the defense as she was not the titleholder of the jewelry.

C. The judge should explain that the defense cannot be raised in retail situations, even when the defendant is a titleholder.

D. The judge should explain that the woman can raise the defense as she was in lawful possession of the jewelry.

379. A man was driving his friend's car and stopped for some gas. As he was filling the tank, a woman came up to the man and loudly accused him of stealing her car. The woman also tried to grab the car keys from his hand.

The man knew his friend was pretty shady and realized that the friend may have stolen the car from the woman. But since he was not certain the car was stolen, he pushed the woman to the ground and quickly drove away.

Was the man entitled to use force in this situation?

A. No; once the woman suggested the car was stolen from her, the man should have called his friend for advice.

B. No; because the man doubted his friend's lawful possession of the car, he could not use force to defend it.

C. Yes; the man had the right to use non-deadly force to keep the woman from taking the car keys and the car.

D. Yes; under the alter-ego rule, if the friend was entitled to use force, the man could have used force as well.

380. A man was sitting on his couch, reading a magazine, when he heard noise coming from his driveway. The man looked up and saw a teenager trying to break into his car. The man grabbed his gun, opened his front door, and yelled at the teenager to stop. The teenager ignored the man so the man shot and killed him.

The man was charged with murder. He told his lawyer that when he shot the teenager, he was only trying to protect his car.

How should the attorney respond?

A. The attorney should explain that deadly force may never be used to protect property, because human life is more valuable than property.

B. The attorney should explain that deadly force can be used to protect property if the force is necessary to avoid destruction of the property.

C. The attorney should explain that deadly force can be used to protect property if the force is used while the defendant is within his home.

D. The attorney should explain that most modern jurisdictions acknowledge that homeowners need to use deadly force to protect property.

381. A woman was driving home from work when a carjacker got into her expensive sportscar. The carjacker pointed his gun at the woman and told her to drive him to a certain bank because he wanted to rob it. The woman did as she was told. While the carjacker was momentarily distracted, the woman pulled out her own gun and shot and killed him.

The woman was charged with murder. At a pretrial hearing, the prosecutor mentioned to the judge that he would vigorously oppose any attempt by the woman to claim defense of property at the trial.

How should the defense attorney respond?

A. The defense attorney should explain that only the jury can decide whether deadly force was justified under these facts.

B. The defense attorney should explain that the woman used deadly force to protect her own life and not defend her property.

C. The defense attorney should explain that the woman was justified in using deadly force to protect her expensive sportscar.

D. The defense attorney should explain that deadly force can be used to defend property when deadly force is used to take property.

382. A college student was sleeping one night when he heard loud singing coming from the shower on the first floor. The college student recognized the singing as coming from his best friend, who sometimes got too drunk to drive home and would sleep on the student's couch instead. The college student was annoyed that his best friend had woken him up, though, and so he went downstairs and shot and killed him.

Was the college student permitted to use deadly force under these circumstances?

A. Yes, because deadly force can always be used to keep someone from entering a private home without an invitation.

B. Yes, because the best friend was drunk and the college student might not have been safe from him.

C. No, because it was not necessary to use deadly force in this situation to protect either habitation or human life.

D. No, because the best friend had an implicit invitation to enter the house, given that he had done so in the past.

383. A woman lived alone; she was reading in bed one night when she heard the sound of breaking glass coming from the first floor of the house. The woman called out but no one answered. The woman grabbed her gun from her safe; she grew more and more frightened as she heard the sound of someone coming up the stairs and closer to her bedroom. The woman called out again but before the intruder could respond, she fired a shot through the bedroom door. The shot killed the intruder, who turned out to be the woman's younger brother.

Later, the woman learned that her younger brother was drunk and had come to her house because he lost his own house keys.

Were the woman's actions lawful under these circumstances?

A. Yes, because the intruder failed to respond to the woman when she initially called out to him after he entered the house.

B. Yes, because the woman was entitled to use deadly force to protect both her home and to defend herself from harm.

C. No, because the woman did not wait for the intruder to respond before she fired the lethal shot through the bedroom door.

D. No, because the woman should have recognized the sound of her younger brother's steps as he climbed the stairs.

384. A man was working in his study when he heard his baby crying in her room. The man went upstairs and found an intruder in the room, standing over the baby's crib with a knife in his hand. The man jumped on the intruder and pushed him to the ground, punching him until he fell unconscious.

Were the man's actions lawful under these circumstances?

A. No, because the man did not stop to inquire why the intruder was in the house, or how he got in.

B. No, because the man failed to call the police first, before taking matters into his own hands.

C. Yes, because the man was entitled to use force to protect both his home and to defend his baby.

D. Yes, because a person is always allowed to use force—deadly or otherwise—to protect a baby.

385. A man learned that two local teenagers had broken into several of his neighbors' houses, and the man vowed that he would not become their next victim. The man rigged a flare gun to fire if anyone tried to force open his back door.

Several nights later, the teenagers attempted to break into the man's house through his back door. The flare gun fired into the face of one of the teenagers, blinding him. The other teenager ran away. The man later told the investigating police officer that he did not think he did anything wrong.

How should the police officer respond?

A. The police officer should tell the man that his actions were not justified because a mechanical device should never be used in place of human judgment.

B. The police officer should tell the man that his actions were only justified because one of the teenagers was shot, instead of an innocent party.

C. The police officer should tell the man that his actions were justified because he would have been permitted to fire the gun himself if he had been present.

D. The police officer should tell the man that his actions were justified because the teenagers were menacing the neighborhood and needed to be stopped.

Insanity, Mental Health, and Intoxication

386. A man murdered his mother and decapitated her. He was captured by the police after he mailed the severed head to his sister. At the man's subsequent trial for murder and abuse of a corpse, the jury found him not guilty by reason of insanity.

What is the legal meaning of the jury's verdict?

A. The jury's verdict recognized that the man was crazy, as only crazy people decapitate their victims and mail body parts.

B. The jury's verdict recognized that the man lacked the *mens rea* for both crimes and was not criminally responsible.

C. The jury's verdict was wrong, because the man committed methodical acts and insane people do not commit planned crimes.

D. The jury's verdict recognized that the man was guilty as charged but also suffered from severe mental illness.

387. A man was arrested and charged with killing his neighbor. During the time he was in jail awaiting trial, the man became very depressed. Over time, the man began to suffer from delusions that he was a king and was being held by his rivals as part of their effort to assume control of his country.

At a hearing a week before trial, the man was brought to court. He interrupted the judge as she was speaking and told her that, as king, he would fight for his country and that she had no right to order his execution.

How should the judge respond?

A. The judge should tell the man that he will be held in contempt if he interrupts her again.

B. The judge should do nothing because it is defense counsel's responsibility to control the man.

C. The judge should find the man not guilty by reason of insanity, because he is legally insane.

D. The judge should order an evaluation to determine if the man is competent to stand trial.

388. A law student was reviewing her Criminal Law notes in preparation for her final exam. The student's notes included the following definition for the *M'Naghten* test for insanity:

> A defendant is legally insane if, at the time he commits the crime, he does not know the nature and quality of his acts or, if he does know, he does not know that what he is doing is wrong.

Are the student's notes correct?

A. No; the definition fails to address the defendant's mental disease or defect.

B. No; the definition should use the word "appreciate" instead of "know."

C. No; the definition should only refer to the ability to tell right from wrong.

D. No; the definition fails to explain the consequences of an insanity acquittal.

389. A man with a long history of mental illness killed and cannibalized his roommate. After the man was charged with murder, he was evaluated to determine whether he was legally insane at the time of the crime. The man explained to the evaluator that he had neither killed nor cannibalized; instead, the man insisted he had only prepared himself a meal and eaten it. When the evaluator confronted the man with what he had done, he insisted that he was a vegan and that he did not eat animal products of any kind.

The evaluator later told the prosecutor that she believed the man's mental illness caused him to believe that his roommate was not a person, but was an ingredient in a vegan recipe. This jurisdiction follows the *M'Naghten* test for insanity.

Should the man be found legally insane?

A. Yes; because of the man's mental illness, he did not know the nature and quality of his actions.

B. Yes; the man cannibalized his roommate and anyone who eats human flesh is legally insane.

C. No; the man is malingering and is using his veganism as an excuse to evade responsibility.

D. No; the man knew the nature and quality of his acts because he knew he'd prepared a meal and eaten it.

390. A woman suffered from hallucinations that told her she needed to kill her daughter in order to save the girl from evil that was certain to happen on her ninth birthday. The woman did not know what form the evil would take, but she knew that it was coming. The woman also knew that it was wrong to kill other people, but she thought that she had to keep her daughter safe from the evil.

The night before the daughter's ninth birthday, the woman killed her. She was charged with murder and, prior to trial, was examined by a forensic psychiatrist. The psychiatrist diagnosed the woman with a mental illness and testified that the woman's hallucinations were caused by her mental illness. He also testified about why the woman believed she had to kill her daughter. The judge then instructed the jury on insanity, using the *M'Naghten* rule.

Should the jury find the woman not guilty by reason of insanity?

A. No, because the woman did not know anything about the form of the supposed evil or what it would do to her daughter.

B. No, because despite the fact that the woman suffered from mental illness and hallucinations, she knew right from wrong.

C. Yes, because the woman suffered from a diagnosed mental illness, which caused her to believe she had to kill her daughter.

D. Yes, because the woman suffered from a diagnosed mental illness and believed she had to kill her daughter to save her from evil.

391. A woman killed her husband. Before trial, the woman claimed she had been legally insane at the time of the killing. The woman's attorney sent the prosecutor a report from the woman's psychiatrist. It stated that the woman suffered from long-standing mental illness, and at the time of the killing, she heard voices in her head that commanded her to kill. The report also explained that the woman had successfully ignored these command hallucinations for many years, but that on the day of the homicide, she could not ignore them anymore.

According to this state's penal code:

> A person shall not be found guilty of a crime when, at the time of the act, omission, or negligence constituting the crime, the person, because of mental disease, injury, or congenital deficiency, acted as he did because of a delusional compulsion as to such act which overmastered his will to resist committing the crime.

Is the woman legally insane?

A. No, because the woman ignored the voices for many years, and so she could have ignored them on the day of the homicide.

B. No, because nothing in the psychiatrist's report indicates that the woman suffered from an injury or congenital deficiency.

C. Yes, because on the day of the homicide, the woman was unable to control her command hallucinations or her actions.

D. Yes, because the woman suffered from a mental illness that caused command hallucinations that she was unable to ignore.

392. A mentally ill man believed that his neighbor was mistreating her two children and that he needed to protect them from her. One day when the children were playing in the street, the man snatched them and hid them in his basement. He kept the children there for several weeks before they were found. The man was charged with kidnapping.

Prior to trial, the man asserted an insanity defense, claiming that his concerns about the children's mistreatment were due to his mental illness, and were so profound that he could not keep from kidnapping the children and keeping them in the basement. The defense expert agreed with these claims; the prosecution expert opined that because of his mental illness, the man could not stop himself from kidnapping the children in the first instance. This jurisdiction follows the "irresistible impulse" test for insanity.

Should the prosecutor concede that the man was insane at the time of the crime?

A. No; the prosecutor should retain another expert who better understands that his job is to disagree with the defense expert.

B. No; the prosecutor should argue that the man acted methodically over several weeks and so he was able to control his actions.

C. Yes; because the prosecution and defense experts agree, the prosecution should just concede and move on to the next case.

D. Yes; the prosecution expert has offered an opinion that supports the man's claims, so there is nothing left to do.

393. After concluding that the state's existing insanity test did not allow adequate inquiry into a defendant's mental illness and the reasons for his actions, a newly elected legislator decided to propose a new test. According to the proposed test, a defendant would be found legally insane if "his unlawful act was the product of mental disease or defect."

The legislator shared his proposed test with a colleague and asked for her criticism.

How should the colleague respond?

A. The proposed test fails to make a distinction between mental illnesses and physical illnesses.

B. The proposed test gives too much power to the jury because insanity is a threshold issue for a judge.

C. The proposed test gives the fact-finder no standard by which to evaluate a defendant's conduct.

D. The proposed test fails to explain the procedure for treating a defendant after he is found insane.

394. A state legislator plans to propose that her jurisdiction replace the existing test for insanity—the *M'Naghten* test—with the Model Penal Code test for insanity. That test states that a defendant is legally insane "if at the time of such conduct as a result of mental disease or defect he lacks substantial capacity either to appreciate the criminality of his conduct or to conform his conduct to the requirements of the law."

In preparation for introducing her legislation, the legislator drafted a memo to her colleagues, explaining the key differences between the two tests.

What sentence should appear in the legislator's memo?

A. "The Model Penal Code test adds a volitional prong to the insanity inquiry and softens the all-or-nothing approach employed under the *M'Naghten* test."

B. "The two tests are identical but because Model Penal Code test is newer, it reflects a more modern perspective on the effects of mental illness on crime."

C. "The *M'Naghten* test is loosely written and allows an insanity acquittal based solely on the defendant's self-serving testimony about his mental health."

D. "The Model Penal Code test restricts the insanity defense to those who suffer from serious mental illness, which will reduce insanity acquittals overall."

395. A woman drowned her son believing that she was saving him from a lifetime of suffering. The woman was charged with murder and was evaluated by a psychiatrist for insanity. The woman told the psychiatrist that she understood the "general rule" that killing is wrong, but explained that she killed her son under an "exception" which permits parents to kill their suffering children.

This jurisdiction has adopted the Model Penal Code test for insanity.

Does the woman meet the Model Penal Code test for insanity?

A. Yes, because the woman was mentally ill and her statements indicate that she was unable to appreciate the criminality of her conduct.

B. Yes, because the woman's statements about a "general rule" and "exception" shows that she could not fully appreciate the criminality of her conduct.

C. No, because the woman's statements about a "general rule" and "exception" are just a convenient excuse for her to get away with murder.

D. No, because the woman told the psychiatrist that she knows that it is wrong to kill, so she appreciated the criminality of her conduct.

396. A state currently follows the *M'Naghten* test for insanity. A state legislator was elected on a platform to reform the criminal law and has proposed that the state adopt the federal test for insanity. That test states, in part:

> It is an affirmative defense to a prosecution ... that, at the time of the commission of the acts constituting the offense, the defendant, as a result of a severe mental disease or defect, was unable to appreciate the nature and quality or the wrongfulness of his acts.

Will adoption of the federal test reform insanity law in the state?

A. Yes; the federal test was only adopted after significant study and reflects current understanding of how mental illness affects behavior.

B. Yes; the federal test offers a modern way to view mental illness and its effects, and rejects the outdated perspective of the *M'-Naghten* test.

C. No; the federal test is identical to the *M'-Naghten* test and offers absolutely no prospects of reform to mentally ill criminal defendants.

D. No; the federal test is substantially the same as the *M'Naghten* test, but adds that the defendant's mental disease or defect be "severe."

397. A young man was found not guilty by reason of insanity after he attempted to steal a jacket from a clothing store. Following the requirements of state law, he was sent to a psychiatric facility for evaluation and treatment and was required to remain there until a psychiatrist deemed him mentally well or no longer dangerous.

If the young man had pleaded guilty, he would have received a maximum sentence of one year.

How long can the young man be kept at the psychiatric facility?

A. The young man must be released immediately, because due process bars any confinement after an insanity acquittal.

B. The young man can be kept at the psychiatric facility for one year, the maximum sentence for commission of the crime.

C. The young man can be kept at the psychiatric facility for two years, twice the maximum sentence for commission of the crime.

D. The young man can be kept at the psychiatric facility indefinitely if he does not meet the criteria for release.

398. A jury in a murder trial was instructed on the insanity defense, but was also instructed on an alternative verdict of guilty but mentally ill. According to the judge's instructions, the jury could find the defendant guilty but mentally ill if it found that the prosecutor had proven the elements of the crime beyond a reasonable doubt and if the defendant established by a preponderance of the evidence that he was mentally ill at the time he committed the offense.

Is the guilty but mentally ill verdict the same as an insanity acquittal?

A. Yes, because both involve a finding that the defendant was mentally ill at the time of the offense.

B. Yes, because both require an inquiry into the defendant's mental state at the time of the offense.

C. No, because the guilty but mentally ill verdict will not result in the defendant's acquittal of the crime.

D. No, because the guilty but mentally ill verdict does not distinguish between different types of mental illness.

399. A woman killed her grandmother and was charged with first degree murder. In this jurisdiction, the sentence for such a conviction ranges from 25 years to life in prison.

At trial, the woman offered an insanity defense, but the jury found her guilty but mentally ill. At the woman's sentencing, the defense attorney argued that the woman should be sent to a state psychiatric hospital until it was determined that she was no longer a danger to herself or others. The prosecutor objected.

How should the judge sentence the woman?

A. The judge should impose whatever sentence the jurisdiction allows for a first degree murder conviction.

B. The judge should follow the defense recommendation and send the woman to a state psychiatric hospital.

C. The judge should have the woman evaluated to determine if she is competent to be sentenced to prison.

D. The judge should impose a reduced sentence, because the woman lacked the *mens rea* for the crime.

400. A woman was charged with the first degree murder of her husband. At the bench trial, the defense expert testified that the woman was suffering from a major depression at the time of the killing and, as a result, could not rationally premeditate or deliberate. The prosecution expert countered that the woman was able to premeditate and deliberate despite her depression. The judge found the defense expert's testimony credible and did not believe the prosecution expert's testimony.

In this jurisdiction, first degree murder is defined as "any wilful, premeditated, and deliberate killing," and second degree murder is defined as "any intentional killing."

What is the appropriate verdict?

A. The judge should find the woman not guilty by reason of insanity because she did not have the *mens rea* for first degree murder.

B. The judge should find the woman guilty of second degree murder because of her diminished capacity at the time of the killing.

C. The judge should find the woman guilty of first degree murder because there is a possibility the prosecution expert is right.

D. The judge should find the woman not guilty because she did not intentionally kill her husband.

401. A man could not sleep and so he drank a large glass of whisky, hoping the alcohol would relax him. Later, when he was in bed, the man heard noises outside his bedroom window. Frightened, he opened the window and fired a few shots into the dark, thinking that the shots would scare away whoever—or whatever—was making the noise.

The shots narrowly missed the man's neighbor, who was taking out the trash. The neighbor called the police and the man was later charged with attempted murder and reckless endangerment, as well as weapons offenses. At his first court appearance, the man told the judge that he was so drunk that he had no memory of firing the shots.

How should the judge respond?

A. The judge should tell the man that the law has little sympathy for people who get themselves into impaired states.

B. The judge should tell the man that he should work with his lawyer to develop a voluntary insanity defense.

C. The judge should tell the man that if he honestly and reasonably believed he was drunk, he has a complete defense.

D. The judge should tell the man that if he honestly and reasonably believed he was drunk, he has a partial defense.

402. A man was charged with arson, based on a fire that began with a pile of leaves in his backyard and spread to his neighbor's house. The man told his lawyer that he had consumed about four beers at the time of the fire and asked about the possibility of a voluntary intoxication defense—which is recognized in this jurisdiction.

How should the lawyer respond?

A. The lawyer should tell the man that four beers would not be enough alcohol for a plausible intoxication defense.

B. The lawyer should explain to the man that voluntary intoxication is a possible defense to specific intent crimes only.

C. The lawyer should tell the man that the law does not reward defendants for their self-induced intoxication.

D. The lawyer should ask the man about the alcohol content of the beer, so he can develop the man's intoxication defense.

403. Late one night, a man went into a bar for a drink. The bartender allowed the man to stay after the bar closed and he had several more drinks. The next morning, the bar owner found the bartender dead inside the bar; she had been killed by a blow to the head. The bar owner found the man passed out nearby with a whisky bottle in his hand.

The man was charged with first degree murder. At trial, he testified that the last thing he remembered of the evening was walking into the bar. On cross-examination, the man conceded that the evidence showed an intentional killing, but he claimed he was too drunk to have premeditated or deliberated. He implored the jury to convict him of third degree murder instead, which only requires an intent to kill.

What is the appropriate verdict?

A. The man should be convicted of first degree murder because his testimony is self-serving and not credible.

B. The man should be convicted of first degree murder because he admitted his guilt during cross-examination.

C. The man should be convicted of third degree murder because he was too drunk to premeditate and deliberate.

D. The man should be convicted of first degree murder because he did not offer proof of how many drinks he had.

404. A young man was at a party, drinking beer. As a joke, the young man's friend put something in his beer. The substance caused the young man to become very aggressive, and he attacked a woman who was standing nearby. The friend and several others pulled the young man off of the woman, but not before he ripped her blouse and pawed at her breasts.

The woman reported the young man to the police and he was arrested and charged with attempted rape. The young man claimed to have no memory of the event.

Does the young man have a plausible defense?

A. No; the young man should have watched his drink more closely and should get himself a better group of friends.

B. No; involuntarily intoxication is only a defense to property crimes, but never to crimes involving sexual violence.

C. Yes; the young man can claim that his voluntary intoxication prevented him from forming the specific intent to rape.

D. Yes; the young man can claim that he was involuntarily intoxicated by the substance his friend put in his beer.

405. A woman was prescribed a new medication to help with her insomnia. At the time he wrote the prescription, the doctor told the woman that she should only take one tablet per night, as the medication was very strong and could have serious side effects. That night, the woman took two tablets. Two hours later, she stabbed her husband as he slept in their bed. The next morning, the woman woke up and saw what she had done. She was horrified and told police that she could not remember anything because of the medication. The woman explained that her doctor had warned her about "side effects," but she thought he was referring to things like rashes and an upset stomach.

The woman was charged with murder and wants to claim that she was involuntarily intoxicated at the time of the crime.

Does the woman have a strong defense?

A. No, because the woman did not take the medication as she was specifically directed by the prescribing doctor.

B. No, because the woman's involuntary intoxication is not a defense to homicide, but voluntarily intoxication can be.

C. Yes, because the woman was intoxicated by the medication and could not remember stabbing her husband.

D. Yes, because the woman only ingested a little bit more of the medication than her doctor advised her to.

Necessity and Duress

406. A woman was sitting in her car, the first in line at a railroad crossing. The railroad crossing was well marked, with signs indicating that drivers were to stay in their cars while the gates were lowered and that criminal fines would be imposed on any driver who did not follow these rules.

As she waited, the woman saw a toddler walking down the middle of the railroad tracks. Seeing that a train was approaching, the woman quickly got out of her car and rescued the toddler. The woman was later charged with violating the ordinance prohibiting drivers from exiting their cars at railroad crossings.

How should the woman defend herself?

A. The woman should argue that she acted out of necessity because the toddler's parents failed to properly supervise him.

B. The woman should argue that she was required by her moral compass to save the toddler from being killed by the train.

C. The woman should argue that she should be treated as a hero for saving the toddler and not charged with a crime.

D. The woman should argue that she acted out of necessity and chose being fined over having the toddler killed by the train.

407. A woman began to read stories online about how global warming might create food shortages in her community. Afraid of what was to come, the woman went to her local store to stock up on food. But the woman did not have enough money to pay for all her groceries, so she placed several expensive items in her backpack without paying for them.

The woman was arrested and charged with larceny. The woman told her lawyer that she wants to use a necessity defense based on her fears about the possible food shortages.

How should the lawyer respond?

A. The defense will not succeed because the woman's fears were speculative at the time she stole from the grocery store.

B. The defense will not succeed because the woman did not conduct any research to determine if the online stories were true.

C. The defense may succeed because global warming is a force that will affect the food supply for many decades to come.

D. The defense may succeed because the woman had a well-founded fear of starving to death due to a food shortage.

408. An activist created a plan to build a new food bank in his town, where many children lived in poverty and did not have enough to eat. To put his plan in action, the activist burglarized the homes of several wealthy residents, taking the food from their refrigerators and cabinets. At each house, the activist left a note stating, "It's hard to imagine not having food. But now you will know what it feels like. Please donate generously." The note also included an address for donations.

The activist was arrested and charged with several counts of burglary. He told his attorney that he wanted to present a necessity defense.

How should the attorney respond?

A. The necessity defense never works in these kinds of do-gooder situations; the activist will be better served by requesting a plea deal.

B. The necessity defense will not work because there is no causal link between the burglaries and the harm the activist sought to avoid.

C. The necessity defense may be an option because the activist broke the law in order to help fix a larger and more troubling social harm.

D. The necessity defense may be an option because the activist broke the law in order to finally cure a larger and more troubling social harm.

409. A woman was camping in a remote area when the temperature dropped drastically and unexpectedly. The woman decided to hike back to her car. On the way, she passed by a small cabin; the woman knocked on the door to gain entry, but no one answered. Shivering with cold, the woman broke a window and let herself into the cabin, reasoning that she would warm up and then return to hiking. But the cabin had no heat and it was colder inside than outside.

Later, the woman was charged with trespass for breaking and entering into the cabin.

Can the woman claim necessity in response to these charges?

A. No, because the woman incorrectly believed the cabin was heated and it was not.

B. No, because the woman should have checked the weather before she began camping.

C. Yes, because the woman reasonably believed the cabin was heated although it was not.

D. Yes, because the woman cannot be held responsible for sudden weather changes.

410. A graduate student began working for a professor who had a grant to conduct research on rabbits; the research protocol involved underfeeding the rabbits. After several months, the graduate student began to believe that his work constituted cruelty to animals, and so he erased all of the data that had been collected from the hard drives on the professor's computer.

The graduate student was later charged with various cybercrimes. At his upcoming trial, the graduate student wants to claim that he had to erase the data to demonstrate the greater harm of animal cruelty.

Will the graduate student's proposed defense be successful?

A. Yes, because the moral cost of animal cruelty outweighs the research value of the data.

B. Yes, because the graduate student chose the lives of the rabbits over the research.

C. No, because the graduate student could have protested the research through legal means.

D. No, because necessity is not a defense to crimes involving animals, only humans.

411. A large dam unexpectedly broke, causing a massive flood in a small town. Several residents of an apartment building saved themselves by running to the roof of the building. The residents expected that they would soon be rescued, but no help came. As darkness fell, the residents became cold and hungry, and so they broke into the top-floor apartment for food and better shelter, destroying the front door and eating all the food from the refrigerator.

The residents were rescued the next day and were later charged with trespass for breaking into the apartment and theft for stealing food from the refrigerator. At trial, the residents asserted a necessity defense, but the prosecutor argued in his closing that there was no necessity because the residents had chosen a greater evil (property damage) over a lesser one (the threat of being cold and hungry).

Will the defense be successful?

A. Yes, because the residents properly chose to protect their lives over damage to property.

B. Yes, because the residents would likely have starved to death if they had not acted as they did.

C. No, because the residents should not have chosen their own lives over the damage to property.

D. No, because the residents were rescued, which proves that they did not face a real choice of evils.

412. One night, a college student got very drunk, fell down in his bedroom, and broke his wrist. In immense pain, the student drove himself to the hospital for an x-ray. On the way to the hospital, police pulled the student over and cited him for drunk driving.

The student told his attorney that he wants to challenge the charge, arguing that he had no other choice but to drive himself to the hospital.

How should the attorney respond?

A. The defense will likely succeed because a medical emergency will always trump a moving violation.

B. The defense will likely fail because necessity is only a defense to common law crimes.

C. The defense will likely succeed because the student had to choose between drunk driving or medical treatment.

D. The defense will likely fail because the student was responsible for getting himself drunk.

413. A man was driving his car when he spotted a motorcycle heading toward him at a high rate of speed. The man quickly realized that the only way to avoid the motorcyclist was to veer onto a sidewalk where a pedestrian was present. Making a split-second decision, the man drove into the pedestrian, killing her. The man survived the accident, and the motorcyclist drove down the road, unharmed. The man was later charged with the murder of the pedestrian.

Does the man have a viable necessity defense?

A. Yes; the man chose the life of one person over the lives of two people.

B. Yes; the man was forced to choose between the motorcyclist's life and the pedestrian's life.

C. No; necessity is not a defense here because the man did not pick the lesser of two evils.

D. No; the man could have used his brakes and the pedestrian would not have been killed.

414. A prisoner serving a 20-year sentence for rape escaped from prison one night after the prison caught fire. The prisoner did not go far, but instead went far enough from the burning building to keep himself safe, and then waited on the side of the road for the authorities to find him. The prisoner was charged with prison escape, and he now wants to offer a necessity defense. In this jurisdiction, necessity is codified in the penal code as:

> Unless inconsistent with other provisions of this penal code, conduct which would otherwise constitute an offense is justifiable and not criminal when it is necessary as an emergency measure to avoid an imminent public or private injury which is about to occur by reason of a situation occasioned or developed through no conduct of the actor, and which is of sufficient gravity that, according to ordinary standards of intelligence and morality, the desirability and urgency of avoiding the injury clearly outweigh the desirability of avoiding the injury sought to be prevented by the statute defining the offense in issue.

Does the prisoner have a viable defense?

A. Yes, because all of the requirements of the statute are met by these facts.

B. Yes, because the prisoner received a 20-year sentence, not the death penalty.

C. No, because the prisoner committed the rape that caused him to be imprisoned.

D. No, because only some of the requirements of the statute are met by these facts.

415. A law student was studying for her final exam and was confused about the differences between necessity and duress. The student emailed the teaching assistant for help.

How should the teaching assistant respond?

A. The two defenses are completely distinct and each has separate requirements.

B. The two defenses are interchangeable and there is no difference between them.

C. The two defenses are related and have several overlapping requirements.

D. The two defenses are interchangeable but each has distinct requirements.

416. A woman was stopped in her car at a stoplight when a stranger got in and pointed a gun at her. He calmly explained that he would kill her unless she drove to a nearby bank and robbed it for him. The stranger said that the bank security guard was working with him, and would make sure that no one called the police. The stranger also cautioned that the guard would be watching the woman closely, and would kill her if she did not follow the directions.

The woman drove to the bank, robbed it, and then gave the proceeds to the stranger. The woman was later arrested and charged with bank robbery.

How should the woman defend herself?

A. The woman should argue that she made a reasoned choice to rob the bank instead of being killed by the stranger or the security guard.

B. The woman should argue that she acted under duress because the stranger's credible threats of death left her no choice but to rob the bank.

C. The woman should argue that the stranger should be charged with bank robbery as well, and that she only did what he told her to do.

D. The woman should argue that the unusual facts of how she came to rob the bank should be considered as mitigation at her sentencing.

417. Police arrested a man for drunk driving as he drove away from a bar. Earlier, the man was hitting on a woman who had been sitting at the bar, repeatedly trying to get her phone number. When the woman declined, the man tried to kiss her, and he grabbed at her breasts. The bartender saw this and told the man that should "leave now or else." Fearing that the bartender might hurt him, the man left the bar.

At his upcoming trial, the man wants to claim that he had to drive while intoxicated in order to protect himself from the bartender.

What defense does the man propose?

A. Necessity, because the bartender's threat left the man with no choice but to drive drunk.

B. Necessity, because the bartender should have known the man was too drunk to drive.

C. Duress, because the man faced threats of serious bodily injury from a person, the bartender.

D. Duress, because the bartender took advantage of the man's condition to threaten him.

418. The law school dean approached the school's chief finance officer and instructed her to skim one percent off the top of all incoming tuition payments and to put the skimmed funds into a separate account. At first, the finance officer refused, but the dean had nude photos of her posing with several different students. The dean warned the finance officer that if she did not cooperate, he would publish the photos online and the finance officer would lose her job.

The finance officer did as she was instructed. Three months later, a routine audit revealed the missing funds and the finance officer was arrested and charged with embezzlement.

Can the finance officer present a duress defense?

A. Yes, because the dean's credible threats left the finance officer no choice but to embezzle tuition money from the law school.

B. Yes, because the finance officer honestly and reasonably believed that she had no choice but to embezzle from the law school.

C. No, because the finance officer was only threatened with public embarrassment and losing her job, not death or serious bodily injury.

D. No, because the dean only threatened the finance officer once, but the finance officer repeatedly embezzled from the law school.

419. A woman was in a residential neighborhood when a carjacker hopped into her car and put a gun to her head. The carjacker instructed the woman to drive to a particular house where a child's birthday party was being held. The carjacker then told the woman that he would kill her unless she drove her car onto the front lawn and into the group of children who were playing there. Tearfully, the woman did as she was told, killing three children. At the woman's upcoming murder trial, she wants to claim duress and ask that she be acquitted.

Will the defense succeed?

A. No, because duress is not a defense to a charge of homicide.

B. No, because the woman could have easily refused the carjacker.

C. Yes, because the carjacker forced the woman to kill the kids.

D. Yes, because she reasonably believed she had to kill the kids.

420. A woman began dealing cocaine. She started with just a few customers, but her business quickly grew. The woman's supplier offered her the opportunity to grow her business even more by transporting a suitcase of cocaine on a plane. The woman refused, but the supplier told her that he would kill her if she did not comply. The supplier also warned the woman that she was being watched at all times, and she would be killed if she contacted the police.

The following week, the woman tried to board a plane with the suitcase of cocaine, but she was arrested before the plane took off. She was charged with various drug crimes, and she wants to claim duress. According to the jurisdiction's penal code:

> It is an affirmative defense that the actor engaged in the conduct charged to constitute an offense because he was coerced to do so by the use of, or a threat to use, unlawful force against his person or the person of another, which a person of reasonable firmness in his situation would have been unable to resist.
>
> The defense provided by this section is unavailable if the actor recklessly placed himself in a situation in which it was probable that he would be subjected to duress. The defense is also unavailable if he was criminally negligent in placing himself in such a situation, whenever criminal negligence suffices to establish culpability for the offense charged. In a prosecution for murder, the defense is only available to reduce the degree of the crime to manslaughter.

Will the woman's proposed defense succeed?

A. Yes, because the woman was coerced to act by a threat to use unlawful force against her, and she could not reasonably resist.

B. Yes, because the woman only negligently placed herself in a situation in which it was probable that she would be subjected to duress.

C. No, because the woman should have known that the threat that she was being watched "at all times" was overblown and not credible.

D. No, because the woman recklessly placed herself in a situation in which it was probable that she would be subjected to duress.

Entrapment

421. An undercover police officer approached a young woman at a bar and struck up a conversation. The two chatted for a while over a couple of beers. During the conversation, the officer revealed that he sometimes used heroin; the young woman replied by asking if he wanted to buy heroin from her. The officer agreed, and the two left the bar and made the exchange in a nearby alley.

Once the sale was concluded, the undercover officer arrested the young woman. She was charged with possession and distribution of heroin and asked her attorney whether she has a plausible entrapment claim.

How should the attorney respond?

A. The entrapment claim will succeed because the undercover officer approached the young woman first, and not the other way around.

B. The entrapment claim will succeed because the undercover officer failed to tell the young woman that he worked with the police.

C. The entrapment claim will fail because the young woman did not ask for the undercover officer's ID before selling him drugs.

D. The entrapment claim will fail because the undercover officer gave the young woman a chance to do what she wanted to do anyway.

422. A man struck up a conversation with a woman he met at the gym. In the course of the conversation, the man complained to the woman that he could not stand his wife. The woman responded: "why don't you do something about that?" The man replied that he had been thinking of hiring someone to kill his wife, and asked the woman if she would kill his wife for $5,000.

What the man did not realize is that the woman was also a police officer. The woman arrested the man and he was later charged with solicitation to commit murder. At his upcoming trial, the man wants to assert a defense of entrapment.

Will the man's defense be successful?

A. Yes, because the woman prompted the solicitation when she asked, "why don't you do something about that?"

B. Yes, because the woman never told the man of his right to remain silent and that his words could be used against him.

C. No, because the man's statement to the woman indicated that he had already developed the idea of killing his wife.

D. No, because entrapment is not a defense to solicitation, only to completed crimes like murder, arson, and rape.

423. A computer hacker's roommate was a police officer who worked in the internet crimes unit. Every night, the police officer would brag to the hacker about his work and how he and his colleagues worked to expose online child pornographers. The police officer also told the hacker that he knew of a way to download photos and not be traced, but that no one else had yet figured it out.

After hearing many, many times about downloading photos without detection, the hacker became curious and wanted to see if he could succeed. One evening after work, the hacker logged into a child pornography site and downloaded several photos using a hack that—he believed—would make his work untraceable. But the hacker was wrong, and he was charged with possession of child pornography. The hacker wants to offer an entrapment defense. This jurisdiction follows the majority rule regarding entrapment.

Does the hacker have a possible entrapment defense?

A. No, because the hacker should have known that every action a person takes online leaves some sort of trail.

B. Yes, because the officer's bragging induced the hacker to commit a crime he would not have otherwise committed.

C. Yes, because the hacker wanted to download child pornography, but he had no intent to possess that pornography.

D. No, because the officer's bragging only made the hacker curious about something he wanted to do anyway.

424. A man was charged with drug possession and claimed entrapment at his bench trial. After closing arguments, the presiding judge reviewed the case with her clerk. The judge explained that she was horrified by the police work in the case, and thought that the overreaching of the lead officer would have led anyone to become curious about drugs and commit the crime. Still, the judge told the clerk that she was also bothered by the fact that the man had a drug possession conviction from a few years before, and was concerned that he was predisposed to commit the crime anyway.

This jurisdiction follows the minority rule regarding entrapment.

What verdict should the judge return?

A. Not guilty, because the lead officer's conduct would have led anyone to become curious about drugs and commit the crime.

B. Not guilty, because the police gave the man the opportunity to commit a crime, even though he was predisposed to it.

C. Guilty, because the man's prior conviction for drug possession shows that he was predisposed to commit this crime.

D. Guilty, because the police gave the man the opportunity to commit a crime he was predisposed to commit anyway.

425. A law review student was writing a student note about the defense of entrapment. As part of the note, the student wanted to include a section about her jurisdiction's entrapment defense, which is codified in the following statute:

> A person is not guilty of an offense if the person's conduct is incited or induced by a public servant or a public servant's agent for the purpose of obtaining evidence for the prosecution of the person. However, this section is inapplicable if a public servant or a public servant's agent merely affords to the person the opportunity or facility for committing an offense in furtherance of criminal purpose that the person has originated.

In the text, how should the student characterize this statute?

A. This statute follows the objective approach as it focuses on the public servant's conduct leading up to the crime.

B. This statute follows the objective approach as it requires evaluation of the all the facts and circumstances.

C. This statute follows the subjective approach as it focuses on each actor's motivation for his individual acts.

D. This statute follows the subjective approach as it focuses on the defendant's predisposition to the crime.

Answer Key

1.	D	26.	A	51.	A	76.	B
2.	B	27.	C	52.	B	77.	A
3.	A	28.	D	53.	B	78.	D
4.	A	29.	D	54.	A	79.	A
5.	D	30.	C	55.	D	80.	A
6.	B	31.	C	56.	D	81.	C
7.	D	32.	C	57.	A	82.	A
8.	B	33.	A	58.	B	83.	C
9.	A	34.	C	59.	A	84.	D
10.	B	35.	C	60.	B	85.	C
11.	C	36.	C	61.	A	86.	A
12.	C	37.	A	62.	D	87.	A
13.	A	38.	B	63.	A	88.	C
14.	B	39.	B	64.	C	89.	D
15.	D	40.	A	65.	D	90.	A
16.	B	41.	B	66.	B	91.	C
17.	A	42.	D	67.	D	92.	D
18.	C	43.	B	68.	D	93.	B
19.	C	44.	A	69.	B	94.	C
20.	C	45.	C	70.	C	95.	C
21.	B	46.	D	71.	B	96.	B
22.	C	47.	A	72.	A	97.	D
23.	A	48.	C	73.	C	98.	A
24.	D	49.	B	74.	A	99.	C
25.	D	50.	C	75.	D	100.	A

101. D
102. C
103. D
104. B
105. A

106. C
107. D
108. D
109. C
110. A

111. D
112. A
113. B
114. D
115. C

116. D
117. D
118. C
119. C
120. B

121. A
122. B
123. C
124. D
125. B

126. C
127. D
128. A
129. C
130. C

131. A
132. C
133. A
134. D
135. A

136. A
137. D
138. B
139. C
140. B

141. D
142. B
143. A
144. D
145. A

146. C
147. C
148. A
149. B
150. D

151. C
152. B
153. B
154. A
155. D

156. C
157. B
158. D
159. A
160. C

161. D
162. A
163. C
164. A
165. B

166. B
167. B
168. D
169. B
170. A

171. D
172. C
173. B
174. D
175. A

176. B
177. D
178. A
179. B
180. C

181. B
182. C
183. A
184. B
185. D

186. C
187. A
188. D
189. A
190. B

191. C
192. B
193. C
194. D
195. B

196. B
197. D
198. B
199. C
200. A

201. B
202. D
203. A
204. D
205. B

206. D
207. B
208. A
209. D
210. C

211. C
212. D
213. C
214. B
215. C

216. B
217. C
218. A
219. D
220. C

221. D
222. A
223. C
224. D
225. A

226. C
227. B
228. A
229. A
230. D

231. D
232. D
233. C
234. A
235. C

236. A
237. B
238. A
239. B
240. D

241. B
242. D
243. A
244. A
245. C

246. D
247. B
248. A
249. B
250. D

251. B
252. A
253. B
254. A
255. C

256. D
257. B
258. D
259. A
260. C

261. D
262. A
263. A
264. D
265. A

266. B
267. B
268. A
269. B
270. B

271. D
272. C
273. B
274. B
275. A

276. C
277. C
278. D
279. A
280. B

281. A
282. D
283. A
284. D
285. C

286. B
287. C
288. B
289. A
290. D

291. D
292. B
293. A
294. C
295. A

296. C
297. D
298. B
299. A
300. B

301. C
302. A
303. C
304. D
305. D

306. A
307. B
308. C
309. D
310. A

311. C
312. A
313. B
314. D
315. B

316. A
317. B
318. C
319. C
320. A

321. C
322. A
323. A
324. C
325. B

326. C
327. B
328. D
329. B
330. A

331. B
332. A
333. C
334. B
335. D

336. B
337. C
338. D
339. C
340. B

341. A
342. C
343. D
344. B
345. D

346. B
347. C
348. D
349. B
350. A

351. D
352. B
353. C
354. D
355. A

356. C
357. A
358. B
359. A
360. D

361. B
362. C
363. D
364. A
365. C

366. A
367. B
368. D
369. A
370. C

371. C
372. B
373. A
374. D
375. C

376. B
377. C
378. D
379. B
380. A

381. B
382. C
383. B
384. C
385. C

386. B
387. D
388. A
389. A
390. B

391. D
392. B
393. C
394. A
395. B

396. D
397. D
398. C
399. A
400. B

401. A
402. B
403. C
404. D
405. A

406. D
407. A
408. B
409. C
410. C

411. A
412. D
413. C
414. A
415. C

416. B
417. C
418. C
419. A
420. D

421. D
422. C
423. B
424. A
425. D

Part IV

Explanations

Introductory Concepts

1. This question tests on the key factor that distinguishes torts from crimes: punishment. Punishment occurs when the government imposes some sort of consequence upon the defendant as a result of his conviction. Punishment may be relatively light and consist of a fine. But punishment may also consist of the government taking a life, such as when a defendant is sentenced to death.

   D is correct because it recognizes that, without a criminal conviction, the man was not punished. He may not like that he has to pay the pedestrian's estate and he may think that the jury punished him when it rendered its verdict. But true punishment only accompanies a criminal conviction.

   A, B, and C are all incorrect because none recognize that punishment is tied to a criminal conviction.

2. This question tests on the goals of punishment: to deter, to incapacitate, to rehabilitate, and to show retribution.

   B is correct because the proposal refers specifically to testing and treatment, and because the author of the proposal has commented on how other drug courts have led to reductions in the recidivism rate. Both of these points show that the proposal is designed to rehabilitate offenders so that they do not reoffend.

   A is incorrect because incapacitation refers to depriving offenders of the ability to commit their crimes, usually by incarcerating them. While reduction in crime may be a goal of specialty courts, the question's reference to reducing recidivism suggests that the author of the proposal wants to reduce crime by addressing the causes of addition, and not through incarceration. **C is incorrect** because the proposal's focus on rehabilitation suggests the opposite of retribution. **D is incorrect** because the proposal focuses on actual offenders and their drug problems, and not on sending a message to other drug users.

3. This question tests on the two types of deterrence: specific and general.

   A is correct because the prosecutor wants to send a message to other parents, and not necessarily to this particular father. As such, the prosecutor's motivation is to generally deter others, and not specifically deter this defendant.

   B is incorrect because the reference to having the "public" learn from the case is a reference to general deterrence and not specific deterrence. **C and D are both incorrect** because bounded and universal deterrence are not recognized goals of punishment.

4. This question tests on utilitarianism, the first of the two theories of punishment. Utilitarians advocate for punishments that will be best for society overall, instead of those punishments that only address the defendant and his crime.

   A is correct because the judge's proposal refers to the cost savings that it will bring, i.e., something that will affect the community as a whole.

   B is incorrect because retributivism places its primary emphasis on the defendant and his crime and not on how possible punishment might affect society as a whole. **C and D are both incorrect** because each refers to a philosophical theory that has nothing to do with punishment or the criminal law.

5. This question tests on the other basic theory of punishment: retributivism. Retributivists believe that punishment should be crafted to "fit the crime," and that other considerations—e.g., rehabilitation—should be secondary.

   D is correct because the legislators opposing the motion are not swayed by information about the cost of capital sentencing. Instead, these legislators want to preserve the death penalty regardless of its cost. This focus on crime and punishment above all else shows a retributive perspective.

   A is incorrect because it makes a value judgment about the "best solutions," which may or may not be correct. **B is incorrect** because the question gives no information about the deterrent effect of capital punishment. **C is incorrect** because the legislators opposing the motion want to retain capital sentencing for its punitive effect and not because of its impact on society.

6. This question tests on utilitarianism and retributivism and the points where the two theories overlap. While there are many situations where utilitarians and retributivists disagree, there are some where they do not. In this question, for example, even the "tough on crime" legislators acknowledge that the proposed penalties for minor drug possession are too harsh.

   B is correct because it recognizes this principle.

   A is incorrect because it assumes facts beyond those given in the question. **C is incorrect** because the expression "tough on crime" refers to all crimes and does not distinguish between crimes against the person and drug crimes. **D is incorrect** because it does not address the question: while prosecutors might have exclusive authority to make charging decisions, the legislature is responsible for drafting the laws.

7. This question tests on the primary sources of American criminal law: the common law, the Model Penal Code, and statutory law. In general, the "common law" refers to both the common law in England and the common law as it developed in America. The Model Penal Code is a code that was drafted by members of the America Law Institute; it was finalized in 1962 and offered as a "model" for states to use in drafting their own penal codes. Finally, "statutory law" refers to the penal codes that have been enacted by individual states. In general, these penal codes rely on common law concepts (and sometimes the Model Penal Code), as modified to reflect more modern approaches to the criminal law.

   D is correct because it lists all three of these sources.

   A, B, and C are all incorrect because each only lists a subset of these three sources.

8. This question tests on how the common law is addressed in penal codes today. The text of this statute is from the Pennsylvania penal code, 18 Pa.C.S. § 107(b), and most state penal codes have similar provisions. This statute signals that the statutory penal code is the exclusive source of crimes in the jurisdiction. But that does not mean the jurisdiction has rejected or abandoned the common law. Instead, the common law will play a significant role in the interpretation of the penal code.

   B is correct because it recognizes that the statute only requires that all crimes be defined in the penal code and not that the common law is rejected entirely.

   A is incorrect for two reasons. First, the statute refers only to the abolition of common law crimes and not a complete rejection of the common law. Second, it would be impossible to determine to what degree this jurisdiction follows the Model Penal Code without reading the penal code in its entirety. **C is incorrect** because the statutory provision makes clear that this jurisdiction has a penal code in effect. **D is incorrect** because there is no constitutional requirement that a state follow the common law. In any event, the statutory provision does not "reject" the common law.

9. This question tests on how the Model Penal Code can be used by a jurisdiction: it is a model only, and states are free to adopt all of it, some of it, or none at all.

   A is correct because it recognizes that no state is required to adopt the Model Penal Code, but that many have adopted parts of it into their penal codes.

   B is incorrect because it is only partially true: the Model Penal Code was intended to be a guide, but it was drafted with the intent that states could and would adopt its provisions. **C and D are both incorrect** because each suggests that the Model Penal Code must be adopted in whole or not at all.

10. This question tests on the principle of legality. That principle is fundamental to the criminal law and holds that conduct cannot be punished by the law unless the conduct has previously been defined as a crime.

    B is correct because the man cannot be prosecuted for bestiality if the penal code does not include a crime addressing bestiality.

    A is incorrect because the issue here is that there is no crime that addresses the man's actions, and the *Ex Post Facto* Clause addresses the retroactive applications of crimes. **C is incorrect** because it directly violates the principle of legality: the issue is not whether the man knew his conduct was wrong, but whether this jurisdiction has defined a crime to proscribe the man's conduct. **D is incorrect** because, even if true, the man cannot be prosecuted for a crime that does not exist.

11. This question tests on what type of conduct can be criminalized. The answer is that almost any conduct can be criminalized, assuming that the law itself does not violate the Constitution. The statute in this question is from the Arkansas penal code. Ark. Code § 5-63-204.

    C is correct because it recognizes that a legislature has the authority to criminalize a wide range of conduct, subject to just one limitation: the Constitution.

    A is incorrect because it is untrue. Indeed, many modern crimes did not exist at common law, e.g., tax evasion, cruelty to animals, embezzlement, cybercrimes, etc. **B is incorrect**

because, by identifying robocalling as a crime, a state legislature can decide that it is not a legitimate business practice. **D is incorrect** because, if the state legislature can criminalize robocalling, it can also categorize the crime as a felony. While there could be concerns about whether the eventual punishment for any crime is disproportionate and violates the Eighth Amendment, the question gives no information about possible penalties in the proposed law.

12. This question tests on one of the limits on defining crimes. In particular, this question tests on the *Ex Post Facto* Clause, which prohibits the retroactive punishment of conduct that was legal at the time it was committed. See U.S. Const. Art. 1, §§ 9, 10. The *Ex Post Facto* Clause also prohibits the retroactive application of new or additional punishments that did not exist at the time the criminal conduct was committed. *Weaver v. Graham*, 450 U.S. 24 (1981).

    C is correct because the woman should be punished (sentenced) according to the law that was in effect at the time she committed the crime.

    A is incorrect because it offers a nonlegal response to a legal question. **B and D are both incorrect** because neither recognizes the *ex post facto* implications of the woman's sentencing.

13. This question tests on another limit for defining crimes—the constitutional prohibition on bills of attainder. A bill of attainder is a criminal law written to retroactively criminalize a specific person's (or class of people's) conduct. See U.S. Const. Art. 1, §§ 9, 10. These bills effectively punish the conduct without the ordinary process associated with a trial.

    A is correct because it properly describes the proposed bill.

    B is incorrect because nothing in the question implicates interstate commerce or its regulation. **C and D are both incorrect** because neither addresses the core issue in this question: that the proposed bill would retroactively criminalize the crematory owner's conduct.

14. This question tests on another limit on defining crimes: the Bill of Rights. The Michigan statute in this question was invalidated in *People v. Boomer*, 655 Mich. App. 255 (2002).

    B is correct because the statute infringes on the young man's right to speech. Although some forms of speech can be limited, most forms are protected.

    A and D are both incorrect because each involves a concession that the young man violated the statute. Instead, the best challenge to the charge is one that results in it being dropped entirely. **C is incorrect** because an equal protection challenge might result in the statute being amended and not being struck as unconstitutional.

15. This question tests on the rule of lenity, a fundamental principle involving the interpretation of criminal statutes. So that people can rely upon and follow the law, criminal statutes must provide fair warning about what conduct is proscribed. But if a statute has any ambiguity, the rule of lenity requires that the ambiguity be resolved in favor of the defense. The facts in this question are derived from *Yates v. U.S.*, 574 U.S. 528 (2015).

    D is correct because the relevant statute appears to refer to the mishandling of various kinds of paperwork and not fish. While one could interpret the statutory definition of a "tangible object" to include fish, the question is whether a person reading the statute would be on notice of that interpretation. As that is unlikely, the rule of lenity requires resolving the motion in the caption's favor.

A and B are both incorrect because each recognizes the ambiguity but neither provides a legal reason to grant the motion. **C is incorrect** because it does not address the captain's argument about the statute's ambiguity.

16. This question tests the core elements of common law crimes: *mens rea*, *actus reus*, causation, and harm.

B is correct because it identifies these requirements, and because it recognizes that the *mens rea* must be concurrent with the *actus reus*, i.e., the *mens rea* must drive the *actus reus*.

A is incorrect because it suggests that a guilty mind and a guilty act alone form a crime. But if the *mens rea* and the *actus reus* are unrelated, no crime has occurred. Likewise, if the *mens rea* and *actus reus* together result in no proscribed harm, then no crime has occurred. **C is incorrect** because it provides inaccurate descriptions of *mens rea* and *actus reus*. **D is incorrect** because it omits the causation element.

17. This question tests on a definition of a crime that requires proof of attendant circumstances, beyond the ordinary elements. In this question, the woman is charged with burglary, which has a nighttime requirement. The prosecutor has established the woman's *mens rea* and *actus reus*, but she must also prove that the crime happened at night.

A is correct because the prosecutor cannot expect a conviction unless she proves that the crime happened at night. That is an attendant circumstance in the definition of the crime.

B is incorrect because burglary does not require a completed crime inside the house; it requires the intent to commit that crime at the time of the breaking and entering. **C is incorrect** because the focus here is not whether the woman stole the jewelry, but instead whether the prosecutor must prove that the crime happened at night. **D is incorrect** because the definition of burglary requires proof of an additional attendant circumstance.

18. This question tests on causation, and on the requirement that the defendant's action be the cause-in-fact of the identified harm. This requirement requires "but for" causation, i.e., but for the defendant's actions, the harm would not have occurred.

C is correct because it is the only answer that recognizes that the woman directly caused her sister's death by shooting her.

A, B, and D are all incorrect because the sister's alleged theft from the estate may have started the chain of events that led to her death, but it did not "cause" her death.

19. This question also tests on causation and the additional requirement that the defendant's action be the proximate or legal cause of the identified harm. This is a foregone conclusion for most crimes, but proximate cause can be an issue when there is a time lapse between the defendant's actions and the resulting harm. Here, the second man died a year after he was shot, so the question is what killed him—the gunshot, the pneumonia, or his drug use? Thus, the proximate cause rule focuses on foreseeability and asks whether the defendant could have foreseen the result at the time he engaged in his criminal conduct. If so, he is the proximate cause of that result.

C is correct because it recognizes that the second man's death was a foreseeable result of the shooting.

A is incorrect because it goes too far in arguing that the first man had "no way of knowing" that his act of shooting the second man in the neck might lead to the second man's death. **B is incorrect** because the intervening causes here were also foreseeable, and so the first man cannot evade responsibility for his actions. By comparison, imagine if the second man died from a shellfish allergy. In that situation, the allergy would be an unforeseeable intervening cause of death, and the first man would not be responsible for the homicide. **D is incorrect** because the defense motion implicates proximate cause and not direct, but-for cause.

20. This question tests on the concurrence requirement, which dictates that the defendant's *mens rea* drive his *actus reus.* In this question, the woman has the *mens rea* for intentional murder, but killed the child by accident. As such, she cannot be convicted of intentional murder because there is no concurrence between her *mens rea* and *actus reus.*

    C is correct because it recognizes this principle.

    A, B, and D are all incorrect because each concedes that the woman killed the child intentionally and suggests a possible mitigating factor for sentencing. But the question asks about trial defenses and not sentencing arguments.

21. This question tests on the two types of common law crimes: misdemeanors and felonies. At common law, the distinction between them was very clear, as misdemeanor convictions carried no more than a year of incarceration. Today, the distinction is less clear, as some misdemeanors in some jurisdictions carry lengthier sentences. But in general, the basic distinction from the common law remains mostly true today.

    B is correct because it recognizes the one-year misdemeanor sentencing limitation, and that such shorter sentences are usually served in jail and not prison.

    A is incorrect because no matter the jurisdiction and how it distinguishes misdemeanors from felonies, the range of penalties in the answer is too harsh for a misdemeanor conviction. **C is incorrect** because the sentence for a misdemeanor is usually one year or less and is served in a jail and not a prison. **D is incorrect** because it is too definitive: while the man's clean record will probably help him at sentencing, there is no guarantee that he "will only be fined."

22. This question tests on *mala in se* crimes, which are crimes that are intrinsically wrong or evil, like murder and rape.

    C is correct because it recognizes that it is wrong for one person to kill another.

    A is incorrect because *mala prohibita* crimes are those that are wrong because they are prohibited. For example, jaywalking is a *malum prohibitum* offense, but there is nothing intrinsically wrong with jaywalking—it is just against the law. **B is incorrect** because *mare liberum* refers to the open seas and has nothing to do with the classification of crimes. **D is incorrect** because *jus commune* is Latin for "common law," which gives a circular answer: murder is a common law crime because murder is a common law crime.

23. This question tests on *mala prohibita* crimes, which describe prohibited conduct. The conduct itself is not morally wrong—as with *mala in se* crimes—but it is still prohibited. The statute in this question is from the East Lansing municipal code. E.L. (MI) Code § 14-37.

A is correct because it is the only answer that accurately responds to the question.

B and C are both incorrect because this statute cannot be identified as a misdemeanor based solely on the college sophomore's punishment. Although an omitted provision in this statute describes it as an infraction, looking at a defendant's sentence is an imprecise way of identifying the underlying conviction. For example, some misdemeanants go to jail and some convicted felons receive probation and avoid incarceration. **D is incorrect** because littering is not morally wrong in the way the traditional *mala in se* crimes—e.g., murder and rape—are.

24. This question tests on "victimless crimes," and relies on a Georgia public drunkenness statute. Ga. Code Ann. §16-11-41. While many crimes include an identifiable harm, some—particularly *mala prohibita* offenses—do not.

D is correct because this statute does not identify a specific harm, like a type of injury. Instead, the statute focuses on a defendant's *actus reus*: his boisterousness, his indecent condition or act, and his possibly vulgar, profane, loud, or unbecoming language.

A is incorrect because it provides a nonlegal response to a legal question. **B is incorrect** because the prosecutor does not need to concede error in this situation, as there is no merit to the man's argument. **C is incorrect** because the statute does not require anyone to hear the man's singing; instead, the statute focuses on the singing itself.

25. This question tests on jurisdiction to prosecute crimes. The federal government has exclusive jurisdiction to prosecute a limited number of federal crimes—e.g., those occurring in a federal territory or in a federal prison—and have concurrent jurisdiction with the states over some other crimes. But the states have exclusive jurisdiction over most of the criminal prosecutions in the United States.

D is correct because this question describes a state murder that lacks any features that would allow the federal prosecutor to assert jurisdiction. Instead, the federal prosecutor only wants to take over the case because he thinks his office could do a better job. While a federal court may review a state crime to determine if it violates the federal constitution, that is different from having jurisdiction to prosecute the case in the first place.

A is incorrect because jurisdiction is about the authority to oversee the case and has nothing to do with funding. **B is incorrect** because the federal prosecutor lacks jurisdiction and so has no rights here. **C is incorrect** because it does not respond to the jurisdictional issue.

26. This question also tests on jurisdiction. When all elements of a crime are committed in one state, that state has exclusive jurisdiction to prosecute the crime.

A is correct because the only state that has jurisdiction to prosecute is the state where the homicide occurred.

B is incorrect because no act associated with the homicide occurred in the man's (victim's) home state. As such, that state lacks jurisdiction to prosecute the crime. **C is incorrect** because the gun was purchased years before, and so the act of purchasing was not associated with the homicide. Thus, the third state lacks jurisdiction to prosecute the crime. **D is incorrect** because it suggests that multiple states have jurisdiction to prosecute this crime, and only one state has jurisdiction.

27. This question also tests on jurisdiction. In this question, some acts associated with the conspiracy occurred in one state, and other acts occurred in a second state. Because conspiracy is an ongoing crime, both states will have jurisdiction to prosecute both crimes.

    C is correct because it recognizes this principle. While there may be advantages to having the case prosecuted in one state or the other, both states may prosecute both crimes.

    A is incorrect because conspiracy is an ongoing crime, which means that the state where the agreement was formed would have jurisdiction to prosecute, as would any state where any act in furtherance of the conspiracy was committed. **B and D are both incorrect** because each misstates the rule about jurisdiction.

28. This question tests on concurrent state and federal jurisdiction, which occurs in situations where either the state or the federal government may prosecute a defendant for a crime. In such situations, either the state or the federal government, or sometimes both, have jurisdiction to prosecute the crime.

    D is correct because the existence of overlapping state and federal bank robbery statutes indicates that this is a crime where there is concurrent jurisdiction.

    A is incorrect because the presence of a federal bank robbery statute demonstrates that the attorney's argument is wrong. **B is incorrect** because successive prosecutions by separate sovereigns for the same crime do not violate the Double Jeopardy Clause. *Gamble v. U.S.*, 139 S. Ct. 1960 (2019). **C is incorrect** because the attorney's argument addresses the right to prosecute the man in the first instance.

29. This question tests on the burden of proof in a criminal case, which requires that the prosecutor prove each element of the charged crime beyond a reasonable doubt. *In re Winship*, 397 U.S. 358 (1970).

    D is correct because the prosecutor conceded that she could not meet her burden when she told the jury that she could not "give ... any real evidence that the defendant committed the crime."

    A is incorrect because, honesty aside, the prosecutor still must meet her burden. **B is incorrect** because, if the prosecutor cannot prove the elements of the crime, the defendant cannot be convicted. That is not harmless error, but the opposite. **C is incorrect** because the prosecutor's inability to meet her burden does not demonstrate the defendant's innocence. Instead, it only demonstrates a deficiency in the prosecutor's case.

30. This question tests on the difference between burdens of proof and burdens of production. The burden of proof requires the prosecutor to prove something exists or is true, e.g., that the defendant acted with an intent to kill or that his actions caused the victim's death. The burden of production is a showing that a party must make to have a particular issue presented to the fact-finder. For example, in this question, if the defendant wants to claim self-defense, he will have a burden of production regarding the necessity of his actions before the jury can be instructed on that issue.

    C is correct because it addresses these principles.

    A is incorrect because it provides a nonlegal answer to a legal question. In any event, while burdens of proof and production are complicated concepts, each can still be explained to a layperson. **B is incorrect** because the prosecution always bears the burden of proof for the elements of the crime, no matter what defense is offered. **D is incorrect** because the law is not unconstitutional because it does not relieve the prosecution of the burden of proof.

31. This question also tests on the prosecutor's burden of proof in a criminal case. The prosecutor can use direct or circumstantial evidence to prove her case, but she must prove the elements of the crime beyond a reasonable doubt.

    C is correct because the prosecutor's comments—referring to the defendant's failure to disprove the circumstantial case—impermissibly shifted the burden of proof. The defendant may want to answer the state's case: he may want to cross-examine witnesses, he may want to offer an alibi, or he may want to point out that his hair is brown and not red. But he is not required to prove his innocence, and the prosecutor's argument suggests that he is.

    A is incorrect because the problem here is the shifting of the burden of proof and not that the prosecutor seeks to convict the man on circumstantial evidence. **B is incorrect** because the prosecutor's argument does more than summarize the witness testimony. **D is incorrect** because the burden of production is not at issue here.

32. This question tests on the proof beyond a reasonable doubt standard, which is the standard by which the prosecution must prove the elements of its case. While the Constitution does not require any particular reasonable doubt definition—or that the standard be defined at all—any reasonable doubt instruction has to be correct. *Victor v. Nebraska*, 511 U.S. 1 (1994).

    C is correct because the judge's instruction here is patently incorrect. By stating that reasonable doubt is "probably more than 50%," the judge left open the possibility that it could be less than that, i.e., less than a preponderance of the evidence. As a result, the instruction reduced—or diluted—the prosecution's burden.

    A is incorrect because there is no such prohibition on quantifying reasonable doubt, although, as this question demonstrates, this might not be a good idea. **B is incorrect** because the problem with the judge's instruction is not that the jurors might be confused; it is that the instruction was wrong. **D is incorrect** because it is untrue: the judge did not instruct the jurors that the defendant was required to prove anything.

33. This question tests on one of the ways in which criminal liability can be imposed. In many criminal cases, the defendant acts alone and so he is prosecuted alone. But a defendant can also be prosecuted for the acts of others, such as when he is a co-conspirator or an accomplice.

    A is correct because the man and his friend were co-conspirators. As such, the man can be prosecuted for the conspiracy and any act committed in furtherance of the conspiracy, regardless of whether he committed those acts himself. *Pinkerton v. U.S.*, 328 U.S. 640 (1946).

    B, C, and D are all incorrect because each misstates the rule from *Pinkerton*.

34. This question tests on another way that a person can be prosecuted for the criminal acts of another person: through vicarious liability. Although vicarious liability is relatively limited

in the criminal law, it can be used in some situations, particularly those involving highly regulated activities and where the penalties for a violation are relatively minor.

C is correct because it recognizes that a prosecution here would be appropriate. Even though the bar owner did not engage in the *actus reus* of the crime, he had the *mens rea* for its commission. And, given that liquor sales are regulated and that the punishment for violation of the statute is so minor, the bar owner can be held vicariously liable for the actions of the bartender.

A is incorrect because it suggests that vicarious liability can never be imposed under any circumstances. **B is incorrect** because the bar owner does not need 100% certainty; instead, knowledge is sufficient. **D is incorrect** because the bar owner should be prosecuted because he had the *mens rea* that the crime be committed and because the underage liquor sales were being made at a bar that he owned and was responsible for. The fact that the bar owner made money from these transactions shows his *mens rea* for the crime, but it is not an independent reason to prosecute him.

35. This question tests on the limits of vicarious liability. In this question, the penalty for a conviction of the statute is a 20-year sentence, which goes well beyond the limits of permissible vicarious liability. Instead, if a defendant faces a sentence of incarceration, the prosecutor will have to prove that he had both the *mens rea* and the *actus reus* for the crime.

C is correct because it focuses on the key to imposing vicarious liability: punishment must be significantly curtailed.

A and D are both incorrect because each suggests that there is no vicarious liability in the criminal law, which is untrue. **B is incorrect** because the felony/misdemeanor distinction is important, but is not dispositive as to whether the business owner can be prosecuted.

Mens Rea

36. This question tests on *mens rea* generally and demonstrates the why it is important to establish the defendant's mental state. Here, the man killed his neighbor. But to punish him properly, we also need to know his *mens rea*. Did the man plan the killing for some time before committing it? If so, the man should be convicted of murder and his punishment should be severe. Did he kill with criminal negligence? If so, he should be convicted of involuntary manslaughter, and the punishment will be less severe. Or did he kill in self-defense? If so, the man should not be punished at all. But without knowing all the attendant circumstances, including the man's *mens rea*, we cannot determine the appropriate punishment.

C is correct because it recognizes this principle.

A, B, and D are all incorrect because each proposes an appropriate punishment. But those proposed punishments cannot be evaluated without knowing the man's *mens rea*.

37. This question tests on the difference between motive and *mens rea*. A defendant's motive is a possible explanation for why he commits a crime. But his *mens rea* is his mental state at the time he commits the crime. A defendant's *mens rea* can be driven by his motive, but having a motive does not necessarily equate to having the *mens rea* for the crime.

A is correct because it recognizes this principle. The young woman had a financial motive to kill her parents, but that does not mean that she also had the intent to kill them.

B is incorrect because "all children" do not inherit money from their parents. In any event, even if "all children" have the same motive, that would still not establish the *mens rea* for any resulting crimes. **C is incorrect** because it conflates motive and *mens rea*. **D is incorrect** because it does not address the legal issue presented by the question, and because it assumes facts about inheritance taxes that are not provided by the question.

38. This question tests on the basic problem with proving *mens rea*: how can anyone know what the defendant was thinking when he committed the offense, unless the defendant explains himself? The answer is that the defendant's *mens rea* can be established by looking at all the attendant circumstances and making reasonable inferences from those circumstances.

B is correct because it recognizes this principle. The senior may refuse to testify, but that does not mean the jury cannot make a finding regarding his *mens rea*.

A is incorrect because formal logic is not required; instead, the jury can just make reasonable inferences from the facts. **C is incorrect** because it states the opposite of the correct rule. **D is incorrect** because this is not about the balancing of constitutional rights. The senior does have a constitutional right to refuse to testify. But the prosecutor can still meet her burden without interfering with that constitutional right.

39. This question also tests on *mens rea*, giving another example of making reasonable inferences from the facts. Here, the man was arrested in the backyard of his enemy's house—a place where he presumably has no reason to be. The man was dressed in dark clothing and is surrounded by fire-making tools. From these facts, the fact-finder could reasonably infer that the man intended to commit arson of the enemy's house. But, at the same time, it would be unreasonable for the fact-finder to infer that the man intended to rape someone inside the house.

B is correct because it recognizes that all the facts, considered together, show a specific intent to commit arson.

A is incorrect because the man is charged with attempted arson and not (completed) arson. Because attempt is an inchoate crime, it requires specific intent to commit the target crime. **C is incorrect** because it goes too far by referring to what "all" reasonable fact-finders will agree to in this situation. **D is incorrect** because it is untrue: the prosecutor cannot force the man to testify in this situation.

40. This question also tests on proving *mens rea* in criminal cases. In this question, the judge instructs the jury that it can "presume" the defendant's *mens rea* from the facts, which goes well beyond making reasonable inferences from those facts. Such an instruction is not permitted, because it relieves the prosecution of its burden of proof. See *Sandstrom v. Montana*, 442 U.S. 510 (1979).

A is correct because it recognizes this principle. If the instruction was correct, then all homicides committed with guns could be treated as intentional murder.

B is incorrect because the judge's instruction referred to a presumption about the defendant's intent and not his actions. **C is incorrect** because it is not "obvious" that people intend the consequences of their actions. They sometimes do, but not in every instance. **D is incorrect** because this is not a harmless error, as the error affects whether the man is convicted of an intentional homicide or not.

41. This question tests on general intent crimes, i.e., those crimes that only require proof of the defendant's awareness of the factors associated with the crime. Here, the woman is charged with arson, which has one of two possible mental states: intent to burn or recklessness regarding a high risk of burning. The woman testified that she did not intend to destroy the building. While her testimony, if credited, may be relevant to sentencing, it is irrelevant to the underlying conviction because arson does not require an additional intent to destroy.

B is correct because the woman's testimony about destruction of the shed has no bearing on whether she intended to burn it in the first place, or was reckless regarding a high risk of burning.

A is incorrect because arson is a general intent crime. Only strict liability crimes omit the *mens rea* requirement. **C is incorrect** because it is untrue: the woman's testimony demonstrates nothing about the neighbor's role in the arson. **D is incorrect** because arson does not have an intent to destroy requirement in its definition.

42. This question tests on general intent crimes. At common law, general intent crimes included:

Common law murder, when described as a "malice" crime

Felony murder, when the underlying felony is a general intent crime

Common law manslaughter

Rape

Arson

Battery

All malice crimes

All criminal negligence crimes

D is correct because it includes three of the crimes from this list.

A is incorrect because it includes burglary, which is a specific intent crime. **B is incorrect** because it includes assault, which is a specific intent crime. **C is incorrect** because it includes the inchoate crimes, which are specific intent crimes.

43. This question tests on specific intent crimes, i.e., those crimes that require proof of the defendant's awareness of the factors associated with the crime, plus some additional intent. Specific intent crimes are also sometimes described as having dual intents: the intent associated with the *actus reus* plus some other intent.

B is correct because the prosecutor has only established that the woman intended to break and enter. But burglary is a specific intent crime, which also requires proof that the defendant intended to commit some other crime once inside the dwelling house. Absent that showing, the prosecutor has not shown the woman had the *mens rea* for the crime.

A is incorrect because the woman does not have to testify in her own defense. In fact, she has a constitutional right to refuse to testify. **C is incorrect** because there are no facts from which to make such an inference, reasonable or not. Maybe the woman broke and entered because she wanted to commit a crime inside the house. But she also could have broken and entered because she needed shelter. Without additional facts, these inferences cannot be made. **D is incorrect** because it restates only part of the definition of burglary, omitting the final requirement: with intent to commit a felony therein.

44. This question also tests on specific intent crimes. At common law, specific intent crimes included:

Felony murder, when the underlying felony is a specific intent crime

Burglary

Assault

All theft crimes

All inchoate crimes

Crimes established by accomplice liability

Crimes that include "with intent to" in their definition

A is correct because it accurately describes the dual intents for conspiracy.

B is incorrect because conspiracy to commit rape is a single crime, and so it involves the *mens rea* to commit that crime, i.e., the intent to agree and the intent that the rape be committed. **C is incorrect** because conspiracy—like all inchoate crimes—is a specific intent crime. **D is incorrect** because conspiracy to commit rape is a distinct crime from rape, and the question asks about the former and not the latter.

45. This question tests on one of the main reasons why it matters if a crime is classified as having general or specific intent: because different defenses operate differently depending on that classification.

C is correct because the attorney is charged with larceny, which has dual intents: the intent to take by trespass and the intent to permanently deprive the owner of his property. But because the attorney believes the ring was abandoned, she lacks that second intent.

A is incorrect because, in the context of criminal law, there is no different standard of proof for attorney-defendants. **B is incorrect** because the question explains that the attorney "sincerely" believed the ring was abandoned, and so what the attorney "should have known" is irrelevant. **D is incorrect** because the question asks about the effect of the attorney's already-formed belief about the status of the ring, and not whether her belief would have changed if she had reported her discovery to the police.

46. This question also tests on general and specific intent crimes and defenses. In this question, the man is charged with rape, a general intent crime; the man claims a mistake of fact regarding the woman's consent. For general intent crimes, an honest and reasonable mistake of fact negates *mens rea*.

D is correct because it restates the rule regarding mistake of fact and general intent crimes. But notice that the man's mistake would probably not result in his acquittal: he may subjectively believe the woman consented, but that belief is not objectively reasonable.

A and B are both incorrect because each misstates the rule regarding mistake of fact and general intent crimes. **C is incorrect** because the man's belief regarding consent is highly relevant to his *mens rea*, because rape requires proof of non-consensual sexual intercourse.

47. This question tests on the transferred intent rule, which dictates that the *mens rea* of one crime cannot be mixed with the *actus reus* of another crime. In this question, the man committed burglary and had the intent to break and enter and also the intent to commit a theft. The man then engaged in the *actus reus* of arson when he burned the house. But to find arson, the jury cannot rely on the *mens rea* associated with the burglary; instead, it would have to find that the man also had the *mens rea* for arson.

A is correct because it reaches the correct conclusion and restates the general rule regarding transferred intent.

B and D are both incorrect because neither responds to the question of whether the judge's instructions were correct or not. While the man may have been lighting matches to help him see, and while his actions may demonstrate the *mens rea* for arson, the question asks whether the *mens rea* for burglary can be used to show the *mens rea* for arson. **C is incorrect** because it is untrue.

48. This question also tests on the transferred intent rule and on what some see as an exception to this rule. In this question, the defendant shoots at one person with intent to kill, but accidentally shoots and kills someone else instead. This type of scenario raises transferred intent issues only if one views intent to kill as victim-specific, instead of more generally as just "intent to kill." Regardless, the defendant is guilty of intentionally killing the eventual victim.

C is correct because it reaches this result and for the right reason.

A is incorrect because it would reward the woman for her bad aim by convicting her of a crime of recklessness instead of an intentional murder. Instead, the fairer result would be to convict the woman of the same crime, no matter if she killed her intended victim or not. **B is incorrect** because it would create a gap where no defendant would be punished unless he completed his intended crime, and as he envisioned committing it. **D is incorrect** because it offers an opinion in response to a legal question.

49. This question tests on an exception to the transferred intent rule: felony murder. In felony murder, malice is constructive only, and is based on the defendant's *mens rea* for the predicate felony; there is no inquiry about his *mens rea* for the homicide. For this reason, felony murder—and misdemeanor manslaughter, which operates in the same way—can be seen as an exception to the transferred intent rule.

B is correct because the judge can find constructive malice based on the woman's bank robbery and her act of killing the baby.

A is incorrect because it overstates the felony murder rule: a defendant is responsible for deaths that occur during the commission of the felony, but not all crimes. **C and D are both incorrect** because each misstates the felony rule. That rule holds a defendant responsible for deaths that occur during the commission of the felony, including those that are accidental and unintentional.

50. This question tests on another crime that is sometimes incorrectly described as an exception to the transferred intent rule: burglary. Burglary is a specific intent crime that requires the intent to break and enter and the intent to commit a felony once inside the house. But the former is not used to prove the latter; instead, the intent to commit a felony inside the house is best considered as an additional element of the crime.

    C is correct because it provides an accurate description of what is required for a burglary conviction.

    A is incorrect because the prosecutor is not seeking to use one *mens rea* to prove the other. **B is incorrect** because it is untrue: specific intent crimes have dual *mens reas*. **D is incorrect** because it misstates the general rule for transferred intent and provides the opposite rule.

51. This question tests on strict liability crimes, i.e., crimes that do not require proof of *mens rea*. Although these crimes were disfavored and rare at common law, they are a part of modern life. Here, the driver was charged with a seatbelt violation, but other, familiar strict liability offenses include speeding, expired parking meters, and jaywalking. Most strict liability offenses are also *mala prohibita* offenses, i.e., offenses that are considered to be "prohibited wrongs," and not those that are considered to be morally wrong.

    A is correct because seatbelt violations were not contemplated or recognized at common law, which suggests that the woman has committed a modern, *mala prohibita* offense. As such, the woman's offense is "most likely" categorized as a strict liability offense.

    B is incorrect because misdemeanors can carry jail time, and it is not "likely" that such low-level conduct would carry such a high potential penalty. **C and D are both incorrect** because the nature of the charge provides enough information to answer the question, without needing to see how the woman's case proceeds in court.

52. This question tests on how to identify a strict liability offense. The statute in this question is taken from a Nevada statute and has been edited slightly. N.R.S. 484B.287(d).

    B is correct because this crime does not have a *mens rea* in its definition, e.g., intentionally, purposefully, maliciously, recklessly, etc.

    A is incorrect because it is worded too broadly: all criminal law statutes prohibit conduct. *Mala prohibita* offenses are just a category of criminal statutes. **C and D are both incorrect** because the question does not provide enough information about the statute to classify the offense as a criminal infraction or a misdemeanor.

53. This question tests on strict liability offenses and defenses that negate *mens rea*. In this question, the woman claims a mistake of fact as to what she read on the posted sign. But her mistake is irrelevant because the statute does not require proof of *mens rea*. Instead, it focuses only on the defendant's *actus reus*.

    B is correct because it recognizes this principle.

    A is incorrect because it suggests that this crime includes a *mens rea*, and it does not. **C is incorrect** because it suggests that the woman's defense has some relevance, and it does not. Regardless, the question does not provide any facts about the officer's ability to dismiss a ticket. **D is incorrect** because, again, the woman would not be permitted to offer a mistake of fact defense in response to this charge.

54. This question tests on the *mens rea* for statutory rape. While some authorities describe statutory rape as a strict liability crime, it is not. That is, the prosecutor still must establish the *mens rea* for the sexually prohibited act. For this reason, it is better to describe statutory rape as "strict liability as to age."

    A is correct because it recognizes that statutory rape still requires proof of the defendant's *mens rea.*

    B is incorrect because statutory rape is not strict liability as to every element. Although the victim's consent is irrelevant—considered a "child," she would not be able to give consent—the prosecutor must still prove the defendant's *mens rea.* **C and D are both incorrect** because each suggests that the college student's claims will impact his conviction, and they will not.

55. This question tests on the limits of strict liability crimes and is based on the facts of *Staples v. U.S.*, 511 U.S. 600 (1994). In general, if a statute is silent as to *mens rea* and if a conviction carries a significant penalty—heavy fines, or any form of incarceration—a court should not presume that the legislature intended to create a strict liability crime. Instead, the court should construe the statute as requiring some proof of *mens rea.*

    D is correct because it recognizes this principle, and that the woman should not face a loss of her liberty without proof of her *mens rea.*

    A is incorrect because it fails to recognize the significant penalties associated with violation of this statute. **B is incorrect** because it does not respond to the question. **C is incorrect** because it goes too far: *Staples* holds that the statute does not need to be found unconstitutional. The court can instead read a *mens rea* requirement into the statute.

Acts and Omissions

56. This question tests on why a criminal conviction requires proof of *actus reus*: because otherwise, defendants would be punished for their thoughts alone.

    D is correct because it recognizes this principle. By fantasizing about killing her supervisor, the employee has not committed any crime. Instead, she can only be guilty of a crime if she acts on those fantasies.

    A is incorrect because it is untrue: nothing in the facts suggests that the supervisor is in "imminent danger." **B is incorrect** because attempt crimes require an *actus reus* and no *actus reus* has occurred here. **C is incorrect** because it provides a nonlegal response and because not "everyone" fantasizes about killing their boss.

57. This question tests on what is required for a criminal *actus reus*: a conscious and voluntary act.

    A is correct because it recognizes this principle. Note, though, that had the woman been awake (i.e., conscious) and had she acted voluntarily, she would be guilty of battery.

    B is incorrect for two reasons. First, it assumes facts that go beyond the fact pattern: i.e., that the woman was "still intoxicated" when she hit her husband and the woman's level of intoxication was enough to render her unconscious. **C and D are both incorrect** because each presupposes that the woman's act was sufficient to meet the *actus reus* of battery. Of course, if she was awake and had acted voluntarily, it would be. But because she was sleeping and acted involuntarily, it was not.

58. This question tests on the requirement of concurrence between *mens rea* and *actus reus*, i.e., the requirement that the defendant's *mens rea* drive his *actus reus*.

B is correct because it recognizes that the man formed a *mens rea* about harming the little girl only after he engaged in the *actus reus* of killing her.

A is incorrect because there was no concurrence between the man's *mens rea* and his *actus reus*. The issue of whether he was able to prevent the accident is secondary to that. **C and D are both incorrect** because each focuses on the content of the man's *mens rea* and not when it was formed.

59. This question tests on another general rule regarding *actus reus*: the failure to act—also known as an "omission"—is insufficient to meet the *actus reus* requirement unless the defendant also has a duty to act.

A is correct because it recognizes that the student here did nothing, other than watch the crime take place. But because he had no duty to act, his omission will not expose him to any criminal liability.

B is incorrect because it is untrue: one person can be held responsible for the criminal actions of another through accomplice and co-conspirator liability. **C and D are both incorrect** because each describes the student's moral duty in this situation, not his legal duty.

60. This question tests on the exception to the general rule about omissions: a defendant's failure to act can expose him to criminal liability where he has a duty to act. The first way a duty can be imposed is through a status relationship with the victim. Examples of these relationships include married partners, parent and child, employer and employee, and host and guest. In each relationship, one party relies on the other.

B is correct because it recognizes that the husband had a duty to act on behalf of his wife, and so his omission can constitute the *actus reus* of a crime.

A is incorrect because the relative ease of acting generally does not matter; instead, when a party fails to act, the relevant question is whether he had a duty to act. **C is incorrect** because a failure to comply with traditional marriage vows is not sufficient to demonstrate the *actus reus* of a crime. **D is incorrect** because this question is about omissions and *actus reus*, not *mens rea*.

61. This question also tests on an omission, and the second way a duty can be created: by contract. In this question, the elder care agency and its employees only have a duty to the elderly mother because they have assumed that responsibility by contract. But without the contract, there would be no duty.

A is correct because it identifies the duty and the omission.

B is incorrect because it addresses a moral duty and not a legal one. **C and D are both incorrect** because neither responds to the question, which asks about the responsibility of the agency and its employees.

62. This question tests on another way a duty to act can be created: by statute. Here, the teacher is mandatorily required to report suspected child abuse, but failed to do so. Because the teacher did not meet her statutory duty, her omission can form the *actus reus* of a crime.

    D is correct because it identifies the duty and the omission.

    A is incorrect because it ignores the teacher's statutory duty. **B is incorrect** because the statute requires the reporting of "suspected" abuse, not confirmed abuse. **C is incorrect** because there is no required proof of but-for causation; instead, criminal responsibility is imposed based on whether the elements of the crime are present or not. Here, the teacher had a duty to act but did not do so, and this will be enough to meet the *actus reus* requirement for the crime.

63. This question tests on another way a duty to act can be created: by assumption of the risk. That is, if a party begins to deliver aid to another, then he has a duty to follow through. While some states have enacted Good Samaritan laws to offer protection to those who offer aid to strangers and act in good faith, the facts in this question show the woman abandoning the jogger so she could go to the mall. As such, even if the question identified a Good Samaritan law, the woman probably would not meet its requirements.

    A is correct because it identifies the duty and the omission.

    B is incorrect because it focuses on what more the woman could have done, instead of her duty after she began helping the jogger. **C is incorrect** because it ignores that both the woman and the other driver can be at fault in this situation. **D is incorrect** because it ignores the woman's duty to act.

64. This question tests on another way a duty to act can be created: by creation of the dangerous situation.

    C is correct because it identifies the duty and the omission.

    A is incorrect because it offers a civil law solution to a criminal law question. **B is incorrect** because the question asks about the man's responsibility after the girl fell into the hole, and not where she was standing when she fell. **D is incorrect** because it focuses on what the man did (gave the girl permission to watch) instead of what he did not do (render aid after she fell into the hole).

65. This question presents a statutory example of how a duty can be imposed. The definition in this question is taken from the Illinois Adult Services Act, 320 Il. C.S. § 20/4, although it has been edited slightly.

    D is correct because it identifies the doctor's responsibilities under the statute: if the doctor has the requisite belief regarding possible abuse, he must make a report within 24 hours of developing the belief.

    A, B, and C are all incorrect because each addresses how the doctor can confirm his suspicions. However, the statute does not require the doctor to do that. Instead, he is required to make a report.

Parties to a Crime

66. This question tests on the basic reason we have accomplice liability: to hold people accountable for their criminal acts even they don't directly commit the crime, e.g., they don't pull the trigger or set fire to the house or perform the prohibited sexual act themselves. As the subsequent questions demonstrate, an accomplice is one who, with intent to provide aid and with the intent that a crime be committed, provides some act of assistance toward the commission of that crime.

B is correct because the supervisor had both the *mens rea* and the *actus reus* to be considered an accomplice: she intended to help, intended that the murder be committed, and provided an act of assistance toward the commission of the murder. Note that without accomplice liability, the supervisor would not be responsible at all for her actions. But with accomplice liability, the supervisor can be held responsible.

A is incorrect because it is worded too broadly and suggests that the supervisor is responsible just because her weapon was used in the crime. But what if the weapon had been stolen from her, or used without her knowledge? Under those circumstances, she would not be responsible. **C is incorrect** because it is worded too narrowly and suggests that the supervisor would only be responsible if she personally committed the crime at issue. **D is incorrect** because it removes the focus from the supervisor's *mens rea* and *actus reus*.

67. This question also tests on basic accomplice liability; in this question, the friend has a culpable *mens rea* and *actus reus*, but he was not present at the crime when it was committed. Still, under accomplice liability, the friend is criminally responsible as if he committed the crime himself.

D is correct because it recognizes this principle: a person can be guilty via accomplice liability even if he does not commit the crime himself.

A and C are both incorrect because each improperly focuses on the friend's "tangible connection" to the crime. As the following questions demonstrate, the proper focus should instead be on the potential accomplice's *mens rea* and *actus reus*. **B is incorrect** because it focuses on the loan being repaid when, again, the proper focus should be on the potential accomplice's *mens rea* and *actus reus*.

68. This question tests on a core tenet of accomplice liability: that the accomplice's liability is not direct, but is instead derivative. As such, accomplice liability is not a substantive crime; instead, it is a means to hold a person responsible for the acts of another.

D is correct because it recognizes that the neighbor should be charged "as" an accessory to the resulting crime of murder.

A and B are both incorrect because each identifies "accessory before the fact" as a substantive crime, which it is not. **C is incorrect** because it fails to identify that the neighbor will be charged through accomplice liability.

69. This question tests on the common law "parties to a crime," which provides a way to describe the various actors and their roles when accomplice liability is involved. The "parties" are (1) principal in the first degree; (2) principal in the second degree; (3) accessory before the fact; and (4) accessory after the fact. Subsequent questions will explore each of these roles.

B is correct because it properly identifies these categories.

A, C, and D are all incorrect because each provides incorrect or incomplete categories.

70. This question tests on whether accomplice liability should be used in cases where a defendant acts alone. It should not. Instead, accomplice liability only comes into use when there are multiple parties associated with the crime.

C is correct because it recognizes that because the woman acted alone, she should just be charged with murder, and not as a principal to murder.

A and B are both incorrect because each implies that accomplice liability applies here, and it does not. **D is incorrect** because there is no need to "reserve" a spot for an accomplice, should one be later arrested. Instead, the prosecutor can always later use accomplice liability to charge that other person, assuming he exists and is identified.

71. This question tests on the difference between the first two parties to a crime, i.e., the two types of principals. The principal in the first degree is the one who, acting with the *mens rea* for the charged crime, commits that crime: he pulls the trigger or sets the house on fire or performs the prohibited sexual act. The principal in the second degree is one who intends to provide aid, intends that the crime be committed, and performs some act of assistance in support of the crime—or fails to act when he has a duty to act. In addition, the principal in the second degree has some sort of actual or constructive presence at the crime. Thus, the principal in the second degree may stand next to the principal in the first degree as he is committing a crime (actual presence) or he may act as a lookout (constructive presence). But he must be close enough to provide aid if needed.

B is correct because the older brother committed the robbery (principal in the first degree) and the younger brother served as the lookout (principal in the second degree).

A is incorrect because it fails to recognize accomplice liability at all. **C is incorrect** because it reverses the brothers' roles. **D is incorrect** because a conspiracy is not identified by "participation" in a crime; instead, a conspiracy is identified by an agreement between the parties to commit a crime.

72. This question tests on the difference between the principal in the second degree and the accessory before the fact. Both parties have the identical *mens rea* and *actus reus*: they each intend to provide aid, intend that the crime be committed, and perform some act of assistance in support of the crime—or fail to act when he has a duty to act. But while the principal in the second degree must be actually or constructively present at the crime, the accessory before the fact has no presence.

A is correct because the mother intended to help and intended that the robbery be committed (*mens rea*), provided the handgun (*actus reus*), but was not present in any way when the brothers robbed the bank.

B is incorrect because it equates the mother's act of assistance—providing the handgun—to constructive presence. **C is incorrect** because it suggests that the mother cannot be an accomplice because she did not commit the robbery. **D is incorrect** because it labels the mother as a principal in the first degree.

73. This question tests on the final party to the crime: the accessory after the fact. This is the person who learns about the crime after it is completed and, with knowledge of the principal's guilt (*mens rea*), helps her to avoid arrest or prosecution (*actus reus*).

C is correct because it recognizes that the father has committed a crime by intentionally trying to help his son avoid arrest.

A is incorrect because it is too narrow: accomplice liability does not depend on the accomplice performing illegal acts. Instead, the focus should be on the accomplice's *mens rea* (intent to help the principal evade arrest) and the *actus reus* (helping to evade arrest). **B is incorrect** because it improperly ties the charging of an accomplice with forensic proof that the crime was committed. While the common law did tie conviction of an accomplice to conviction of the principal, see questions 75 and 76, the accomplice can still be charged without that conviction. **D is incorrect** because it is worded too broadly: while the son may be a fugitive, nothing in the question suggests that the father also had a duty to report him to the police.

74. This question tests on the innocent instrumentality rule in the context of accomplice liability. That rule provides that when a person uses a non-culpable agent to commit a crime, the person who used that agent is responsible for the crime.

A is correct because it recognizes that the boyfriend lied to the best friend and so she was unaware that she was helping him to commit a crime. Because the best friend lacks any sort of culpable *mens rea*, she cannot be charged as an accomplice, and the boyfriend should be charged as if he acted alone.

B and C are incorrect because each suggests that the best friend has some form of criminal liability, and she does not: she has no *mens rea* associated with the boyfriend's crime. Indeed, she does not even know she is committing a crime. **D is incorrect** because car theft is a crime, and so is the type of situation where a prosecutor should get involved.

75. This question tests on a common law rule regarding liability of an accomplice in relation to the liability of the principal: that the principal be convicted before the accomplice. The reason is because of the derivative liability associated with accomplice liability: without a principal to the crime, there could be no accomplice to that crime. At common law, there were a number of these rules; for a summary, see Dressler, *Understanding Criminal Law* (8th Ed. 2018), §§ 30.03[B] and 30.06.

D is correct because the woman—the principal—must be convicted first, no matter how sound the reasons are for delaying her trial.

A is incorrect because the fact of marriage is irrelevant to the legal issue presented by the question. **B is incorrect** because the trials can be held together, but don't have to be. **C is incorrect** because it focuses on the woman's diagnosis and not the common law rule regarding trials of accomplices.

76. This question tests on a related common law rule regarding the liability of accomplices and principals: if the principal was acquitted, the accomplice could not be prosecuted. For more information about these common law rules, see Dressler, *Understanding*, §§ 30.03[B] and 30.06.

B is correct because it recognizes that accomplice liability is based on derivative liability and so requires a finding of the principal's guilt.

A is incorrect because the woman's acquittal does not necessarily mean that the jury did not believe a crime occurred. Instead, the jury could have acquitted because it found the woman had a viable defense. **C is incorrect** because no additional testimony is necessary to decide this purely legal question. **D is incorrect** because it provides a nonlegal response to a legal question.

77. This question tests on the *mens rea* for accomplice liability: the accomplice must intend to provide an act of assistance and must also intend that the target crime be committed. Because of these dual intents, crimes proven via accomplice liability are specific intent crimes.

    A is correct because the recording only establishes that the woman was "glad" about the killing of her ex-husband, and not that she intended his death. As the woman was charged as an accomplice in his murder, the prosecutor would have to establish that she intended for her husband to be killed.

    B is incorrect because the question asks about *mens rea* and not *actus reus*. **C is incorrect** because the motion should be granted and not denied. **D is incorrect** because it provides a nonlegal response to a legal question.

78. This question also tests on the *mens rea* for accomplice liability.

    D is correct because it recognizes that the woman was only a "feigning accomplice:" she lent the handgun out of fear and had no intent for the husband to be killed. As such, the woman only had one of the two necessary intents.

    A is incorrect because it does not distinguish between knowledge and intent; to be an accessory before the fact, the woman must also intend that the husband be killed. **B is incorrect** because trying to dissuade the man from acting is irrelevant to the question of the woman's liability. **C is incorrect** because categorizing the woman as an accessory before the fact depends on her *mens rea* and *actus reus*, and not on how quickly the man acted in killing his husband.

79. This question also tests on the *mens rea* for accomplice liability and underscores that the accomplice must intend that a specific crime be committed—and not crimes in general.

    A is correct because by telling the jury that the woman only needed to intend "a crime"—instead of the specific crime of arson—the judge impermissibly relieved the prosecution of its burden of proof.

    B is incorrect because it provides a nonlegal response to a legal question. **C is incorrect** because the instruction is not vague as a matter of law; it is overbroad. **D is incorrect** because the instruction does not need to address the woman's testimony. Instead, it is the jury's task to apply the testimony to the law.

80. This question also tests on the *mens rea* for accomplice liability and focuses on the difference between knowledge and intent. While a person may know of a crime being committed—a teen who drinks alcohol before turning 21, a friend who drives over the speed limit, or a family member who uses illegal drugs—that is not enough to become an accomplice to

those crimes. Instead, the person must assist with the intent that the crime be committed. See also *U.S. v. Peoni*, 100 F.2d 401 (2d Cir. 1938). In short, knowledge alone is not sufficient.

A is correct because it recognizes that the sister lacked the *mens rea* to be an accomplice.

B is incorrect because it focuses on presence, which is how a principal in the first degree is distinguished from a principal in the second degree. The focus of this question is whether the sister can be considered a party to this crime at all. **C is incorrect** because it suggests that knowledge is sufficient for the sister to be an accomplice. **D is incorrect** because it focuses on the sister's *actus reus*, when the focus should instead be on her *mens rea*.

81. This question also tests on the *mens rea* for accomplice liability and whether one can intend to commit an unintentional crime. Ordinarily, the prosecutor must show that the accomplice intended to commit the target crime. But accomplice liability to an unintentional crime—here, involuntary manslaughter, which has a *mens* rea of criminal negligence—presents a conundrum because a defendant cannot specifically intend an unintentional crime. The law on this issue is confusing, with no clear common law rule. See Dressler, *Understanding*, § 30.05[B][3]. Under modern law though, most courts would allow the conviction to stand. *Id.*

C is correct because, if the judge did dismiss the charges, it would be on the basis of the bartender's *mens rea*.

A and D are both incorrect because neither addresses accomplice liability. **B is incorrect** because "knowledge with certainty" is not required for accomplice liability.

82. This question tests on the *actus reus* requirement for accomplice liability: an act of assistance toward the commission of the target offense.

A is correct because the friend provided the man with a car so he could sell drugs, which plainly meets the *actus reus* requirement.

B is incorrect because it focuses on the importance of the friend's act to the target offense, which is not a requirement. Instead, to be liable, the friend must only provide some assistance. **C is incorrect** because it improperly shifts the focus from the friend's *actus reus* to what the man did with the car. **D is incorrect** because it suggests that the woman was an innocent instrumentality and did not know why the man needed the car. But the question indicates that when the man asked to borrow the car, he explained that he wanted to use it for the drug sale.

83. This question also tests on the *actus reus* for accomplice liability and the form of assistance. The act can be substantial and tangible, such as providing a weapon to commit a homicide. But a less substantial, intangible act will also suffice, such as providing a pep talk to the principal in the first degree.

C is correct because it recognizes that the father's words assisted the woman in her commission of the crime.

A is incorrect because it fails to recognize that the father's words encouraged the woman to commit a crime. **B is incorrect** because a tangible, physical act is not necessarily required; any act will do. **D is incorrect** because "but for" causality is not required. Instead, the accomplice must provide an act of assistance.

84. This question also tests on the *actus reus* for accomplice liability and whether "mere presence" at the crime is enough to turn an innocent bystander into a principal in the second degree. It is not.

D is correct because it recognizes this principle, and that the second boy just stood and watched. Even if the second boy enjoyed watching the first boy smash the windows, that is not enough; instead, to be an accomplice, the second boy would have to do something beyond being merely present during the crime.

A is incorrect because the second boy did not offer to be a lookout or act as one. **B and C are both incorrect** because each focuses on whether the second boy gave a warning or not. But since the second boy never offered to be a lookout or had the opportunity to be one (in the absence of offering to do so), he did not have the *actus reus* for accomplice liability.

85. This question also tests on *actus reus* and mere presence.

C is correct because it recognizes that the friend's agreement to serve as a lookout was an act of assistance beyond mere presence—even though the friend never had to text the man as he robbed the bank.

A is incorrect because it focuses on whether the friend assisted the man by texting him or not, and ignores the fact that she assisted him just by agreeing to be a lookout in the first place. **B is incorrect** because it fails to recognize why the friend was sitting in the parking lot: because she had agreed to serve as a lookout. **D is incorrect** because the *actus reus* is met here because the friend agreed to serve as a lookout, not because she stayed in the car.

86. This question tests on *actus reus* and omissions, i.e., the failure to act. In general, the *actus reus* requirement for crimes requires an affirmative act and a person will not be liable for failing to act unless the law also imposes a duty to act.

A is correct because there is no indication that the man had a duty to act in this situation. As such, his failure to act cannot be held against him.

B is incorrect because the question asks about the man's failure to act and not his mere presence. **C is incorrect** because the judge decides questions of law and not the jury. **D is incorrect** because the focus should be on the man's *actus reus,* and not whether the woman was helped by his failure to call the police.

87. This question also tests on *actus reus* and omissions.

A is correct because it recognizes that the law imposed a duty on the coach, and so the *actus reus* requirement is met by her failure to fulfill that duty.

B is incorrect because the law required the coach to report suspected abuse, not suspected possible homicides. **C and D are both incorrect** because the law required the coach to report suspected abuse "without exception," and so the student's age or the coach's ignorance of the law are irrelevant.

88. This question tests on the scope of accomplice liability. Principals in the second degree and accessories before the fact are responsible for the crime for which they provide assistance and all other natural and probable consequences of that crime.

C is correct because it recognizes this principle: the man robbed a gas station with the roommate's gun, and it was a "natural and probable" consequence to believe that someone might be shot and killed during the robbery.

A and B are both incorrect because each focuses too narrowly on what the roommate knew or could have known. Instead, the focus should be on the natural and probable consequences of the crime. **D is incorrect** because it focuses too broadly on what "probably" would have happened in the robbery, and the clerk's death was not a foregone conclusion.

89. This question also tests on the scope of accomplice liability and what constitutes a natural and probable consequence.

D is correct because, without additional facts, it is nearly impossible to link the vandalism to the home invasion or the theft.

A, B, and C are all incorrect because each ties the vandalism to an irrelevant fact: teenagers doing "stupid things" (A and B) and that the teams were rivals (C). In addition, A and B refer to incorrect standards, and not the natural and probable consequences standard.

90. This question tests on the punishment for principals in the second degree and accessories before the fact: because these parties are liable as if they committed the crime themselves, they face the same punishment as principals in the first degree.

A is correct because it recognizes this principle: the man was convicted of first degree murder and so faces the same sentence as if he had committed that crime directly.

B is incorrect because it provides an opinion instead of a legal response. **C is incorrect** because the sentences can be the same, regardless of which person pulled the trigger. **D is incorrect** because, while sentences should be individualized, they can be the same under these circumstances.

91. This question tests on the punishment for accessories after the fact: because these parties only learn of the crime after its completion, they faced reduced sentences relative to the other parties to that crime.

C is correct because it recognizes this principle. While the best friend helped the woman after the fact, knowing about the crime, she is still less culpable than if she had assisted with the commission of the crime.

A is incorrect because it provides a nonlegal response to a legal question. **B is incorrect** because it states an improper rule for sentencing accessories after the fact, and because the question does not give sufficient facts to tell whether the woman impeded the police investigation. **D is incorrect** because there is no indication that the woman had a duty to act in this situation. As such, her failure to act cannot provide the basis of an enhanced sentence.

92. This question tests on the overlap between accomplice and co-conspirator liability. Most of the time—but not always—there is complete overlap. This question illustrates a situation with complete overlap.

D is correct because the man and the woman formed a conspiracy when they agreed to commit a crime, and the man acted as a principal in the second degree when he intentionally served as the lookout for the robbery.

A, B, and C are all incorrect because they recognize one form of liability of the other, but not both.

93. This question also tests on the overlap between accomplice and co-conspirator liability. In this question, the customer is an accomplice but there is no conspiracy.

B is correct because it correctly describes the customer's *mens rea* and *actus reus.*

A is incorrect because it suggests that an agreement was formed between the woman and the customer. Although conspiracy does not depend on a verbal agreement, the question does not indicate that the woman even knew the customer was in the store. **C is incorrect** because it improperly focuses on whether the woman and the customer knew one another. **D is incorrect** because it fails to recognize that the customer can still be a principal in the second degree, even if the woman did not know about her or the help she provided. She cannot be a co-conspirator, though.

94. This question also tests on the overlap between accomplice and co-conspirator liability. In this question, a conspiracy exists, but there is no accomplice liability.

C is correct because it recognizes that the woman and her brother formed a conspiracy, but that the woman provided no assistance to him after the agreement was formed. As such, she is not an accessory to his crimes.

A is incorrect because it makes no sense: nothing in the facts suggests that the brother was involved in the woman's drug crime. **B is incorrect** because it does not recognize the conspiracy. **D is incorrect** because it identifies the woman as her brother's accessory.

95. This question tests on the way a modern jurisdiction deals with accomplice liability: to abolish the distinctions among the first three parties, but to retain the category of accessory after the fact. Thus, most jurisdictions today recognize only three parties to a crime: (1) principal, (2) accomplice (sometimes also referred to as an accessory or an aider and abettor), and (3) accessory after the fact.

C is correct because it recognizes that the statutory provision, by referring to those who aid in the commission of the offense, excludes accessories after the fact. By definition, an accessory after the fact learns about the crime after it has been completed.

A is incorrect because it fails to recognize that the statutory provision includes accessories before the fact. **B and D are both incorrect** because each includes accessories after the fact, and the statutory provision excludes this group.

Model Penal Code

96. This question tests on the Model Penal Code as a source of the criminal law. When the Model Penal Code was introduced in 1962, it was offered as a resource for states to use in building their own penal codes. But no state was required to adopt the Code, either in whole or in part. Over time, many states have adopted select provisions of the Model Penal Code and, in some instances, have adapted these provisions to best fit into their penal codes.

B is correct because the state was free to change "extreme mental or emotional disturbance" to "extreme emotional disturbance."

A, C, and D are all incorrect because each provides a nonlegal response to a legal question.

97. This question tests on the four mental states included within the Model Penal Code. Although the Model Penal Code presented many reforms, "[n]o aspect of the Model Penal Code has had greater influence on the direction of American criminal law" than the provision listing and describing these mental states. Dressler, *Understanding* § 10.07. While the mental states associated with the common law are often confusing, the Model Penal Code's mental states include clear definitions.

D is correct because it acknowledges the Model Penal Code approach and lists the same four mental states provided in § 2.02 of the Code.

A and B are both incorrect because each suggests that the Model Penal Code retains common law terminology, and it does not. **C is incorrect** because it is untrue: mental states are highly relevant under the Model Penal Code, just as they are under the common law.

98. This question tests on the first of the Model Penal Code's mental states: purposely. See § 2.02(2)(a). Note that this definition has two components: the defendant's view of his conduct or its result, and the defendant's view of the attendant circumstances associated with the crime. Regardless, both describe "intentional" circumstances.

A is correct because it recognizes the link between acting intentionally at common law and acting purposely under the Model Penal Code.

B and C are both incorrect because "premeditatedly" and "deliberately" are not common law terms. Instead, each first came into use in the Pennsylvania homicide statute of 1794. **D is incorrect** because it is untrue: the Model Penal Code did not "reject" common law concepts.

99. This question tests on the purposely mental state under the Model Penal Code, using the robbery provision from § 222.1 of the Code.

C is correct because it identifies the correct components from the definition of purposely and the definition of robbery. That is, the man's "conscious object" was to engage in conduct that would lead to the type of fear described in the robbery statute.

A is incorrect because the robbery statute does not require the man to use a "real" weapon. Instead, if he commits a theft while "purposely" putting the victim "in fear of immediate serious bodily injury," he will be guilty of robbery. **B is incorrect** because the robbery statute does not require that the woman's fear be objectively reasonable, although it probably is in this situation. **D is incorrect** because the man used a cell phone, so he could not have intended to "to threaten her with immediate serious bodily injury." But he did intend for her to have a fear of that injury.

100. This question tests on the second of the Model Penal Code's mental states: knowingly. See § 2.02(2)(b). This definition also has two components: the defendant's view of his conduct or the attendant circumstances, and the defendant's view of the result of his conduct.

A is correct because the man knew from his experience with guns that the gunshot would probably kill his husband. Note that, under this definition, the man did not have to intend that his husband die.

B is incorrect because there is no indication that the man lied to the police. **C is incorrect** because the man did not have to intend his husband's death to be guilty of knowingly causing his death. **D is incorrect** because absolute certainty is not required; instead the man only needed to be "aware that it is practically certain that his conduct will cause such a result."

101. This question tests on the knowingly mental state under the Model Penal Code, using the felonious restraint provision from § 212.2 of the Code.

D is correct because the woman knew that she was restraining her friend: she took his car keys and prevented him from leaving. Additionally, the woman knew the friend had diabetes and needed his medication, so she was also aware of the risk of serious bodily injury associated with his detention.

A is incorrect because it is untrue: the woman knew about the friend's diabetes and his need for medication. **B is incorrect** because the woman did not need to know how sick her friend might become, only that he faced a risk of serious bodily injury. **C is incorrect** because it focuses only on the woman's *actus reus*, and omits any reference to her *mens rea*.

102. This question tests on the third of the Model Penal Code's mental states: recklessly. See § 2.02(2)(c). This definition also has two components: a substantial and unjustifiable risk, and a conscious disregard of that risk.

C is correct because driving 6 MPH above the posted highway speed limit on a sunny day does not pose a "substantial and unjustifiable risk" to other drivers.

A is incorrect for two reasons. First, it suggests that the woman's driving posed a substantial and unjustifiable risk, and it did not. Second, it refers to the woman's failure to be aware of that risk. But the Code's definition of "knowingly" requires a conscious disregard of the risk, not ignorance of it. **B and D are both incorrect** because each states that the woman's driving posed a substantial and unjustifiable risk, and it did not.

103. This question also tests on the Model Penal Code's definition of "recklessness" and what it means to have a conscious disregard for a certain risk.

D is correct because the nurse's concession demonstrates that she was aware of a "substantial and unjustifiable risk" from the home surgery. While the nurse claims she was not aware of the risk that the woman would die of a heart attack, the statute does not require her to be able predict the final result with complete accuracy. Instead, she simply needs to be aware of the risk that it will result.

A is incorrect because it would reward the nurse for being willfully blind to a relatively predictable risk of harm. **B is incorrect** because it does not respond to the question. **C is incorrect** because it fails to tie its conclusion to the language of the statute.

104. This question tests on the fourth and final of the Model Penal Code's mental states: negligently. See § 2.02(2)(d). This definition also has two components: a substantial and unjustifiable risk, and a failure to be aware of that risk.

B is correct because the only difference between the two provisions is whether the defendant is aware of the risk or not. When a defendant acts recklessly, he consciously disregards the risk; when he acts negligently, he fails to be aware of the risk. But both provisions require the same degree of risk: "a substantial and unjustifiable risk that the material element exists or will result from his conduct."

A, C, and D are all incorrect because each suggests that the risk is different between the two provisions, and it is not.

105. This question tests on the negligently mental state under the Model Penal Code, using the simple assault provision from § 211.1 of the Code.

A is correct because the facts suggest that the teenage boy was not aware of the risks of his conduct: he did not know the gun (a deadly weapon) was loaded, and his finger slipped on the trigger.

B is incorrect because it states that the teenage boy "consciously disregarded" the risk, and the facts suggest the opposite. **C is incorrect** because it focuses on the title of the crime and does not apply the statute to the facts. **D is incorrect** because it offers a reason why the teenage boy should not be convicted of the crime—because it was an unfortunate accident—but the question asks whether he can be convicted.

106. This question tests on Model Penal Code murder. See § 210.2.

C is correct because it lists all three forms of murder.

A is incorrect because it omits reckless murder. **B is incorrect** because it fails to recognize that, in the quoted provision, "recklessly" is modified by the phrase, "circumstances manifesting an extreme indifference to the value of human life." **D is incorrect** because, under the Model Penal Code, a killing that occurs during the commission of an enumerated felony is presumed to constitute murder—but may also be manslaughter. A killing that occurs during the commission of an enumerated felony is just one type of reckless murder.

107. This question tests on the recklessly mental state under the Model Penal Code, using part of the murder provision from § 210.2.

D is correct because this provision "presumes" the defendant acts recklessly under circumstances manifesting extreme indifference to the value of human life when he kills while committing an enumerated felony. But presumptions are not the same as conclusions, and the question explains that the jurors thought the killing was an accident. As such, the presumption is overcome, and the man is not guilty of the charged crime.

A is incorrect because it suggests that the Model Penal Code's reckless murder provision operates in the same way as common law felony murder, but it does not. The Code permits a presumption that a defendant who kills while committing an enumerated felony is guilty of murder, but that is all. **B and C are both incorrect** because each uses "extreme indifference to the value of human life," but untethers that phrase from the recklessness requirement. But, as demonstrated by the statutory provision, these two go together.

108. This question tests on manslaughter under the Model Penal Code. § 210.3. This provision is similar in some respects to common law voluntary manslaughter, but differs in others.

D is correct because it lists the differences between the second form of Model Penal Code manslaughter and common law voluntary manslaughter.

A and B are both incorrect because the two crimes are not identical, or nearly so. **C is incorrect** because the two crimes are not as far apart as the answer suggests.

109. This question tests on how the Model Penal Code uses degrees to classify crimes. Under the Code, felonies are classified into degrees—first, second, and third—and then those degrees are used for sentencing. So, for example, Model Penal Code murder is a felony of the first degree, but manslaughter is a felony of the second degree. Then the Code has separate sections listing possible sentences for each degree of crime.

C is correct because it recognizes these principles.

A and B are both incorrect because they are untrue. **D is incorrect** because, despite its age, the Model Penal Code is still very influential.

110. This question tests on negligent homicide under the Model Penal Code. §210.4. This provision is identical to common law involuntary manslaughter. Notably, the drafters of the Model Penal Code did not include criminally negligent killings in the manslaughter definition, but carved out a new category for these crimes.

A is correct because it recognizes that common law involuntary manslaughter is provided for in the Model Penal Code.

B is incorrect because criminally negligent killings are not included in the Code's definition of murder. **C is incorrect** because the two crimes are the same, and the Code's version is not more restrictive. **D is incorrect** because it is untrue.

Homicide (Common Law)

111. This question tests on the definition of homicide: the killing of a human being by another human being.

D is correct because the hunter did not kill another human being; he killed an animal. As such, the hunter did not commit a homicide.

A and B are both incorrect because each suggests that the hunter may have committed a homicide. But because the hunter killed an animal, there was no homicide. **C is incorrect** because it suggests that the hunting violation is relevant to this question, and it is not.

112. This question tests on an important aspect of homicide: that it is not necessarily against the law. Instead, "homicide" is a neutral term that can refer to both lawful and unlawful killings.

A is correct because the woman (a human being) was executed (killed) by her executioner (another human being). As such, the woman died by homicide, although it was state-sanctioned and therefore legal.

B and C are both incorrect because "culpable" and "criminal" homicides are against the law, and this killing was state-sanctioned. **D is incorrect** because euthanasia refers to ending the life of a person who is suffering from a significant illness or is brain dead, and not a legal punishment for a person who has been convicted of a crime.

113. This question tests on the two basic types of criminal homicide: murder and manslaughter. Under the common law, murder is a killing with malice aforethought, and manslaughter is a killing without malice aforethought. As such, the presence or absence of malice is what distinguishes murder from manslaughter. While malice aforethought is a broad and ambiguous term, the following questions will explore its meaning.

B is correct because the woman intentionally killed her husband without justification, excuse, or any legitimate mitigating circumstances. As such, the woman has killed with malice aforethought.

A and D are both incorrect and for two reasons. First, common law crimes were not separated into degrees, and both answers refer to second degree crimes. Second, both answers refer to a reduced degree of crime because the husband "provoked" the woman by calling her delusional. But under the common law, verbal insults are not considered to be adequate provocation. **C is incorrect** because the woman killed with malice, and so her crime cannot be described as manslaughter.

114. This question tests on the definition of murder: a killing with malice aforethought, express or implied.

D is correct because it reiterates this definition.

A and C are both incorrect because the Latin phrases, *malum in se* and *malum prohibitum*, refer to larger categories of crimes, and not the mental state for a type of homicide. **B is incorrect** because it is too narrow: as demonstrated below, a defendant may still exhibit malice, even without the intent to harm another person.

115. This question tests whether a murder defendant must exhibit malice (the *mens rea* of murder) for an appreciable period of time before committing the crime, i.e., whether she must have the *mens rea* "aforethought." Although a time element may have been required at very early English common law, it is not a requirement for the American common law. Instead, malice can be formed in an instant.

C is correct because it recognizes that no set time was required for the woman to develop malice aforethought (here, an intent to kill).

A is incorrect because it suggests the opposite: that some appreciable time period is required. **B is incorrect** because the attendant circumstances make it easy to determine the woman's *mens rea*: by pointing a gun at the man and shooting him in the chest, she demonstrated an intent to kill. **D is incorrect** because the woman's failure to give the man a chance to return the bananas does not address whether or not the law requires time to develop malice aforethought.

116. This question tests on the four types of malice. Express malice exists when (1) a defendant kills intentionally, and implied malice exists when he (2) has an intent to cause great bodily harm that causes death, or (3) shows an extreme indifference to a very high risk of death and causes death ("depraved heart"), or (4) kills while committing or attempting to commit a particular felony ("felony murder"). Each form of malice is addressed in the questions that follow.

D is correct because it restates the four forms of malice, although in an abbreviated way.

A is incorrect because, while malice can be express or implied, the *mens rea* for murder is not bilateral, or shared between two parties. **B is incorrect** because it misstates two of the forms of malice. First, the defendant must have intent to commit some significant bodily harm and not just any bodily harm. Second, the third form of malice is usually described as "depraved" heart, and not as "corrupt" heart. While modern dictionaries may list the two words as synonyms, the common law traditionally used the word "depraved." **C is incorrect** because, while malice can be express or implied and express malice includes intent to kill, it does not include negligent killings.

117. This question tests on one of the overarching issues in the criminal law: how to assess a defendant's *mens rea* when the only person who knows what is in the defendant's mind is the defendant himself. In the context of homicide, a fact-finder will consider the circumstances surrounding the killing, e.g., the type of weapon or instrument and how it was used, whether the defendant was aware of how risky his conduct was, or whether he should have been aware of the risk, etc. But no matter what crime is being considered, the fact-finder is only permitted to make *reasonable inferences* from the facts and is prohibited from *presuming* that the facts prove an element of the crime. *Sandstrom v. Montana*, 442 U.S. 510 (1979). Instead, in criminal cases, the prosecution bears the burden of proof for each element of the offense. *In re Winship*, 397 U.S. 358 (1970).

D is correct because it explains that the fact-finder can make an inference from the facts.

A is incorrect because even though the facts here are quite limited, they are sufficient to reach a conclusion about the young man's *mens rea*. That is, because the young man used a deadly weapon to shoot his roommate in the head, the fact-finder can infer an intent to kill. **B is incorrect** because testimony from an eyewitness or the defendant is not necessary to secure a conviction Instead, a defendant can be convicted based on direct evidence, circumstantial evidence, or a combination of the two. **C is incorrect** because the fact-finder cannot *presume* intent to kill from the use of a weapon; to do so would relieve the prosecution of part of its burden of proof.

118. This question tests on another way a fact-finder can make a reasonable inference about the defendant's *mens rea* in a homicide case: by asking whether the defendant should have foreseen that the natural and probable consequences of his actions would be the victim's death. If so, then the fact-finder can infer that the defendant had the intent to kill the victim. In this question, the retired man knew the rat poison was highly toxic, but he hoped that his wife would only become sick and not die.

C is correct because the wife's death was foreseeable: the retired man knew the consequences of using the poison, and just hoped the result would be illness and not death.

A and B are both incorrect because each ignores the fact that the retired man knew the rat poison could cause death. **D is incorrect** because the retired man's claims are not completely implausible; instead, his knowledge of the toxicity of the rat poison outweighs his hope that his wife would survive the poisoning.

119. This question tests on the so-called "deadly weapon rule," which is really just a way of evaluating the facts of a case to determine if a crime is more severe (deadly weapon used) or less severe (no deadly weapon used). Under the rule, a fact-finder considers the weapon or device at issue and (1) whether it was manufactured to cause death or serious bodily injury, or (2) used in a way that was intended or likely to cause death or serious bodily injury.

For example, guns are considered to be deadly weapons because they are manufactured for killing, and are often used for the same. Beyond guns, though, the rule is necessary because virtually every tangible object—a car, a pen, a can of food, a computer power cord—can be used to cause death. But while each of these objects can be used to kill, the defendant using them may have had no intent to kill or cause any harm to the victim. And if not, the defendant should be charged with a lesser crime, or not at all.

C is correct because it addresses the facts and accurately describes what happened: the sophomore intentionally drove her car at her victims, which means that she used the car in a manner calculated to cause their deaths.

A and B are both incorrect; while each is a true statement, neither addresses the sophomore's actions. **D is incorrect** because it is worded too broadly: if D were correct, then every killing—no matter how performed—would be committed with a deadly weapon.

120. This question also tests on the deadly weapon rule and illustrates why not every object that causes death can be considered a deadly weapon.

B is correct because although the impact of the hockey puck caused the college student's death, the puck itself was not intended by anyone—its designer, its manufacturer, or the friend—to be a deadly weapon. By comparison, if the friend had shot the college student in the face with a gun, no one would dispute that the gun was a deadly weapon.

A is incorrect because, while a true statement, it does not address how the puck was used. **C is incorrect** because it only addresses causation. **D is incorrect** because it is worded too broadly: if D were correct, then every killing—no matter how performed—would be committed with a deadly weapon.

121. This question tests on the second way that malice can be established: by showing the defendant intended great bodily harm to the victim that resulted in death.

A is correct because smacking someone across the face with a lamp demonstrates an intent to cause great bodily harm. And, since the friend died as a result, the teenage boy can be convicted of murder.

B and D are both incorrect as each focuses on whether it is appropriate to hold a teenager criminally responsible for an adult crime. While this is a legitimate policy question, this question focuses on the teenage boy's *mens rea*. **C is incorrect** because it suggests that the only way to establish malice is with an intent to kill. But malice can be established in other ways as well: through an intent to cause great bodily harm, a "depraved heart," or felony murder.

122. This question tests on the level of harm intended in "great bodily harm" murders. A defendant must intend some significant harm to his victim and not just some harm.

B is correct because the man intended to teach the roommate a lesson, and did not intend to harm her at all. Although the question asks about "common law murder," which could include any one of four types of murder, only one form—intent to cause great bodily harm murder—potentially applies to these facts. And the harm intended here, if any, was minimal.

A and D are both incorrect because each provides a nonlegal answer to a legal question. **C is incorrect** because there was a causal link between the man's actions and the roommate's death.

123. This question tests on an issue related to causation: how the criminal law addresses a crime victim who is weakened or has some sort of trait or characteristic that plays a role in the events. Here, the first man is charged with murder, presumably on the theory that he intended great bodily harm to the second man. In the criminal law, the defendant must "take the victim as he finds her," which means that criminal liability will usually be imposed if the defendant has the *mens rea* and *actus reus* for the crime.

    C is correct because it recognizes that the first man's ignorance of the second man's medical condition is not a valid excuse. If the second man did not have a brain abnormality and had died from the punch anyway, the first man could still be found guilty of intent to cause great bodily harm murder. So why should the first man evade responsibility because of the second man's medical condition?

    A and D are both incorrect because each addresses apportioning blame between the two parties; that is a tort law concept. **B is incorrect** because it assumes facts that were not given—what the first man "likely knew"—and also because it does not address the question of how to evaluate his *mens rea* and *actus reus*.

124. This question tests on the third way that malice can be established: by showing the defendant acted with a "depraved heart." That phrase is as ambiguous as "malice aforethought" and so, over time, "depraved heart" has been interpreted to include two basic requirements. First, the defendant must be engaged in extraordinarily risky behavior. Second, the defendant either must know and ignore that his behavior carries a high risk of death, or he should be aware of the risk (because his conduct is so risky).

    D is correct because it describes the seniors' *actus reus* (they acted recklessly) and *mens rea* (they were indifferent to any harm they might cause) and also recognizes the causal connection among their *mens rea*, *actus reus*, and the eventual harm.

    A is incorrect because it suggests that the only forms of murder are intent to kill or intent to cause great bodily harm. **B is incorrect** because contributory negligence is a tort law concept, which does not apply here. **C is incorrect** because it suggests that murder is an appropriate charge any time a dangerous act leads to death.

125. This question tests on the first requirement for depraved heart murder: that the defendant be engaged in very risky behavior. All conduct carries some risk; if any risk would meet the requirements for depraved heart murder, every killing involving risk could be categorized as murder. For that reason, depraved heart murder is reserved for situations where the defendant takes a substantial and unjustifiable risk to human life.

    B is correct because it recognizes that the risk here was relatively limited, even if it did lead to the loss of life.

A is incorrect because criminal law does not evaluate contributory negligence—tort law does. **C is incorrect** because the man's risk was not "significant;" instead, it was the type of risk that many drivers take every day. For the same reason, **D is incorrect**.

126. This question also tests on the required degree of risk for depraved heart murders. Again, the risk must be significant, and well beyond the ordinary risks we all take in our everyday lives. The example here—intentionally shooting into a residence, even with the belief that it is unoccupied—is one of the classic examples of risky behavior that will support a depraved heart murder conviction.

C is correct because it provides an accurate statement of the facts and law: the guest's conduct was very risky and, because of that, his belief about the occupancy of the house is irrelevant.

A is incorrect because criminal law does not evaluate contributory negligence—tort law does. **B is incorrect** because it suggests that good intentions can make up for extraordinarily risky conduct, which is not true. Instead, a defendant's claim that he was unaware of the risk of his behavior becomes less and less plausible as the risk increases. **D is incorrect** because the guest's culpability is judged by the risk he took and the resulting harm, and not by whether he followed some other code of conduct, i.e., basic weapons safety rules.

127. This question tests on the second requirement for depraved heart murder: that the defendant know that his behavior carries a high risk of death, or he should be aware of the risk—because the risk to human life is so high.

D is correct because it accurately describes the risk to the daughter's life ("significant"), and also the father's attitude toward that risk ("aware of and ignored").

A is incorrect because ordinary negligence and breach of duty are tort concepts. **B is incorrect** because, according to the facts, the father knew of the risk to his daughter's life. **C is incorrect** because there is nothing in these facts to support an intent to kill.

128. This question tests on the fourth and final way that malice can be established: when the defendant kills during the commission or attempted commission of a particular felony. In the United States, the original predicate felonies for felony murder included burglary, arson, robbery, and rape.

In felony murder, malice is constructive only, and is based on the defendant's *mens rea* for the predicate felony; there is no inquiry about his *mens rea* for the homicide. For this reason, some sources refer to felony murder as a strict liability crime, i.e., one without any required mental state. But since a *mens rea* for the predicate felony must be established, it is more accurate to say that felony murder is strict liability as to the *mens rea* for the homicide.

A is correct because it recognizes that malice is demonstrated by a killing committed in the course of a robbery.

B is incorrect because there is no indication in the facts that the woman intended any harm to the bank teller; in fact, the facts describe the woman as a pacifist. **C is incorrect** because the accidental discharge of the gun does not negate the fact that the woman robbed the bank teller. **D is incorrect** because it suggests that the only forms of murder are intent to kill or intent to cause great bodily harm.

129. This question tests on the felony murder rule and demonstrates why it is often so controversial. Under the rule as originally established, any death that occurs during the commission of the predicate felony is considered a murder. It does not matter whether the victim is the felon, a co-felon, an innocent bystander, or a police officer, and it does not matter if the victim died at the hands of the felon, a co-felon, an innocent bystander, or a police officer. Instead, the only relevant inquiry is whether the death occurred during the commission of the predicate felony. As will be demonstrated in later questions, statutory reforms have tried to soften the felony murder rule somewhat.

C is correct because it provides an accurate statement of the common law felony murder rule.

A is incorrect because the felony murder rule does not evaluate whether the death was reasonably foreseeable or not. **B is incorrect** because the felony murder rule addresses whether a death occurred, and not the identity or status of the victim. **D is incorrect** because the judge decides questions of law, not the jury.

130. This question tests on the original felony murder rule, and why its unfairness did not capture attention until relatively recently. The original felony murder rule dictates that any death that occurs during the commission of the predicate felony is considered a murder. But since the punishment for commission of a felony was death anyway, it did not matter that felony murder was also punished with death.

C is correct because it recognizes this principle.

A is incorrect because few common law scholars, if any, found the felony murder rule to be unfair. Instead, because capital punishment was then so widely used, many of the problems of the felony murder rule evaded attention. **B is incorrect** because common law scholars were not focused on developing a model penal code; instead, that effort began in the 1950s, with the American Law Institute. **D is incorrect** because "fairness" is a concept that pre-dates the common law.

131. This question tests on the felony murder rule's requirement that the death occur during "the commission" of a felony. Under the *res gestae* rule, the felon is responsible for a death as long as there is a causal relationship between the felonious behavior and the death, and if the felon has not yet reached a point of safety after engaging in the felonious behavior.

A is correct because the robbery had not been fully committed—for felony murder purposes—until the police were no longer chasing the man and he was safe. But since the death of the minivan driver occurred before that happened, the man is responsible for that death.

B is incorrect because *corpus delicti* is irrelevant here; that term refers to the rule that the prosecution first prove a crime was committed before a person can be convicted of that crime. **C is incorrect** because it does not account for the *res gestae* rule. **D is incorrect** because it improperly places the blame for the chase on the police.

132. This question tests on the three types of common law manslaughter: voluntary manslaughter, involuntary manslaughter, and misdemeanor manslaughter. Each is explored in the questions that follow.

C is correct because it identifies these three forms of manslaughter.

A is incorrect because there is no such thing as "*amicus curiae* manslaughter." Instead, *amicus curiae* refers to a nonparty "friend of the court," who provides help to a court by offering information or an opinion, often in a legal brief. **B is incorrect** because common law crimes were not separated into degrees. **D is incorrect** because strict liability crimes do not require *mens rea*, and all homicide crimes require a *mens rea*—even felony murder.

133. This question tests on the key difference between murder and manslaughter: the presence or absence of malice aforethought. If a homicide requires proof of malice, it is a murder. But if the homicide does not require proof of malice, it is manslaughter.

A is correct because it recognizes this principle.

B is incorrect because this distinction—originally part of the common law—still exists in many penal codes today. **C is incorrect** because, while there may be other ways to distinguish murder from manslaughter, the question asks about the "primary" distinction between the two. **D is incorrect** because when a defendant kills intentionally and when the crime is labeled as manslaughter, there is no malice.

134. This question tests on the definition of voluntary manslaughter: it is an intentional killing, committed during a "heat of passion" that arises due to "adequate provocation." In voluntary manslaughter, the defendant reacts swiftly to provocation from the victim and kills him, failing to reflect before acting. Because voluntary manslaughter and intentional murder share the same *mens rea*—intent to kill—a murder conviction can be mitigated to voluntary manslaughter, assuming the other requirements for voluntary manslaughter are met.

D is correct because it recognizes that the woman killed intentionally and the killing can be mitigated by the woman's discovery of her husband engaged in adultery; it also identifies the correct crime to be charged.

A is incorrect because it assumes that an intentional killing can "only" be prosecuted as murder. **B is incorrect** because it identifies the incorrect crime to be charged: involuntary manslaughter instead of voluntary manslaughter. **C is incorrect** because it assumes that possession of an unlicensed weapon is a predicate felony for common law felony murder.

135. This question tests on the most common rationale for the existence of voluntary manslaughter: out of the recognition that humans can sometimes be weak and can respond the wrong way to difficult circumstances.

A is correct because it properly articulates this rationale.

B is incorrect because it fails to address the question. **C is incorrect** because there are not enough facts to determine whether the jury deliberately ignored the law when it returned its verdict. **D is incorrect** because there are no facts to support the idea that the woman was mentally ill when she killed her husband.

136. This question tests on the "heat of passion" required for voluntary manslaughter. Because voluntary manslaughter gives a defendant who kills intentionally a break—by reducing a conviction from murder to manslaughter—there are strict requirements that must be first be met. The first of these is heat of passion, which is the type and degree of emotion that causes a person to kill without thinking.

A is correct because it recognizes that the man was only annoyed by his wife's actions. That is not enough for a heat of passion.

B is incorrect because it suggests that the man's plan to divorce his wife gave him an excuse to kill her. **C is incorrect** because the judge should make decisions on the facts in front of her, and not what "probably" happened. **D is incorrect** because it focuses on the provocation, and not whether the man labored under a heat of passion.

137. This question tests on adequate provocation. Not every provocative act is enough to support a voluntary manslaughter conviction; instead, the provocation must be legally adequate. The common law recognized only a few categories of provocation, such as seeing one's spouse engaged in adultery, mutual combat, witnessing a crime against a close relative, and aggravated battery. This has the effect of limiting voluntary manslaughter, because not every angry defendant should have his conviction reduced from murder to manslaughter.

D is correct because the man did not see his wife engaged in adultery; he only thought that the hug meant that she was cheating on him.

A is incorrect because the facts show the wife hugging the second man to greet him, and not necessarily as part of an adulterous act. **B is incorrect** because it focuses on heat of passion, and not whether the provocation was adequate under the law. If the provocation is not legally adequate, then the defendant will not be excused for his acts performed under a heat of passion. **C is incorrect** because it suggests a requirement for voluntary manslaughter—verification—that does not exist. And, if the man had taken time to verify what he saw, that would also be time to reflect and "cool off."

138. This question tests on adequate provocation. At common law, words alone could not be adequate provocation. The reason for this is simple: if name-calling was adequate provocation, then any verbal fight that ended with an intentional killing could potentially be voluntary manslaughter.

B is correct because it recognizes that words alone—even hurtful words, like the ones used here—are not considered legally adequate provocation.

A and C are both incorrect because the wife's denial and whether the man had enough proof of the affair are irrelevant; instead, the issue is whether the law will recognize the wife's words as provocation. **D is incorrect** because it misstates the facts: the man was provoked by his wife's words. Still, the issue is whether her words are legally adequate.

139. This question tests on the standard by which to assess the provocation faced by the defendant in a voluntary manslaughter case. At common law, that standard was the objective, reasonable person.

C is correct because it is the only answer that refers to a purely objective standard.

A is incorrect because it refers to a hybrid objective and subjective standard: a reasonable person (objective) in the young man's position (subjective). **B is incorrect** because it focuses on the fact that the young man was provoked, instead of on whether a reasonable person would have been provoked. **D is incorrect** because it provides a factual response to a legal question.

140. This question tests "misdirected retaliation," i.e., when a provoked defendant, acting in a heat of passion, kills a third party by mistake. At common law, when a defendant killed the wrong person by mistake, he could not be convicted of voluntary manslaughter. Instead, for the defendant to be convicted of voluntary manslaughter, he had to kill the person who provoked him.

B is correct because it recognizes that the homicide victim was not the person who provoked the woman.

A and D are both incorrect because, while each may be true, neither addresses the legal question presented in this question. **C is incorrect** because it fails to recognize that the person who provoked the woman is different from person she shot and killed.

141. This question also tests on provocation from third parties: here, the man suffered from a heat of passion due to inadequate provocation (having his loan application denied) but did not experience any provocation from or feel a heat of passion toward the person he did kill (the security officer), even though he was adequately provoked (punched in the face) by that person. Because the man's heat of passion was not due to the security officer's actions, a charge of voluntary manslaughter would be incorrect.

D is correct because it recognizes that the man's heat of passion came from the denial of the loan application, and not the punch in the face.

A is incorrect because it fails to recognize the respective roles played by the loan officer and the security officer. **B is incorrect** because, although true, it does not address the origins of the man's heat of passion. **C is incorrect** because it articulates a made-up rule. In the absence of a statute in the question addressing "intentional killings on or near bank property," do not assume such a rule exists.

142. This question tests on another requirement for voluntary manslaughter: that the defendant act quickly in response to the heat of passion and adequate provocation, and not have time to "cool off" or reflect on her actions. If the defendant does have time to cool off and reflect and still intentionally kills the victim, then the resulting crime is murder and not voluntary manslaughter.

B is correct because it recognizes that the woman did have time to cool off—and did cool off—while she was sitting in the car. Thus, when she returned to the coffee shop and intentionally killed the man, she was no longer acting under the heat of passion required for a voluntary manslaughter conviction.

A is incorrect because it makes no sense: a person may act deliberately when he commits voluntary manslaughter, but it is the presence of the heat of passion and adequate provocation that distinguishes the crime from an intentional murder. **C is incorrect** because, while the man's conduct was aggressive, offensive, and outrageous, it reaches a factual conclusion and does not provide a legal answer. **D is incorrect** because it does not address the time the woman spent in her car calming herself.

143. This question also tests on "cooling off" for voluntary manslaughter. In this question, the woman had time to cool off but did not.

A is correct because even though the woman did not cool off, she had enough time to do so. As such, the resulting crime is murder and not voluntary manslaughter.

B is incorrect because the woman's awareness of her short temper would not negate a voluntary manslaughter charge, assuming the other requirements were met. By restricting provocation and judging heat of passion objectively, voluntary manslaughter already compensates for defendants with short tempers. **C is incorrect** because it fails to address the time it took for the woman to walk around the block, and it reaches the wrong conclusion. **D is incorrect** because it offers an opinion and not a legal response.

144. This question tests on the need for concurrence between the requirements of voluntary manslaughter: the provocation must cause a heat of passion and also generate the intent to kill. But if the defendant had a preexisting intent to kill, she cannot claim that it was formed due to the adequate provocation.

D is correct because it recognizes that the woman already intended to kill her husband.

A and B are both incorrect because neither acknowledges the woman's preexisting intent to kill her husband. **C is incorrect** because it offers an opinion and does not provide a legal response.

145. This question tests on the definition of involuntary manslaughter: a killing due to criminal negligence. As with depraved heart murder, involuntary manslaughter focuses on the defendant's risky conduct and his attitude toward that risk. In depraved heart murder, the risk of death or danger to human life is very high, and the defendant either is aware of the risk and ignores it or should be aware of the risk. In involuntary manslaughter, the risk of death or danger to human life is lower—although still above ordinary, everyday risk—and the defendant fails to be aware of that risk.

A is correct because two cues in the question—heavy rain and the high rate of speed—suggest that the man took a risk to human life. But, at the same time, nothing in the question suggests that the man knew of the risk to life and deliberately ignored it, or that he should have been aware that he might harm or kill someone.

B is incorrect because it provides a policy answer to a legal question. **C is incorrect** because the man was driving 20 MPH over the speed limit, which was more than a "slight" violation of the posted speed limit. **D is incorrect** because it illogically suggests that the man should have continued with one risky and illegal behavior (speeding) to avoid a risky result (hydroplaning).

146. This question tests on the difference between tort or ordinary negligence, and criminal negligence. Tort negligence looks at four elements: duty, breach, causation, and harm. By contrast, criminal negligence addresses risky behavior and measures the defendant's attitude toward that risk.

C is correct because it best describes what happened here: in retrospect, the man failed his child by not seeking immediate medical attention and this failure caused her death. But that means that the man was negligent under tort law, and not criminally negligent.

A is incorrect because it describes the young man's tort liability, and the question asks about his criminal liability. **B is incorrect** because the failure to seek prompt medical care may not even be a deviation from the standard of care, let alone a "gross" deviation. Most parents do not rush to the doctor when their kids first get a fever, because it often goes away after a day or so. **D is incorrect** because the young man's failure to be aware of the risk weighs in favor of an involuntary manslaughter conviction, and not against it.

147. This question tests on the standard by which to assess the defendant's *mens rea* and *actus reus* in an involuntary manslaughter case. At common law, that standard was the objective, reasonable man.

C is correct because the proposed standard is a hybrid one, including both objective ("ordinary") and subjective ("sleep-deprived, new parent") criteria. Instead, the reasonable man is a completely objective standard.

A is incorrect because the proposed standard is not fully objective. **B is incorrect** because, if the proposed standard describes the mother and her attributes, it cannot be a fully objective standard. **D is incorrect** because it provides a factual response to a legal question.

148. This question tests on the distinction between depraved heart murder and involuntary manslaughter—which is often a very fine line. In general, the difference depends on the defendant's attitude toward his risky conduct: the more the defendant is or should be aware of the risk to human life, the more likely his *mens rea* is malice and not criminal negligence.

A is correct because it focuses on the teenager's knowledge about the weapon, and about how risky his conduct was. While in retrospect it may have been unwise for the teenager to rely on his father's assurances that the weapon was unloaded, it is also generally reasonable for a child to rely on the word of his parent.

B is incorrect because charging the father with a crime does not address whether the teenager should also be charged. **C is incorrect** because the teenager would be better served by conviction of a lower degree of homicide, instead of a mitigation argument at his sentencing for murder. **D is incorrect** because the facts provide no information about the teenager's exact age, and because it provides a policy answer to a legal question.

149. This question tests on misdemeanor manslaughter, which is also sometimes referred to as "unlawful act manslaughter." Misdemeanor manslaughter requires that a death occur during the commission of a non-felonious act, and so is comparable in some ways to felony murder. It was not a widely prosecuted crime at common law and is not widely prosecuted today.

B is correct because it properly categorizes the underlying offense as a misdemeanor, and recognizes that killing during the commission of a misdemeanor is a crime.

A is incorrect because it describes the mental state for depraved heart murder, and the risk the woman took does not rise to that level. **C is incorrect** because it fails to recognize the crime of misdemeanor manslaughter. **D is incorrect** because it offers an opinion, and does not respond to the question.

150. This question tests on a more realistic use of misdemeanor manslaughter, as the underlying misdemeanor involves an inherent risk to human life. The statutory provisions in this question come from the Washington penal code. R.C.W. 9A.36.050 and 9A.08.010(1)(c).

D is correct because the student was aware of the number of people in the car, how she was driving the car, and that the seat belts in the back seat were broken.

A is incorrect because the reckless endangerment statute does not require a drive-by shooting, but instead refers to acts that do not involve drive-by shootings. **B and C are both incorrect** because each concludes that the student should be charged with involuntary manslaughter. But with that crime, the defendant fails to be aware of the risk she is taking, and the facts in this question suggest the opposite. Still, depending on the student's testimony, it could be a close call as to the appropriate charge.

Homicide (Modern and Statutory)

151. This question tests on why a jurisdiction might try to refine common law categories of crime and alludes to Pennsylvania's 1794 penal code, which introduced "degrees" of murder.

C is correct because it is the only answer that articulates a possible valid reason for the statutory change. Indeed, the reason given in this answer is the reason why the Pennsylvania legislature changed its statute: to restrict the use of capital punishment to the most egregious killings, i.e., those classified as first degree murder.

A is incorrect because remembering the four basic types of malice is not an "onerous" task. **B is incorrect** because separating murder into degrees does not necessarily mean that the resulting statute is "progressive" or "reflects modern norms and values." Instead, one would need to review the text of the statute to make that determination. **D is incorrect** because separation of murder into degrees will provide the public (including those who commit crimes) with some information about crime and punishment, but not necessarily the "security" described by the answer.

152. This question tests on the Pennsylvania "degrees of murder" statute enacted in 1794, which still serves as a model for many murder statutes nationally. Under the 1794 statute, felony murder was expressly included under first degree, but felony murder has been omitted from this one.

The 1794 statute carved out a subset of intentional or "willful" killings—those that were also premeditated and deliberate—and elevated them to first degree murder. But the statute also relied on the common law, and so second degree murder's reference to "all other forms of murder" required looking to the common law to see what forms of murder were not included with first degree murder. Thus, under this statute, second degree murder includes (1) intentional killings that are not premeditated and deliberated; (2) intent to cause great bodily harm killings; (3) depraved heart killings; and (4) felony murders.

To categorize a crime that might fall under this type of statute, one must first determine how the common law would categorize the killing, and then determine how that type of murder is classified under the statute.

B is correct because intentional (or "willful") killings are part of the second degree "all other forms of murder" category.

A is incorrect because, although "intentional" and "willful" are synonyms, the woman did not premeditate or deliberate, and both are required for first degree murder. **C is incorrect**

because the statute clearly states what is required to elevate an intentional killing to first degree—premeditation and deliberation—and so information about other attendant circumstances is not required. **D is incorrect** because it is untrue; intentional (only) killings fall within second degree murder.

153. This question tests on statutory homicide generally and illustrates that there is no set format for a homicide statute. Instead, jurisdictions can draft their statutes in many different ways. Under this statute, first degree murder focuses on the status of the victim. Killings that are "willful, premeditated, and deliberate" are included within second degree murder, instead of first degree, where most statutes place them. Third degree murder includes felony murder, and "all other forms of murder"—i.e., those forms of common law murder that aren't described in the first, second, and third degree categories—fall into fourth degree murder. Thus, under this statute, fourth degree murder includes (1) intentional killings that are not premeditated and deliberate and where the victim does not otherwise meet the criteria listed in first degree murder; (2) intent to cause great bodily harm killings; and (3) depraved heart killings.

B is correct because the man certainly killed intentionally, but we need more information to determine if the killing was also premeditated and deliberate. The man did bring a weapon to the meeting, but that fact alone does not conclusively establish premeditation and deliberation.

A is incorrect because the mayor was a local official, and first degree murder requires that the victim be elected to state office. **C is incorrect** because it fails to recognize that the killing here could fall under second or fourth degree, depending on the circumstances. **D is incorrect** because its reference to "only" is too restrictive; the man's actions certainly fall under fourth degree murder, but they may also fall under second degree murder.

154. This question tests on the meaning of the words, "willful, premeditated, and deliberate." As explained earlier, "willful" is a synonym for intentional. Additionally, premeditation means to "think about beforehand" and refers to quantity of thought. *People v. Morrin*, 31 Mich. App. 301, 329 (1971). Deliberation means to "measure and evaluate," *id.*, and refers to quality of thought. Some jurisdictions give independent meaning to each adjective, but others do not.

A is correct because all three requirements are met here: the woman "decided to kill her boss," so she premeditated. She decided to act before he placed the evaluation in her personnel file, which means that she deliberated. And she killed using a bow and arrow, so we can infer that she acted intentionally (willfully).

B is incorrect because it only addresses willfulness, and not premeditation and deliberation. **C is incorrect** because the statute does not require that the killing be committed with poison; instead "killings by means of poison" are examples of "willful, premeditated, and deliberate" killings. **D is incorrect** because the statute focuses on the defendant's *mens rea*, and not the weapon used to commit the killing.

155. This question also tests on the meaning of the words, "willful, premeditated, and deliberate."

D is correct because it recognizes that the killing was accidental and not intentional (willful). But this answer also recognizes that premeditation and deliberation could "arguably" be established by the man's past planning and contemplation of killing the neighbor. Because the man had planned to shoot the neighbor, he also "arguably" did not premeditate and deliberate this death.

A, B, and C are all incorrect because the killing was accidental and not intentional (wilful).

156. This question tests on how long it takes to premeditate and deliberate. Different jurisdictions take different approaches: some jurisdictions require some appreciable period of time beyond that required to form the intent to kill, and others require less time, blurring the line among intent, premeditation, and deliberation. But some additional time is required beyond the time needed to develop the intent to kill.

C is correct because the woman's demand for a "few minutes" to form the *mens rea* for first degree murder is unworkable, no matter what approach this jurisdiction takes to premeditation and deliberation. Under the woman's proposed rule, defendants who wait two and a half minutes before killing would not be guilty of first degree murder, but those who wait three minutes and 15 seconds would be. A better approach would be to evaluate all of the attendant facts and circumstances, instead of employing such a rigid rule.

A is incorrect because the woman did have the necessary time for premeditation and deliberation when she asked her husband to reconsider his answer, and then waited for him to respond. **B is incorrect** because it illogically suggests that the time period required for deliberation is longer than that required for premeditation. **D is incorrect** because it does not respond to the question.

157. This question tests on a statutory definition of "willful, premeditated, and deliberate," where the statute defines premeditation and deliberation. The definition in the question—requiring that "the defendant maturely and meaningfully reflected upon the gravity of his or her act"—comes from the California first degree murder statute. Cal. Penal Code § 189(d).

B is correct because it recognizes that if, as the prosecutor argues, premeditation and deliberation do not have separate meanings, then there is no meaningful distinction between first and second degree murder.

A is incorrect because the statute's reference to "mature[] and meaningful[] reflection" indicates something more than intent to kill, which defeats the prosecution's "plain language" argument. **C is incorrect** because courts are supposed to interpret the law, and so the court's ruling would not violate the separation of powers doctrine. **D is incorrect** because it does not respond to the statutory interpretation issue raised by the question.

158. This question tests on a degrees of murder statute and how it treats depraved heart murders—another form of common law murder. Under this statute, first degree murder includes a subset of intentional or "willful" killings, i.e., those that are also premeditated and deliberate. Second degree murder includes felony murders. Thus, depraved heart murders fall under the third degree definition ("all other forms of murder").

D is correct because the man committed a depraved heart killing, and those killings are included within this statute's third degree murder category.

A is incorrect because the question does not indicate whether voluntary intoxication is a valid defense in this jurisdiction. **B is incorrect** because it does not respond to the question. **C is incorrect** because it assumes that the high rate of speed shows intent to kill. While the prosecutor might make that argument, it is not clear that intent to kill can definitively be established here.

159. This question also tests on a degrees of murder statute. The crime here has been described as "extremely reckless," which is a modern and more precise label for depraved heart murders.

A is correct because, given the prosecutor's description of the crime, the man should be prosecuted for second degree murder as it falls into the "all other forms of murder" category.

B and C are both incorrect, and for two reasons. First, the prosecutor has indicated that this was essentially a depraved heart killing. Second, while Russian Roulette may often lead to death, there is no indication in the facts that this killing was willful, premeditated, and deliberate. **D is incorrect** because it fails to recognize that extreme recklessness is another way of describing a depraved heart.

160. This question tests on felony murder and shows why many modern jurisdictions have limited the possible predicate felonies to those that are inherently dangerous to human life. At common law, the pool of possible predicate felonies was necessarily limited. But the pool of modern predicate felonies is quite large and includes so many non-violent crimes. As such, the potential reach of the felony murder rule could be quite broad if any felony could qualify as a predicate felony.

C is correct because this statute does not appear to place any restrictions on predicate felonies, and because the hacker committed a felony that led to a death. While the hacker's conviction is permitted under the statute, there are legitimate policy questions as to whether his crime should be classified as a form of murder or not. That is why most modern jurisdictions limit predicate felonies to those that are dangerous to human life.

A and B are both incorrect; while both are true, the statute appears to allow the prosecution to proceed. **D is incorrect** because the judge decides questions of law, not the jury.

161. This question tests on how to determine whether a predicate felony is inherently dangerous or not. Some modern jurisdictions will examine the felony in the abstract to determine if it can be committed without danger to human life. If so, the felony cannot support a felony murder conviction. But most modern jurisdictions will examine the felony in the abstract and also the way it was committed in the particular case.

D is correct because arson—a crime against habitation and thus a crime that interferes with the right to be secure in one's home—is both dangerous in the abstract and in the way that it was committed here. Thus, no matter which approach this jurisdiction follows, the arson should be considered inherently dangerous to human life.

A is incorrect because the woman's intended or anticipated result is irrelevant. Instead, the focus should be on the danger associated with the arson. **B is incorrect** because the woman's precautions are irrelevant if the crime itself is inherently dangerous to human life. **C is incorrect** because this is a legal question, and so should be decided by the judge.

162. This question tests on a second modern statutory limitation to felony murder: the restriction of predicate felonies to those that are "independent" of the homicide. If the homicide cannot be committed without committing that felony, then the felony is not independent and it "merges" into the homicide. For example, assault is generally defined as an attempted battery, and so neither assault nor battery is considered independent of homicide. Most jurisdictions today impose some version of this limitation.

A is correct because assault with a deadly weapon is not independent of murder.

B and C are both incorrect because each focuses on the reasons why the man shot his husband. Voluntary manslaughter may be a more appropriate charge on these facts, but the question asks about appellate issues and neither answer responds to that question. **D is incorrect**—an appellate court cannot just vacate a conviction because it disagrees with a prosecutor's charging decision. Instead, the court must have a legal reason to vacate the conviction.

163. This question also tests on the independent felony limitation to felony murder.

C is correct because, on these facts, there was an alternative route to convict the father of murder: by arguing that he committed an intent to cause great bodily harm murder. The existence of that alternative route undercuts the father's argument about fairness.

A is incorrect because it is not clear that the father could be convicted of intentional murder on these facts—although the prosecutor could certainly try to make that argument. **B is incorrect** because it ignores the prosecutor's possible argument regarding a conviction for great bodily harm murder. **D is incorrect** because, by referring to convictions of two additional forms of murder, it presupposes an intentional murder conviction.

164. This question tests on another modern approach to felony murder: instead of trying to restrict predicate felonies to the inherently dangerous or independent felonies, a jurisdiction could lift all restrictions and allow any felony to be used as a predicate felony. Only a few jurisdictions ever followed this approach.

A is correct because it recognizes that, under second degree murder, the predicate felony can be "any assaultive felony not specifically enumerated in the first degree statute." Here, the predicate felony was felonious assault, which meets this definition exactly.

B is incorrect because the trial judge has to respond to the woman's motion. While he might deny the motion and she might appeal, the judge must issue a ruling. **C is incorrect** because felonious assault is a form of battery, and as such, there is nothing to restrict it from merging with the homicide. **D is incorrect** because the statute plainly provides for felonious assault ("any assaultive felony not specifically enumerated in the first degree statute").

165. This question tests on the felony murder rule and killings committed by non-felons, demonstrating one of the ways in which the felony murder rule can be unfair.

B is correct because the felony murder rule holds felons and co-felons responsible for deaths committed during the commission of their felonies.

A is incorrect because the felony murder rule does not focus on what a felon should have known or anticipated; instead, the rule focuses on whether a predicate felony was committed and a killing occurred during the commission of that felony. **C is incorrect** because the felony murder rule does not require proof of actual malice; instead, the malice associated with felony murder is constructed from the intent to commit the felony and the ensuing death. **D is incorrect** because there is no such restriction in the felony murder rule. A jurisdiction would be free to impose such a restriction—by statute or case law—but none is given in the question.

166. This question tests on the way a majority of modern jurisdictions address the issue of killings by non-felons: by holding the felon responsible for those deaths only if the non-felon was acting as the felon's agent.

B is correct because the question asks about the "majority rule" and this answer articulates that rule and correctly applies it to the facts.

A is incorrect because the majority rule does not inquire about reasonable foreseeability; instead, the only inquiry is whether the non-felon was acting as the felon's agent when he (the non-felon) committed the killing. **C is incorrect** because it articulates the minority rule for these cases. **D is incorrect** because the judge decides questions of law, not the jury.

167. This question tests on the way a minority of modern jurisdictions address the issue of killings by non-felons: by holding the felon responsible for those deaths only if the felon was the proximate cause of the killing.

B is correct because the woman—who robbed the liquor store, which created a situation where the officer intervened—created the events that caused the clerk's death.

A is incorrect because the woman is permitted to file a motion to dismiss the charges; she should not have to wait until after she is convicted for a ruling. **C is incorrect** because it ignores that the question asks about the proximate cause rule. **D is incorrect** because it articulates the majority agency rule, and the question asks about the minority proximate cause rule.

168. This question tests on a variation on the felony murder rule, where the statute itself lists potential defenses for less-culpable co-felons. This statute is taken from the Maine penal code. Me. Stat. tit. 17-A, § 202.

D is correct because the facts indicate that the sister knew about her brother's weapon. As such, she cannot meet the requirements of subsection (3), which requires a reasonable belief that no other participant was armed.

A is incorrect because it is untrue: the sister did not take "every possible precaution" because she knew her brother was armed. **B is incorrect** because the brother's promises are irrelevant under the statute. **C is incorrect** because it is written too broadly: under this statute, a defendant can "help" with a felony and still have a valid defense if she meets the requirements in subsections (1)–(4).

169. This question tests on one of the ways to address the potential unfairness with the felony rule: reject constructive malice. Under this modern variation of felony murder, used in Michigan, a felony murder conviction requires proof that the defendant had some form of "actual malice" at the time of the killing, i.e., an intent to kill, an intent to cause great bodily harm, or a depraved heart. *People v. Aaron*, 409 Mich. 672 (1980).

B is correct and demonstrates how use of the *Aaron* rule—here, codified in the statute—can limit the unfairness that is sometimes seen in felony murder cases. The man committed a robbery and a bank customer died in the robbery; in many jurisdictions, this could be prosecuted as felony murder based on the man's constructive malice. But because he did not have actual malice, he cannot be convicted under the given statute.

A is incorrect for two reasons: we do not know that the bank customer was "clumsy" and it is inaccurate to say that the man had "nothing" to do with the death. **C is incorrect** because forcing the customers into the office doesn't show malice, at least as that term is legally defined. **D is incorrect** because this is not an ordinary felony murder statute; instead, the statute requires "actual malice."

170. This question also tests on the *Aaron* rule and demonstrates how it applies to a more ordinary felony murder scenario.

A is correct because, by holding the gun to the pharmacist's head, the woman demonstrated the intent to kill. Since such intent is a form of actual malice, the woman can be convicted of felony murder under this statute.

B is incorrect because it does not address the statute's requirement of "actual malice;" instead, it presumes an ordinary felony murder statute. **C is incorrect** because it ignores that the woman held the gun to the pharmacist's head and the meaning of that act. **D is incorrect** because it addresses sentencing, and not whether the woman can be convicted in the first instance.

171. This question also tests on another modern approach to felony murder: to abolish the rule altogether. Only a handful of states have taken this approach.

D is correct because it recognizes that many felony murders can be prosecuted as other forms of murder.

A and C are both incorrect because, while the proposed legislation might save tax dollars, it will not stop "all" or "most" of the described prosecutions. For example, if a defendant shoots and kills a clerk while robbing a store, or if a defendant burglarizes a home and beats and kills the homeowner, these crimes can still be prosecuted as murder. **B is incorrect** because it makes no sense: if a killing occurs during the commission of a felony, it will not fall within the definition of manslaughter.

172. This question tests on modern reforms to voluntary manslaughter, which is an intentional killing, committed during a heat of passion that arises due to adequate provocation. The question focuses on adequate provocation, which, under modern law, is not as narrowly constructed as at common law. Today, the question of adequate provocation is often a jury question. Regardless, legal conduct on the part of the victim is still not considered to be adequate provocation. If it was, then voluntary manslaughter could expand to include almost any intentional killing.

C is correct because it recognizes that the defense argument goes too far, and argues for an infinitely expandable definition of adequate provocation.

A is incorrect because it does not address the defense argument that the speaker provoked the woman. In any event, even if the defense argued that the woman was partially provoked by the cheering of the crowd—i.e., legally protected speech—her argument would still fail. **B is incorrect** because provocation can still be adequate even when it is not directed at the defendant, such as when a defendant witnesses physical harm to a close relative. **D is incorrect** because it does not respond to the legal question.

173. This question tests on modern voluntary manslaughter, relative to the common law. Now, as then, most jurisdictions do not consider "words alone" to be adequate provocation. Otherwise, any verbal fight that resulted in an intentional killing could be treated as voluntary manslaughter.

B is correct because it recognizes that provocation requires more than words. As such, the "critical fact" will be that the driver threatened the bicyclist with physical harm. At common law and today, that is sufficient for adequate provocation.

A is incorrect because it suggests that words are enough for adequate provocation. **C is incorrect** because that fact alone is not critical to the manslaughter assessment. **D is incorrect** because whether the driver cooled off or not is irrelevant to whether the bicyclist committed voluntary manslaughter.

174. This question tests on how modern jurisdictions deal with "misdirected retaliation," i.e., when a provoked defendant, acting in a heat of passion, kills a third party by mistake. Now, as then, most jurisdictions do not allow a defendant to use this as an excuse. The statute in this question is from Pennsylvania, 18 Pa. C.S. § 2503(a), and represents a minority approach.

D is correct because the statutory exception is inapplicable here. The mother was slapping the other driver, and then intentionally shot the neighbor when he intervened. For the mother to take advantage of the statute, she would have needed to "endeavor to kill" the driver of the other car.

A is incorrect because, while it correctly describes the statute, it does not address the facts. **B is incorrect** because the mother was not trying to kill the driver of the other car; she was slapping him. **C is incorrect** because the mother acted intentionally, not recklessly.

175. This question tests on how modern jurisdictions approach the reasonable person in the context of voluntary manslaughter. At common law, the standard was an objective one. Today, more jurisdictions include some subjectivity in the analysis, looking at how a reasonable person in the defendant's shoes would respond to the situation.

A is correct because the standard proposed by the defense is far too subjective. Instead, it appears that the defense has proposed a standard that is identical to the woman.

B and D are both incorrect because neither responds to the question. **C is incorrect** because, although true, it does not provide a legal response to the question.

Rape

176. This question tests on the definition of common law rape, which can be committed in several different ways: forcibly and without the victim's consent, through fraud or deception, or against a victim who is incapable of giving consent. Regardless of how committed, the core definition is the same: rape is the carnal knowledge of a woman, by force and against her will. Subsequent questions will explore this definition.

B is correct because it includes all the necessary elements. Although the answer refers to "without consent" instead of "against her will," the two phrases mean the same thing.

A and C are both incorrect because each identifies the victim of this crime as "another," and common law rape required a female victim. Thus, common law rape requires carnal knowledge "of a woman." **D is incorrect** for two reasons. First, it focuses on the rape of a child victim, and the question asks about the broader crime of "common law rape." Second, because children are incapable of consenting to sexual acts, rape of a child does not require proof that the child did not consent.

177. This question tests on the requirement at common law that only a woman could be a victim of rape.

D is correct because no matter how egregious the manager's actions, they were not committed against a woman and so do not constitute common law rape.

A, B, and C are all incorrect because they focus on the wrong issue, i.e., the medical examination results or how the head chef's drinking affected his credibility. Instead, the issue here is whether the common law would recognize a man as a victim of rape at all.

178. This question tests on another gender-related aspect of common law rape: that only a man can commit this crime. While this is not an express part of the definition, only a man can engage in "carnal knowledge of a woman."

A is correct because it recognizes this principle.

B and D are both incorrect because each focuses on the sleeping woman's ability to accurately testify as to what happened to her. But if the other woman cannot be charged with the crime, the sleeping woman's testimony is irrelevant. **C is incorrect** because no matter what the other woman did to the sleeping woman, she is not a proper defendant for a common law rape charge.

179. This question tests on the marital exemption to common law rape, which holds that a man cannot be charged with the rape of his wife. Although seemingly antiquated, the marital exemption is still a part of many state rape and sexual assault statutes. For more, see Dressler, *Understanding* § 33.06[B].

B is correct because it recognizes that the marital exemption would defeat a rape charge against the husband.

A is incorrect because it focuses on whether the prosecution will successfully proceed, and not whether the husband should be charged in the first instance. **C is incorrect** because, while it accurately describes the husband's actions, it does not address the marital exemption. **D is incorrect** because it suggests that there is a rebuttable presumption that can be applied to the marital exemption. Instead, the marital exemption was absolute: if the male perpetrator was married to the female victim, he had an absolute defense to the charge.

180. This question tests on the *actus reus* of rape: sexual intercourse ("carnal knowledge") committed without the victim's consent and with force. While these latter two elements are often considered together—proof of one can provide proof of the other, and vice versa—they are distinct requirements. To establish lack of consent, the prosecutor must prove that the victim outwardly indicated that she did not want to have intercourse, or that she was subjected to force or threats of force that prevented her from doing so. To establish force, the prosecutor must prove that the victim resisted the defendant, or demonstrate that she did not do so because she faced threats of death or serious bodily injury.

C is correct because it recognizes that neither the consent nor the force requirements are established by these facts. First, the woman never told the man that she did not consent; instead, she remained silent only because she was afraid and not because of any force used against her. Second, the man did not use force—beyond that required to accomplish the sexual act—to engage in sexual intercourse with the woman.

A is incorrect because, at common law, the woman was required to resist her attacker or be prevented from doing so by force or threat of force. Being legitimately afraid did not excuse the woman from this requirement. **B is incorrect** because consent at common law focused on what the woman communicated to the man, and not what the man should have responsibly inferred. **D is incorrect** because it only addresses lack of consent and not the lack of force.

181. This question also tests on the *actus reus* for common law rape: carnal knowledge, which is another way of describing sexual intercourse. To meet the carnal knowledge requirement, any act of penetration was enough, and no emission of semen was required.

B is correct because it recognizes that oral sex is different from sexual intercourse.

A is incorrect because it focuses on consent, instead of the sexual act. And, given that the facts state that the woman "kicked and screamed" before the man overpowered her, her lack of consent was communicated to the man. **C is incorrect** because it does not address that oral sex is insufficient for common law rape. **D is incorrect** because it focuses on force although, again, the issue is whether the sexual act was sufficient.

182. This question also tests on the *actus reus* for common law rape. In this question, the man "fondled" the woman, but he did not have sexual intercourse with her. While this might be a battery at common law, it was not rape.

C is correct because it recognizes that fondling does not meet the *actus reus* requirement for common law rape.

A and B are both incorrect because each suggests that fondling will meet the *actus reus* for common law rape. **D is incorrect** because it focuses on the quality of the prosecutor's evidence, and not whether the charge is appropriate in the first place.

183. This question also tests on the *actus reus* for common law rape and underscores that "carnal knowledge" does not require ejaculation.

A is correct because it recognizes this principle.

B is incorrect because it focuses on whether or not the man had consent to enter the woman's "house and her bed," which is not part of the requirement for common law rape. **C is incorrect** because carnal knowledge may be found even without ejaculation. **D is incorrect** because it is untrue: the acts of breaking into the woman's house and having intercourse with her while she slept demonstrate force.

184. This question tests on the force required for common law rape. To prove force, the victim had to resist or demonstrate that she did not do so because she faced threats of death or serious bodily injury.

B is correct because it recognizes that being subjected to nonconsensual sexual intercourse, alone, does not establish force.

A is incorrect because the woman's consent to the date would not provide blanket consent for all of the other events that occurred that evening. Instead, the woman could consent to the date but not consent to sexual intercourse. **C is incorrect** because common law rape requires more than nonconsensual sexual intercourse. **D is incorrect** because the delay between the sexual act and its report is irrelevant if the man's actions do not meet the elements of common law rape.

185. This question also tests on the force requirement. At common law, this required that the victim actively resist:

> The prosecutrix, if she was the weaker party, was bound to resist to the utmost. Nature had given her feet and hands with which she could kick and strike, teeth to bite, and a voice to cry out. All these should have been put in requisition in defence of her chastity. [*Prokop v State*, 148 Neb. 582; 28 N.W.2d 200 (1947), abrogated, *Reavis v Slominski*, 250 Neb. 711; 551 N.W.2d 528 (1996).]

While the resistance requirement is no longer so strictly defined, the law regarding resistance is still somewhat in flux. For more, see Dressler, *Understanding* § 33.04[B][2].

D is correct because it recognizes that the woman's resistance was minimal. If anything, the woman's resistance demonstrated her lack of consent instead of the man's use of force.

A is incorrect because it makes no sense: the prosecutor should look to the woman's actions to determine whether she consented, and not at what the man thought about her consent. **B is incorrect** because whether or not the intercourse occurred is not the issue here; instead, the issue is whether the other requirements of common law rape have been met. **C is incorrect** because the facts do show that the woman withheld her consent: aside from saying no, she pushed the man away twice.

186. This question tests on the role of fear in the force analysis. In short, a victim's fear is irrelevant, because fear is a subjective emotion and cannot be used to prove force. Instead, a victim would have to resist.

C is correct because it recognizes that one of the elements of common law rape cannot be established on these facts.

A is incorrect because, despite the college student's fear, the force requirement must still be established. **B is incorrect** because the prosecutor cannot prove a rape occurred based just on the lack of consent. Instead, the prosecutor would also need to show force. **D is incorrect** because the college student's consent to go on the date cannot be reasonably be construed as consent to being raped.

187. This question also tests on the force requirement. In this question, the woman faced threats of death or serious bodily injury, so she would be excused from resisting her attacker.

A is correct because it recognizes that the woman would not have to resist while the man had such ready access to a gun.

B is incorrect because force at common law required more than nonconsensual sexual intercourse. **C is incorrect** because the man did use force when he pointed the gun at the woman and kept it in his hand during intercourse. **D is incorrect** because the man's use of the weapon is a sufficiently specific threat to the woman's life.

188. This question tests on consent and common law rape. To prove lack of consent, the prosecutor was required to prove that the victim indicated that she did not want to have intercourse, or that she was subjected to force or threats of force such that she could not do so.

D is correct because the woman stayed silent throughout the sexual encounter, and did not indicate in any way that she did not consent to the sexual act.

A is incorrect because consent to enter an apartment for a drink cannot be reasonably be construed as consent to being raped. **B is incorrect** because it does not present a legal argument; while the defense might make this argument, the stronger argument would be one that attacks an element of the offense. **C is incorrect** because forcible rape can occur between acquaintances as well as strangers.

189. This question tests on rape and fraud. Because the common law did not treat seduction as rape, a man who lied to a woman so she would have sex with him was not a rapist. Instead, because the woman had consented to the sexual act, no rape occurred. On the other hand, if the man lied about the sexual act he would perform, the woman's consent was invalid and the man would be guilty of rape.

A is correct because the young woman did consent to sexual intercourse. She just did not consent to having sexual intercourse with the brown-eyed twin.

B is incorrect because any delay in reporting does not affect whether or not the elements of the crime have been met. **C is incorrect** because the twins' motivation is irrelevant to the question of whether a crime has occurred. **D is incorrect** because it suggests that the young woman could never be raped by the brown-eyed twin, due to her relationship with the blue-eyed twin.

190. This question tests on rape where the victim is incapable of giving consent. The common law treated these situations as rape, with the force committed constructively instead of actually.

B is correct because it recognizes that the woman was unconscious and could not give or withdraw consent. As a result, the night nurse's sexual intercourse with her was committed by force.

A is incorrect because the woman was unconscious, and so it would have been impossible for the night nurse to secure her consent. **C is incorrect** because it is ludicrous: the voluntary placement of woman in the care facility cannot be reasonably construed as consent to sexual intercourse. **D is incorrect** because it ignores that having sexual intercourse with an unconscious person is a forceful act.

191. This question tests on rape of a child, which is more commonly referred to as "statutory rape." Because a child under the age of consent cannot give consent to a sexual act, the intercourse is considered to be constructively forceful and non-consensual.

C is correct because it recognizes that the girlfriend's age trumps her willing participation in the sexual act.

A is incorrect because the girlfriend is not too young to be reliable. Although the common law did recognize that very young children were unreliable, the girlfriend is in her mid-teens. **B is incorrect** because the focus should be on the girlfriend's age, and not that of the sophomore. **D is incorrect** because there is no requirement of forensic evidence; instead, the prosecutor may use any admissible evidence to prove the elements of the offense.

192. This question tests on statutory rape and the relevance (if any) of a defendant's mistake about the victim's age. Such a defense is more generally described as a mistake of fact. While this defense is generally available in response to other criminal charges, it is not a defense to statutory rape. Instead, statutory rape is "strict liability as to age," which means that the defendant must have the *mens rea* for the crime, but his beliefs about the victim's age are irrelevant.

B is correct because it acknowledges this point.

A is incorrect because the larger crime of statutory rape is not classified as a strict liability crime. **C and D are both incorrect** as each suggests that the mistake of fact defense is a possibility on these facts, depending on whether the man's belief is subjectively or objectively held.

193. This question tests on a modern sexual assault statute that has expanded the prohibited *actus reus*, from "carnal knowledge" to (among other things) "nonconsensual sexual contact." The definition in this question is taken from the Michigan criminal sexual conduct statute. M.C.L. § 750.520a(q). For a more thorough discussion of the ways modern jurisdictions have expanded their rape and sexual assault statutes, see Dressler, *Understanding* § 33.04[B][2].

C is correct because the man's act of grabbing the woman's breasts and buttocks is an act of "intentional touching ... of the clothing covering the immediate area of the victim's ... intimate parts." In addition, on these facts, it is reasonable to conclude that the touching was "for the purpose of sexual arousal or gratification." As all the statutory elements have been met, it seems likely that the colleague will likely be convicted.

A is incorrect because it focuses on sexual intercourse, and the statute is worded more broadly to encompass other acts. **B is incorrect** because the statute does not require "proof" of sexual arousal; instead, it requires less: that the touching "reasonably be construed" for arousal or gratification. **D is incorrect** because it focuses on the colleague's kiss, which is not prohibited by this statute.

194. This question tests on the marital exemption as well as a modern statutory definition of a sexual crime. Although this statute retains elements of the common law—it requires sexual intercourse—its title, use of degrees, and reference to "forcible compulsion" indicate that it departs from the common law, too. The definition of forcible compulsion in this question is based on the Pennsylvania rape statute, 18 Pa. C.S. § 3101, although it has been edited somewhat.

D is correct because the husband had sexual intercourse with his wife; she "struggled" and so indicated that she did not consent; and he held her arms down, which constitutes express physical force, used to accomplish the prohibited act.

A is incorrect because, given the way that the statute departs from the common law, it would be unwise to think that the marital exemption exists in this jurisdiction. **B is incorrect** because the statute does not require injuries; it requires forcible compulsion. **C is incorrect** because it relies on the common law definition of rape, and the question supplies an alternative, statutory definition.

195. This question also tests on a modern sexual assault statute. In this question, the sexually prohibited act includes far more than the common law's "carnal knowledge of a woman." The statute also refers to the defendant as an "actor," which signals both men and women can be charged with this crime. The definition in this question is taken from the Michigan criminal sexual conduct statute. M.C.L. §750.520a(r).

B is correct because it recognizes that, under this statute, a man can be convicted of sexually assaulting another man.

A and D are both incorrect because neither responds to the issue presented by the question. **C is incorrect** because it refers to the common law, and the question instead supplies a statutory definition.

Assault and Battery

196. This question tests on assault, which was defined at common law as an attempted battery. There are two forms of criminal assault. First, the attempt can be made, as here, to cause fear and apprehension in the victim, but with no intent to make actual contact. But second, as the definition implies, the attempt can be unsuccessful, as when a person tries to hit another person but misses.

B is correct because it recognizes that the woman assaulted her wife when she tried to hit her with the soda can and missed.

A is incorrect because battery requires contact with the victim, and the wife ducked and missed being hit with the can of soda. **C and D are both incorrect** because each refers to the crime of mayhem, a form of aggravated battery that at common law required disfigurement.

197. This question tests on the *mens rea* for the first type of assault: the intent to create fear or apprehension in the victim.

D is correct because it recognizes this form of assault.

A and B are both incorrect because each suggests that assault is restricted to a failed battery. **C is incorrect** because it misstates the facts.

198. This question tests on the *actus reus* for the first type of assault. In general, "words alone" are insufficient to support an assault conviction, because insulting words are not enough to create fear or apprehension in a victim. If they were, the crime of assault would necessarily occur anytime one person got into a disagreement with another person.

B is correct because it recognizes that, while the crossing guard might have been offended when the father called her an idiot, a reasonable person would not have been offended.

A and D are both incorrect because each refers to "fighting words," which are words that are so provocative and insulting that they are not protected by the First Amendment. *Chaplinsky v. New Hampshire*, 315 U.S. 568 (1942). This is a very narrow class of words, and "idiot" is not included within it. **C is incorrect** because it recognizes that the crossing guard may have been insulted, but she could not reasonably have felt "fear or apprehension" because of the insult.

199. This question also tests on word-based assault. In this question, the words are not insulting but are instead threatening. Threatening words can be sufficient for an assault conviction, but they must be accompanied by the present ability to carry out the threat.

C is correct because it recognizes that the man's words were just that: words spoken over the phone and nothing more. While the words might have been threatening, the facts do not suggest that the man knew where the clerk lived or even how to find him.

A and B are both incorrect because each focuses on the man's motivations for his threat, and not whether the elements of the crime have been met. **D is incorrect** because the man's words were not vague and did threaten harm. Although the man did not specify how he would make the clerk "pay," it is reasonable to infer that he was referring to some form of physical harm.

200. This question tests on the *mens rea* for the second type of assault: the intent to batter the victim or the intent to engage in a harmful or offensive touching. With this type of assault, a battery is attempted, but it fails.

A is correct because it best describes what happened: the rival fan tried to hit the man but missed.

B and D are both incorrect because the rival fan did more than try to scare the man. Instead, according to the facts, he tried to hit the man in the face with a bottle. **C is incorrect** because the question asks about assault, which does not require contact.

201. This question tests on whether an assault occurs when the victim is unaware of the defendant's actions. For the first type of assault (intent to create fear or apprehension), the victim must be aware and must experience the fear or apprehension. For the second type of assault (unsuccessful battery), the victim does not need to be aware.

B is correct because it recognizes that an assault did not occur here. While the neighbor may have intended the man to hear him, he did not.

A is incorrect because even if the neighbor "only" intended a threat, the man did not hear his words. **C is incorrect** because the neighbor's threat alone is not a violation of the criminal law. **D is incorrect** because the 60-foot distance between the neighbor and the man suggests that the neighbor did not intend to batter the man at the time he made his threat.

202. This question also tests on the awareness of the victim in an assault. In this question, the woman intended to hit her mother and would have if the nurse had not intervened. For this type of assault, the victim does not need to be aware of the impending battery.

D is correct because it recognizes that an assault occurred, regardless of the mother's unconscious state.

A is incorrect because this form of assault does not require the victim to be aware of the defendant's actions. **B is incorrect** because the assault did happen, but the battery did not. **C is incorrect** because it focuses on the woman's motive, which is irrelevant.

203. This question tests on the definition of battery: the unlawful use of force that results in injury or offensive touching.

A is correct because it describes what the woman did: she slapped the man (use of unlawful force), which led to an injury (a reddened face).

B is incorrect because assault is an attempted battery, and the woman's hand actually touched the man's face when she slapped it. **C is incorrect** because the man does not have to suffer a "real injury;" instead, he has to suffer an injury or be touched in an offensive manner. **D is incorrect** because any assault that occurred in this situation merged into battery when the woman's hand touched the man's face.

204. This question tests on the first of three different mental states required for battery: the intentional application of force.

D is correct because it is the only answer that addresses *mens rea* and tracks the definition of battery.

A and C are both incorrect because each provides a nonlegal response to a legal question. **B is incorrect** because the fact that the man did not need stitches does not mean that he was not battered.

205. This question tests on the second possible mental state for battery: criminal negligence. This is more than ordinary tort negligence and involves the defendant's failure to be aware of a significant risk of injury or harm to the victim.

B is correct because it is the only answer that addresses the facts and ties them to the definition of battery.

A is incorrect because committing battery in the past does not establish that the plastic surgeon committed a battery in this case. **C is incorrect** because it suggests that medical malpractice cannot also constitute criminal battery, which is untrue. **D is incorrect** because it does not respond to the question, which asks about charging the doctor.

206. This question tests on the third possible mental state for battery, which occurs when the defendant does not intend harm and is not acting with criminal negligence, but where she has the *mens rea* for some other unlawful act. In this question, the unlawful act is exceeding the speed limit.

D is correct because it explains the causal link between the woman's unlawful act (exceeding the speed limit) and the pedestrian's injury.

A and B are both incorrect because each addresses the pedestrian's fault for the accident, and the question addresses the driver's fault. **C is incorrect** because it addresses an omission (failure to brake in time), and the question provides no information about the driver's duty to use her brakes.

207. This question tests on how to assess the injury or offensive touching associated with a possible battery. Concrete injuries are easy to assess, but it can be more difficult to determine if a touching is offensive or not. Consistent with other aspects of the common law, the harm for battery is judged objectively, according to the reasonable man standard.

B is correct because it addresses the correct standard.

A is incorrect because this does not appear to be a case of sexual harassment, and so the prosecutor's explanation is misplaced. **C is incorrect** because the prosecutor should not advise the woman to file a police report if it is clear that no crime occurred. **D is incorrect** because it provides nonlegal advice in response to a legal question.

208. This question tests on the issue of consent in battery. In some situations, people consent to a certain amount of jostling, injury, and offensive touching. For example, football players tacitly consent to conduct that would be deemed battery if that same conduct occurred off the football field. But that does not mean that football players consent to every injury or offensive touching on the field; these nonconsensual acts can be considered crimes.

A is correct because it accurately described what happened here: the student used force beyond what the other player tacitly consented to, which caused a broken cheekbone and a concussion.

B is incorrect because the rules of hockey do not dictate whether the student committed a battery or not. That is, while it is relevant that the student violated the rules, it is not dispositive of whether a battery occurred or not. **C is incorrect** because the other player's consent presumably did not extend to a broken cheekbone and a concussion. **D is incorrect** because the lack of a penalty call is not dispositive of whether a battery occurred or not.

209. This question tests on a modern statute addressing assault and battery. This statute combines common law forms of assault and battery into a single crime of "simple assault," as the statute refers to both the attempted and completed crime. The statute in this question is derived from the Pennsylvania simple assault statute and has been edited somewhat. See 18 Pa. C.S. §2701(a).

D is correct because, at most, the woman's actions here are an attempt, because she did not touch the greeter in any way. The facts in the question do not give enough information by which to determine if the spitting was intended to place the greeter in fear of bodily injury. Did the woman spit at the greeter? On the ground in front of the greeter? The facts are silent on these details, so the best answer is that the woman's actions do not meet the attempt provisions of the statute.

A is incorrect because the statute recognizes "simple assault," even if the statute does not. **B is incorrect** because there is no constitutional prohibition on a statute describing multiple crimes in the same provision. **C is incorrect** because it only addresses one part of the statute and a part that is not relevant to these facts.

210. This question tests on another modern statute addressing assault and battery. The statute in this question is based on a Michigan statute, M.C.L. §750.84, but has been edited somewhat.

C is correct because the teenager both assaulted and battered her father. But, most importantly, she did so with the intent to cause him great bodily harm, but without the intent to kill.

A is incorrect because the statute does not require information about the father's injuries. **B is incorrect** because the statute does not require intent to kill; it requires intent to cause great bodily harm less than murder. **D is incorrect** because the teenager did not intend to kill her father.

Burglary

211. This question tests on the common law classification of burglary. Common law burglary—defined as a breaking and entering of the dwelling house of another, at night, with the intent to commit a felony once inside—is classified as a crime against habitation. That is, it is a crime that interferes with the right to be secure or live peacefully in one's home. While a crime against the person or against property can be committed in conjunction with a burglary, burglary itself is a crime against habitation.

C is correct because it properly classifies burglary as a crime against habitation.

A, B, and D are all incorrect because each classifies burglary incorrectly.

212. This question tests on the definition of breaking, the first required element of burglary. To break, the defendant must create a breach or opening in the dwelling house, or remove some barrier that prevents him from entering the house. An actual breaking occurs when the defendant himself breaks, and a constructive breaking occurs when he, through coercion or fraud, causes someone else to create the breach or opening.

D is correct because the man used the key to open the door without the homeowner's consent. In other words, a breaking occurred when the man created an opening into the house that he was not entitled to create.

A is incorrect because it suggests that a breaking requires force or destruction of valuable property; neither is required for a breaking. **B is incorrect** because it does the opposite and suggests that by not using force, no breaking occurred. **C is incorrect** because it focuses on the wrong thing: the man's actions toward the flower pot instead of his actions toward the house.

213. This question tests on constructive breaking: where the defendant, through coercion or fraud, causes someone else to create the breach or opening.

C is correct because it recognizes that the woman lied, and the effect of that lie: it induced the neighbor to open the door and create a breach to her house.

A is incorrect because it ties breaking to destruction of property, which is not required for burglary. Instead, the defendant must create a breach or opening in the property. **B is incorrect** because it does not address the woman's lie in any way. **D is incorrect** because it suggests that the woman is guilty of burglary even though all the elements of the crime are not present.

214. This question also tests on breaking. When a homeowner consents for his home to be opened in a certain way and the person does only what he is authorized to do, no breaking occurs. But when the person exceeds the scope of the homeowner's consent, then the resulting action is trespassory and is considered a breaking. Here, the woman gave the builder a key, but the builder exceeded the limits she placed on its use.

B is correct because the builder exceeded the limits the woman placed on the use of the housekey. As such, the builder's actions are no different from the woman's actions in the previous question.

A is incorrect because it does not address that the key was used without consent. **C is incorrect** because it does not respond to the question, which asks about breaking, and not felonious intent. **D is incorrect** because the scope of the agreement is the relevant issue here, not how the agreement was formed.

215. This question also tests on breaking and the limits of how secure the home must be for the homeowner to claim protection under the law. While the common law did not require the homeowner to lock every door and window, no breaking occurred if a door or window was left open and the homeowner invited an entry. This question presents a middle ground: the main door was left open, but the closed screened door covered the entry to the house.

C is correct because it recognizes that the screen door was a legitimate barrier to the house, and the teenage son breached that barrier when he opened the door.

A is incorrect because it does not recognize that the screen door closes the house to intruders. **B is incorrect** because it focuses on the type of door (screened versus solid), instead of the position of the door (closed). **D is incorrect** because it places the focus on consent to enter when the fact pattern gives no indication of any consent.

216. This question tests on two concepts: constructive breaking and the innocent instrumentality rule. The former is defined above. The latter provides that when a person uses an unwitting agent to commit a crime, the person who used that agent is responsible for the crime—not the agent.

B is correct because it recognizes that the woman herself is responsible for the breaking because she used her daughter (an "innocent") to do the breaking for her.

A is incorrect because it provides a factual response to a legal question. **C and D are both incorrect** because neither answer recognizes that the mother used her daughter to commit the crime for her, nor addresses how to respond to that fact.

217. This question tests on the causal relationship between breaking and entering, which requires that entry be gained through the breach or opening previously created—and not some other breach or opening. In this fact pattern, the teenager broke on one day and entered the next, but there was a causal relationship between the two acts.

C is correct because it recognizes this principle.

A is incorrect because it refers to a nonexistent time requirement between the breaking and the entry, where all that is required is that there be a causal relationship between the two elements. **B and D are both incorrect** because each refers to the teenager's juvenile status, but the fact pattern gives no information about her exact age or the laws in this jurisdiction for prosecuting juveniles.

218. This question tests on the common law rules for entries committed via chimneys. Even though a chimney is effectively an opening into a house—like an open window or door—the common law did not treat chimneys this way. Instead, at common law, if one entered via a chimney, a breaking occurred because an open chimney is not an invitation to enter like an open window or door might be.

A is correct because it recognizes that no breaking occurred here, and why.

B is incorrect because it provides a policy-based answer to a legal question; as the common law provides a direct answer to the question, there is no reason to resort to public policy. **C is incorrect** because does not respond to the question: the attempted sale of the painting shows the man's possession of the stolen property but does not address how he gained possession in the first instance. **D is incorrect** because it misstates the common law rule.

219. This question tests on the temporal scope of the "dwelling house," which includes curtilage, i.e., buildings close enough to the house to be included in a fence surrounding the property. Although the precise contours of the curtilage are sometimes difficult to determine, a shed close to the house would certainly qualify.

D is correct because it recognizes the proximity between the shed and the home, and that the shed is part of the home's curtilage.

A is incorrect because it does not recognize that buildings close to the home (i.e., on the curtilage) are considered part of the "dwelling house." **B and C are both incorrect** because each suggests that a burglar must commit a crime once inside the dwelling house, but all that is required is that he intend to commit a crime at the time of the breaking and entering.

220. This question tests on whether a dwelling house loses its character when the owner is not living in the house. At common law, burglary did not require the homeowner to be present in the house at the time of the breaking and entering. Indeed, the homeowner could be away for an extended period of time, as here, and the home would still be protected.

C is correct because it recognizes this principle.

A is incorrect because it suggests that the common law imposed a strict time limit on homeowner vacations, and it did not. **B is incorrect** because the gap of time between the crime and its discovery may affect the prosecutor's ability to secure a conviction, but the question asks about whether the man committed a burglary or not. **D is incorrect** because it is too narrow; the home could cease to be a dwelling house for other reasons too, e.g., if it was abandoned or became uninhabitable.

221. This question tests on the type of property that must be broken and entered into: the dwelling house of another. Because burglary is a crime against habitation, it requires a dwelling house.

D is correct because it recognizes that the restaurant is not a dwelling house.

A and B are both incorrect because this question asks about common law burglary, which requires a dwelling house. Without additional facts that someone lives in this structure, the restaurant is just a business. **C is incorrect** because the question does not ask about alternative charges, but instead asks whether the cook committed burglary.

222. This question tests on whether a mixed-use property will qualify for burglary purposes. At common law, if the structure was used solely for business, it would not be considered a dwelling house. But if the structure was also used for habitation—i.e., if the owner slept there at night—it was a dwelling house.

A is correct because it recognizes this principle: the baker's house was a mixed-use building, and so qualifies as a dwelling house for burglary purposes.

B is incorrect because it ties the baker's profit to the dwelling house issue, and there was no such requirement at common law. **C and D are both incorrect** because they do not recognize the common law rules regarding mixed-use buildings.

223. This question tests on the requirement that the breaking and entry be of the dwelling house of another. Put a little differently, one cannot commit burglary against oneself because burglary is a crime against habitation, i.e., the right of *another* person to be secure or live peacefully in his home.

C is correct because it recognizes the common law requirement that the crime occur in the dwelling house of another.

A and B are both incorrect because, by focusing on breaking and entering, neither answer addresses the issue of whether one can burglarize oneself. **D is incorrect** because the woman clearly had the intent to commit a criminal act; however, in the end, she did not commit a burglary.

224. This question tests on the nighttime requirement for common law burglary. At common law, that requirement dictates that there not be enough natural light in the sky to see the potential intruder. While the presence of moonlight or a light from a street lamp might allow the homeowner to see the intruder, the common law focused on sunlight only.

D is correct because a lack of light in the sky equates to "nighttime."

A is incorrect because the door was closed, and so there was no invitation to enter. **B and C are both incorrect** because the sunrise (or sunset) is not the relevant criteria; instead, whether the nighttime element is met depends on the amount of light in the sky.

225. This question also tests on the nighttime requirement for common law burglary. In this question, the neighbor could see the man (the burglar) because of a street light. But the common law focused on natural sunlight only, not artificial light, and so this crime still happened "at night," even though the man's actions were illuminated by the streetlamp.

A is correct because it correctly identifies the issue (whether the light from the streetlamp has any relevance) and reaches the correct conclusion (it does not).

B and D are both incorrect because each addresses a possible claim of right defense, which would only be relevant if the man was charged with a theft offense. **C is incorrect** because it presents an incorrect statement of the common law rule regarding artificial light and burglary.

226. This question tests on the required *mens rea* for burglary: that the defendant both intend to commit a breaking and entry into the dwelling house, and also that he intend to commit

a felony once inside the house. The requirement is literal: the intent must be to commit a felony (not a misdemeanor) inside the house. The defendant does not have to commit the crime, he just needs to intend to commit it.

C is correct because the man was looking for a place to rest and had no apparent intent to commit a felony at the time he broke into the house. At most, he had the intent to commit a simple trespass which, at common law, required a breach of the peace.

A is incorrect because the question asks about burglary and not felonies in general. **B is incorrect** because the man had no intent to commit a felony inside the house; instead, the man appeared to be looking for a place to spend the night. **D is incorrect** because the facts only explain that the man was too drunk to drive, not that he was too drunk to form "any" *mens rea.*

227. This question also tests on the *mens rea* for burglary. In this fact pattern, the camper lacked the *mens rea* for burglary at the time she broke and entered into the cabin, but formed the *mens rea* for theft later, after she broke and entered. This is not sufficient, because burglary requires that criminal *mens rea* be present at the time of the breaking and entering.

B is correct because it recognizes that the camper formed a criminal *mens rea* only after she broke into and entered the cabin.

A and C are both incorrect because the condition of the cabin is irrelevant to the question of whether the camper committed a burglary or not. **D is incorrect** because it suggests that the camper might be guilty of burglary even without the required *mens rea.*

228. This question again tests on the *mens rea* for burglary. In this question, the issue is what crime must be intended at the breaking and entry. At common law, the intended crime must have been a felony, and not some other crime.

A is correct because the incumbent did not intend to commit any known common law felony at the time she broke and entered.

B is incorrect because, while factually accurate, it does not provide a legal response to the question. **C and D are both incorrect** because campaign finance law did not exist at common law.

229. This question also tests on the *mens rea* for burglary. The issue in this question is whether the intended felony must be completed, or whether intent alone is enough. At common law, the intent alone was sufficient.

A is correct because it recognizes that the woman's intent to take the wine is sufficient for burglary.

B is incorrect because it addresses what the woman "would have" done when the proper focus should be on her *mens rea.* **C and D are both incorrect** because burglary only requires intent to commit a felony at the time of the breaking and entering, and does not require that the envisioned crime be completed.

230. This question tests on a modern statutory variation of burglary, which is very different from the common law definition. This is not surprising, as the common law definition is limited, and does not address a variety of modern situations. In this statute, the breaking, dwelling house, and nighttime requirements have all been eliminated.

D is correct because the woman entered the store with the intent to shop for clothing and had no apparent intent to commit a crime at the time of her entry. Although the woman later committed a crime and remained unlawfully in the store (i.e., she remained after she was told to leave), the statute appears to require that she enter the store with a criminal *mens rea*.

A, B, and C are all incorrect because each refers to an element of common law burglary that is not part of the statutory definition.

Arson

231. This question tests on the definition of common law arson: the malicious burning of the dwelling house of another. Subsequent questions will explore this definition further.

     D is correct because it provides the complete common law definition.

     A, B, and C are all incorrect because each omits at least one component of the definition.

232. This question tests on the classification of arson, which is a crime against habitation. That is, arson is a crime that interferes with the right to be secure or live peacefully in one's home.

     D is correct because it provides the proper classification for arson.

     A, B, and C are all incorrect because each classifies arson in the wrong way.

233. This question tests on the *mens rea* for arson: malice. The definition of malice for arson is similar to the definition of malice for common law murder: it means that the defendant either acted (a) intentionally or (b) with a reckless disregard for a high risk of burning. In this question, the sister acted intentionally.

     C is correct because it recognizes that malice includes intentional acts.

     A is incorrect because it suggests that malice does not include intentional acts, and it does. **B is incorrect** because the sister's provision of the key does not mean that she consented to the burning of her house. **D is incorrect** because it omits the *mens rea* requirement entirely.

234. This question tests on the alternative definition of malice for arson: a reckless disregard for a high risk of burning. This requires a significant risk of burning, and that the defendant be aware of the risk and ignore it. This formulation likely sounds familiar, as it is very close to the *mens rea* for depraved heart murder.

     A is correct because the woman took a risk in burning the leaves, but she did not ignore the risk. Instead, the woman burned the leaves in a "relatively isolated" spot at the "bottom" of her "large" yard and monitored the fire. These facts show that she knew of the risks associated with leaf burning and tried to mitigate them. This is the opposite of reckless disregard.

     B is incorrect because the sparks traveling from the trees to the roof were the sole cause of the fire and not an intervening cause. **C is incorrect** because the failure to obtain a permit only shows that the woman ignored the local laws, and not necessarily that she acted with a reckless disregard for a high risk of burning. **D is incorrect** because it is not obvious that the woman failed to tend to the fire; the fire may have spread even while she was paying attention.

235. This question also tests on the reckless disregard *mens rea* for arson. Here, the junior knew of the high risk of burning and ignored it—apparently because he was bored.

C is correct because it recognizes that the facts demonstrate the two key components required for the reckless disregard *mens rea*: extreme risk-taking behavior and a conscious disregard of that risk.

A is incorrect because it focuses on the junior knowing the result of his actions, which suggests more certainty than is required here. Instead, the junior must be aware of the risk he is taking, and ignore that risk. **B is incorrect** because it suggests that bored teenagers cannot commit criminal acts, and they can. **D is incorrect** because—by referring to "ill will" and not "reckless disregard"—it does not provide an accurate legal response.

236. This question tests on the burning requirement for arson, which requires some type of fire. Smoke alone is insufficient.

A is correct because it recognizes this principle.

B is incorrect because it puts the focus on when the fire was extinguished when it should instead be on whether any burning occurred. **C is incorrect** because it puts the focus on the man's *mens rea*, instead of on the burning requirement. While the man acted intentionally, the lack of burning (fire) means that he is not guilty of arson; instead, he may be guilty of attempted arson. **D is incorrect** because arson does not require a grave risk to human life.

237. This question also tests on the burning requirement, and whether an explosion that does not include any fire meets that requirement. It does not.

B is correct because it recognizes this principle.

A is incorrect because the young man arguably did have the *mens rea* for arson: by building and storing an unstable bomb in his house, he showed a reckless disregard for a high risk of burning. **C is incorrect** because arson focuses on whether the dwelling house was burned or not, and not how much of the dwelling house was damaged. **D is incorrect** because it ignores that there are two possible *mens reas* for arson: intent to burn and a reckless disregard for a high risk of burning.

238. This question tests on the damage required for arson: burning or charring of the dwelling house or its permanent fixtures (e.g., a porch). Smoke damage alone or damage to temporary fixtures (e.g., a couch) was not sufficient.

A is correct because the flaming bottle caused fire damage (charring) to the wood flooring of the house.

B is incorrect because it puts the focus on the woman's *mens rea* instead of the damage caused by the fire. **C is incorrect** because it compares the fire damage to the water damage. But these facts demonstrate that an arson occurred, even though the water damage was more significant than the fire damage. **D is incorrect** because it focuses on the degree of damage to the dwelling house, rather than the type of damage.

239. This question also tests on the damage required for arson. In this question, the only damage was to a temporary fixture in the house, i.e., the curtains.

B is correct because it recognizes that burning of the curtains, alone, is insufficient for arson.

A is incorrect because it provides a nonlegal, procedural answer to a legal question. **C is incorrect** because it ignores that there are two possible *mens reas* for arson: intent to burn and a reckless disregard for a high risk of burning. **D is incorrect** because the facts—by referring to leaf burning on a windy day—suggest more than a mere accident.

240. This question tests on the meaning of a "dwelling house," and whether a partially built house meets that definition. Because arson is a crime against habitation, someone must live or have lived in the dwelling house for the structure to be classified as such.

D is correct because it recognizes this principle.

A is incorrect because it suggests that the half-built house is a dwelling house. **B is incorrect** because it improperly focuses on setting fire to the bulldozer, which is not a dwelling house. **C is incorrect** because the contractor was hired to build the house, and so even in its half-built state, it belonged "to another."

241. This question tests on the temporal scope of the "dwelling house." As with common law burglary, dwelling houses include curtilage, i.e., buildings close enough to the house to be included in a fence surrounding the property. Although the precise contours of the curtilage are sometimes difficult to determine, sheds and similar outbuildings on residential property usually qualify as curtilage.

B is correct because the components of arson are met: the *mens rea* (here, a reckless disregard for a high risk of burning) and the *actus reus* (burning of the dwelling house of another).

A is incorrect because the sons' failure to pay attention shows only that they had the *mens rea* for arson, and does not address the other elements of the crime. **C is incorrect** because it fails to recognize that curtilage is included within the definition of "dwelling house." **D is incorrect** because it provides a nonlegal response to a legal question.

242. This question also tests on the dwelling house requirement for arson, and that it be the dwelling house "of another." That is, if the defendant burned her own house, she could not be guilty of arson.

D is correct because it recognizes this principle.

A is incorrect because it misstates the definition of arson: there is no nighttime requirement. **B is incorrect** because it focuses on the woman's motive for burning her house, which is irrelevant. **C is incorrect** because it focuses on the strength of the woman's alibi after she started the fire and while the house was burning, which is also irrelevant

243. This question also tests on the dwelling house requirement. In this question, the landlord owns the dwelling house, but the woman is its long-time inhabitant.

A is correct because it recognizes that the prosecutor should respond in a way that suggests that the dwelling house is effectively the woman's, and not the landlord's.

B is incorrect because if the prosecutor concedes that the dwelling house does not effectively belong to the woman, the landlord is not guilty of arson. **C is incorrect** because it does not address the issue presented on these facts: whether the landlord burned his dwelling house, or the woman's. **D is incorrect** because it focuses on reckless endangerment to human life, which is not a requirement for arson.

244. This question tests on a modern statutory definition of arson. As with many other crimes, these modern definitions expand upon the rigid common law concepts and are often better suited to modern situations. Still, one can see the common law origins within these statutory definitions. These statutes come from the Michigan penal code. M.C.L. §§750.71 and 750.73.

The definition of second degree arson here expands the common law definition to include explosions and damage to the contents of a dwelling house, and not just the dwelling house itself. But it still requires damage to the dwelling house "of another," and the definition of "damage" is essentially the same as the definition of burning at common law.

A is correct because it recognizes that the man's intentional act of setting a fire within the friend's house resulted in "damage" within the meaning of the statute.

B is incorrect because it focuses on what could have happened, instead of what did happen. **C is incorrect** because it focuses on sentencing, and not whether the prosecutor can show that the elements of the crime were met. **D is incorrect** because it suggests that the man cannot act intentionally if he was also joking around.

245. This question also tests on a modern statutory definition of arson and is taken from the Michigan penal code. M.C.L. §750.75. The statutory definition expands arson to include burning of "any" personal property of a certain value. The property does not need to be "of another;" instead, burning of "any" personal property of a certain value will suffice.

C is correct because it properly describes what the woman did: she burned her husband's $5,000 bicycle.

A is incorrect for two reasons. First, the question does not identify the bicycle as marital property. Second, the statute refers to "any" property. **B is incorrect** because this statutory definition suggests that arson includes crimes against possession and not just crimes against habitation. **D is incorrect** because it focuses on the time of day that the burning occurred, and that is not a statutory requirement.

Theft

246. This question tests on the basic definition of larceny: the (1) trespassory taking and (2) carrying away of the (3) personal property (4) of another (5) with the intent to permanently deprive. Subsequent questions will explore the meaning of each of these elements.

D is correct because it is the only answer that recognizes that the man committed larceny and because it provides a definition that includes all the necessary elements of this crime.

A is incorrect because it assumes that a business entity cannot be a victim of larceny. **B is incorrect** because it does not respond to the question: the issue here is what crime has been committed, and not whether the officer had the authority to make the arrest. **C is**

incorrect because the man did not have lawful possession of the frozen dinner; instead, as subsequent questions will demonstrate, the man only had custody—a lesser property interest—over the frozen dinner.

247. This question tests on the classification of common law larceny, which is a crime against possession. That is, larceny is a crime that interferes with the right of lawful possession of property.

B is correct because it provides the proper classification for larceny.

A is incorrect because a crime against nature is a sexual crime, and no sexual offenses were committed here. **C is incorrect** because no force or threats of force were used, and so no crimes were committed against the girl's person. **D is incorrect** because, while the girl was standing on the curtilage of her home, the man's act did not interfere with her right to peaceful habitation.

248. This question tests on custody, one of the three basic interests one can hold in property; the other interests are possession and title. Understanding these interests is key to understanding theft crimes.

When a person has custody over property, she has a restricted property interest in that property. Although there is no bright-line test to determine when a person has custody, substantial restrictions on use of the property usually signal custody. In this question, the lawyer has some control over the computer as it sits in her office and she will presumably use it for her work. But she is not in control of the computer password; the system administrator is. In addition, the computer itself is a desktop PC, which means that it is not readily portable and it would be somewhat unusual for the lawyer to move it out of her office.

A is correct because it recognizes these limitations and reaches the correct conclusion.

B is incorrect because it places too much emphasis on changing the password, and not on the fact that the password was not one of the lawyer's choosing. **C is incorrect** because the lawyer does not own the computer; the law firm does. **D is incorrect** because it goes too far: by loaning the lawyer a computer for her in-office work, the law firm did give the lawyer some rights over the computer.

249. This question tests on possession, again focusing on a computer provided by an employer to an employee. In this question, the nature of the computer (a laptop, which is readily portable) and the terms of the doctor's employment contract signal that she has much more control over that computer than the lawyer did in the previous question. In other words, the doctor in this question has possession over the laptop.

B is correct because it recognizes this point.

A is incorrect because it suggests that the mere fact of having an employment contract restricts the doctor's interest in the laptop. Instead, the contract must be evaluated to determine how its terms affect the doctor's possessory rights. **C is incorrect** because the employment contract clearly indicates that the university maintains title to the laptop. **D is incorrect** because it suggests that since the university has title to the laptop, the doctor cannot also have a possessory interest in it. But multiple people can have possessory interests in the same property, as here.

250. This question also tests on possession.

D is correct because it best describes what the professor is permitted to do with the textbook. Although she did not pay for the textbook and although it appears to ultimately belong to the law school, there are no other apparent restrictions on its use.

A is incorrect because the question of who paid for the textbook is not dispositive of the question of the professor's possessory interest in the textbook. Instead, one needs to look at all the facts and circumstances to evaluate her interest. **B is incorrect** because it places too much emphasis on the university's purchase of the textbook and does not address how the professor used the textbook. **C is incorrect** because, while the university may not want a used textbook, the university paid for it and so is still the titleholder.

251. This question tests on actual possession, which requires having direct physical control over property.

B is correct because the woman was no longer in actual possession of the bracelet when it was on the ground. While the next question addresses constructive possession, the original definition of common law larceny did not recognize this concept. Thus, if property was not taken from the victim's actual possession, there was no trespassory taking.

A is incorrect because the woman did not know the bracelet fell from her wrist, and abandonment requires an affirmative act. **C is incorrect** because the man had the *mens rea* for larceny, i.e., the intent to permanently deprive. **D is incorrect** because it fails to address the man's act of picking up the bracelet and hiding it in his pocket.

252. This question tests on constructive possession, which is a legal fiction that describes when a person has possession over property without being in direct physical control over it. In this question, the clerk had actual possession over the sweater when she initially picked it up, and she retained her possessory right when she handed it to the customer to inspect. That is, the clerk retained constructive possession when she handed the sweater to the customer, and he took custody over the sweater at that point.

A is correct because it recognizes that the clerk did not give up her possessory interest in the sweater when she handed it to the customer to try on.

B and D are both incorrect because each fails to address the legal issue presented by the motion to dismiss. **C is incorrect** because the clerk gave the customer custody and not any form of possession.

253. This question tests on title, which is the greatest possessory right one can have in property. Here, because the attorney owns the store, he is the titleholder of its inventory.

B is correct because it recognizes this point.

A and C are both incorrect because each ties the attorney's possessory interests to whether he controls the store's daily operations. **D is incorrect** because it focuses on the attorney's ethics, and the question asks about possessory interests.

254. This question tests on a trespassory taking, drawing on the previous questions about custody, possession, and title. To take by trespass means to take possession unlawfully, or without consent.

A is correct because it accurately describes what the woman did: by taking the wallet, she took unlawful possession, and her actions indicate that she had the *mens rea* for larceny. The woman has more than custody because she is able to use the wallet (unlawfully) without restriction, but she does not have title because the true owner of the wallet retains that interest.

B is incorrect because it conflates the trespassory requirement from the definition of larceny with the crime of trespass. **C is incorrect** because larceny requires the taking of property of another, not from another. **D is incorrect** because the wallet still has value, even if there is no cash inside it.

255. This question also tests on trespassory taking. Here, the taking was with the owner's consent, and so there was no trespass.

C is correct because it recognizes this principle.

A is incorrect because the friend intended both to help his friend and to permanently deprive her of the car. **B is incorrect** because it does not present a defense; instead, it presents a strategy for a reduced charge. **D is incorrect** because the identity of the "mastermind" is irrelevant; instead, the critical question is whether the elements of larceny have been met.

256. This question tests on the carrying away requirement, which is also sometimes referred to as "asportation." The movement required for carrying away can be slight, but the movement has to be performed in support of the trespassory taking. Other types of movement will not suffice.

D is correct because it recognizes this principle. By hiding the ring under his hand and with the intent to steal it, the man moved the ring so that he could take it by trespass.

A is incorrect because the man concealed the ring by moving it under his palm so he could take it without the clerk's consent. This meets the definition of carrying away, even if the man did not "carry" the ring anywhere. **B is incorrect** because it does not respond to the question, and it places the focus on the clerk's actions instead of the man's actions. **C is incorrect** because the judge is supposed to decide legal issues. The jury, by contrast, decides factual issues.

257. This question also tests on the carrying away requirement. In this question, the woman moved the earrings when she picked them up off the floor. But this movement was not in support of her dispossession of the earrings; instead, the woman picked them up to help the clerk.

B is correct because it recognizes this point.

A is incorrect because it suggests that the woman could only be guilty of larceny if she removed the earrings from the store. But the asportation requirement can be met by lesser movements. **C is incorrect** because the woman's lie is not relevant to asportation. **D is incorrect** because it focuses on the theft of the bracelet, and the question asks about possible theft of the earrings.

258. This question tests on the personal property element of larceny, which requires tangible personal property—not realty, and not intangible property.

D is correct because the paper deed is paperwork that represents real property, and so the deed—by itself—is not personal property.

A is incorrect because the monetary value of the paper deed is unknown. **B and C are both incorrect** because each represents personal advice, and the question asks for a legal response.

259. This question also tests on the personal property element of larceny. In this question, the student watched a football game for free when she should have paid. This is an example of taking something intangible, and so is not considered to be personal property under the definition of larceny.

A is correct because it recognizes that the student did not steal personal property.

B is incorrect because physical trespass to land is not an element of larceny. **C and D are both incorrect** because each assumes that the elements of larceny exist, and each questions the evidence offered in support of those elements. But because the student stole something intangible—she watched the football game for free—the elements of larceny have not been met.

260. This question tests on the next element of larceny: that the personal property be "of another," i.e., that it not belong to the defendant.

C is correct because it recognizes that the woman cannot commit a larceny against herself.

A is incorrect because it presupposes that the woman can commit larceny and burglary against herself. But both crimes require a defendant to act against someone else. **B is incorrect** because it likewise presupposes that the woman can commit attempted larceny against herself. **D is incorrect** because the lack of a report to the insurer is irrelevant to the larceny issue.

261. This question tests on the *mens rea* for larceny: the intent to permanently deprive.

D is correct because the teenager clearly borrowed his mother's car. As such, he did not have the *mens rea* for larceny.

A is incorrect because the teenager did not have to pick up his date to be guilty of larceny, assuming the elements of the crime otherwise existed. **B is incorrect** because it is untrue. **C is incorrect** because the mother's awareness that the teenager had her car would not negate any of the elements of larceny, assuming each existed.

262. This question also tests on the *mens rea* for larceny.

A is correct because if the man did not have the intent to permanently deprive, he is not guilty of larceny. The man's story many seem preposterous, but note that the answer is conditioned on the fact-finder believing his claim.

B is incorrect because it is untrue: in some cases, a prosecutor will consider the defense in making the charging decision, but the prosecutor is not required to do so. **C is incorrect** because the man's claim, if believed, would show that he lacked any the intent to permanently deprive. **D is incorrect** because the laptop owner was in constructive possession of the laptop when it was taken, and so he did not have to take it directly from her for the trespassory taking element to be met.

263. This question also tests on the *mens rea* for larceny. In this question, the man took the watch but gained no benefit: he did not sell the watch or keep it for himself. Instead, he threw it away. That will suffice for the *mens rea* requirement because the defendant need only intend to permanently separate the rightful owner from his property.

A is correct because it recognizes this principle.

B is incorrect because, while the man's motive provides additional proof of his *mens rea*, it is not necessary to prove that he had the *mens rea*. Instead, the man's act of tossing the watch in the trash will suffice. **C is incorrect** because the two facts cited—that the watch stayed in the brother's house and that it was quickly recovered—do not address whether the *mens rea* has been met. **D is incorrect** because it suggests that throwing the watch in the trash was not enough.

264. This question tests on the issue of when the crime of larceny is complete: when all the elements are met.

D is correct because it recognizes that as soon as the teenager passed through the cash register without paying for the video game, all the elements of larceny were met.

A is incorrect because the teenager did not need to leave the store. While some stores might delay stopping would-be shoplifters until after they leave the store, that is not a requirement for larceny. **B is incorrect** because the mother's parenting style has nothing to do with whether or not the teenager stole the video game. **C is incorrect** because the teenager paid for the groceries and so he did not steal them.

265. This question tests on how larceny law treats lost property. At common law, property was either abandoned or constructively possessed. If a defendant took abandoned property, he was not guilty of larceny because he was not dispossessing anyone of her property. But if he took constructively possessed property, he could be guilty of larceny. In general, the two factors to assess in lost property situations are (1) the possessory interest of the title-holder at the time the property is found, and (2) the finder's state of mind at the time he finds the property.

A is correct because the facts make clear that the wallet was constructively possessed by its owner, the second woman. It held items of value—cash, but also an ID and credit cards—and was left open in a spot where one would expect people to rest property while they washed their hands.

B is incorrect because there is no common law "legal obligation" to report discovered property, although there may be a moral one. **C is incorrect** because the woman's ineffectual attempt to find the owner of the wallet should not shield her from prosecution. **D is incorrect** because, while the woman may not have had a legal obligation to report the missing wallet, the facts demonstrate that she knew (or reasonably should have known) that the wallet was constructively possessed by someone.

266. This question also tests on whether a person who discovers and takes seemingly lost property is guilty of larceny.

B is correct because it addresses the student's *mens rea* at the time she discovered the sweat-shirt. The location of the sweatshirt and its condition both suggest that it had been abandoned. But if the student thought someone owned the sweatshirt and kept it anyway, that suggests that she might have stolen it.

A is incorrect because it only addresses what might have happened in the past, and does not provide information about the student's state of mind when she found the sweatshirt. **C is incorrect** because the student's history does not help identify what she did in this situation. **D is incorrect** because the student does not need a witness.

267. This question addresses how larceny law treats bailment situations. A bailment is created when an owner or lawful possessor (the "bailor") gives control over his property (the "bail") to a third party (the "bailee"), and for a specific purpose, e.g., to deliver goods to a market. Since the bailor gives the bailee lawful possession over the bail, it would not be larceny if the bailee then took those goods.

B is correct because it is the only plausible response: that the assistant was given possession over the case and its contents, so he cannot be guilty of larceny.

A is incorrect because being put in charge of the logistics for the trip would not provide a defense; instead, the assistant needs a defense that addresses the control he was given over the jewelry case and its contents. **C is incorrect** because it provides a nonlegal justification and not a legal defense. **D is incorrect** because the delay doesn't demonstrate reasonable doubt.

268. This question also tests on bailment situations and demonstrates the legal fiction created by the common law—"breaking bulk"—to resolve them. Under this doctrine, the bailor gives possession to the bailee of the container that encloses the bail, but only custody over the bail itself. Thus, when the bailee opens the container and takes the bail, he commits a trespassory taking.

A is correct because it shows how breaking bulk works: the mover had possession over the bags but only custody over the contents of those bags.

B is incorrect because whatever the responsibility of the mover, it likely did not include stealing a dress. **C is incorrect** because nothing in the facts suggests that the museum gave title to the mover. **D is incorrect** because it provides a nonlegal answer to a legal question.

269. This question tests on larceny by trick, a common law crime that evolved from larceny. In larceny by trick, the defendant tricks the lawful possessor of the property into providing (what appears to be) lawful possession over the property. But the possession is not lawful because it is based on fraud or a lie.

B is correct because it recognizes that the woman's possession was not lawful, but only appears to be so because she lied to the rental agency.

A is incorrect because the fact pattern does not provide any information about a legal duty imposed on the woman at the time she signed the contract. **C is incorrect** because it suggests that the woman had lawful possession over the car for some time. Instead, because the rental itself was based on a fraud, the woman's possession was unlawful from the start. **D is incorrect** because it fails to recognize the impact of the woman's lie.

270. This question tests on a gap in larceny law that led to the creation of a new crime, larceny by continuous trespass—a crime based on a legal fiction. With larceny by continuous trespass, the defendant's initial taking is by trespass, but he forms the intent to permanently deprive at some later point. Under the legal fiction, each moment the defendant is in possession of the property is a new moment of trespassory taking. Then, when the defendant forms the intent to permanently deprive, all the elements of larceny are present and the crime of larceny by continuous trespass is complete.

B is correct because it identifies this gap in larceny law.

A is incorrect because it focuses on the general problem with proving *mens rea* in any criminal case, and not the precise issue in this case. **C is incorrect** because the woman did not commit larceny by trick: although the woman took the earrings by trespass, she had no intent to permanently deprive at the time of the taking. **D is incorrect** for two reasons. First, the type of event does matter, as the friend would not have lent the earrings had she known where they would be worn; this is what makes the taking trespassory. Second, the answer fails to recognize that the woman lacked the *mens rea* for larceny at the time of the trespassory taking.

271. This question tests on the difference between larceny by trick and larceny by continuous trespass. In both crimes, the initial taking is trespassory because it is based on a lie or some sort of fraud. But the crimes differ as to when the *mens rea* is formed. In larceny by trick, the *mens rea* is present at the time of the taking; in larceny by continuous trespass, the *mens rea* is formed after the taking is completed.

D is correct because it recognizes that the initial taking was trespassory and that the *mens rea* was formed after the taking was complete. As such, the man has committed larceny by continuous trespass.

A and B are both incorrect and for two reasons. First, each suggests that the initial taking was not trespassory. Second, each ignores the *mens rea* issue. **C is incorrect** because it also ignores the *mens rea* issue.

272. This question tests on larceny by false pretenses, another common law crime that evolved from larceny. In larceny by false pretenses, the defendant tricks the victim out of title, not possession.

C is correct because it recognizes that the customers gave title to their money, not possession. The key is to look at the possessory interest the customers thought they were providing. That is, when the customers put money in the jar, did they believe they were giving up the money completely (title), or with some limitations (possession)?

A is incorrect because it blames the customers for being victims of crime, instead of placing blame on the owner. **B is incorrect** because larceny by trick involves taking unlawful possession and not unlawful title. **D is incorrect** because the owner's goal from the start was to keep the money his customers put in a jar.

273. This question tests on one of the important differences between larceny by trick and larceny by false pretenses. In the former, the defendant takes unlawful possession, but in the latter, he takes title.

B is correct because it accurately describes the senior's possessory interest in the car after she lied to her father to get access to the keys.

A is incorrect because the senior did not take title; even though she intended to keep the car forever, her father still retained his possessory interest in the car. **C is incorrect** because all of the elements of the crime were complete when the senior left the house in the car. **D is incorrect** because it fails to recognize that the senior took possession of her father's car by fraud, with the intent to permanently deprive him of the car.

274. This question also tests on the difference between larceny by trick and larceny by false pretenses. In this question, the statement on the flyers is very specific about how the donations will be used and indicates that "all donations" would be given to the landlord. As such, when the neighbors gave donations based on this false promise, they intended to give the woman possession only, and for the landlord to receive title.

B is correct because it recognizes this principle.

A is incorrect because the woman has committed a crime. **C is incorrect** because the woman only tricked her neighbors out of possession, not title. **D is incorrect** because, by focusing on the core crime of larceny, it fails to recognize that the woman tricked her neighbors into donating money. And, when the trespass is accomplished by trick or fraud, the resulting crime is not ordinary larceny.

275. This question tests on another gap in larceny law: when the defendant has lawful possession of property and converts it for his own use. In these situations, no larceny occurs, because the defendant's possession is lawful, not unlawful.

A is correct because it recognizes that the woman cannot be guilty of larceny if she had lawful possession of the outfit.

B is incorrect because it only guesses about the woman's right to take from the store's inventory. **C is incorrect** because, again, the woman had lawful possession of the store's inventory. As such, her actions can't be compared to a shoplifter, who takes possession unlawfully. **D is incorrect** because the woman had possession over the store's inventory, not just custody.

276. This question tests on the same gap in larceny law and introduces the statutory crime of embezzlement. Embezzlement occurs when the defendant has lawful possession of property and converts it for his own use.

C is correct because it identifies embezzlement as the correct crime, and because it recognizes that the chief financial officer—by virtue of his job—has possession over the corporation's bank accounts.

A is incorrect because it identifies the wrong crime, and because the chief financial officer did not lie about his authority; instead, he lied about what the CEO authorized him to do. **B is incorrect** because the corporation retained title to the money. **D is incorrect** because it is too simplistic and does not address the factual nuances presented in the question.

277. This question also tests on embezzlement. As with other forms of larceny, the crime is complete when all the elements are met, and the defendant does not have a defense if he later changes his mind and returns the property. Return of the property can mitigate punishment, but it does not eliminate guilt.

C is correct because it recognizes that the treasurer's repayment of the money—even with interest—is irrelevant to whether she committed the underlying crime.

A and B are both incorrect because each focuses on the elements of embezzlement, and neither focuses on the impact of the treasurer's repayment of the embezzled money. **D is incorrect** because the treasurer did not need the president's permission to either take or repay the money: the treasurer had lawful authority over the account, and so could act on her own.

278. This question tests on the primary defense to larceny: claim of right. When a defendant asserts this defense, he claims that he lacked the *mens rea* for larceny because he believed the property belonged to him. The defendant's belief does not need to be objectively reasonable; it just needs to be sincerely or honestly held.

D is correct because it recognizes that the woman's belief that the watch was hers negates the *mens rea* for larceny.

A is incorrect because the two watches do not need to be identical; instead, the woman just needed to sincerely believe the watch was hers. **B is incorrect** because it provides a nonlegal response to a legal question. **C is incorrect** because it suggests that a claim of right requires that the woman's belief be objectively reasonable, and all that is required is a sincere, subjective belief.

279. This question tests on robbery, a common law crime. Robbery includes all the elements of common law larceny, plus two more: the taking must be from the person or the area of his actual control, and the taking must be accomplished by force or threats of bodily harm to the victim, his family member, or someone in his presence. In this sense, robbery is an aggravated form of larceny.

A is correct because it identifies the correct crime and proves the correct definition.

B, C, and D are all incorrect because each identifies non-common law crimes which, if they exist, must be defined by statute. As no statute was provided with the question, none of these answers is correct. In addition, D also incorrectly states that the woman took title over the bank's money, and the woman took unlawful possession over the money.

280. This question also tests on robbery and the force or threat of force element. In robbery, the threat must be to the victim personally, and not to her property.

B is correct because it recognizes that the man's threats were insufficient for a robbery conviction. While the clerk was frightened by the man's threats, they were focused on her car, not her.

A is incorrect because the vegetables have value, just not a high value. **C is incorrect** because the man does not have to take the vegetables from the clerk's hands, just her presence, which he did. **D is incorrect** because it provides a nonlegal answer to a legal question.

281. This question also tests on the force requirement for robbery.

A is correct because it recognizes that the young woman did not use force to take the laptop, even though the laptop was taken directly from the young man's presence.

B is incorrect because the focus here should be on the young woman's actions, not the young man's failure to protect his property. **C is incorrect** because interfering with someone's "personal space" is insufficient for a robbery charge; instead, the interference must be by force or threat of force. **D is incorrect** because it inaccurately describes the facts.

282. This question also tests on robbery and the requirement that the property be taken from the victim's control or an area within his control.

D is correct because the neighbor only had constructive control over her house at the time the second man took the jewelry.

A and B are both incorrect because both fail to recognize that the neighbor was nowhere near her home when the jewelry was stolen. **C is incorrect** because it is possible for people in distinct locations to be prosecuted for the same crime, e.g., accomplices, co-conspirators, etc.

283. This question tests on claim of right as a defense to robbery. At common law, claim of right was a defense to all theft crimes, including robbery. Today, modern jurisdictions do not recognize claim of right as a defense to robbery.

A is correct because it recognizes that claim of right is a defense in this situation.

B is incorrect because it suggests that the woman could only be charged with robbery if she used a weapon against the former roommate. **C and D are both incorrect** because each suggests that claim of right is not a defense to common law robbery.

284. This question tests on "consolidated theft," which is a phrase used to describe how modern jurisdictions deal with theft crimes. Instead of having multiple crimes with narrow differences, most jurisdictions combine these crimes into one larger crime that addresses all of these variations. The statute in this question is based on the Maryland theft statute, Md. Code Ann., Crim. Law § 7-104, although it has been edited somewhat.

D is correct because it accurately describes the man's actions: he intentionally took the motorcycle without permission ("willfully ... obtains unauthorized control over property") and intentionally hid the motorcycle from the neighbor ("willfully ... conceals ... the property in a manner that deprives the owner of the property").

A is incorrect because it focuses on "carrying away," which is not required by this statute. Instead, the statute focuses on concealment and abandonment. **B is incorrect** because it focuses on the general problem with proving *mens rea* in any criminal case, and not the statutory issue presented here. **C is incorrect** because it uses the language of common law larceny and not the statutory language.

285. This question also tests on consolidated theft and a common way such statutes divide crimes into degrees: by value of the property stolen. Here, the dividing line between misdemeanor and felony is $1,500.

C is correct because the facts make clear that the laptop was worth $1,700, and so the friend should be charged with a felony. The friend might have a plausible argument if the laptop was old or broken or in poor condition, but the facts indicate that it was brand-new.

A is incorrect because the only indication that the (brand-new) laptop is worth less than $1,000 is the friend's unsupported claim. **B is incorrect** because it fails to recognize that the laptop had been purchased just a couple days before it was stolen. **D is incorrect** because the statute focuses on the objective financial value of stolen property and not the subjective emotional value of that property.

Solicitation

286. This question tests on the definition of the first of the inchoate crimes, solicitation. A solicitation occurs when a person asks, commands, incites, counsels, induces, urges, or encourages another person to commit a crime, with the intent that the crime be committed. There are two relevant aspects of this definition. First, the solicitor is asking someone else to commit the crime, and is not trying to commit the crime himself, or asking for help in committing the crime. Second, the solicitor must have the *mens rea* that the crime actually be committed.

B is correct because it provides the proper definition.

A is incorrect—or perhaps just incomplete—because it fails to reference the full *mens rea* for solicitation. **C and D are both incorrect** because, in each, the solicitor anticipates committing the crime himself, and is only looking for help. But with solicitation, the solicitor does not anticipate participating in the target crime.

287. This question tests on the *mens rea* for solicitation, which requires (1) intent to commit the *actus reus* (the asking, commanding, etc.), and (2) intent to commit the target crime. Because of the dual intents, solicitation is a specific intent crime.

C is correct because the facts state that the friend was joking when she made her comment about killing the boyfriend. As such, the friend had sufficient *mens rea* for the *actus reus*—to counsel the woman to kill her boyfriend—but no intent that the crime be committed.

A is incorrect because it fails to recognize that the friend was joking when she made her comment, and so had no intent that the crime be committed. **B is incorrect** because the effect of the defendant's words on the listener is irrelevant; instead, to determine whether a solicitation occurred, the focus should be on whether the defendant had the requisite *mens rea* and *actus reus*. **D is incorrect** because it also focuses on the woman, and the focus should instead be on the friend.

288. This question tests on the *actus reus* for solicitation: asking, commanding, inciting, counseling, inducing, urging, or encouraging another person to commit a crime. Assuming the *mens rea* is also present, the crime of solicitation is complete as soon as the *actus reus* is committed.

B is correct because the husband counseled the man to commit a crime when he suggested that the man slash the supervisor's tires.

A and C are both incorrect because the man was seeking reassurance from his husband, and was not asking him to commit a crime. **D is incorrect** because, while the husband's second statement provided additional reassurance to the man, the solicitation was complete when he made his first statement.

289. This question also tests on the *actus reus* for solicitation and focuses on the need for the solicitor to ask—or command, etc.—someone else to commit the crime. If the solicitor intends to commit the crime himself, then no solicitation has occurred.

A is correct because it recognizes that the wealthy woman intended to commit the murder herself. As such, she did not solicit the gardener to commit a crime.

B is incorrect because, since there was no solicitation, the merger doctrine is inapplicable. **C is incorrect** because providing a weapon for use in a crime is not necessarily a crime by itself. Instead, providing a weapon makes the gardener an accomplice to the woman's crime. **D is incorrect** because the wealthy woman's exploitation of her employee is irrelevant to the question of whether she solicited him to commit a crime or not.

290. This question tests on uncommunicated solicitations. That is, what happens when the solicitor takes steps to ask—or command, etc.—another to commit a crime with the intent that the crime be committed, but where the other person never learns of the solicitation? The answer to this dilemma is to instead describe the crime as an attempted solicitation.

D is correct because the solicitation was not communicated to its intended recipient, as required by the statute. This answer also provides a correct alternative: to charge the prisoner with attempted solicitation.

A is incorrect because it suggests that the prisoner should be convicted, regardless of the express requirement in the statute that the solicitation be communicated. **B is incorrect** because it recognizes some of the language in the statute ("solicits another") but ignores other language ("A solicitation must be communicated"). **C is incorrect** because solicitation does not require settled negotiations or a complete plan. Instead, the crime of solicitation is complete as soon as the *actus reus* is committed.

291. This question tests on the innocent instrumentality rule in the context of solicitation. Under that rule, when a defendant uses a nonculpable agent to commit a crime, the defendant is responsible for the crime as if he had committed it himself. In other words, the defendant cannot hide behind someone he has duped into doing his work for him. But solicitation requires that the defendant ask—or command, etc.—someone else to commit a crime. And so, if the defendant "solicits" a nonculpable agent, he is just using the person to commit the crime himself. As such, a defendant who "solicits" a nonculpable agent is not guilty of solicitation.

D is correct because it recognizes that the professor asked the student to step into her shoes and commit her crime.

A is incorrect because it ignores that the professor is using the student to do her work for her. **B is incorrect** because the student cannot become complicit in the crime simply because he was asked if he would join it; instead, to have some sort of liability, the student would have to have his own criminal *mens rea* and *actus reus*. **C is incorrect** because it ignores that the professor is attempting to steal a car, and not just move it.

292. This question tests on application of the merger doctrine to solicitation when the request to commit a crime is accepted. In that situation, a conspiracy is formed, and the solicitation merges into the conspiracy.

B is correct as it recognizes that when the woman accepted the man's request, they had an agreement to commit a crime. And, since the solicitation merged into the conspiracy, the man should not be charged with both crimes.

A is incorrect because it does not acknowledge that the woman accepted the man's request. **C is incorrect** because the woman's report to the police is irrelevant to the question of how the man should be charged. The woman's report is relevant, if at all, to her culpability. **D is incorrect** because this question focuses on the possible merger of the solicitation into the conspiracy. Merger of conspiracy would only be a possible issue if the target crime had been completed. And, even then, the conspiracy would not merge because conspiracy does not merge with a completed crime.

293. This question also tests on the merger doctrine, where there is a solicitation and the target crime is later committed. In this situation, the solicitation merges into the completed crime. And, while the solicitor is not guilty of the crime of solicitation, he does not evade responsibility: he becomes an accomplice to the person who committed the target crime.

A is correct because it recognizes these principles.

B and D are both incorrect because each looks at the link between the woman's offer and the brother's actions, and each asks whether he really acted at her behest. But the question is about the sister's liability and not the brother's actions. **C is incorrect** because it does not address the fact that murder was later committed.

294. This question tests on use of the abandonment defense in response to a solicitation charge. Because the crime of solicitation is complete as soon as the defendant asks—or commands, etc.—it cannot be abandoned.

C is correct because it recognizes this principle.

A is incorrect because it suggests that abandonment is a defense to solicitation, and it isn't. **B is incorrect** because the woman's stress does not appear to be enough to negate the *mens rea* for the crime. With that said, the larger circumstances surrounding the crime and woman's retraction of the post would be relevant to sentencing. **D is incorrect** because the reason abandonment is not a defense to solicitation has nothing to do with the means used to commit the solicitation.

295. This question tests on one possible defense to solicitation: legislative exemption. Under this defense, a person who is protected by a criminal statute cannot be convicted of solicitation of a violation of that statute. *E.g.*, *Gebardi v. U.S.*, 287 U.S. 112 (1932) (applying legislative exemption rule to conspiracy charge).

A is correct because it recognizes this principle.

B is incorrect because the girl's "suggestion" would constitute solicitation, but for the fact that she is legislatively exempt. **C is incorrect** because it suggests a misuse of the criminal law. **D is incorrect** because it fails to address that the girl is legislatively exempt from statutory rape.

Attempt

296. This question tests on the definition of second of the inchoate crimes, attempt. An attempt occurs when a defendant, with the intent to commit a specific crime, takes a substantial step beyond mere preparation toward the commission of that crime. The "substantial step" phrasing is taken from the Model Penal Code and is used here because it concisely summarizes the *actus reus* for the crime. But no matter what definition is used, it must recognize that the defendant's actions have to go beyond mere preparation for the resulting crime to be considered an attempt.

C is correct because it articulates this definition.

A is incorrect because attempt crimes are incomplete, and the answer refers to a completed crime. **B and D are both incorrect** because preparation alone is not enough for attempt. Instead, the defendant must go beyond "mere preparation."

297. This question tests on one of the biggest difficulties with attempt crimes: determining how close the defendant must get to the target offense before it can be said that he has committed an attempt. As the following questions demonstrate, thinking bad thoughts or preparing to commit a crime is not enough; the defendant must do more, but identifying how much more is not always easy. And the closer the defendant gets to the target crime, the more danger he creates. Ideally, the defendant needs to be stopped someplace between "too soon" and "too late."

D is correct because the defendant here is only guilty of thinking bad thoughts, and our criminal law does not penalize that. Instead, it is only when people act on their bad thoughts that the criminal law will potentially impose punishment.

A and B are both incorrect because each suggests that the *actus reus* of the crime is irrelevant. **C is incorrect** because the reason the man cannot be properly prosecuted is that he has not committed a crime, not because he has committed a crime and might have a valid defense.

298. This question tests on another key aspect of attempt: it is not a standalone crime, and always must be paired with another crime, i.e., the target offense.

B is correct because it recognizes that the college student intended to murder her roommate, and by putting the poison on the pizza, she took a substantial step beyond mere preparation toward that murder. As such, the college student has attempted to commit a murder.

A and C are both incorrect because neither refers to the target crime of murder. **D is incorrect** because the roommate didn't have to eat the pizza for the college student to be guilty of attempting to kill her.

299. This question tests on the merger doctrine, which provides that when a defendant completes his intended target crime, the attempt merges with the completed offense. Put a little differently, when a defendant completes his intended target crime, he is only guilty of the target crime—and not attempt as well.

A is correct because it recognizes that the man completed his intended target crime, and so the attempted robbery merged with the completed robbery.

B and C are both incorrect because, while the man may have planned to use the proceeds from the robbery to pay his debts, his crime was in robbing the bank. **D is incorrect** because it fails to acknowledge that the attempt merged with the completed crime.

300. This question tests on the *mens rea* for attempt, which requires (1) intent to commit the *actus reus* (the substantial step beyond mere preparation), and (2) intent to commit the target crime. Because of the dual intents, the *mens rea* for attempt is described as "specific intent."

B is correct because it recognizes that the boyfriend had no intent to kill, and that *mens rea* would be required for an attempted murder conviction.

A and D are both incorrect because they address reasonable foreseeability, which is irrelevant to the issue of whether the boyfriend had intent to kill. **C is incorrect** because it focuses on *actus reus* instead of *mens rea*.

301. This question also tests on the *mens rea* for attempt, and focuses on an issue that arises in many criminal cases: how to prove *mens rea* when a defendant herself will not explain her thoughts and actions. The answer is to look at the attendant facts and circumstances and make reasonable inferences from them.

C is correct because it addresses all the circumstances surrounding the woman's actions, and not just one or two of those circumstances in isolation.

A, B, and D are all incorrect because each addresses just some of the facts, but not all of them together.

302. This question tests on the *mens rea* for attempt, and the interplay between specific intent and felony murder. In felony murder, the intent to commit the predicate felony is combined with the homicide to create a constructive form of malice—the *mens rea* for murder. But attempt requires the specific intent to commit the target crime. This begs the question: can a defendant be guilty of attempted felony murder when all he intends is to commit a felony? Currently, few jurisdictions recognize this crime. (For the same reason, attempted misdemeanor manslaughter is not a cognizable offense.)

A is correct because a majority of jurisdictions recognize that attempted felony murder—where the defendant otherwise has no intent to kill—is not a cognizable offense. Instead, as with all other attempt crimes, the defendant must have the specific intent to commit the target offense.

B and D are both incorrect because malice and reckless indifference are irrelevant to attempt, which requires a different *mens rea*. **C is incorrect** because it focuses on the woman's *actus reus*, and this question addresses her *mens rea*.

303. This question also tests on the *mens rea* for attempt. In this question, attempt is combined with acts usually classified with depraved heart murder. As with attempted felony murder, attempted depraved heart murder is a mismatch, trying to combine specific intent to commit a crime with reckless indifference to human life. For that reason, attempted depraved heart murder is not a cognizable offense. (For the same reason, attempted involuntary manslaughter is also not a cognizable offense.)

C is correct because it identifies the problem with combining attempt and depraved heart murder: one cannot specifically intend to commit an accident.

A is incorrect because, while true, it does not address the *mens rea* problem presented by attempted depraved heart murder. Of course, had the young woman died, there would be no problem with charging the man with the completed crime of depraved heart murder. **B is incorrect** because malice is irrelevant to attempt, which requires a different *mens rea*. **D is incorrect** because the question asks about the propriety of an attempted depraved heart murder charge, and not whether the man knew the house was inhabited or not.

304. This question tests on the *actus reus* for attempt: a substantial step beyond mere preparation toward the commission of the target crime. The "substantial step" test comes from the Model Penal Code, but it is used here because it provides an accurate description of what the common law required: some sort of significant act beyond preparation in furtherance of the target crime.

D is correct because it recognizes that the woman has only engaged in preparation for the crime, which is not enough to establish the *actus reus* of attempt. Instead, the woman would have to go beyond that point—e.g., travel to the boyfriend's house—to be guilty of attempted arson.

A and B are both incorrect because each suggests that preparation, alone, is sufficient for an attempt. **C is incorrect** because it suggests that the woman would actually have to commit arson to be guilty of attempted arson.

305. This question also tests on the *actus reus* for attempt. In this question, the man has the intent to commit a burglary and has engaged in some preparation for the burglary (following the jeweler home from work), but it is unclear if his actions are a substantial step or not. While the actions that constitute a substantial step do not have to be illegal, the actions here are relatively ambiguous and a prosecutor would have difficulty proving that they were made in furtherance of the burglary.

D is correct because it is unclear what the man was doing when he parked his car a block from the jeweler's house.

A and B are both incorrect because they both assume that the man was going to burglarize the house that same night. **C is incorrect** because it is unclear if the man was done with his preparation or not. What is clear, however, is that the man had not gone beyond preparing to commit the crime.

306. This question also tests on the *actus reus* for attempt. In this question, the woman has taken a substantial step and more. The woman was only prevented from committing the crime because the intended victim (the co-worker) saw her and called the police.

A is correct because it recognizes that by crouching behind the bush with a weapon in her hand, the woman was no longer "just" preparing to commit the crime.

B is incorrect because a defendant having a motive for a crime does not also establish that he has the required *mens rea*. In any event, this question is about *actus reus* and not *mens rea*. **C is incorrect** because the woman's arrest is independent of the question of whether she took a substantial step. **D is incorrect** because the woman did fully exhibit her *mens* *rea* when she hid behind the bush with a weapon in her hand. While the woman could have changed her mind, that would not negate the actions she did take.

307. This question tests on the first of two defenses for attempt: impossibility. This defense comes into play when the intended crime can never be completed—no matter how hard the defendant tries to commit the crime. In general, there are two types of impossibility defenses, factual and legal, and each type can be broken down into additional subcategories. See Dressler, *Understanding* § 27.07. At common law, factual impossibility was not a defense, but legal impossibility was.

Factual impossibility occurs when the defendant intends to commit a crime, but the crime cannot be committed (or is impossible) due to some fact unknown to him or outside of his control. For example, if a defendant shoots into a building with the intent to kill someone inside—but no one is inside—the defendant can claim that the crime of attempted murder is impossible because he was unaware that the intended victim was not in the building.

B is correct because it is the only plausible defense on these facts: the woman intended to kill her neighbor, but did not know that she cannot commit that crime by sticking pins into a doll.

A and D are both incorrect because the facts give no information about the woman's mental health. As such, the strength of these mental health defenses cannot be evaluated. **C is incorrect** because it does not present a defense, but instead presents a fact that might be useful at sentencing.

308. This question tests on the second type of impossibility: legal impossibility. Legal impossibility occurs when the defendant intends to commit a crime but makes a factual mistake regarding a legal circumstance relevant to the crime. Here, the man's factual mistake is that there is no underaged girl, and the legal circumstance is that the charged crime requires that the pornographic material be sent to a minor.

One difficulty with the impossibility defense is that, in some situations, it can seem like the otherwise dangerous defendant is receiving a windfall. But this result leaves many uneasy, as the defendant "gets lucky" just because the intended victim happened to be elsewhere at the time of the shooting. That is why most modern jurisdictions have abandoned impossibility defenses.

C is correct because it recognizes that a modern jurisdiction would not permit the defense, and why.

A is incorrect because it articulates the result under the common law, and the question asks about modern law. **B is incorrect** because the man's arrival at the mall is irrelevant to the charged crime. **D is incorrect** because it focuses on whether the attempt occurred or not, and the question asks about defenses.

309. This question tests on the second of two defenses for attempt: abandonment. The common law did not recognize this defense, as the crime of attempt would necessarily have been completed by the time the defendant changed his mind about committing the intended crime.

D is correct because it recognizes that the common law would not have accepted the woman's defense, and why.

A and B are both incorrect because each assumes that the abandonment defense would be allowed. **C is incorrect** because it looks at the woman's motivation for leaving the bank. As demonstrated in the next question, that is a concern for modern jurisdictions and was not relevant at common law.

310. This question also tests on abandonment. To the extent that modern jurisdictions recognize this defense, the abandonment must be voluntary and complete. The former requirement means that the defendant must renounce his criminal purpose on his own volition and not because of pressure from third parties; the latter requirement means that he must abandon his criminal purpose forever, and not momentarily.

A is correct because the man's statement to his wife shows a genuine and permanent change of heart, and so his abandonment was both voluntary and complete.

B is incorrect because it fails to recognize that attempted murder can occur even when no death occurs. **C is incorrect** because it focuses on whether the attempt occurred or not, and the question asks about defenses. **D is incorrect** because it doesn't respond to the question.

Conspiracy

311. This question tests on the definition of the third inchoate crime, conspiracy. A conspiracy is an agreement between two or more parties to commit a crime or to commit a legal act in an illegal manner. At common law, a conspiracy conviction only required an agreement.

C is correct because it recognizes that the two men agreed to rob a bank. And, since bank robbery is a crime, the two men are guilty of conspiring to commit a crime.

A is incorrect because "criminal attempt" is not a crime; instead, attempt crimes are described in terms of the target offense, e.g., attempted robbery or attempted rape. **B is incorrect** because by collecting weapons and face masks, the men were still preparing to commit a crime, and attempt requires an act beyond preparation. **D is incorrect** because it fails to recognize that by merely agreeing to commit a crime, the men have entered into a conspiracy.

312. This question also tests on the definition of conspiracy, and focuses on the second part of the definition: an agreement to commit a legal act in an illegal manner. Here, the sorority sisters have decided to accomplish a legal goal (charity fundraising) through illegal means (theft).

A is correct because it recognizes that by agreeing to steal money from the grocery fund, the sorority sisters agreed to commit a crime—regardless of the fact that their ultimate goal was to raise money for charity.

B is incorrect because there is no crime of "deceit" or "deception." **C is incorrect** because it focuses on the result of the sorority sisters' actions (charity fundraising) and not the means they agreed to use to reach their goal (theft). **D is incorrect** because it assumes certain facts—that the sisters "likely" contributed to the grocery fund—and also suggests that their contribution to the fund confers a right to steal from it.

313. This question tests on the merger doctrine, which provides that when a co-conspirator completes his intended target crime, the conspiracy does not merge with the completed offense. By comparison, a completed target crime merges with attempt and solicitation, the other two inchoate offenses.

B is correct because it recognizes that the woman agreed with her sister to commit a crime (a conspiracy) and then intentionally killed the renter (murder).

A and D are both incorrect because the renter was killed, so any attempt would merge with the completed homicide. **C is incorrect** for two reasons. First, without knowing what the first degree statute requires, it is unclear if the woman's actions fall within it. Second, this answer omits conspiracy.

314. This question tests on why conspiracies are so dangerous: because when defendants act together in groups, they are more dangerous than when they act alone. There are several reasons for this: conspiracies may be more efficient because they use pooled talent and resources; due to peer pressure, co-conspirators may be less likely to abandon their crimes; and multiple people acting together can usually do more harm than a single person acting alone.

D is correct because it recognizes these principles.

A is incorrect because it makes no sense: if the women have not committed a crime, maintaining crime statistics is irrelevant. **B and C are both incorrect** because each addresses the result of any punishment that might be delivered, and not why the women should be charged and punished in the first place.

315. This question tests on the *mens rea* for conspiracy, which requires (1) intent to commit the *actus reus* (the agreement), and (2) intent to commit the target crime. Because of the dual intents, the *mens rea* for attempt is described as specific intent.

B is correct because it recognizes that the gymnasts had these dual intents: the intent to agree to commit a battery, and the intent to commit that battery.

A is incorrect because it focuses on the line between preparation and perpetration, which is an issue for attempt and not conspiracy. **C is incorrect** because purchasing the poison was an act of preparation, and the gymnasts have not yet committed an attempted battery. **D is incorrect** because it suggests that some extra, affirmative act must be shown to establish the conspiratorial agreement. But if the parties agree to commit a crime, that is sufficient.

316. This question also tests on the *mens rea* for conspiracy, focusing on the need for a plurality, i.e., for both parties to the conspiracy to have the intent to agree.

A is correct because it acknowledges that although the sister told her brother that she would participate, she was only feigning her agreement. As such, there was no plurality.

B is incorrect because, while the sister lacked the *mens rea* for the robbery, the issue in this question is whether she had the *mens rea* for conspiracy. **C is incorrect** because it makes no sense: a person can still be guilty of conspiracy even if the target crime is not committed. **D is incorrect** because it fails to recognize that the sister's "agreement" was not based on her intent to commit, but instead on her intent to get off the phone with her brother and call the police.

317. This question also tests on the *mens rea* for conspiracy, focusing on the modern approach to the plurality issue. Under that approach, a conspiracy can be formed if one party believes that he is entering into an agreement to commit a crime. In other words, the agreement can be unilateral instead of bilateral—as is required by the common law.

B is correct because it recognizes that a unilateral agreement is all that is required and that such an agreement was formed on these facts.

A is incorrect because it places the focus on the police officer's *actus reus* (pretending to agree), when instead the focus should be on the drug ring member's *mens rea* (believing that he was entering into an agreement). **C is incorrect** because modern law requires only a unilateral agreement, and not a bilateral agreement. **D is incorrect** because there is no entrapment on these facts; instead, the drug ring member proposed the crime, and the undercover officer did nothing to induce him to commit a crime.

318. This question also tests on the *actus reus* for conspiracy: the agreement. Unlike other areas of law, the criminal law does not require the conspiratorial agreement to be formal or express.

C is correct because it recognizes this principle. In this question, the two men formed their agreement through gestures—nodding at the clerk and then smiling at one another—which is sufficient.

A is incorrect because the conspiracy can be established without the first man's testimony; for example, the clerk could testify to what he saw when the two men walked into the store. **B is incorrect** because it fails to recognize the importance of the brief exchange between the two men before the first man drew his weapon. **D is incorrect** because there is no "doctrine of *mortui non morden*." Translated from Latin, that phrase means "dead men tell no tales."

319. This question tests on the *actus reus* for conspiracy. At common law, all that was required was an agreement to commit a crime or to commit a legal act in an illegal manner. No additional *actus reus* was required.

C is correct because it recognizes that only the agreement is required.

A and B are both incorrect because no additional act is required for a conspiracy, and no concrete plans are required. Instead, only the agreement is required. **D is incorrect** because the co-workers agreed to commit the killing—and not just to try it.

320. This question also tests on the *actus reus* for conspiracy and focuses on the requirements under modern law: (1) an agreement and (2) an overt act in furtherance of the agreement.

A is correct because it recognizes that the man and woman have only agreed to commit a crime, and have done nothing else. While this agreement would suffice for a conspiracy at common law, the question asks about modern law.

B is incorrect because the question does not provide enough facts to determine how intoxicated the man and woman were, or whether they were "clearly" not serious about their agreement. **C is incorrect** because it fails to recognize that this question asks about modern law, and not the common law. **D is incorrect** because it fails to recognize that there was an agreement between the man and the woman; as such, if the man is guilty of conspiracy, the woman must be also.

321. This question tests on the overt act requirement under modern law. Unlike attempt law, which limits the types of acts that can qualify for the *actus reus*, an overt act for conspiracy can be any act, as long it is committed in furtherance of the conspiracy.

C is correct because it recognizes that the phone call, although legal, was committed with the goal of furthering the conspiracy. As such, it qualifies as an overt act, and the woman and the hit man have engaged in a conspiracy.

A is incorrect because it suggests that legal acts cannot qualify as overt acts, and they can. **B is incorrect** because it suggests that preparatory acts cannot qualify as overt acts, and they can. By comparison, preparatory acts are insufficient to form the *actus reus* for attempt crimes. **D is incorrect** because it fails to recognize that there was an agreement between the woman and the hit man; as such, if the woman is guilty of conspiracy, the hit man must be also.

322. This question tests on the scope of conspiratorial liability: each conspirator is liable for (a) the conspiracy, (b) acts falling within the scope of the conspiracy, and (c) all other reasonably foreseeable acts committed in furtherance of the conspiracy. *Pinkerton v. U.S.*, 328 U.S. 640 (1946). This is often referred to as "*Pinkerton* liability."

A is correct because it articulates the rule from *Pinkerton*.

B is incorrect because it limits the man's liability to those crimes he "personally committed," and *Pinkerton* is broader than that. **C is incorrect** because it expands the man's liability to all acts committed by his co-conspirators, regardless of foreseeability. **D is incorrect** because it limits the man's liability to those crimes committed before his arrest. But as *Pinkerton* makes clear, a co-conspirator continues to be liable as long as the conspiracy continues.

323. This question also tests on *Pinkerton* liability. In this question, the man committed a reasonably foreseeable act—murder—while committing an armed robbery. But he also committed a sexual assault, which was not part of the conspiratorial agreement and was not reasonably foreseeable.

A is correct because it recognizes that the woman could not have reasonably foreseen that the man would commit a sexual assault.

B is incorrect because it fails to recognize that the murder was foreseeable, and so the woman is liable for that crime under *Pinkerton* liability. **C and D are both incorrect** because they each go too far; while the scope of *Pinkerton* liability is broad, it does not extend to "all crimes." Instead, *Pinkerton* liability is limited to acts falling within the scope of the conspiracy and all other reasonably foreseeable acts committed in furtherance of the conspiracy.

324. This question tests on the parties to a conspiracy, which is important because of *Pinkerton* liability. In a small conspiracy with just two people, each defendant will have relatively limited liability. But if more people are included in the conspiracy—each committing his own acts in furtherance of the conspiracy—the greater the sentencing exposure for each co-conspirator.

There are generally two basic ways to model a conspiracy: as a chain or as a wheel. (Many large conspiracies are actually hybrids, and include both chain and wheel components.)

In a chain conspiracy, co-conspirators are linked together, with each person serving a role to further the conspiracy. As co-conspirators are added to the chain, the links become weaker, and it becomes more difficult to prove a connection between distant links. Wheel conspiracies are addressed in the next question.

C is correct because the facts present a classic chain conspiracy, with each person serving a distinct role in that conspiracy: the farmer grew the marijuana, the woman sold the marijuana, and the college student bought the marijuana.

A is incorrect because although the prosecutor could charge a two-person conspiracy between the woman and the college student, that is not the "only" charging option. **B and D are both incorrect** because co-conspirators do not need to know one another—and often, in multiple-actor conspiracies, they do not.

325. This question tests on the other basic model of conspiracy: the wheel conspiracy. This model of conspiracy requires (a) a central hub; (b) co-conspirators at the ends of each spoke; and (c) a rim around the wheel, i.e., some sort of shared criminal objective between the co-conspirators at the end of each spoke. Without a rim, there is no wheel, and a prosecutor will only be able to prove a series of two-person conspiracies between the hub and the co-conspirators at the end of each spoke.

B is correct because it articulates all the requirements for a wheel conspiracy: a hub (the agent); co-conspirators at the ends of each spoke (the physicians); and a rim (shared interest in insurance fraud). Note that the motions to dismiss did not argue that the physicians were unaware of the fraud, but only that they did not realize the magnitude of the fraud.

A is incorrect because it focuses on whether the physicians knew one another. While the facts indicate that they did know one another, this is not a requirement to establish a conspiracy. **C is incorrect** because it supports the defense motion in alleging several two-person chain conspiracies. **D is incorrect** because it suggests the rim can be established based on the existence of a central hub. Instead, the rim needs to be separately established.

326. This question tests on one of the advantages the prosecution has when it charges a conspiracy. This question addresses venue for a conspiracy prosecution, which can be any jurisdiction where a conspiratorial agreement was formed, or where any act in furtherance of the conspiracy was committed. In a small conspiracy, this may not matter much, but in a larger conspiracy, an individual defendant may be forced to appear in a venue far from his home. *Hyde v. U.S.*, 225 U.S. 347 (1912). Other prosecutorial advantages include relaxed hearsay rules, joint trials for all co-conspirators, and the ability to rely on one overt act to prove a conspiracy between many defendants. For more, see Dressler, *Understanding* § 29.07[B].

C is correct because it recognizes that because a pipe was sold in Pennsylvania, the charges can be brought there.

A is incorrect because the venue selection here is proper, no matter how unfair it might seem from the man's perspective. **B is incorrect** because *forum non conveniens*—a civil procedure concept that allows a court to decline jurisdiction if it appears that another court might be better suited to handle the case—is inapplicable here. Regardless, this answer also suggests that the venue would be changed just because the man made a "demand" for a change of venue. **D is incorrect** because it provides a nonlegal response to a legal question.

327. This question tests on one of the possible defenses to conspiracy: abandonment, or withdrawal from the conspiracy. The common law did not recognize this defense, as the crime of conspiracy would necessarily have been completed by the time the defendant changed his mind about the conspiracy, and about committing the intended crime. Most modern jurisdictions follow suit. But when the defense is recognized, it can shield a defendant from *Pinkerton* liability for the future acts of his co-conspirators, assuming the defendant has communicated his withdrawal to the other members of the conspiracy.

   B is correct because it recognizes that the nonparticipating player still agreed to commit a crime, and so he is responsible for the conspiracy. But because he told the other two players that he did not want to continue, he should not be held responsible for their actions after he communicated his withdrawal to the others.

   A is incorrect because it suggests that withdrawal from a conspiracy can negate the already-formed conspiracy and "exonerate" the defendant, which goes too far. Instead, the withdrawal can only shield a defendant from liability for future crimes. **C is incorrect** because the question explains that the defense was successful, so it had to have some impact at the trial—and not just at sentencing. **D is incorrect** for the same reason. In addition, the nonparticipating player's withdrawal does not require "independent proof." Instead, he could testify to what happened in the parking lot.

328. This question tests on another defense to conspiracy: Wharton's Rule. Under this rule, conspiracy to commit a particular crime cannot be prosecuted if that crime itself requires the same number in the conspiracy. Without Wharton's Rule, defendants who act in groups would be otherwise doubly punished: once for the conspiracy and once for the target crime.

   D is correct because it recognizes this principle. Since commission of adultery requires at least two people, Wharton's Rule dictates that the prosecutor would need to charge the woman and her co-worker and at least one more person if she wanted to also charge a conspiracy.

   A is incorrect because it presents a post-verdict strategy, and the question asks about a trial defense. **B is incorrect** because the chances are quite low that the defense attorney could accomplish this task before the start of trial, and because it doesn't present a trial defense. **C is incorrect** because it presents a sentencing argument, and the question asks about a trial defense.

329. This question tests on a third defense to conspiracy: legislative exemption. Under this defense, a person who is protected by a criminal statute cannot be convicted of conspiring to violate that statute. *Gebardi v. U.S.*, 287 U.S. 112 (1932).

   B is correct because it recognizes this principle: the sophomore cannot be convicted of conspiring to violate a law designed to protect him.

   A is incorrect; while neuroscience does show that the brain finishes its development after adolescence, e.g., *Miller v. Alabama*, 567 U.S. 460 (2012), this does not mean that a teenager cannot form the *mens rea* to commit a crime. **C and D are both incorrect** because neither provides a defense to conspiracy—which is about the agreement to commit a crime.

330. This question tests on a fourth possible—and controversial—defense to conspiracy: impossibility.

A is correct because it recognizes that to permit an impossibility defense here would unjustly reward the women for the ex-husband's unexpected absence from his house.

B is incorrect because it does not address the women's claim of impossibility. Instead, the explanation in the answer would be relevant to a defense of abandonment, where the fact-finder needs to assess whether the defendant genuinely and permanently changed her mind. **C is incorrect** because it does not address impossibility, but instead addresses good police work. **D is incorrect** and shows one of the problems with impossibility as a defense to conspiracy: the ex-husband's absence makes his killing impossible, but does not make the underlying conspiracy impossible.

Classification of Defenses

331. This question tests on one of the three basic types of affirmative defenses: justifications. The other two types—excuses and crime-specific defenses—are addressed in later questions. When a person offers a justification defense, he is essentially claiming that he made the right choice under the circumstances. With a justification defense, the focus is on the defendant's actions, rather than on the defendant himself.

B is correct because self-defense is a justification defense: when all the requirements are met, a defendant who uses force to protect himself is justified in the use of that force.

A is incorrect because self-defense is not an excuse defense. **C is incorrect** because it provides a nonlegal response to a legal question. **D is incorrect** for two reasons. First, the facts do suggest an intentional killing. Second, it does not respond to the question.

332. This question also tests on justification defenses. In this question, the woman claims a necessity defense, and that she made the right decision to drive without a valid license and in violation of her probation, relative to the greater harm of not seeking medical attention for her unconscious wife. If the fact-finder accepts this defense, the verdict indicates that the woman's actions were justified under the circumstances.

A is correct because it describes the woman's position.

B and C are both incorrect because the woman is not asking that she be excused, a position that suggests that she did something wrong and should be forgiven. Instead, the woman here claims that she did the right thing. **D is incorrect** because the woman's defense assumes that the prosecutor can meet her burden; the defense is a response to the prosecutor's case.

333. This question tests on the second basic type of affirmative defense: excuses. When a person offers an excuse defense, he claims that his actions should be forgiven for some recognized reason, e.g., because he was legally insane at the time he committed the crime, or because he made a mistake of law or fact. With an excuse defense, the focus is on the defendant, rather than his actions.

C is correct because the meaning of the woman's insanity acquittal is that she lacks the *mens rea* for the crime. As such, she is not morally culpable for her actions.

A and D are both incorrect because each suggests a reason for the verdict that goes beyond the facts offered in the question. **B is incorrect** because it suggests that insanity is a justification defense, but it is an excuse.

334. This question also tests on excuse defenses. In this question, the man claims that his voluntary intoxication prevented him from forming the *mens rea* for murder. He is not suggesting that the killing was justified in any way, but instead that he should be partially excused for what he did.

B is correct because it recognizes these principles.

A is incorrect because it describes a justification, not an excuse. **C and D are both incorrect** because each suggests that voluntary intoxication is not an excuse.

335. This question tests on the third basic type of affirmative defense: those that are specific to individual crimes. Where justifications and excuses can be offered in defense of almost any crime, defenses in this third category cannot be used so broadly. For example, this question addresses Wharton's Rule, a defense that is only available in response to a conspiracy charge. Other defenses in this category include impossibility (a defense to attempt crimes) and withdrawal (a defense to conspiracy).

D is correct because it recognizes that Wharton's Rule is a specialized defense to conspiracy. Under the statute in the question, two parties are required for a substantive conviction: the peace officer who receives the payment, and the defendant who makes the payment. As such, conviction under this statute requires a plurality. But under Wharton's Rule, conspiracy to commit a particular crime cannot be prosecuted if that crime itself requires the same number as are charged in the conspiracy. As the substantive offense here requires two people in order to be completed, a successful conspiracy charge would require three.

A, B, and C are all incorrect because each improperly categorizes Wharton's Rule as a justification and/or an excuse.

Mistake

336. This question tests on the basic difference between a mistake of fact defense and a mistake of law defense, and uses a provision from the Maine penal code. Me. Stat. tit. 17-A, § 359. When a defendant asserts a mistake of fact defense, he acknowledges that he was aware of the law, but he claims that he misunderstood some factual circumstance, which in turn led him to break the law. But when a defendant asserts a mistake of law defense, he claims that he did not know what the law required.

B is correct because the student is claiming a mistake about a factual circumstance: that the property was stolen.

A is incorrect because it misstates the college student's claim: he is not arguing that he should have been told the property was stolen, but instead that he did not know the property was stolen. **C and D are both incorrect** because the college student has not claimed any mistake or ignorance of the law.

337. This question tests on the effect of a successful mistake of fact mistake or law defense: the defendant will be acquitted because a successful mistake of fact defense shows that the defendant lacks the *mens rea* for the crime.

C is correct because it recognizes that a man who believes he had consensual sex is not guilty of rape.

A is incorrect because the man in this situation will not receive something "to which he is not entitled." Instead, because rape requires proof of a *mens rea*, a defendant who lacks that *mens rea* actually deserves an acquittal. **B is incorrect** because the mistake here establishes that the man lacked the *mens rea* for rape, which is far from a "technicality." **D is incorrect** because the man's mistake is linked to his *mens rea* and not his *actus reus*.

338. This question tests on the mistake of fact requirements for a general intent crime: the defendant's mistake must be both honest (subjectively held) and reasonable (objectively appropriate).

D is correct because the contractor is charged with a general intent crime (arson), and the woman's email demonstrates his honest and reasonable mistake. The mistake is honest because the contractor believed he was supposed to burn both buildings. But the mistake was also reasonable because the woman's email can be read in two different ways: that she did not like the view of the barn and wanted it to be destroyed, or that she hoped the view of the barn from her new house will be different.

A is incorrect because the issue here is whether the contractor's belief was honest and reasonable, and not what the woman meant when she wrote the email. **B is incorrect** because mistake of fact is a potential defense for any crime involving a *mens rea*. **C is incorrect** because an honest (subjectively held) belief is not enough to secure an acquittal for a general intent charge.

339. This question tests on the mistake of fact requirements for a specific intent crime: the defendant's mistake must only be honest (subjectively held), and does not need to be objectively reasonable.

C is correct because the attorney is charged with a specific intent crime (embezzlement) and she honestly believed she had linked the autopay for her electricity bill to her personal account. As such, she lacked the *mens rea* for embezzlement, i.e., the intent to convert the funds of another for her own use.

A is incorrect because mistake of fact is a defense available to any defendant, including attorneys. **B is incorrect** because mistake of fact is a potential defense for any crime involving a *mens rea*. **D is incorrect** because it states the mistake of fact requirements for a general intent crime. While the mistake in this situation might also be objectively reasonable, it does not have to be.

340. This question tests on the mistake of fact defense, offered in response to a statutory rape charge. Rape is a general intent crime. While some authorities describe statutory rape as a strict liability crime, it is not; instead, statutory rape is strict liability as to age only. Regardless, mistake of fact is not accepted as a defense when it is offered to show that the defendant was mistaken about the victim's age.

B is correct because it recognizes that the defense is not available to the young man.

A is incorrect because it addresses the reasonableness of the young man's mistake, and suggests that if he checked the young woman's ID, he would have a plausible defense. C

is incorrect because it reaches the wrong conclusion, although it does accurately describe the nature of the young man's mistake. **D is incorrect** because it reaches the wrong conclusion, and because it misstates the requirements for a mistake of fact defense.

341. This question tests on a particular type of mistake of fact defense: claim of right. This is a potential defense to theft crimes, which require proof of specific intent to permanently deprive. When a defendant asserts a claim of right, he is arguing that he believed the property at issue belonged to him, and so lacked the *mens rea* for the crime.

A is correct because it reaches the right conclusion and also recognizes that the woman's belief that the tennis racquet was hers only needs to be honestly held.

B is incorrect because it suggests that the woman's belief has to be objectively reasonable. But instead, because the woman is charged with a specific intent crime, she only needs to have an honest, subjectively held belief that the racquet belongs to her. **C is incorrect** because it assumes facts beyond those given in the question: that the woman is lying about her honestly held belief. **D is incorrect** because it imposes a nonexistent requirement on the mistake of fact defense. Of course, a fact-finder is free to reject a defendant's claim that he made an honest mistake of fact. But the facts in this question do not permit that inference.

342. This question tests on mistake of fact offered in defense to a strict liability charge. Because a successful mistake of fact defense establishes that the defendant lacked the *mens rea* for the crime, this defense can only be offered to crimes that have a *mens rea* requirement. Put a little differently, mistake of fact is not a defense to strict liability crimes.

C is correct because it recognizes that the woman's mistake—no matter how honest or how reasonable—does not matter here, because the statute has no *mens rea* associated with it.

A and B are both incorrect because each assumes that mistake of fact is a defense in this situation, and it is not. **D is incorrect** because it focuses on the woman's credibility. But if the woman cannot assert a mistake of fact defense, her credibility is irrelevant.

343. This question tests on the general rule for mistake of law: ignorance of the law is not a defense and all are presumed to know the law. Later questions will explore the exceptions to this general rule.

D is correct because it restates this general rule.

A, B, and C are all incorrect because each offers a misstatement of the general rule. As later questions will show, mistake of law can be a defense in some situations but none of these answers addresses these situations.

344. This question tests on the rationale for the general rule about mistake of law, which assumes a lot about a person's knowledge. But if the criminal law did not expect everyone to know the law, it would be difficult to distinguish between those who were truly ignorant of the law and those who use ignorance as a way to avoid following the law. As a result, all are presumed to know the law, subject to the exceptions discussed in the following questions.

B is correct because it articulates the primary justification for the general rule about ignorance of the law.

A is incorrect because it is untrue: mistake of law continues to be a defense. **C is incorrect** because of its reference to "technicalities." The mistake of law defense, when it is accepted, establishes that the defendant lacked the *mens rea* for the crime. But proof of *mens rea* is an essential component of the criminal law and hardly a "technicality." **D is incorrect** because it suggests that the rationales for limiting the mistake of law defense are outdated. But these rationales apply with equal force today.

345. This question tests on the first exception to the general rule regarding mistake of law: a person can claim ignorance of law when the law is not yet published and publicly available. The statute in this question is based on a Virginia statute, 13 V.S.A. §352, but has been edited slightly.

D is correct because the law was posted on the state's official website, and so it was available for the public to review. As such, while the woman may not have been aware of the law, its public posting means that she cannot claim ignorance of the law.

A is incorrect because there is no 72-hour grace period unless the state's penal code has a separate statute creating one. But in the absence of such a statute, the law is either published or it is not. And here, the law was published. **B is incorrect** because it imposes a requirement that the new law appear in print. While the common law certainly could not have anticipated that laws would be published online, publishing online is sufficient to inform the public today about new laws. **C is incorrect** because it ties ignorance of the law to the subject matter of the law, i.e., dog ownership. Instead, the availability of the defense is tied to more objective criteria.

346. This question tests on the second exception to the general rule regarding mistake of law: a person can claim ignorance of the law when she relies on an interpretation of the law by one whose job it is to interpret and enforce the law. Here, the woman sought and obtained an opinion from the district attorney and so she is permitted to rely on that opinion.

B is correct because it recognizes this principle. And this makes sense: if the woman could not rely on the district attorney's official interpretation, then the district attorney serves no purpose in the criminal justice system.

A is incorrect because otherwise, mistake of law would be an available defense for every well-meaning defendant. **C is incorrect** because the fact that the attorney general disagrees with the district attorney does not mean the woman received "bad advice." Regardless, because the district attorney's job is to enforce the law, the woman can rely on his interpretation. **D is incorrect** because it is not necessarily true to say that the attorney general outranks the district attorney. Instead, each officer serves different roles in the state's executive branch.

347. This question tests on a variation on the second exception to the general rule regarding mistake of law. In this question, the woman relied on advice from her retained attorney and the advice turned out to be wrong. The woman cannot claim mistake of law under these circumstances because the retained attorney's job does not include the official enforcement and interpretation of the law.

C is correct because it recognizes this principle. If the woman was allowed to rely on the retained attorney's advice, the mistake of law defense would expand considerably, and would create a big loophole for would-be criminal defendants.

A is incorrect because it suggests that the retained attorney can be an authority for the woman's mistake of law defense. **B is incorrect** because it suggests that the availability of the mistake of law defense depends on the complexity of the underlying law. **D is incorrect** because the estate funds may or may not eventually go to the woman. But the estate could also have significant debts, and the woman might not inherit anything. Regardless, the estate money does not belong to the woman until the estate gives it to her.

348. This question tests on the third exception to the general rule regarding mistake of law: a person can claim ignorance of the law when his mistake would negate specific intent. Thus, to claim this defense, the defendant must be charged with a specific intent crime, and must assert an honestly held belief that he was not aware that he was violating the law. *Cheek v. U.S.*, 498 U.S. 192 (1991). Of course, a fact-finder is always free to reject the defendant's claims about his honestly held belief.

D is correct because the young man cannot "voluntarily and intentionally violate[] a known legal duty" if he sincerely believes he does not owe that duty.

A is incorrect because it states the general rule regarding ignorance of the law, and this question tests on an exception. **B is incorrect** because focusing on what the young man "should have known" does not address what he claims he did not know. **C is incorrect** because it misstates the requirements for this exception: the defendant's mistake must be honestly held, and does not need to also be objectively reasonable.

349. This question tests on the fourth exception to the general rule regarding mistake of law: a person can claim ignorance of the law when his mistake is not based on the criminal law, but some other area of law. Here, the woman knows that she can only be married to one person at a time. Her mistake was based on family law, though, and in assuming she was divorced from her first husband.

B is correct because it reaches the correct conclusion and because it articulates a legal reason why that conclusion is correct.

A is incorrect because it restates the facts, and does not give a legal reason for the conclusion. **C is incorrect** because it states the general rule regarding ignorance of the law, and this question tests on an exception. **D is incorrect** because it reaches the wrong conclusion, although it does correctly restate the applicable exception to the general rule.

350. This question tests on mistake of law offered in defense to a strict liability charge. As with mistake of fact, a successful mistake of law defense establishes that the defendant lacked the *mens rea* for the crime. As such, even though the mistake of law defense is very limited, it can only be offered to crimes that have a *mens rea* requirement and so is not a defense to strict liability crimes.

A is correct because it recognizes this principle.

B is incorrect because it offers an opinion and not a legal response. **C is incorrect** because it does not respond to the question, which focuses on mistake of law. **D is incorrect** because it suggests that mistake of law is a defense to strict liability crimes.

Self-Defense and Defense of Others

351. This question tests on the basic concept of self-defense: the right to use deadly or nondeadly force to protect oneself from an imminent attack.

D is correct because it recognizes that the woman can claim that she had the right to use force to protect herself.

A is incorrect because it refers to what a person "should" do, and not what this woman can do. **B is incorrect** because, while relative fault is important when evaluating a self-defense claim, that inquiry usually focuses on who began the altercation that led to the use of force. It is unlikely that the firearms violation would defeat the woman's defense. **C is incorrect** because it is worded too broadly; indeed, there are many situations where deadly force cannot be used against an attacker.

352. This question tests on the principle that self-defense is limited to situations where a defendant is faced with unlawful force being used against her. Here, as the woman will concede that the officer did not use excessive force and was acting lawfully, she had no right to use force in response.

B is correct because it recognizes this principle.

A and D are both incorrect because an officer's qualified or governmental immunity from a civil suit has nothing to do with the woman's defense to a criminal charge. **C is incorrect** because there are some circumstances where a person can use lawful force against an officer.

353. This question tests on the principle that self-defense encompasses the use of both deadly force and nondeadly force. The questions that follow first address the use of deadly force and then nondeadly force.

C is correct because it recognizes that nondeadly force can be used in self-defense.

A is incorrect because it provides an antiquated, nonlegal response to a legal question. **B is incorrect** because it suggests that self-defense is only a defense to homicide, which is untrue. **D is incorrect** because it does not respond to the question, which asks about self-defense and not mental illness.

354. This question tests on the first of three requirements for use of deadly force in self-defense: that it be necessary for the defendant to use force. The necessity requirement has three components: the defendant cannot be of the initial aggressor, the requirement of an imminent threat, and the duty to retreat. Although different authorities break down these requirements differently, all agree on the same basic requirements.

Assessing the identity of the initial aggressor is not always easy, because most self-defense situations involve complicated facts—words can be exchanged, the situation can escalate and de-escalate, one party might retreat and later return, multiple parties might be involved, etc. The facts in this question are relatively straight-forward, though, because the stranger pulled a gun on the man and so the stranger was the initial aggressor.

D is correct because it recognizes this principle.

A is incorrect because the man's rudeness does not bar him from claiming self-defense. Instead, the issue is who brought the force to the situation. **B is incorrect** because it suggests that the man's rudeness makes him the initial aggressor in this situation, and it does not. **C is incorrect** because it is untrue: the man's self-defense claim cannot be evaluated without looking at his actions.

355. This question also tests on assessing the initial aggressor. In this question, the first man began the altercation when he confronted the second man and punched him in the face. Judging the facts in isolation, this makes the first man the initial aggressor. But then he retreated and lost that status. After an interval of time, the second man approached the first man with a gun in his hand. As such, the second man became the initial aggressor.

A is correct because it credits the first man's retreat and recognizes that the second man later became the initial aggressor.

B and C are both incorrect because each fails to address the first man's retreat, suggesting that the two men fought in a single, uninterrupted episode. That does sometimes happen, but it did not happen here. **D is incorrect** because the identity of the initial aggressor can change, depending on whether one party retreats from the scene or otherwise ends his aggression.

356. This question tests on assessing the initial aggressor, where a fight between two parties escalates from shouting to plate-throwing to a shooting. In these situations, the initial aggressor is the one who brings the final deadly force to the situation.

C is correct because it recognizes that the interaction between the roommate and the senior changed completely when the roommate pulled out his gun. By contrast, imagine if the roommate did not use a gun, but instead threw a plate at the senior. With those changed facts, the senior would keep his status as the initial aggressor and the roommate would be able to claim self-defense.

A is incorrect because it looks at the facts in isolation. While the senior did throw a plate, the roommate's use of a weapon qualitatively changed the interaction. **B is incorrect** because the roommate had other choices available to him. **D is incorrect** because it provides a non-legal response to a legal question.

357. This question tests on the second component of the necessity requirement for deadly force: that the defendant who claims self-defense face an imminent threat. Because self-defense authorizes the use of force, it should only be used in limited circumstances. Thus, when a defendant faces only a vague threat, there is no necessity to respond with force.

A is correct because the co-worker gave no indication that he was going to follow through with his threat, or that he even was able to do so. While the woman was frightened by the threat, the co-worker's threat appears to have been an idle one.

B is incorrect because the problem here is not that the threat was conditional, but instead that the threat did not suggest any imminent harm. What if the co-worker made the same threat, but with a gun in his hand? Adding that fact demonstrates that conditional words are not the problem here. **C is incorrect** because it would allow a person to kill in self-defense anytime she felt afraid or threatened, which would expand self-defense considerably. **D is incorrect** because it fails to address the fact that there was no imminent threat.

358. This question tests on the third component of the necessity requirement for deadly force: the duty to retreat. That duty requires that, before resorting to the use of force, the defendant try to leave the situation if he can. At common law, the duty was absolute and the defendant had to "retreat to the wall," but this rule has been relaxed over time. Regardless, in this question, the woman was in a car and the man was on foot; she could have easily left the situation. Instead, the woman chose to stay and fight.

B is correct because it recognizes that the woman cannot both ignore her easy escape route and claim self-defense.

A, C, and D are all incorrect because they do not address the woman's duty to retreat. Even if the man was the initial aggressor and even if the woman had a credible fear that he had a gun, the woman cannot claim self-defense unless all the requirements for the defense are met.

359. This question tests on the duty to retreat, but where a defendant is in her own home. In such a situation, the "castle doctrine" dictates that the defendant has no duty to retreat but can instead stay in place and confront the intruder.

A is correct because it recognizes that the castle doctrine protected the college professor's right to stay in the kitchen and that she was not required to leave through the back door.

B is incorrect because it fails to address the castle doctrine. **C and D are both incorrect** because each focuses on the fact that there was a way for the professor to retreat: through the back door, conveniently located right where she was standing when she heard the intruder. But while the college professor could have retreated, the castle doctrine dictates that she did not have to.

360. This question tests on the second requirement—after necessity—for use of force in self-defense: that the defendant use force that is proportional to the force used against him. Put a little more simply, the defendant cannot legitimately respond to a punch by using a gun or a knife, but he can legitimately respond by punching back.

D is correct because the women used identical force against one another.

A is incorrect because it provides a nonlegal response to a legal question. **B is incorrect** because the proportionality for force requirement focuses more on the device used—e.g., fists, knives, plates, guns, hangers—instead of the precise injuries received. **C is incorrect** because the prosecutor's motion was focused on proportionality of force, not the identity of the initial aggressor. In any event, the second woman struck the first blow, and so she is likely the initial aggressor.

361. This question also tests on proportionality of force. In this question, the senior used disproportionate force when he used a knife to respond to a punch.

B is correct because it recognizes this principle.

A is incorrect because self-defense can be used to defend against any crime involving violence to the person. **C is incorrect** because, while probably true, it does not provide a legal answer. **D is incorrect** because it is worded too loosely. What if the freshman had hurled a plate at the senior? In that situation, the freshman would have "used a weapon," but the senior would still not be privileged to stab him in self-defense.

362. This question tests on the third requirement—after necessity and proportionality of force—for self-defense: that the defendant reasonably believe that he must use deadly force to protect himself. A reasonable belief does not need to be accurate; it just needs to be reasonable under the circumstances.

C is correct because the woman's belief was reasonable under the circumstances: a burglar had entered her house in the middle of the night and was in her bedroom. While it is possible that the burglar meant no harm—anything is possible—it is reasonable to believe that he did.

A is incorrect because the woman did not need to know precisely what the burglar wanted, she just needed to reasonably believe that he meant to physically harm her in some way. **B is incorrect** because the woman's belief was more than merely subjective; it was also objectively reasonable. **D is incorrect** because it is untrue, and there is no such presumption.

363. This question also tests on the reasonable belief requirement. In this question, the man's belief about the woman reaching for a gun was wrong. But, as long as his belief was reasonable, the requirement will be met.

D is correct because it recognizes this principle.

A is incorrect because it equates reasonability with accuracy. **B is incorrect** because it cites a wholly subjective standard, and because it requires that the man's belief be accurate. **C is incorrect** because it focuses on the man's sincere belief, which is a wholly subjective standard.

364. This question tests on the effect of a "perfect" self-defense claim, i.e., one that meets all the requirements. In such a situation, the defendant will be acquitted of the charged crime.

A is correct because it recognizes the proper result if the jury accepts the woman's self-defense claim: she will be acquitted.

B is incorrect because an acquittal is not the same as an exoneration. With a perfect self-defense claim, the defendant is acquitted because his actions were justified. But there is no dispute that the defendant engaged in the acts that constitute the underlying crime. When a defendant is exonerated, that means he did not commit the crime at all. **C is incorrect** because a finding that a defendant acted in self-defense means that she is not criminally responsible for her acts at all, not that she is responsible for a lesser crime. **D is incorrect** because it presupposes that the jury would find the woman guilty. But, if the jury believed the woman acted in self-defense, she should be acquitted and not convicted.

365. This question tests on modern "imperfect" self-defense: a self-defense claim offered in response to a homicide charge, but where one or more of the requirements of self-defense are not met. In such a situation, the defendant should be convicted of a lesser-included homicide offense out of the recognition that he made the wrong choice under difficult circumstances.

C is correct because a voluntary manslaughter conviction would recognize that the man killed intentionally and hold him responsible for his acts, but would also recognize that at least some of the other requirements for self-defense were present. Of course, if few of the requirements for self-defense were met and if it appeared that the defendant's actions were completely unjustified, the defendant should be convicted as initially charged.

A is incorrect because the question does not give enough information to determine if this is true or not. **B is incorrect** because it suggests that imperfect self-defense does not exist. **D is incorrect** because the man killed intentionally, and so it does not make sense to convict him of an unintentional homicide.

366. This question tests on modern "stand your ground" statutes, which relax or completely eliminate the common law duty to retreat. These statutes generally say that if a defendant is in a place where he is entitled to be, he has no duty to retreat.

A is correct because the only apparent obstacle to the man's self-defense claim would be the duty to retreat. But once that requirement is eliminated, he would be able to claim self-defense.

B is incorrect because the common law imposed a duty to retreat. **C is incorrect** because proportionality of force is not an issue on these facts. **D is incorrect** because the man was in his car and not his home, and so the castle doctrine is irrelevant.

367. This question tests on the reasonable belief requirement as codified in a modern self-defense statute. This provision is taken from the New York penal code and has been edited slightly. N.Y. Penal Law § 35.15.

B is correct because the statute's reference to what "he or she reasonably believes" indicates that the fact-finder should examine both the defendant's subjective beliefs ("he or she... believes") and whether those beliefs are objectively reasonable ("reasonably believes").

A is incorrect because it provides a nonlegal response to a legal question. **C and D are both incorrect** because each addresses one part of the relevant phrase from the statute, but not the phrase in its entirety.

368. This question tests on the problems with self-defense law that have given rise to the so-called Battered Woman's Defense. That is, long-term abusive relationships often have dramatic ebbs and flows and deeply traumatize their victims, but the rigid requirements of self-defense do not take any of this into account.

D is correct because the woman does not have a viable self-defense claim. The homicide was not necessary because the man was asleep. The force was disproportionate because the man was not using any force against the woman when she set the bed on fire. And a reasonable person would not have been in fear when the woman set the bed on fire because, again, the man was sleeping at that moment.

A, B, and C are all incorrect because each suggests that the woman would have a viable defense if she can produce enough credible witness testimony. But the problem here is that the woman killed the man while he was sleeping, and not that she does not have enough witnesses to support her claim.

369. This question tests on how the Battered Woman's Defense can work in a jurisdiction that recognizes it in some form. In this question, the male victim wants to offer testimony to show how the years of abuse affected his perspective on the power and control of his abuser. If that testimony is permitted, it would help to show why he believed he needed to kill her and why he believed his use of force was proportional.

A is correct because it recognizes this principle.

B is incorrect because it provides a value judgment about the wife, and the question asks for a legal response. **C is incorrect** because it is untrue: although most of these cases involve battering of a woman by a man, men can be victims of abuse, too. **D is incorrect** because the husband is not trying to blame his wife for what happened; he is instead trying to provide a more complete context for the fact-finder, to explain why he killed her.

370. This question tests on use of nondeadly force in self-defense. Similar to use of deadly force, a defendant who uses nondeadly force must reasonably believe that the force he uses is necessary to protect against an imminent threat of unlawful force.

C is correct because it meets all these requirements.

A is incorrect because self-defense can be used to defend against any crime involving violence to the person. **B is incorrect** because the niece was threatening unlawful force, although that force may not have entailed physical pain. **D is incorrect** because the woman's perception of a threat, alone, is not enough for her to claim self-defense.

371. This question tests on the duty to retreat in nondeadly force situations. In short, there is no such requirement.

C is correct because it recognizes this principle.

A is incorrect because it addresses the "ability" to retreat, which is not a legal obligation—although it might have been best if the first man had retreated. **B is incorrect** because there was no duty to retreat. **D is incorrect** because regardless of the witnesses agreeing with one another, the requirements for self-defense must still be met for the first man to have a viable claim.

372. This question tests on use of force to defend third parties, which is also called defense of others. In general, the defense has the same contours as self-defense.

B is correct because it recognizes that there are times when a person can use force to defend someone else.

A is incorrect because it addresses sentencing, and the question asks about a trial defense. **C is incorrect** because it is untrue, and there are instances when a person can and must intervene. For example, teachers and doctors are mandatory reporters, and are required by statute to report suspected child abuse. **D is incorrect** because it suggests an unworkable rule. What if the sister had beaten her teenage son until he was unconscious? Or what if he was a baby and was unable to ask for help?

373. This question tests on a common law restriction on defense of others: that the person using force be in some sort of recognized status relationship with the person he seeks to protect. Most modern jurisdictions no longer impose this requirement.

A is correct because it recognizes that the senior did not know the woman, and so was not privileged to use force in her defense.

B is incorrect because it refers to the right to eavesdrop, not the right to use force. **C and D are both incorrect** because each reaches an incorrect conclusion for a common law jurisdiction.

374. This question tests on the "alter-ego rule," which holds that a person can use force to defend a third party only to the extent the third party would be entitled to claim self-defense. And so, if the third party misjudged the situation and came to the defense of someone who could not claim self-defense, the third party would not have a defense, either.

D is correct because the legal assistant was the initial aggressor, and so would not have been able to claim self-defense. Under the alter-ego rule, the lawyer would then not be able to use deadly force in the legal assistant's defense.

A is incorrect because it does not respond to the legal issue presented by the question. **B is incorrect** because it fails to recognize the alter-ego rule. **C is incorrect** because it suggests that defense of others does not apply in situations involving deadly force.

375. This question tests on a modern defense of others statute from the Texas penal code; the statute has been edited slightly. Tex. Penal Code § 9.33. The statute replaces the alter-ego rule with the requirement that the defendant "reasonably believe" that he needs to use force.

C is correct because it uses the "reasonably believe" language from the statute and reaches the correct conclusion.

A and B are both incorrect because each focuses on what actually happened, and not what the neighbor reasonably believed. **D is incorrect** because the Latin phrase makes no sense here.

Defense of Property and Habitation

376. This question tests on the right to use nondeadly force to defend against unlawful dispossession of property. At common law and today, use of force in such situations is permitted. But, while permitted in modern jurisdictions, using violence to engage in self-help is also discouraged.

B is correct because it recognizes this principle.

A, C, and D are all incorrect because each provides a nonlegal response to a legal question.

377. This question also tests on the right to use nondeadly force to defend against unlawful dispossession of property. In this question, the man seeks to use force well after he was dispossessed of the property—which is not permitted. Instead, if force is used to reclaim property, it must be used at the time of the possible dispossession.

C is correct because it recognizes that the man's opportunity has passed, and so he cannot use force to reclaim the briefcase.

A is incorrect because it suggests that the man had an ongoing right to use force to reclaim the briefcase. **B is incorrect** because it is untrue: a person cannot "always" use force to defend property. Instead, there are limits on the use of that force. **D is incorrect** because the sentimental value of the property is not relevant here. Instead, what matters is that the man acted too late to reclaim his briefcase.

378. This question also tests on the right to use nondeadly force to defend against unlawful dispossession of property where the defendant is not the titleholder to the property. Force in these situations is permitted, even if the defendant only has lawful possession of the property.

D is correct because the woman can use force to protect herself from being dispossessed of the jewelry, even if she is not the titleholder to that property.

A is incorrect because the jury does not decide questions of law; the judge does. **B is incorrect** because it misstates the rule. **C is incorrect** because the common law did not distinguish between retail and non-retail situations.

379. This question also tests on the right to use nondeadly force to defend property where the defendant has reason to believe that the person who claims that property has a superior right to it. This use of force is not permitted.

B is correct because the man suspected his friend stole the car. As such, he cannot use force to defend it.

A is incorrect because it does not respond to the question. While it might be a good idea for the man to reach out to his friend, the question asks whether he was entitled to use force. **C is incorrect** because it ignores the fact that the man suspected his friend of stealing the car. **D is incorrect** because the alter-ego rule applies to use of force to defend third parties, and not the use of force to defend property.

380. This question tests on the use of deadly force to defend property. Deadly force is not permitted in these situations, at common law or today.

A is correct because it recognizes this principle.

B is incorrect because this rule does not change if the property is about to be destroyed. **C is incorrect** because the defendant's location is not relevant if he only faces a threat to his property—and not one to human life. **D is incorrect** because it misstates the rule.

381. This question tests on the overlap between defending property and defending life. In the previous question, the defendant used force to defend property (only). But in this question, the force was used to defend life as well as property. Since life is more important than property, however, the woman's right to protect herself will trump.

B is correct because it recognizes that this is really a case of self-defense, and not defense of property. While the woman may have been afraid the carjacker was going to steal her car, he also threatened her life when he pointed a gun at her. As such, she had the right to use deadly force to defend herself.

A is incorrect because the prosecutor's comment presents a legal question, which should be decided by the judge. Juries decide factual issues. **C is incorrect** because the woman would not be entitled to use deadly force to defend her sportscar. **D is incorrect** because it misstates the rule regarding the right to use force to defend property.

382. This question tests on the right to use deadly force to defend a home, also called defense of habitation. At early common law, this was permitted, although the "scope of this privilege has changed over time, and no single rule universally applies today." Dressler, *Understanding* §20.03[B].

C is correct because the question makes clear that the college student used deadly force only because he was annoyed at his best friend for waking him up. In other words, the only thing the college student sought to protect was his sleep.

A is incorrect because it is worded too broadly. **B is incorrect** because it conflates the best friend's drunkenness with the college student's safety. Without additional facts, there is no reason to believe the college student was not safe. **D is incorrect** because the question does not give enough facts by which to assess if there was an implicit invitation or not.

383. This question also tests on defense of habitation. The rules regarding this defense significantly differ by jurisdiction. Dressler, *Understanding* § 20.03[B] and [C]. Regardless, the use of deadly force to protect habitation usually also raises the issue of self-defense and defense of others, and so the issue rarely presents itself in isolation.

B is correct because it recognizes the overlap between defense of habitation and self-defense, and that the woman here was privileged to use deadly force to protect her own life.

A is incorrect because the right to use force does not depend on the intruder responding to the woman. Instead, that is one fact among many that requires analysis. **C is incorrect** because it suggests that the woman had to come perilously close to danger before she would have been allowed to use deadly force. **D is incorrect** because it is unclear how the woman would be able to recognize footsteps as belonging to her brother.

384. This question also tests on defense of habitation, but with an overlap of defense of others.

C is correct because the man correctly—and reasonably—believed that the intruder was about to harm the baby. As such, he was allowed to use force to protect her.

A and B are both incorrect because each suggests that the man had to take some additional steps before he employed force against the intruder. But no such steps were required because the intruder was plainly about to harm the baby. **D is incorrect** because it is written so broadly that it is untrue.

385. This question tests on spring guns, which are devices rigged to fire when their rigging is tripped. Spring guns were permitted at common law if the human behind the gun would have been permitted to use force in that situation. But spring guns are not permitted today. The reason is simple: a spring gun cannot evaluate an emergent situation like a human and cannot refrain from firing if the situation warrants. Instead, if the rigging is tripped, the spring gun will fire.

C is correct because it restates the common law rule.

A is incorrect because, while probably true, it does not provide the common law rule. **B is incorrect** because it offers circular reasoning, i.e., the man was allowed to use a spring gun because it shot the intended target. But that response does not address the propriety of using a spring gun in the first place. **D is incorrect** because it provides a nonlegal response to a legal question.

Insanity, Mental Health, and Intoxication

386. This question tests on the insanity defense and what it means for a defendant to be found not guilty by reason of insanity, or NGRI: that due to the manifestation of mental illness, he lacked the *mens rea* to commit the charged crime. As a result, the defendant—called an insanity acquittee—is not held responsible for his acts.

B is correct because it recognizes this principle.

A is incorrect because it describes the verdict informally and imprecisely, and does not respond to the legal question. **C is incorrect** for two reasons. First, it argues with the question and does not respond to it. Second, mentally ill individuals can and do act methodically. **D is incorrect** because a person who is found NGRI is not "guilty as charged." Instead, an insanity verdict acquits the defendant of the charged crimes.

387. This question tests on the key difference between the insanity defense and threshold competency to stand trial. The former tests the defendant's mental state at the time of the offense, and the latter tests his mental state at the time of trial. Because mental illness is fluid and can change, a person can meet one standard but not the other.

D is correct because it recognizes that the man's behavior raises questions about his present mental state, and identifies how his mental state might affect the proceedings.

A and B are both incorrect because, while each is potentially true, neither addresses the man's apparent mental illness and how it potentially affects the proceedings. **C is incorrect** because the issue here is the man's present mental illness, and the question does not indicate that the judge has any information about the man's mental state at the time of the crime.

388. This question tests on the *M'Naghten* test for insanity, which was developed in response to defendant Daniel M'Naghten's insanity acquittal in the mid-nineteenth century. The *M'Naghten* test is the common law test for insanity; it is also the most commonly used insanity test today. The *M'Naghten* test is referred to as the "cognitive" test for insanity because it evaluates what the defendant was thinking at the time of the offense. The full test states:

> [T]o establish a defence on the ground of insanity, it must be clearly proved that, at the time of the committing of the act, the party accused was labouring under such a defect of reason, from disease of the mind, as not to know the nature and quality of the act he was doing; or, if he did know it, that he did not know he was doing what was wrong. [*M'Naghten's Case*, 8 Eng. Rep. 718, 722 (H.L. 1843).]

The test has two components. First, the defendant must suffer from some form of mental illness. In the original test, this is described as a "defect of reason" and "disease of the mind," but modern versions of the *M'Naghten* test often just describe this as a "mental disease or defect." Second, and due to that mental disease or defect, the defendant must lack the ability to either "know the nature and quality of the act he was doing," or to know what "he was doing ... was wrong." The *M'Naghten* test presents a very limited view of mental illness, as a defendant can be very mentally ill and still know what he is doing or know right from wrong.

A is correct because the test provided in the question only includes the second part of the test, but it omits any reference to the defendant's mental illness.

B is incorrect because the *M'Naghten* test focuses on the defendant's knowledge, which demands more than mere appreciation. **C is incorrect** because the *M'Naghten* test refers to knowing the nature and quality of acts as well as the ability to tell right from wrong. **D is incorrect** because the question asks about the test for insanity, and not about the procedural consequences of an insanity acquittal.

389. This question tests on the meaning of the *M'Naghten* test's requirement that the defendant not know the nature and quality of the act he was doing. In such a situation, the defendant must not understand what he is doing.

A is correct because the man in this question did not believe he was killing and cannibalizing; instead, he thought he was cooking with vegan ingredients. As such, he did not know the nature and quality of the acts he was doing.

B is incorrect because it provides a conclusion and a value judgment, and does not apply the legal test to the facts. **C is incorrect** because the question states that the evaluator believed the man, and so judgments about possible malingering are inappropriate here. **D is incorrect** because it misinterprets the *M'Naghten* test: the issue is not whether the man knew what he was cooking and eating, but whether he knew he had killed a person and was cannibalizing that person.

390. This question tests on one of the primary problems with the *M'Naghten* test: because it does not always take a realistic view of mental illness, it can exclude some mentally ill defendants. In this question, the woman was mentally ill and suffered from command hallucinations that forced her to act, even though she knew her actions were wrong. But none of that is relevant, as the *M'Naghten* test instead focuses on whether the woman knew what she was doing or whether she knew right from wrong.

B is correct because it recognizes that since the woman knew that it was wrong to kill, her insanity defense will fail.

A is incorrect because the woman's inability to describe the evil is irrelevant, as the *M'-Naghten* test focuses on something else entirely. **C and D are both incorrect** because they ignore the *M'Naghten* test and its requirements.

391. This question tests on a second test used to determine insanity: the irresistible impulse test. Like the *M'Naghten* test, the irresistible impulse test requires the defendant to suffer from some sort of mental disease or defect. But with irresistible impulse, the mental disease or defect must affect the defendant's behavior and not his cognition. For this reason, the irresistible impulse test is referred to as a "volitional" test for insanity. The statute here is taken from the Georgia penal code. Ga. Code § 16-3-3.

D is correct because it addresses all the components from the statutory test: (1) mental disease, and (2) a delusional compulsion, that (3) overmastered (i.e., overcame) the woman's will to resist.

A is incorrect because it ignores the statutory language about "overmaster[ing]" the will to resist. **B is incorrect** because the statute does not require the woman to have an injury or congenital deficiency, assuming she has a mental disease. And, since the psychiatrist diagnosed the woman with a "long-standing mental illness," the requirement of the statute is satisfied. **C is incorrect** because it omits reference to the woman's mental illness, and focuses only on her actions. But under the statutory test, both are required.

392. This question tests on one of the problems with the irresistible impulse test: because it focuses on a mentally ill defendant's ability to control his actions, it can exclude those who act methodically or who exhibit planning behavior. Yet those defendants can be just as mentally ill as those who act suddenly, out of an irresistible impulse.

B is correct because the prosecution expert's opinion leaves room for the prosecutor to argue that the man's mental illness cannot account for the continued detention of the children.

A is incorrect for two reasons. First, it provides a nonlegal response to a legal question. Second, the job of the expert is to help the fact-finder by providing insight and expertise, not to act as an adversary. **C is incorrect** because the prosecution and defense experts are not in full agreement. Instead, the facts indicate that they agree about the man's mental illness and its role in the initial kidnapping. But the prosecution expert has not offered an opinion about how the man's mental illness influenced his decision to keep the children in his basement. **D is incorrect** because it suggests the experts are in full agreement, and they are not.

393. This question tests on a third test used to determine insanity: the *Durham* product test. Although this test is most often associated with a District of Columbia case, *Durham v. U.S.*, 214 F.2d 862 (D.C. Cir. 1954), it has its origins in New Hampshire case law. The *Durham* court's impetus for adopting the test was to permit a deeper inquiry into the defendant's mental health, and to move away from the cognitive and volitional tests—both of which limit an inquiry into the defendant's mental health problems.

Under the *Durham* product test, a defendant is legally insane if "his unlawful act was the product of mental disease or defect." Although no United States jurisdiction currently uses this test, it remains influential.

C is correct because it articulates the primary criticism of this test: it is too broad to be workable because most conduct is a "product" of some thought process.

A is incorrect because the quoted test does make the requisite distinction, referring to "mental disease or defect." **B is incorrect** because insanity is a question for the jury to decide. By contrast, competency to stand trial is a threshold question for the judge. **D is incorrect** because the question asks about the test for insanity and not about the procedural consequences of an insanity acquittal.

394. This question tests on the Model Penal Code test for insanity:

> A person is not responsible for criminal conduct if at the time of such conduct as a result of mental disease or defect he lacks substantial capacity either to appreciate the criminality of his conduct or to conform his conduct to the requirements of the law. [M.P.C. §4.01(1).]

As with other insanity tests, the Model Penal Code test requires the presence of a "mental disease or defect." It also includes components from the cognitive (*M'Naghten*) and volitional (irresistible impulse) tests. But instead of taking an all-or-nothing approach and focusing on what the defendant knows or not, the Model Penal Code test addresses his "substantial capacity to appreciate" the surrounding circumstances.

A is correct because it recognizes these principles.

B is incorrect because the *M'Naghten* and Model Penal Code tests are not identical. **C is incorrect** because it is untrue: the *M'Naghten* test is quite restrictive. And neither test prevents a defendant from being acquitted based solely on his own testimony, although the defendant will most often rely heavily on expert testimony. **D is incorrect** because the Model Penal Code test is not restricted to those with "serious" mental illnesses.

395. This question tests on an application of the Model Penal Code test for insanity. Here, the woman knows the "general rule" that it is wrong to kill, but she also believes in an "exception" that permitted her to kill her son. As such, the woman lacks the substantial capacity to appreciate that killing her son was against the law.

B is correct because it recognizes these principles. Note that this answer refers to the woman's ability to "fully appreciate" the criminality of her conduct, which corresponds to the Model Penal Code test's reference to the defendant's substantial capacity to appreciate the same.

A is incorrect because the Model Penal Code test requires that the woman lack the substantial capacity to appreciate the criminality of her conduct, not that she be completely unable to appreciate it. **C is incorrect** because it assumes the woman is malingering, and does not provide a legal response to the question. **D is incorrect** because it ignores the woman's explanation about the "general rule" and the "exception."

396. This question tests on the test for insanity used by the federal courts in the United States. This test was adopted in 1984 after John Hinckley was found not guilty by reason of insanity for shooting President Reagan and others. That test states, in part:

> It is an affirmative defense to a prosecution ... that, at the time of the commission of the acts constituting the offense, the defendant, as a result of a severe mental disease or defect, was unable to appreciate the nature and quality or the wrongfulness of his acts. [18 U.S.C. § 17(A).]

Like other insanity tests, the federal test requires the presence of a "mental disease or defect." But the federal test adds that it must be "severe." Otherwise, the standard is identical to the *M'Naghten* test.

D is correct because it recognizes these principles.

A is incorrect because it assumes facts that are not given in the question. **B is incorrect** because the federal test refers to a "mental disease or defect," just as the *M'Naghten* test does. **C is incorrect** because the federal test is not identical to the *M'Naghten* test—it requires a severe mental illness and the *M'Naghten* test does not—and the question does not provide enough information to determine whether the new test will provide "absolutely no prospects of reform."

397. This question tests on the consequences of an insanity acquittal: the defendant will be sent to a psychiatric hospital for treatment until he is deemed well enough to be released. There is no limit on how long he can be held, and he can be forced to stay in the hospital much longer than he would have been, had he been found guilty of the crime. *Jones v. U.S.*, 463 U.S. 354 (1983). Indeed, the facts in this question are derived from *Jones*, where the defendant's case reached the Supreme Court a decade after his insanity acquittal for attempted theft of a jacket.

D is correct because the young man's continued detention at the psychiatric facility is dependent upon his mental health status, and not the maximum sentence for the underlying crime.

A, B, and C are all incorrect because *Jones* does not place any time limit on the young man's continued detention. While due process requires periodic evaluation of the young man's mental health status, he can still be detained if he does not meet the mental health standards for release.

398. This question tests on the "guilty but mentally ill" verdict—also referred to as GBMI—which has been adopted by some states as an alternative to the insanity defense. When a defendant is found GBMI, the verdict expressly recognizes that he is mentally ill. But the defendant will be sent to an ordinary prison and is not guaranteed any mental health treatment unless the institution offers it to him. By comparison, if a defendant is found NGRI, he is acquitted and will receive mental health treatment at a psychiatric facility until he is deemed well enough for release.

C is correct because it recognizes the key difference between these two verdicts.

A and B are both incorrect because inquiry into the defendant's mental illness—or a finding that he was mentally ill at the time of the offense—does not mean that the two verdicts are the same. Instead, they differ as to what happens to the defendant after the verdict is rendered. **D is incorrect** because it is untrue: while a fact-finder considering either verdict will hear testimony about the defendant's particular mental illness, the verdicts themselves do not make this distinction.

399. This question tests also tests on the GBMI verdict, and what it offers to a mentally ill defendant. In short, the verdict does not offer mental health treatment unless the prison where the defendant is incarcerated offers such services.

A is correct because there is no special sentencing for GBMI defendants. While a jurisdiction may provide special sentencing and targeted treatment, nothing in the question suggests that this jurisdiction does.

B is incorrect because this jurisdiction requires a prison sentence for a first degree murder conviction, and so it does not appear that the judge can sentence the woman to a state psychiatric hospital. **C is incorrect** because there is no such standard. Instead, a defendant can be evaluated to determine his mental state at the time of the offense and his mental competency to stand trial. **D is incorrect** because it is untrue: unlike an NGRI verdict, the GBMI verdict does not mean that the defendant lacked the *mens rea* for the crime.

400. This question tests on the diminished capacity defense, which is followed by some states. With diminished capacity, the defendant claims that, due to mental illness, he lacked the ability to form the specific intent required to commit the crime. As such, when the diminished capacity defense is recognized, it is only recognized in response to specific intent crimes.

B is correct because, if the woman could not premeditate and deliberate, then she cannot be convicted of first degree murder. But as premeditation and deliberation are what distinguish first from second degree murder, the woman can instead be convicted of second degree murder.

A is incorrect because it conflates diminished capacity with insanity, and they are different defenses. **C is incorrect** because, if the judge discredits the prosecution expert's testimony, he should not use it as a basis for the verdict. **D is incorrect** because it is untrue.

401. This question tests on the voluntary intoxication defense, which allows a limited defense to defendants who voluntarily ingest drugs or alcohol, or both. As might be expected, the defense is controversial, as it permits a defendant to evade responsibility because of his own choice to become intoxicated.

A is correct because it represents the prevailing view regarding the voluntary intoxication defense.

B is incorrect because there is no such thing as a voluntary insanity defense. **C and D are both incorrect** because, even when the voluntary intoxication defense is accepted, it does not rely on the defendant's honest and reasonable beliefs about his intoxication. Instead, the defense focuses on whether the defendant was intoxicated, and to what degree.

402. This question also tests on the voluntary intoxication defense. Like diminished capacity, voluntary intoxication—when recognized—is a defense to specific intent crimes only.

B is correct because it recognizes this principle. And, since the man was charged with a general intent crime (arson), the defense is not available to him.

A and D are both incorrect because each focuses on the degree of the man's intoxication. But as he was charged with a general intent crime, the defense is not available to him. **C is incorrect** because the facts indicate that this jurisdiction will accept the defense.

403. This question tests on a voluntary intoxication defense offered in response to a homicide charge. While voluntary intoxication is a limited defense, many jurisdictions recognize it as a defense to homicide, assuming it would reduce the ultimate conviction and not lead to an acquittal.

C is correct because it recognizes the effect of the man's intoxication: he still had the intent to kill, but he lacked the ability to premeditate and deliberate. As such, he should be convicted of third degree murder instead of first degree murder.

A is incorrect because the question gives no reason to believe the man's testimony was not credible. **B is incorrect** because the man only conceded that the evidence demonstrated an intentional killing, but he never admitted his guilt to the elements of first degree murder. **D is incorrect** because the issue is whether or not the man was intoxicated, and not how many drinks he had. With that said, the jury would be free to find that he did not have enough alcohol to become intoxicated.

404. This question tests on involuntary intoxication, which occurs when the defendant is intoxicated, but not by his own actions. Although cases of involuntary intoxication are very rare, it is a complete defense. In this question, someone slipped something into the young man's drink, but involuntary intoxication can occur under other circumstances as well. Dressler, *Understanding* § 24.06[A].

D is correct because it identifies the correct defense (involuntary intoxication), and why it is available to the young man (because of the friend's actions).

A is incorrect because it provides a nonlegal response to a legal question. **B is incorrect** because there is no such restriction on the involuntary intoxication defense. **C is incorrect** because involuntary intoxication is a defense to any crime that requires proof of a mental state, i.e., it is a defense to both general and specific intent crimes.

405. This question also tests on involuntary intoxication. In this question, the woman became intoxicated when she took some prescription medication. While the woman would have a defense if she took the medication as directed, she ignored the directions. These facts then present a voluntary intoxication situation and not one of involuntary intoxication.

A is correct because it recognizes this principle.

B and C are both incorrect because neither addresses the fact that the woman ignored the instructions about taking the medication. **D is incorrect** because the woman did not just take a "little bit more of the medication"—she took a double dose.

Necessity and Duress

406. This question tests on the necessity defense, which is sometimes also called the "choice of evils" defense. With necessity, the defendant is justified in committing a crime because some greater harm will occur if he does not. Although different authorities break down the requirements for this defense differently, all agree on the same basic requirements, which are explored in subsequent questions.

D is correct because it was necessary for the woman to break the law (get out of the car and save the toddler) to avoid a greater harm (follow the law and allow the toddler to die).

A is incorrect because it assumes that the toddler's parents were inattentive, but the question gives no facts about the parents. **B and C are both incorrect** because neither provides a legal response.

407. This question tests on the first requirement for the necessity defense: that the defendant face some sort of imminent harm. Because the necessity defense allows a defendant to evade responsibility for what would otherwise be criminal conduct, it should only be used when the defendant had no other choice but to break the law. But if the defendant does not face imminent harm, then it is not necessary for him to break the law.

A is correct because the woman's fears about food shortages due to global warming, no matter how sincere, were not imminent at the time she stole from the store. By comparison, imagine if the woman had survived a terrible hurricane, was cut off from any aid and had not had food for days. In that situation, the harm would be imminent.

B is incorrect because it suggests that the woman's necessity defense would fail because it is not based on objective, scientific research. But the defense is about the situation as the defendant perceives it. Regardless, the woman here only perceived a threat, not an imminent threat. **C is incorrect** because it does not address the imminence of the threat. **D is incorrect** because the woman's fear must be more than well-founded: it must also be that the threat is an imminent one.

408. This question tests on the second requirement for the necessity defense: that the defendant reasonably believe that his conduct will prevent the harm he seeks to avoid. That is, the defendant cannot use the necessity as a reason to break the law if his actions were not designed to directly prevent the harm he seeks to avoid.

B is correct because the required causal link is missing: while the activist may be able to use the food he stole to stock the food bank, he was not faced with a situation where he had to break the law to prevent a greater harm.

A is incorrect because it is impossible to say whether the necessity defense "never" works when the defendant is motivated by altruism. **C and D are both incorrect** because each suggests that necessity is a plausible defense in this situation. But again, the facts here indicate that the activist broke the law by choice and not because he had to.

409. This question also tests on the second requirement for necessity. In this question, the woman trespassed because she believed she could get warm inside the cabin. In the end, the woman's belief was wrong, but that does not mean her belief was an unreasonable one.

C is correct because it recognizes the causal link between the woman's actions and the harm she sought to avoid.

A is incorrect because it suggests that the woman's belief had to be correct. It does not; instead, the woman's belief only needs to be reasonable. **B is incorrect** because the necessity defense will not be defeated by the woman's failure to check the weather. And, in any event, the facts indicate that the temperature dropped "unexpectedly." **D is incorrect** because the woman is not being held responsible for the weather; she is being held to answer for why she broke the law.

410. This question tests on the third requirement for the necessity defense: that the defendant have no legal alternative available to him at the time he broke the law.

C is correct because the facts show that the graduate student is seeking to use necessity to defend his act of civil disobedience. But the graduate student could have protested legally by addressing his concerns to the professor or to the funding agency. For more about the use of necessity in cases of civil disobedience, see Dressler, *Understanding* § 22.03.

A is incorrect because it makes a value judgment and, by doing so, ignores the requirement that the graduate student had legal options he could have taken. **B is incorrect** because it only addresses the choice the graduate student made, and not whether the requirements of necessity have been met. Note that if this answer were correct, every necessity defense would be successful. **D is incorrect** because there is no such restriction on the defense of necessity.

411. This question tests on the fourth requirement for the necessity defense: that the defendant choose the lesser of the two evils he faces. While it may sometimes be difficult to ascertain which evil is greater and which is lesser, it will almost always be more important to protect life instead of property.

A is correct because the residents made a choice to protect human life over property damage. In this situation, the choice was clear.

B is incorrect because the facts do not support the claim that the residents would have "likely have starved to death" if they had not broken into the apartment. **C is incorrect** because it suggests that the property damage was the greater evil. **D is incorrect** because the residents only needed to reasonably believe that they were making the right choice under the circumstances.

412. This question tests on the final requirement for the necessity defense: the defendant cannot be at fault for creating the situation. If he is, he cannot claim necessity.

D is correct because the dilemma here—drunk driving or medical treatment—was created by the student, and not by some other force. Note that while this question focuses on whether the student had clean hands, the necessity defense here would also fail because the student could have called a sober friend or an ambulance to take him to the hospital.

A is incorrect because it is not true that a medical emergency will "always" trump a moving violation. This question, for example, presents a situation where it does not. **B is incorrect** because there is no such restriction on the necessity defense. **C is incorrect** because it only describes the student's choice, but does not address why the student was faced with the prospect of drunk driving in the first place.

413. This question tests on necessity as a defense to an intentional homicide. This situation rarely arises and is most often presented as a hypothetical. See Dressler, *Understanding* § 22.04.

C is correct because it recognizes that the man was presented with two equivalent evils—the motorcyclist's life or the pedestrian's life—and chose one over the other. While there can be some interesting issues presented when necessity is discussed in terms of human life, this question does not present a necessity situation.

A is incorrect because the facts do not suggest that two lives were at stake; instead, the facts state that the man was forced to choose between the motorcyclist's life and the pedestrian's life. **B is incorrect** because when a defendant is faced with two equal choices, the necessity defense does not apply. Instead, necessity involves choosing the lesser of two evils. **D is incorrect** because it assumes facts beyond those given in the question.

414. This question tests on necessity, using a provision from the Colorado penal code. Colo. Rev. Stat. § 18-1-702.

A is correct because the prisoner faced an imminent threat, bore no fault for the fire, and reasonably believed it was better to break out of prison than burn to death. Note also that the prisoner simply removed himself from the fire and then waited for the authorities; he did not use the fire as an excuse to leave the jurisdiction. While that latter point is not addressed by the statute, the fact that the prisoner did not go far bolsters his necessity defense.

B and C are both incorrect because the prisoner's conviction and sentence are irrelevant to the question of whether he had a necessity defense. **D is incorrect** because all the statutory requirements are met.

415. This question tests on the duress defense and its relationship to necessity.

C is correct, as the following questions will demonstrate.

A is incorrect because the defenses are related, with some overlapping requirements. **B and D are incorrect** because the defenses are not interchangeable. If they were, there would be no point in having two defenses.

416. This question tests on the duress defense, which is available when a defendant claims he was forced by another person to break the law. Here, the carjacker made a threat that he would kill the otherwise-innocent woman unless she robbed a bank. The woman reasonably believed the threat to be credible and that she had no alternative, and so she did as she was told. This shows she acted under duress. Note the similarities to necessity: an imminent threat, a reasonable belief about the need to break the law, and an inability to select a legal alternative.

B is correct because it recognizes all of these factors.

A is incorrect because the woman is claiming that she had no choice but to rob the bank, not that she made a "reasoned choice." **C is incorrect** because charging the stranger with bank robbery "as well" does not help the woman defend herself in any way. **D is incorrect** because it presents a sentencing argument, and the question asks about a trial defense.

417. This question tests on one of the key differences between necessity and defense. With necessity, the force on the defendant comes from a natural (or non-human) source, e.g., the aftermath of a hurricane that forces a man to steal food for his children. But with duress, the force comes from a human.

C is correct because the man claims that he was forced by the bartender (a human) to drive drunk. Note that the question asks which defense the man proposes, and not whether the defense will be successful.

A and B are both incorrect because each states that the man proposes a necessity defense, and he instead proposes a duress defense. **D is incorrect** because no matter what type of defense is proposed, the man is not claiming that he was taken advantage of.

418. This question tests on another distinct requirement for duress: that the defendant face threats of death or serious bodily injury to himself or his family members.

C is correct because the law school dean's threats were not enough for the finance officer to invoke the duress defense.

A and B are both incorrect because the finance officer did have choices: she could face public embarrassment, she could lose her job, or she could report the law school dean to the police. **D is incorrect** because the quantity of threats is not important; instead, the quality of the threat is.

419. This question tests on whether duress is a defense to homicide. It is not.

A is correct because it recognizes this principle.

B is incorrect because rejecting the carjacker would not have been an "easy" choice. **C and D are both incorrect** because each concludes that the woman would have a complete duress defense.

420. This question tests on duress, using an edited provision from the New Jersey penal code. N.J. Rev. Stat. § 2C:2-9.

D is correct because the woman here does not have clean hands, as the statute requires: as a small-time drug dealer, she cannot complain when she is threatened and told she must commit other, related criminal acts.

A is incorrect because it fails to address the second paragraph of the statute, which explains when the defense is not available. **B is incorrect** because it labels the woman's involvement in drug dealing as merely negligent. But the woman's intentional establishment of her own drug business suggests more culpability than ordinary negligence. **C is incorrect** because it focuses on the quality of the threat, and not whether the statutory requirements are met.

Entrapment

421. This question tests on entrapment, a narrow defense that allows a defendant to demonstrate that the intent to commit the crime did not originate with the defendant, but with the police. Successful entrapment cases involve very detailed facts, but the following questions address some of the core issues associated with the defense.

D is correct because the young woman wanted to sell heroin, and sold heroin to an undercover officer. That is not entrapment, just good police work.

A is incorrect because the entrapment defense does not depend on whether the officer approached the defendant first, or whether the interaction began the other way around. Instead, the content of the interaction will dictate whether a defendant has a viable defense. **B is incorrect** because the undercover officer was not required to give this information to the young woman. **C is incorrect** because the failure to request ID is not fatal to the young woman's defense. Instead, her defense would fail because the undercover officer did not steer her into doing anything she was not inclined to do all along.

422. This question tests on the viability of the entrapment defense when the defendant generates the criminal idea or plan. While some jurisdictions may place less emphasis on this point, there is generally no entrapment under these circumstances. Note that in this question, just as in the previous question, the officer simply gave the defendant the opportunity to do what he already wanted to do.

C is correct because the man's reply indicates that he had been planning to hire someone to kill his wife even before he met the woman at the gym. Thus, as the man was predisposed to commit the crime, he cannot blame the police for giving him the chance to solicit his wife's murder.

A is incorrect because the woman's question was ambiguous, and could have been a suggestion to divorce or legally separate. In any event, it would be difficult to find entrapment when an officer made a single statement and the defendant jumped at the opportunity to commit a crime. **B is incorrect** because it suggests that the woman was required to give the man his *Miranda* warnings, but such warnings would only be required if the man was subject to custodial interrogation. *Miranda v. Arizona*, 384 U.S. 436 (1966). As the man and the woman were having a casual conversation at the gym, there was no custodial interrogation. **D is incorrect** because there is no such limitation on the use of the entrapment defense.

423. This question tests on the modern majority rule regarding entrapment, which focuses exclusively on whether the defendant was predisposed to commit the crime. "When the Government's quest for convictions leads to the apprehension of an otherwise law-abiding citizen who, if left to his own devices, likely would have never run afoul of the law," entrapment will be found. *Jacobson v. U.S.*, 503 U.S. 540, 553–554 (1992). This test is called the "subjective" test for entrapment.

B is correct for two related reasons. First, the roommate/police officer created the desire to commit the crime where none existed before. Second, nothing in the facts suggests that the hacker was predisposed to commit this crime.

A is incorrect because it does not respond to the question of whether the hacker was entrapped. **C is incorrect** because it suggests that the hacker lacked the *mens rea* for possession, and the question asks about his entrapment defense. **D is incorrect** because there is no indication in the facts that the hacker was predisposed to commit this crime.

424. This question tests on the modern minority rule regarding entrapment, which focuses on the government's overreaching in inducing the defendant to commit the crime. The particular defendant may be predisposed to commit the crime, but the focus is instead on whether a fictional innocent person would have been swayed by the police misconduct. This test is called the "objective" test for entrapment.

A is correct because it recognizes the key criteria under the objective test: the police overreaching and whether it would induce an otherwise innocent person to commit the crime.

B, C, and D are all incorrect because the references to giving the man the "opportunity" to commit and his predisposition to that crime underplay the police misconduct here—which is the relevant issue under the objective test.

425. This question tests on an example of an entrapment statute. The statute in this question is taken from the Montana penal code. M.C.A. § 45-2-213.

D is correct because the statute concisely describes the subjective test for entrapment: evaluate the government conduct, but only allow the defense when the defendant is not predisposed to commit the crime.

A and B are both incorrect because each refers to the objective test for entrapment. **C is incorrect** because the statute does not look at the motivation for the public servant's acts; instead, it only looks at the public servant's conduct.

Index of Authorities

Cases

Constitutional provisions

Statutes

Index